# EASTERN VALLEY

## The Story of Torfaen

# EASTERN VALLEY

## The Story of Torfaen

Chris Barber

First Published 1999

ISBN 1 872730 23 X

BLORENGE BOOKS

Blorenge Cottage, Church Lane, Llanfoist,
Abergavenny, Gwent NP7 9NG
Tel: 01873 856114

Printed by Mid Wales Print Group,
Units 10/13, Pontyfelin Industrial Estate., New Inn,
Pontypool, Torfaen NP4 ODQ
Tel: 01495 750033

Front Cover picture: An Autumn scene at Cwmavon in the Eastern Valley. Chris Barber FRGS

Back Cover picture: A Pontypool mural depicting a once famous local industry. Chris Barber FRGS

All present day pictures also taken by Chris Barber unless otherwise stated.

This book was commissioned by Torfaen County Borough Council as a commemorative publication to celebrate the millennium and to provide a detailed record of some of the events and remarkable people that have helped to shape the course of history in the Eastern Valley.

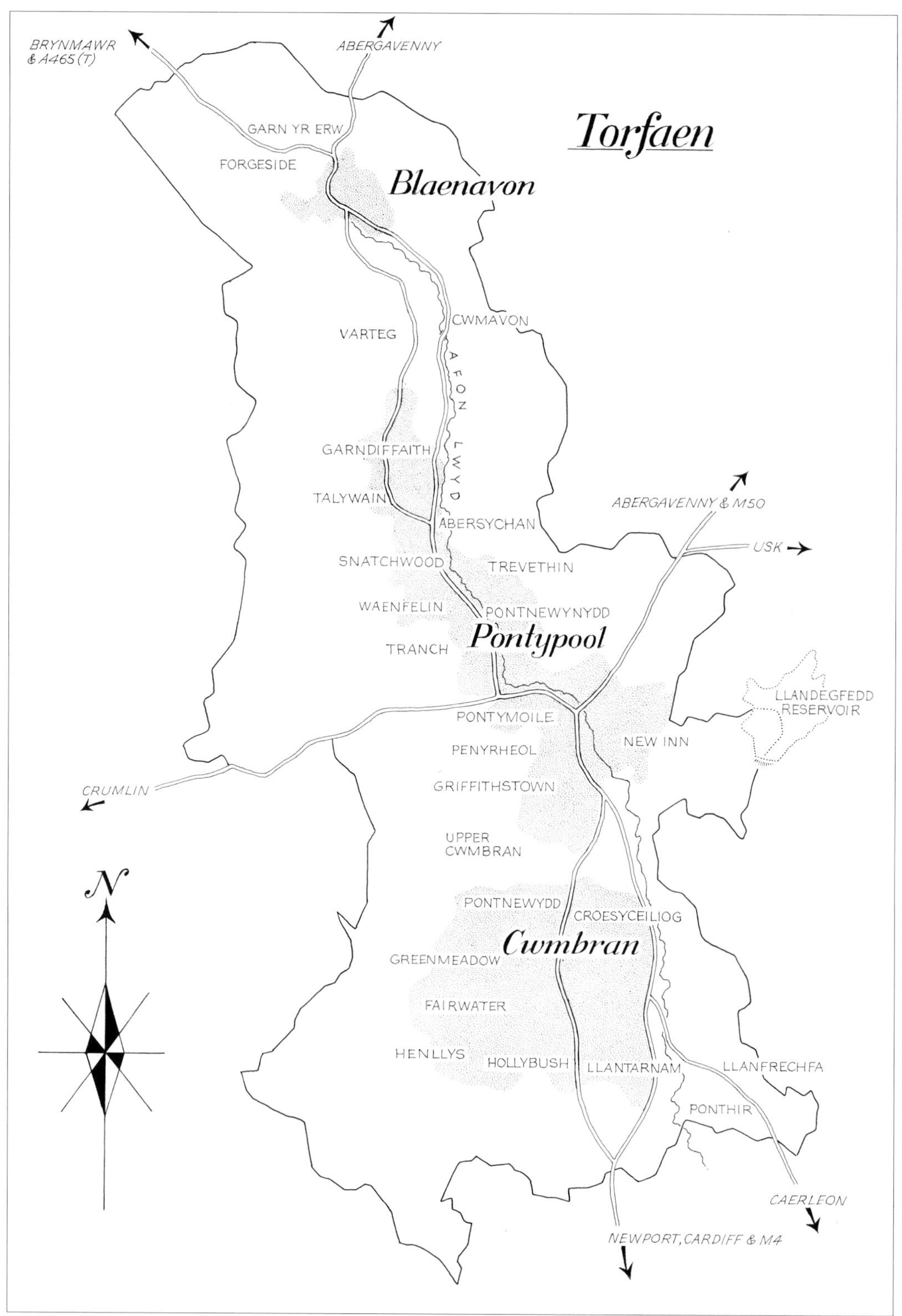


The County Borough of Torfaen comprises a 12 mile long valley from Blaenavon in the north to Ponthir in the south and covers an area of approximately 126 square kilometres.

# CONTENTS

Pontypool Folly. Drawing by Michael Blackmore.

# FOREWORD

Torfaen and the Eastern Valley, embracing as they do both the oldest industrial town in Wales, and a New Town founded just 50 years ago, have long deserved a proper history. That the two communities have blended so well says much for the wisdom of many people, although the more convenient shopping in Cwmbran has not been kind to the older retail sector in Pontypool. Who will remember in a few years time that Pontypool once boasted the best department store and the best ironmonger in Monmouthshire?

Chris Barber has managed to bring together a vast amount of information on the long history of iron and coal, and of the inward migration that has shaped the Eastern Valley, and has made a most readable narrative of it. He has brought to life not only those who were prominent in the community, but also as much as can be recovered of the story of the humbler people whose work brought the plans of the prominent to fruition, and who all too soon suffered from the mistakes of those who should have known better.

Pontypool people have always had a strong sense of humour through thick and thin, and it is good that space has been found for some characteristic stories. I know this book will find a wide readership, for who will not be interested in the eventful history of this community which has been so important in the history of Wales?

Sir Richard Hanbury-Tenison KCVO
Lord Lieutenant of Gwent

Stone viaduct at Pontypool carrying the Brecknock and Abergavenny Canal over the Afon Lwyd

# INTRODUCTION

A peaty moorland plateau, known as Milfraen Flat, to the northwest of Blaenavon is the source of a fast flowing mountain stream bearing the descriptive name Afon Lwyd (Grey River). In the days before industry came to this area, it was a sparkling stream cascading through a beautiful unspoilt valley and, due to its rate of flow over a continuously rocky bed, it was known as the Afon Torfaen (breaker of stones).

It is difficult, however, to determine which is the original name of the river for not only do opinions vary but the historical evidence is also rather confusing. William Rees, in his 14th century map of Monmouthshire, gives 'Afon Lwyd' as the name of the river. Christopher Saxton, the father of British cartography, who travelled through this area, making his surveys for his map which was published in 1577, shows fautologically 'Avon flu' (flu = fluvius, the Latin word for 'river'. Avon also = river, so river river!). Saxton's notation is repeated on John Speed's map of 1611 and *The Royal English Atlas* of 1762 also shows the river as 'Avon'

On 8 December, 1792, a certain Tom Jones gave an address at The Theatre, Pontypool, in which he made reference to the river as 'Torvaen's pale flood.' Being a native of Pontypool he was very familiar with the history of the area and his family had lived in the town for a very long time. By way of explanation, he went on to say that, 'Torvaen or Tormaen, from its rugged or stony bed is the true British name for the river, now called Avon Llwyd, or Gray River, from the colour of the water.'

It is interesting that it is only after 1800 that maps of Monmouthshire begin to include the word 'Torfaen' as the name of this river. This may be due to William Coxe, who in his *Historical Tour in Monmouthshire*, published in 1801, wrote that the 'the church of Llantarnam is so-called from its position near the river Avon Lwyd or Gray River, the original appellation of which is Torfaen - or breaker of stones.'

Local government re-organisation in 1974 resulted in the amalgamation of Blaenavon, Pontypool and Cwmbran Urban District Councils to form the new Borough Council which adopted the name Torfaen. Twenty years later another administrative change resulted in the local authority becoming the Torfaen County Borough Council, which covers an area of 28 square miles, stretching from Ponthir in the south to Garn-yr-erw in the north. It includes the towns of Cwmbran, Pontypool and Blaenavon and has a population of about 91,000.

The heart of Torfaen is the Eastern Valley, so-named because it is the most easterly of the old South Wales coal producing valleys. But what makes this valley really special is the fact that it divides two worlds. The once heavily industrialised upland areas lie to the west while on its eastern side are the pleasant pasturelands of rural Monmouthshire.

During the period of the Industrial Revolution, this valley developed from a Welsh speaking agricultural community into an area populated by a mixture of incomers, particularly Irish and English, who came here in search of employment and higher wages. These were turbulent and exciting times in which the Eastern Valley undoubtedly played a very important role, for this was the birthplace of numerous inventions, pioneering processes and manufactured products which were exported throughout the world.

However, the story of this remarkable valley is not only one of industrial achievement, but it must also be a record of its brave and determined people, whose lived through times of hardship and prosperity to lay the foundations of the communities which exist in Torfaen today. To tell the complete story in one volume is not an easy task and when I was invited by Torfaen County Borough Council to write this book, I was very conscious of the massive amount of research that would be necessary to even begin to do justice to such a history.

It has indeed been a daunting task and with a deadline to publish the book at the end of the millennium, it was necessary for me to complete my delvings into old books, newspapers, journals and other varied sources within a comparatively short time. My piles of notes and references grew at an alarming rate and it soon became clear that it was going to be more of a problem to decide what to leave out rather than which items to include.

Roaming with my camera, I explored all the intimate corners of Torfaen, following ancient tracks, forgotten tramroads and recently waymarked walks. I photographed an assortment of historic buildings and fascinating curiosities. The industrial heritage of this valley is indeed remarkable. Where else for example can tourists descend in a pit cage to the bottom of a coal mine, view the remains of a multi-furnace ironworks dating from 1789 or explore one of the best examples in the world of a landscape created by late eighteenth-century coal mining and ironmaking.

Torfaen is packed with locations of historic interest, while at the same time the varied countryside with its wooded hillsides, wild moorland and breathtaking views provides opportunities for a wide range of outdoor activities. Rugby enthusiasts will boast of the deeds of the famous 'Pontypool Front Row', while golfers can practise their skills on the second highest golf course in Wales, near Trevethin and in Pontypool Park skiers perform on the longest artificial ski slope in Wales.

Writing this book has involved me in an intensive but fascinating period of research and I am grateful to many Torfaen residents for their assistance. I have no doubt that some readers will point out my errors and some of the places or events that have not been included. This is the first time that such a book covering the whole of the Eastern Valley from end to end has been attempted and I hope that my omissions or errors will be forgiven.

At the time of writing, the end of the millennium is just four months away and I have endeavoured to complete my task in time for this book to be published as a tribute to the many people, who through the passing centuries have contributed to the remarkable story of the Eastern Valley, which forms the heart of the new County Borough of Torfaen.

Chris Barber
August 1999

**Author's Note**

Whilst compiling this book I was faced with the dilemma of choosing which spelling to use for certain place-names because many of the old Welsh names have been anglicised over the years.

Blaenavon for example should be spelt Blaenafon for no 'V' exists in the Welsh language. However the spelling of this name with a 'v' became so well established during the 18th / 19th centuries that it would be inaccurate to alter it when writing about the 'Blaenavon Ironworks Company'. The first known map (Coltman 1790) on which the name is shown, (and also on all 19th century maps) gives it as Blaen Avon. Present day Ordnance Survey maps use the 'Blaenavon' spelling.

In April 1988, Blaenavon Town Council took a vote on a proposal to adopt the Welsh spelling for the town, but after much discussion the suggestion was rejected, because the majority of local people were so used to spelling the name with a 'v'.

Other examples are Cwmavon, Varteg and Pontypool which are all anglicised names and might be spelt: Cwmafon, Ffarteg and Pont y Pwll.

Pontymoile is another interesting example and it has been variously spelt Pont-y-moel, Pontymoil, Pontymoyle, Pontymoel and Pontymoile. My choice has been to use the spelling of names as shown on Ordnance Survey maps of the area.

Pontnewynydd - Drawn by Fred Hando

The Afon Lwyd (Grey River) rises in the peaty moorland plateau above Garn-yr-erw, known as Milfraen Flat. From this point, 1,000 feet above sea level it tumbles for 18 miles to join the River Usk near Caerleon upon Usk.

## ---1---

# The Afon Lwyd

*'The old chroniclers affirm that prior to the advent of the coal and iron industries the Afon Lwyd was a pure streamlet, not contaminated by mineral or other refuse, its banks being thickly clothed with sturdy timber and assorted fruit trees, while trout and grayling sported playfully in its eddying pools and shallows.'*

Lewis Browning 1906

It is said that the Afon Lwyd, or Grey River derived its original name of Torfaen ('Rockbreaker') from the destructive nature of its waters. Before industry came to the Eastern Valley it was a sparkling clear tributary of the Usk with banks thickly clothed with trees. Trout and grayling were much in evidence until the growth of industry caused the river to become become a murky polluted channel devoid of all life.

When William Coxe visited the Eastern Valley in 1799 during his 'Tour in Monmouthshire' such changes had not taken hold and the description of his journey from Blaenavon to Pontypool provides us with a picture of a wild and unspoilt valley:

> 'We continued our route down the valley of the Afon Lwyd, on the railroad to Pontypool. The road runs through a narrow vale, bounded by sloping heights, clothed with underwood and watered by the Afon Lwyd, or Grey River, which from a little rill is gradually swelled with mountain streams into a rapid torrent. The vale is at first a deep and narrow glen, wholly occupied by the torrent, but soon expands, and becomes cultivated; the right side is steep, the left gradually shelving to the river, and both are richly covered with trees, and hanging thickets of alder, beech, ash and oak. The left side exhibits a succession of neat farmhouses, with small inclosures of corn and pasture, forming recesses in the wood; these little demesnes are mostly freehold.
>
> In the whole valley, which is five miles in length, there is scarecely a foot of land not cultivated, or overspread with wood, excepting a single patch of rock or heath, which is finely contrasted with the surrounding verdure. Though the scene is wild, nothing is rugged or abrupt, except the torrent foaming over its craggy channel, in a hollow abyss half obscured by trees.'

The Afon Lwyd is one of the fastest flowing rivers in Wales and this is not surprising when one considers that its journey from a source just north of Garn-yr-erw, at an altitude of about 1500 feet, down to the Usk at Caerleon, just a few feet above sea level, is completed within a distance of eighteen miles.

From the geologist's point of view, the valley through which the Afon Lwyd flows, is of considerable interest for there are about half a dozen different types of rock outcropping and each rock gives its own character to the valley. On the western side are all the rocks of the coalfield while Pennant sandstone forms the mountains like Coity and Mynydd Farteg Fawr.

On the eastern side and in the bed of the river are the limestone upland rocks, millstone grit which forms the 'Devil's Heap of Stones' on Mynydd Garn y Clochdy and the rock outcrops on Garn Wen. Also in evidence is the Carboniferous Limestone which gives the valley its quarries, springs, caves and of course, its nam; Afon Lwyd, the Grey River.

Starting as a mere trickle in the area of Milfraen Bog the river doesn't become anything substantial until the geology of the valley changes at Blaenavon. Here the flow is increased by water from the mines on the western side and caves on the eastern side of the valley. The highest feeders of water to the infant Afon Lwyd are below Blaenavon in the valley between the town and Forgeside.

Near the old brewery at Cwmavon the river reaches limestone for the first time and springs in the hillside swell the flow considerably. The brewery was sited at this location to take advantage of the copious flow of good quality spring water.

All the way down from Cwmavon to Pontnewynydd there are springs feeding the river from both sides and also from its bed, issuing from caves and fissures in the limestone. As a result by the time the Afon Lwyd reaches Pontnewynydd, its volume of water has swelled considerably.

Until 1994 the only caves known to be associated with the Eastern Valley were in the quarries on the valley sides known as Ginger's Jackdaw, Nant Maelor and Limekiln. The water feeding these caves came to the surface again in the river at Cwmavon, Victoria Village, Abersychan and Pontnewynydd. It was the discovery at Pwlldu of the entrance to a massive cave system named Ogof Draenan which provided a completely new concept of the hydrology of the valley and its relationship with caves. Springs which had never before been thought to be linked with caves were suddenly identified as part of the Ogof Draenan system. The water flowing through Ogof Draenan comes to the surface at Pontnewynydd where some impressive springs occur.

Pontypool is situated at the junction of two valleys; one running southwards from Blaenavon, with a sharp bend at Abersychan, ending with the Old Red Sandstone plain, just below Pontypool; the other almost at right angles to the first, extending from Crumlin, cuts across the strata in a transverse direction. If one faces towards Blaenavon, the town is flanked on the right by a ridge composed of Old Red Sandstone on the east side and of Carboniferous limestone on the west. This commences at Cae Brest, just above Pontypool Road Station, and ends in the Blorenge, the 'great corner-stone of the South Wales coalfield,' a distance of about seven miles. On the left appears the rounded outline of the coalfield, terminating in the Tranch Hill. The Glyn Valley thus separates what would otherwise be a continuous coal basin

On the slopes of Cwmnantddu Valley, is the site of the Llanerch Colliery and the fossilferous character of its coal was of interest. Ferns such as Neuropteris, Sphenopteris, and Pecopteris; Calamites, Lepidodendrons, and Sigillaria being abundant, with specimens obtainable from the tippings. This colliery, situated on the Lower or Ironstone Series, contained a quantity of clay-ironstone nodules, traversed with veins of calcite and many beautiful crystals of the nail-head and dog-tooth type could be obtained .

The Millstone Grit appears in many places and crops out in the side of the brook which runs down through Cwmnyscoy. On the hill, near the Race Works, large boulders, thickly studded with quartz pebbles of various sizes, are strewn about in all directions, being relics of many a landfall and deluge of past ages. In some of these blocks the pebbles present a flat joint face, as if having been sliced through with a knife, thus showing the tremendous force which must have been in operation.

Situated near Lamb Row, Blaenavon, this iron bridge spanning the infant Afon Lwyd once carried trams from a nearby level to the tramroad which ran down the valley to Pontnewynydd Basin.

The Afon Lwyd between Blaenavon and Cwmavon.

It has been suggested by a geologist that the Afon Lwyd, in far distant times, rose on the Beaufort Moors, ran to Pontypool on a bed a little higher than its present one and then turned right down the Glyn Valley to join the River Ebbw at Crumlin. The deep Glyn Valley which links Crumlin and Pontypool, is now virtually dry, but long ago it must have been a major outlet for easterly-flowing water or ice.

One may conjecture that if only there had been a large chunk of rock where Pontymoile bridge now stands, then the Afon Lwyd would not have broken its banks and and rushed on down through New Inn to Caerleon, but would have flowed through Glyn Trosnant and the Crumlin Valley to join the Ebbw - a course it had taken for tens of thousands of years before it started to wander.

After passing through Pontypool the Afon Lwyd flows acroad a broad plain over a distance of 12km to join the River Usk near Caerleon. During its 24km journey from its source near Garn-yr-erw at an altitude of approximately 381m (1250 ft), the Afon Lwyd descends 376m, which gives an average gradient of 1 in 63 for the entire course of the river. This rapid descent is particularly visible to the observer after heavy rain.

When G. W. Wade visited the Eastern Valley in 1909 he observed that the Afon Lwyd was little more than an open sewer which carried away the effluent of the various works and collieries along its banks and that 'the colour of its waters bears testimony to the nature of the occupations carried on beside them.'

In 1949 the British Field Sports Society, reporting on the pollution affected rivers in England and Wales, commented:-

> 'This is probably the most poisonous stream in South Wales. It is polluted by coal from near its source and from Blaenavon down, there is a constant succession of forges, iron works and collieries. By the time it gets to Pontypool it is red with acid from the ironworks, the colour staining every rock and stone on the bottom. The river is of course quite devoid of life. It has no chance of self-purification; all the way down, past Caerleon to its junction with the estuary, its banks carrying a red stain, wherever the flood water has extended, showing that even when swollen by spates it is still sufficiently acid to leave its mark. Even rats have deserted its bank.'

During the last three decades steps have been taken by local authorities and government agencies to reduce pollution of the Afon Lwyd wherever possible. A *Free Press* report in March 1961 was headed:-

**Man catches a trout in the Afon Lwyd**

> 'Bystanders were intrigued to see a man fishing in the Afon Lwyd near the swimming baths at Pontnewynydd. When they saw him catch two fine trout, one weighing 12 oz and the other a pound-an-a-quarter. The man photographed the fish and then returned them to the water. One observer remarked: 'Not so many years ago it would have seemed ridiculous to think that fish could live and thrive in the Afon Lwyd, but at last the time has arrived.'

But unfortunately some pollution problems are very difficult to resolve. In particular with the closure of deep coal mines, the pumping of minewater ceased, resulting in the rising of ground water levels within the mineshafts. Contaminated minewater eventually finds a route out of the flooded workings and enters surface waters. Such discharges inevitably result in a characteristic orange staining of stream beds due to the precipitation of insoluble iron compounds.

Industrial estates and certain factories also have the potential to cause water pollution which may include detergents and various types of oils. These enter the watercourses via surface water drainage systems, and are usually the result of inadequate storage or careless handling and disposal, The Environment Agency has assesed all the premises which pose a potential risk to the aquatic environment and these are carefully monitored. Routine chemical water quality samples are now taken on a regular basis from the Afon Lwyd in order to assess its compliance with water quality targets and European Union Directives.

In the lower reaches of the river there is reasonable coarse fish available and anglers enjoy a degree of success with chub, dace and roach. Otters have also been seen on the river between Ponthir and Caerleon.

Spawning of salmon has been reported as far upstream as Pontypool in recent years, but the weir formed by the footings of the Pont-y-moel aqueduct present an impossible barrier to the migration of salmon, brown trout and sea trout. Access is thus prevented to a significant length of the Afon Lwyd which would be suitable as spawning grounds. Perhaps a fish pass at the weir will be introduced one day to change this situation.

**Ogof Draenan ('The Cave of Thorns')**

The insignificant entrance of this extensive cave system is situated in the hillside below Pwlldu and it was first investigated in the mid 1980s by Cwmbran Caving Club. They found it to be very tight and were only able to progress for a distance of about 10 metres. Further investigations were undertaken in 1991 by members of the Cardiff based Morgannwg Caving Club who realised that there was potentially a major cave system to be entered. After three years of determined digging, with progress described as 'excruciatingly slow' they at last broke into a chamber on th 6th October 1994 and within3 moths had surveyed 15km of passage.

Intriguing names were given to the various chambers and passages that the first explorers entered and these are shown on the detailed survey that has been produced. 'Rifleman's Chamber' is situated beneath the Rifleman's Arms in Blaenavon; 'Raider's Passage' was named after a scene in Steven Spielberg's film 'Raiders of the Lost Ark' which also inspired 'Indiana Highway'.

Fluorescin dye placed in the main streamway was found to surface four days later at Snatchwood Bridge Risings near Pontnewynydd, a distance of 9km from the entrance.

It was not long before the surveyed length of the cave was 20.9km which made it the fifth longest cave in Britain. Without doubt this has been the fastest growing cave in the history of British caving.

The discoveries continued at a rapid rate and names of new passages and chambers included 'Galería Garimpeiros,' 'Elliptic Passage,' 'Wonderbra Bypass' (named after suspended boulders), 'Gone with the Wind' (situated beneath Keeper's Pond), 'Midwinter Chambers' and 'The Lost Sandwich' to name but a few.

By 1996 the total length of the cave surveyed had reached 47.9km. Ogof Draenan was now the 34th longest cave in the world and the third longest in Britain. It is of interest that at one time Carlsbad Caverns in the USA was the longest known cave systems in the world, but wasthenrated 32nd and just 1.8km longer than Ogof Draenan.

Some bones discovered in 'Perseverance' by members of Wessex Caving Club were identified by the National History Museum as bear. The brown bear died out in Britain in the 10th century so they must be at least 1,000 years old.

Gilwern Passage in Ogof Draenan. Chris Howes FRPS.

Galeria Garimpeiros, Ogof Draenan. Chris Howes FRPS.

In June 1996, two explorers entered a massive fossil passage which they named 'War of the Worlds'. It added a further 1.2km to the cave and is the largest passage found to date. The only bigger one in Britain is the 'Time Machine' in Ogof Daren Cilau, another major cave system in Mynydd Llangattwg above Crickhowell.

Further discoveries continued and by August 1997, Ogof Draenan was 62km in length and rated the second longest cave in the country. In due course explorers will no doubt extend it even further to become this most extensive cave system in Great Britain.

Caving is a very specialised sport which presents opportunities for participants to tread where no man has ever been before. It also also offers the attractions of beautiful formations such as stalactites, stalacmites, calcite crystals, lofty chambers and underground waterfalls.

In this dark and secret part of Torfaen is an amazing world which is only accessible to the serious caver. The entrance to Ogof Draenan is securely gated in order to prevent access by novices and the difficulties of access make it most unlikely that the cave will ever be opened up as a tourist attraction. It is vital that this remarkable cave and its unique features should be conserved and a management committee has been set up for this purpose.

### The Waen Felin Iron Mine

Bill Gascoine, an enthusiastic caver, geologist and hydrologist has a made a special study of the Eastern Valley and in 1993 when the Pontypool by-pass was being constructed he was provided wih an opportunity to explore an old iron mine which had not been entered for many years. He described his involvement as follows:-

> 'During the construction of the Pontypool by-pass contractors were excavating the bed of the existing road at Pontnewynydd. There had always been a tunnel visible just above road level opposite the Pavillion Garage but it was partially bricked up and you certainly couldn't get into it. I found it interesting that every winter on occasions after heavy rain it would give out loads and loads of Ferrugerrous water - bright orange water which would flood over the road. Several times the garage had trouble with floods.
>
> It was quite obvious that when they started to excavate the bed of the road for the new by-pass, they were going to hit water and sure enough that is exactly what they did on a Friday afternoon in April 1993, they dug into the tunnel and released so much Ferrugerrous water - iron stained water that the river was bright orange from Pontypool right the way through Cwmbran.
>
> Basically, what the contractors had done was to de-water about a mile and a half of ironstone workings underneath Waen Felin and Tranch. When the water subsided, Taylor Woodrow who were doing the road wondered what to do about this problem, thinking that this would put a fair amount of money on the cost of the road. So they got in touch with the Council and the Council got in touch with me - being the only one daft enough to put a wet suit on and go paddling in this waist deep water. So I did and happily walked into some of the finest ironstone workings I have ever seen. In due course I found out that they dated back to as early as maybe 1580 or so. Certainly the people who dug this iron mine burnt charcoal for their brews, so there cannot have been coal mines in the area at that time, otherwise I am sure that they would have used coal - so that puts the mine at a very early date.
>
> Giving talks about the iron mine has turned up some fascinating little additions to the information that I had already researched. One that really stands out in my mind is that about 100 yards inside the tunnel from Pontnewynydd, there is a bank of shale which comes out of a cavity in the roof of the tunnel. So you could climb up this shale and go into

a steeply sloping rift. Now I had never been able to climb it, but I have pictures of the place and in 1996, I was giving a talk to a Probus club (retired business men) in Panteg, just south of Pontypool. I showed a picture of this shale bank and an elderly gentleman, who was sitting in the front row, immediately said, "I've been there."

Now, when I have been working on this iron mine over the years, several local people have told me that on at least one occasion, coal miners have come out of this tunnel. But, I have never found any connections between this tunnel and a coal mine. However this elderly gent put it right. In 1937, when he was 14 years of age, he went to work in the Elled Colliery and within a few weeks of him starting, he and a bunch of other lads along with an elderly and experienced miner were caught behind a roof fall. The elderly miner immediately said that he knew a way out and he took these lads down long abandoned coal workings and down into long abandoned ironstone workings, and this 'lad' distinctly remembers sliding down a very steep rift and down a bank of shale to thankfully walk out through chest-deep water and emerge onto the main road at Pontnewynydd. He was really delighted that I had shown this picture because he said that day when he was 14 years old was etched into his memory and he would never forget it for at the time he was really terrified.

It was very satisfying to tie up these loose ends because I didn't think that there was any evidence of men having been in this iron mine since it ceased being worked in early 1800 - well it was disused by 1811. But there we are, it was used as an escape route for the Elled Colliery and I met a *young* man who had actually escaped.'

Lamb and Fox Chamber, Ogof Draenan. Chris Howes FRPS.

## --- 2 ---

# Industrial Heritage

*'Pontypool may be said to possess a history of great interest to persons of nearly every taste; but more particularly to the antiquarian and historian of ancient industries, as connected with its early history of the manufacture of iron, wire, Japan and tin-plate.'*

Dan Griffiths 1883

Iron was first produced in the Eastern Valley at Pontypool by the cousins David and Ieuan Graunt in 1425. Formerly of Glamorganshire they claimed descent from Sir Guyon Le Graund, a Spaniard who was directly related to one of the Dukes of Seville.

The two cousins probably established their small bloomery forges at Pontymoel beside the Afon Lwyd which would have provided the power for operating the bellows supplying the blast to their forge. Close at hand was an abundant supply of trees for making charcoal; ironstone was readily obtained and also limestone which was necessary for fluxing.

In due course, the Graunts as a result of their occupation became known locally as the Gofs (i.e. smiths) and a century later one of David Graunt's descendants apparently dropped the name of Graunt and adopted that of Gough.

Around 1565 the newly established Company of Mineral and Battery Workers commissioned two of its members to go down to South Wales and start up the iron works at Tintern, formerly owned by the monks. The attempt failed and the two men returned having run up debts of £3,620 with nothing to show for it. The Company was ready to give up any interest in South Wales but were dissuaded by some of its members, including Richard Hanbury and his friend John Wheeler of Droitwich. In 1570 these two, together with Francis Heton and Andrew Palmer, travelled down to Tintern and managed to get production started. Both Heton and Palmer had many other interests, however, and soon faded away, while John Wheeler died in 1575. Thereafter Hanbury, who as a Goldsmith had ready access to capital, became senior partner, together with a Wheeler nephew, Edmund, and Hanbury's uncle, John Brode of Dunclent, in Worcestershire. From the start they were also involved in operating ironworks of their own, some no doubt on sites pioneered by the Goughs, so that in 1577 Hanbury could be described as having acquired 'two or three ironworks there (in Monmouthshire) whereat he made much merchant iron to great gaine'. Within a few more years Hanbury was operating ironworks at Pontypool, Trosnant, Abercarn, Monkswood, Llanelly and beside the Taff in Glamorgan. At the same time he was lessee, together with Richard (later Sir Richard) Martyn, of the Tintern works, which were doing well thanks to the highly ductile Osmond iron which Hanbury was mining on the flanks of the Blorenge and processing at Monkswood.

In 1573 the Tintern lease expired and was regranted by the Company of Mineral and Battery Workers to John Challoner together with an undertaking from Hanbury and Wheeler that they would supply sufficient Osmond iron to keep the Tintern wireworks profitable. This led to interminable disputes and there seems little doubt that Hanbury, by then more interested in his own works than Tintern, short changed the Tintern works.

Osmond iron was expensive to produce and was also useful for scythe blades, shears and a number of other products of Hanbury's own works.

Early ironworks required large quantities of charcoal and in 1576 Hanbury secured at least some of his fuel needs by leasing from the Earl of Pembroke 900 acres of land in the Glyn Valley and at Abercarn, then, as now, heavily forested. The rent was to be 21 shillings or 32 sound oxen of the Welsh Breed. This lease also gave Hanbury and his partners the right to extract iron and coal. The Pembroke lease was continued by the Hanburys until the early 18th century, when the land was acquired outright.

The problem of charcoal supplies landed Hanbury and Wheeler in serious trouble in 1577, when they were accused of felling quantities of large diameter timber on lands leased from the Earl of Pembroke, mainly in the Glascoed area. The issue at stake was whether Hanbury had breached the law which forbade the use of large trees for making to charcoal. Hanbury was faced with a fine of £1,000 if found guilty but he then counter-claimed against the Overseer of Crown Woods, John Leake, that the evidence brought against him was false in that any large trees felled had been for the construction of some houses for workmen, saddles for pack horses and other permitted uses. It is, of course, well known that any tree much over 12" in diameter is unsuitable for converting into charcoal. When Hanbury appealed to the Exchequer Court in London, which would have involved the cost of witnesses travelling to the metropolis, the case against him collapsed.

Dan Griffiths, once a well known Pontypool antiquarian, examined the site of Richard Hanbury's blast furnace at Glyn Trosnant (Old Furnace) in 1885 and commented:-

> 'The ruins of these works are still extant and are in a good state of preservation. But the plan and arrangement, as they appear to us at the present time, are by no means the same as when originally erected; for tradition tells us that the old forge was partially demolished in the time of the Civil War by the troops of Cromwell. It was after that however, rebuilt because we learn that iron was manufactured as late as the year 1831. What now remains of the old Glyn Furnace are a blast furnace in a very dilapidated condition, and the roofless ruins of the old mill.'

The site was excavated by members of the Pontypool & District Local History Society in 1973 and they revealed part of the charging platform and evidence of the early blast furnace. A garage was later built on the site.

Two large ponds existed a short distance above the site and they would have supplied the works with a steady supply of water, while extensive woods close by, would have provided an ample means of making charcoal. This site is of particular interest for it was one of the last of the old charcoal furnaces to be operated in South Wales.

**Blaendare Iron Works**

When John Hanbury died in 1784, his widow leased the Pontypool works toDavid Tanner. This lease included:- 'all that Furnace or Iron Work for the making of Sow or Pig Iron called Trosnant Furnace or Pont Pool Furnace and also all that Forge or Iron Work for the making of Bar Iron called the Town Forge or Old Forge and also all that other Forge or Iron Work called the Osborn Forge and also all that other Forge or Iron Work called the Park Forge and also all those Mills or Works for making Iron Wire called the Wire Works and all those works hereinafter mentioned that is to say one Rolling Mill, one Slitting Mill, one Tiling Forge, with the stamper at the said furnace for stamping and separating Scoria Scurf or Scrap Iron and Shot Iron and also all that meadow ground called the Brick Kiln

Meadow and all that... Dwelling House in the possession of William Davies all which works and premises are in or near Pontypool... and also all that other Iron Furnace called Llanelly Furnace with the stamper there and all that Forge or Iron Work called Llanelly Forge in the parish of Llanelly in the Co. of Brecon and also all that ware house and slip of ground near Caerleon together with all the coal houses workmen's houses outhouses shops and yards.' The term was eleven years at a yearly rental of £44 7s 7d for the Town Forge, £200 for the Osborne Forge, £30 for the wire works and £290 for the remainder. This was a surprisingly small amount to pay for such a large industrial concern, but John Hanbury, as an active Member of Parliament and keen sportsman, took little interest in the ironworks which by now had become very old fashioned and run-down. David Tanner began well and built two coal fired blast furnaces on his own land at Blaendare. He had, however, never paid for the stock and implements taklen over at the start of his lease and when that lease expired Jane Hanbury sued him for £16,000 and won.

Shortly afterwards Tanner was declared bankrupt and he departed for the Middle East. John Barnaby, of Herefordshire bought the two blast furnaces from the receivers and then exchanged the land with Capel Hanbury Leigh for two acres of flat ground adjoining the Crumlin Road which he needed as a coal depot. Capel Hanbury Leigh then added two more blast furnaces and began the first deep mines in the Pontypool area, to supply the necessary coal.

Pig iron produced at the Blaendare works (or the Old Furnace) was carried by pack horses up the track by the Wentsland cottage, over Borchhill and down Sow Hill to cross the market place and then down Crane Street. From there it was taken either through Trosnant to the Park Forge or up George Street and around Twyn-tyu-du and Wainfelin to the old Osborne Forge. Here it was converted into iron bars which were then transported to the rolling mills at Pontymoel.

**Varteg Ironworks**

Erected on land that was sub-let by Thomas Hill and Thomas Hopkins these works began operation in 1803. Records show that 81 tons of iron were transported down the Monmouthshire Canal to Newport during the first year of production.

Three years later a forge to serve the works was erected beside the Afon Lwyd at Cwmavon and also a terrace of cottages, known appropriately as Forge Row, built to accommodate the workers. The manager of the forge resided at nearby Cwmavon House. Today, there are few traces of the forge and only scanty information about it has survived, but it may be assumed that it was only in operation for about ten years.

By mid 1819 the Varteg Ironworks were in the hands of Fawcett, Whitehouse and Co., who in that year applied to the Monmouthshire Canal Company for a reduction of tonnages. On 2nd May 1820, the canal solicitor was instructed to take proceedings against the firm unless their tonnages were paid within 14 days. By October of that year the firm had a wharf on the canalside at Pontnewynydd, and were given permission by the Canal Company to run a branch from the Blaenavon Rail Road into it. This branch was taken over by the Canal Company in January 1828, when the Varteg Iron Co. was paid 16s 8d in respect of the rails and stone blocks.

By 1830 the works had five blast furnaces in operation and the owners were Kenrick & Co., with George Kenrick as managing director. By about 1843 the works had fallen into disuse and were advertised for sale by auction in 1844.

## Pentwyn Ironworks

These works were set up by the Hunt brothers in 1825 when three blast furnaces were built below the site of the later Pentwyn School. They were close to the British Ironworks and these two companies competed with each other for the mineral rights owned by the Wentland and Bryngwyn Estate. In 1836 the Pentwyn Ironworks transported over 8,000 tons of iron a year on the canals and tramroads of the Monmouthshire Canal Company.

In 1838 the Pentwyn Company amalgamated with the Golynos Iron Company and the new company was called the Pentwyn and Golynos Iron Company. By 1839 they were transporting 12,533 tons of iron a year on the canal and in 1840 production rose to 17,783 tons.

## Cwmffrwdoer Iron Works

In 1825 when the Hunt brothers were clearing a site for the foundations of the Pentwyn furnaces, the remains of a smelting furnace were revealed. It had been erected in 1579 by Richard Hanbury, who set up furnaces both here and at Trosnant to make use of the Blaenavon ore. Three years previously he had acquired large tracts of woodland between the Ebbw and the Usk, which included iron mines belonging to the Earl of Pembroke. In addition, he leased many of the woods near Tintern. He already controlled the only source of Osmond iron and by 1580 he had built additional furnaces at Abercarn and Monkswood.

Two large ponds supplied the Cwmffrwdoer Works with a good quantity of water and the extensive woods in the valley provided ample means of making charcoal. In the early 1970s it was still possible to see a half section of the stone furnace and remains of stone buildings nearby. The site was excavated in 1973 by Pontypool Local History Society who discovered part of the charging platform and evidence of the early blast furnace. Soon afterwards the site was covered with tipped material prior to the construction of a garage on the site.

## Golynos Ironworks

Situated near the Ffrwd Brook above Garndiffaith this works opened in 1837 and a year later its three blast furnaces were combined with the Pentwyn Ironworks to form the Pentwyn and Golynos Iron and Coal Company, thus operating a total of six blast furnaces.

William Williams took over the concern in 1844 and at about the same time also leased Varteg Ironworks. He ran the ironworks and also a forge and rolling mill at Pontnewynydd until he went bankrupt in 1852. The works were then all closed with the result that nearly four thousand Eastern Valley men became unemployed.

Later that year Crawshay Bailey of Nantyglo took over the Golynos, Varteg and Pontnewynydd works, but the Pentwyn Ironworks was abandoned and never opened again. Crawshay Bailey continued to operate the Golynos Works until 1863 with William Williams retained as manager. The lease was then taken up by G. E. Bevan and Co., of Northampton and the works finally closed when he died in 1866.

## The British Ironworks

This ironworks was originally known as the Abersychan Ironworks and it was established in 1826 by Shears, Small and Taylor on land leased from the Wentsland estate. In 1829 the works were taken over by the new British Iron Company which consisted of two to three thousand people who bought shares at £50 each, but they must have been disappointed in their investment for the Company made no profit during the first eleven years.

The works consisted of six blast furnaces with refineries, puddling train, intermediate train for mill bars, and three rolling mill trains together with collieries and mines. In the early days the average weekly output was about 70 - 80 tons per furnace, with all the iron produced by cold blast. There were no coke ovens and all the coke used in the furnaces was made in the open air from large coal, the loss in coking amounting to 43%. Four-fifths of the pig iron was refined and then, combined with the remaining fifth, passed through the puddling process for conversion into puddled bars. A ton of finished iron required about 28 - 29 cwt of pig iron.

Iron rails were first made at these works in 1840 and both rails and bars in various proportions continued to be made until 1850, when production of bars ceased, except for home use, and rails became the sole product, being in particular demand for the great railways of America.. The selling price fluctuated from 1841 to 1851, between £5 2s 6d per ton, and £10 0s 9d per ton, the price of bars varying from £4 10s 7d to £6 7s 6d during the same period.

In 1848, hot air was introduced into the blast furnaces, and although coal was used in the stoves - the waste gases not yet being utilised - the heated air soon proved to be an important factor in both the saving of fuel and increasing the output, which soon reached 120 or 130 tons per furnace weekly. Open coking was next abandoned and coke ovens substituted, by which a further saving of 30 per cent was made in the quantity of coal used to produce a ton of coke.

The iron was transported in horse-drawn trams along the Tram Road (now Manor Road) and down to the canal head at Pontnewynydd, to be conveyed by narrow boat to Newport docks for shipment.

All the ironworkers resided in a nearby village which was known as The British and had been constructed specially for them. It consisted of several terraces which were given such names as Monmouth Row, Elizabeth View, East View, Norfolk Row, York Place, John's Row, Dublin Row, King's Parade, Queen's parade and Mount Pleasant. The foremen or over men lived in a larger house at the end of each row and had the additional benefit of having gas piped to their homes from the forge coke ovens.

Iron smelting was thirsty work and at one time there were twelve public houses and one drinking club within this locality. They were The Commercial, The Constabulary, The White Horse, The Vulcan, The Golynos, The Globe, The Greyhound, The Albert, The Railway, The Nag's Head, The Britannia and The Black Horse.

In 1851 the British Iron Company went bankrupt, after spending £400,000 on improvements to the works and following a drop in prices the works was sold to the Ebbw Vale Company for £8,500, a paltry sum which represented just one-fifth of the value of the concern. It was said at the time that the stock of ironstone on the pit banks alone represented a sum equivalent to the purchase price.

Within a short time the Ebbw Vale Company proceeded to construct the necessary railroads for connecting the works with the Monmouthshire line, which had just been opened.

The British Iron Company's furnaces at Abersychan were built in 1825. Michael Blackmore.

To make a junction with the main line, which was considerably below the level of the works, the railway company constructed an incline plane from Talywain to a point on the line called Twynyfrwd, about mid-way between Varteg and Abersychan.

This incline, completed in 1854, was worked by a stationary engine sited near 'Bank House,' Talywain and a special rate of 3d per ton plus the tolls was charged by the railway company on all traffic conveyed on it.

Various improvements, costing large sums of money, were carried out at the works by the Ebbw Vale Company, the most important being the application to the blast furnaces of the cup and cone. This arrangement enabled the waste gases to be collected and applied to the heating of the hot air stoves and blast engine boilers, for which purpose coal had previously been used.

Not only did this method result in a large saving in fuel, but it also increased production which rose to 200 tons, and finally, just before the closure of the works, in 1876, to about 250 tons per furnace, per week.

When the demand for iron rails declined in about 1868 - 70 due to the popularity of steel, the British Ironworks went into decline and closed in 1876 putting a large number of people out of work. Soon afterwards the works were completely dismantled, the buildings, plant and machinery, being broken up and sold.

A three-storey Cornish type engine house, built in 1845, survives on the site. It was built to house a Cornish Beam Engine which, powered by steam, was used to drain the Company's mines. The location of the furnaces is recognised by the remains of masonry and evidence of ironmaking on the ground - iron ore, coal, coke, limestone and a large lump of charge (containing these ingredients) can also be seen.

This Cornish Beam pumping engine-house was built by the British Iron Company to drain its mines. Three storeys high, it is built of sandstone and inside some of the timber beams, cast and wrought iron brackets, bolts and plates have survived. Scheduled as an ancient monument this building is a rare example in Wales of a Cornish engine house.

# The Pontypool Forges and Tinplate Works

## The Town Forge

The Town Forge was situated on the south-west side of the Town Bridge in Park Road and within 200 yards of the Cross, which used to be considered the centre of Pontypool. An inn known as the Forge Hammer stood nearby and took its name from the works. This was one of the first forges belonging to the Hanbury family who built 'Ynys-glen-Torfaen' (The island in the valley of the river Torfaen) close by as dwellings for the forge men. The Town Forge, like the Park Forge was used for the conversion of pig iron into wrought iron.

It had four waterwheels which were powered by the pond north of the road and there were coal houses and sheds, a charcoal yard, stables, seven houses for workmen and a manager's house.

In 1827 when the bridge was being rebuilt, the Town Forge was demolished and what remained of the houses was also cleared away. The site was then planted as a shrubbery. According to Dan Griffiths, writing in 1883, remains of the works were still to be seen, the boundary of the pond could be clearly traced and the wooden shafts of the water-wheel were still in evidence. Soon after the Old Town Forge was demolished, the New Forge in Osborne Road was re-named the Town Forge.

An ornamental cottage (Grove House) now stands on the site formerly occupied by the old house and it was apparently built from stone taken from the demolished furnaces. There is evidence of iron in the stones clearly visible.

## The Park Forge

This small works was established during the 1570s to make sheet from the pig iron produced at the blast furnaces owned by the Hanbury family. It was situated on the east bank of the river at the bottom of Trosnant and comprised six small buildings standing at the head of the Forge Pond. One of these buildings housed the main workshop where patterns were made and repairs carried out to machinery. There was a bridge across the river giving access to Trosnant.

The works are shown on the first Ordnance Survey map of Monmouthshire, published in 1833, but it is believed that production stopped in 1831. Capel Hanbury Leigh, whilst carrying out improvements to the Park, demolished the buildings in 1833 and transferred the workforce to the rebuilt tin-plate works (the Upper Mill) west of the river at Pontymoel. It would seem that the Hanbury family had become tired of the constant annoyance arising from the smoke and noise of the forge hammer and decided that life would be so much better without it.

The men who had been employed at the Park Forge were sent to the plating mill, which in turn was called 'The Town Forge' on the upper side of the river nearest the town. The Park Forge lay uner the present day Leisure Centre and considerable foundations were uncovered when the Centre was built.

**Osborne Forge**

In all probability this small forge was built long before the Town Forge and it used to stand below the river bridge at Pontnewynydd. Local people referred to it as the 'Little Forge' and it was celebrated for the production of the 'Osborne,' or as it was anciently called, 'Osmond' iron. This iron was of very good quality and in the 17th century essential for the manfacture of wire. It was considered to be the most malleable and ductile iron then known in England. According to H.R. Schubert, the most suitable ore for making Osborne iron was to be found on Elgam Hill to the north of Blaenavon.

Workers at Osborne Forge, Pontypool, 1906. Torfaen Museum Trust.

King George VI and Queen Elizabeth at the Town Forge, Osborne Road, Pontypool in 1947.
Torfaen Musem Trust.

**The New Town Forge**

In about 1844 the Town Forge in Osborne Road was converted into a tin-plate works by Messrs Partridge Jones and John Paton Ltd., who were known throughout the world for the quality of their products. The site had originally been named the New Forge, but when the Old Town Forge was demolished the New Forge confusingly became known as the Town Forge.

It is of interest that in November 1886 a novel experiment with electric lighting was tried at this forge. It was claimed that electricity gave a light which was far superior to gas and at a reduced cost. Ten arc lights and 35 incandescent lights were put into operation at the works to give an exceedingly vivid light which was far more brilliant that that given by many gas jets. It enabled the workmen to pursue their occupations at night with almost the same ease and comfort as in the day time.

In December 1941 the Pontypool Town Works was visited by King George VI and Queen Elizabeth, both of whom chatted with employees, including several women tin-plate workers. The works still belonged to the Partridge, Jones and John Paton group, although Richard Thomas and Baldwins had now taken over the Iron and Steel Realisation Agency's shares.

During Coronation year (1953) the Town Forge celebrated 250 years of tinplate-making in the town It was claimed, on no real evidence, that sheets were being tinned here as far back as 1703 when Queen Anne was on the throne. In the office of Mr. R.D. Powell, the general manager of the works at this time could be seen a portrait of Major John Hanbury, who was said to be the 'Father of the English Tinplate Trade.'

At its peak it had employed nearly 600 people and it eventually closed down in 1957, throwing 180 out of work.

**Pontymoel Tinplate Works**

Sometime during the period 1720 to 1727, Major John Hanbury and later his son Capel, developed this site for the manufacture of tinplate, and it was the first tinplate works in Britain. During the eighteenth century a large number of visitors who were interested in manufacturing processes were attracted to this works. Richard Pococke, the Bishop of Meath in Ireland came here in 1756 and recorded his impressions:-

> 'They take a piece of red hot iron about four inches broad and five inches long and put it between the rollers which roll it thinner; then they double it and heat it, and so continue doubling and putting it between the rollers until it is thin enough for the purpose.'

In 1807 the Pontypool Bar Iron and Tinplate Co. was formed at Pontymoel with Capel Hanbury Leigh contributing £8000 and the land and buildings. His partners Watkin George and Robert Smith put up £4000 each.

The original buildings were altered and modernised under the direction of Watkin George who had previously been employed as an engineer at the Cyfarthfa Works in Merthyr Tydfil. He also constructed a large water wheel for power purposes, modelling it on the famous wheel that he had built at Cyfarthfa.

Watkin George's father had been a native of Mynyddislwyn and he came to Pontypool as a forge carpenter under John Hanbury. Watkin was born at 'The Ship' in Crane Street, which was kept by his father. He became the finest mechanic of his day in Wales. As a young man he left Pontypool and went to work at Cyfarthfa Ironworks in Merthyr Tydfil. He improved the blast at Crawshay's works by constructing a giant water wheel. It was highly successful and Crawshay was so pleased with Watkin's achievements that he gave him shares in the works. After amassing a fortune of £67,000 Watkin George returned to Pontypool in 1807 and lived in a house on the edge of the Park, where now stands the Library.

During the next fifteen years he carried out many improvements to the works at Pontypool, but succeeded in spending most of his money. He died on 12th August 1822, aged 63.

Robert Smith died in 1825 leavingCapel Hanbury Leigh as the only share-holder. The Town Forge and the Pontymol Tinplate works were connected by a tramroad on the west side of the Afon Lwyd with, for a short period, a loop over the river to take in the Park Forge, until that was demolished. At one point the tramroad ran through a tunnel, which still exists.

The Pontymoel site was, in 1852, leased with the rest of the Pontypool iron and tin works to Messrs Dimmack, Thompson and Firmstone, ironmasters from Staffordshire. These soon got into trouble, however, and sold out their leasehold interest to the Ebbw Vale Steel, Iron and Coal Co. to whom the Pontypool Park Estate granted a new lease in 1877.

Galvanised sheet was produced here until the late 1920s and during the war the buildings were used for storage. Afterwards they were demolished and the site was cleared for redevelopment in 1980.

**Pontyfelin Works**

It is not known where the first rolling mill for the reduction of slab iron to sheets was situated, but somewhere in Pontypool Major John Hanbury and his foreman, Thomas

Cooke, built such a mill, visited by the antiquary, Humphrey Llwyd, on 15 June 1697. Previousl;y the only method for the production of black plate was by hammering - the great invention at Pontypool, allowed the rolling of thinner, smoother and cheaper iron plates than ever before available. Some twenty years later this led to the introduction, at Pontypool, of the industrial production of tinplate, since nowhere else was there sufficiently regular plate for tinning. This tinning would seem first to have been carried out at Pontyfelin, where a former corn-mill was adapted for the purpose by Major Hanbury in about 1720.

The production of tinplate at the time was a dirty business. Each sheet of black plate had to be scoured by hand with a mixture of sand and vinegar before dipping into the tin couldron and further scoured and polished after the tin had adhered. As time went on, qucker and cleaner methods were adoped at Pontyfelin but when David Tanner leased the Pontypool works in 1796 tinplate production at Pontyfelin had ceased.

Some years later a new tinplate works was built by Capel Hanbury Leigh at Pontymoel but by then, of course, the tinplate industry was becoming widespread in South Wales.

**Tin Works in the vicinity of Cwmbran**

In about 1770 the Pontnewydd Ironworks was bought by John Jenkins who had worked as manager for John Butler of Caerleon. With him came George Conway who was to play a large part in the growth of Pontnewydd and Pontrhydyrun. In 1802 he converted the Pontnewydd Ironworks into a tinplate works and it was soon followed by the Edlogan Works, a mile up river at the bottom of Chapel Lane in Pontrhydyrun. This was established by his eldest son John in 1806. At this time the other tinplate works in Monmouthshire were at Pontypool, Ponthir and Caerleon.

By the early 1820s, tinplate was being used for making tin cans. It was an ideal material for packing and preserving foodstuff for it was strong, light and cheap to make. It did not rust easily and was non-toxic.

The Conways were a deeply religious family with a great sense of public duty and responsibility. They constructed workmens' cottages and developed a flourishing community with a chapel and school to serve the inhabitants. Their family home was Pontrhydyrun House which stands at the bottom of Chapel Lane, adjacent to the site of the works.

George Conway died in 1822, but the family continued their association with the tinplate works and Pontrhydyrun Baptist Chapel, which they had founded. Many of the Conway family, including George are buried in a section of the Chapel burial ground, which was specially reserved for them and known as the 'Conway Yard.'

The descendants of George and John Conway eventually took over the Tynewydd and Avondale Tin-plate works which developed about the middle of the nineteenth century on the opposite side of the river. By 1877 there were four tinplate works operating in the Cwmbran area. These were the Lower Pontnewydd Works, the Edlogan Works, the Tynewydd Works and the Avondale Works. The Edlogan Works was one of the last water mills to be run by the Afon Lwyd, but in dry weather there was often insufficient water to turn the wheel. Various firms owned the Tynewydd Works, until it was bought by the Redbrook Tinplate Company in 1898. This works was to have the first electricity-driven tinplate mills in the world and gained a world-wide reputation for manufacturing the finest, thinnest tinplate available.

**Pontypool Japan Ware**

Around 1660 Thomas Allgood, originally from Northamtonshire, was appointed by Major John Hanbury as principal manager of the Pontypool ironworks. Coxe tells a story that Allgood, soon after his appointment, had 'repaired to Woburn (where there was an iron-works) in the character of a beggar, and acting the part of a buffoon gradually obtained access to the workshops and was permitted to inspect the various processes, by which means he acquired the art of making the leys, the principal ingredient for giving a brilliant polish to the iron wire, which was the only desideratum in the Pontypool works. Although Thomas Allgood is credited with the invention of Pontypool Japan, he had not been able to start production before he died in 1716. Production, in fact, could only begin when the Pontypool works began, around 1720, to produce tinplate (the essential ingredient for Pontypool Japan) on a large scle. Thin sheets of tinplate were cut and moulded as required, before coating with several layers of lacquer, originally for the most part black or red and derived from coal. This lacquer had to be applied by hand and each coat was then subjected to slow, low-level firing. Finally the surface would be varnished and stoved. This laborious technique produced wares of unique durability and attractiveness. Early Pontypool is now eagerly sought by collectors and much of it is in the United States.

In the 18th century there was a considerable demand for oriental lacquered wares and enterprising manufacturers in several parts of the country had attempted to produce their own oriental-type goods, with an imitation lacquered surface on wood or metal. Such a technique became known as 'Japanning' and as early as 1690 there are records of 'lackered' iron boxes being made at Bilston and in Sheffield.

It is unfortunate that no records exist of the first designs of the Pontypool Japan ware which is said to have been produced in West Place, Crane Street, in a part of Pontypool which later became known as Old Japan. However, W. H. Greene, writing in 1870, maintained the the building where the Japan ware was manufactured was not in Crane Street but in a premises at the bottom of Lower George Street, immediately below The Cross. 'Here, in close proximity to Major Hanbury's Town Forge, on the Grove, the Allgoods carried on the manufacture from the beginning to the end. The workshops extended along the lower part of the buildings facing the river, and in a little house the finished ware was sold.

What was pointed out as 'The Old Japan House' in Crane Street was in the 18th century the private residence of a lady named Macnamara and it stood in its own grounds a little distance back from the street. The Allgoods at one time rented part of it as a warehouse for their goods, and it thus became known as The Old Japan House.'

One of the earliest accounts of the manufacture of Japan ware at Pontypool was recorded by Mr R. Angerstein, a Swedish visitor, who inspected a number of British iron-works in 1755. He recorded in his diary:

> 'At Pontypool there are two brothers, named Edward and Thomas, who, from black plates, manufacture Bread baskets, tea trays, butter dishes, Powder boxes and all sorts of Tin articles which are cut and designed in circular shapes and afterwards scoured, dried and varnished and also painted in the same manner as at "Mr Baskerville's factory in Birmingham.'

An ordinary butter dish with a little yellow rose painted thereon sells for two shillings, a smaller one for 18 pence. Tea trays are sold at prices ranging from 4 shillings to 18 shillings.'

The early Japan Works in Trosnant.

In September 1756, another visitor to Pontypool was Richard Pococke, Bishop of Meath and he wrote in his diary:

> '....they make salvers and candlesticks and many other things which they japan; I am told the light parts of this in imitation of tortoise shell is done with silver leaf. They adorn them with Chinese landscapes and figures in gold only, and not with colouring, as at Birmingham. This ware is much better than the Birmingham, but is dear, there being only two brothers and their children, who make it and keep it a secret. They will also japan copper boxes, or anything made in copper which they cannot well work in iron.'

The later Japan Works in Lower Crane Street.

In 1801, a London traveller calling himself 'Mr. M.' came to Pontypool and later wrote:

> 'We entered one of the manufactories of the Japan ware that bears the name of Pontypool but it did not answer our expectation. The first coating of japan is put on the Tin or Copper Vessel which is then placed in an oven and at a fixed period taken out and polished. The ornaments are neatly drawn with a hair pencil and a particular size which when a little dried is covered with leaf Silver. It is then varnished which changes the Silver into Gold, for they use not Gold leaf in any of their works. The process is very simple but tedious and we did not consider ourselves compensated for our journey.'

When Edward Allgood retired from the business in 1761 his three sons continued producing the decorated Japan ware, no doubt still under their father's watchful eye. It is believed that Edward died at the Llanfrechfa home of his sister in 1763 at the age of 82 and was possibly buried in the local churchyard. But due to another family argument, his tombstone for some reason was not erected, for it was discovered many years later, lying face downwards, in use as a hearth stone in the house of a Mr Williams in Caerleon. This stone is now at the National Museum, Cardiff and the inscription on it reads:

> 'Near
> this place
> is interred ye Body of
> ELIZA ye Wife of Edwd Allgood
> of this Parish Deceased
> Nov ye 4th 1754 aged 66 years.
> Also the body of Edwd Allgood who first
> invented the Pontypool Japan
> and also ye art of tinning iron
> sheets in England. Deceased
> (J)an ye 9th 1763 aged 82 years.'

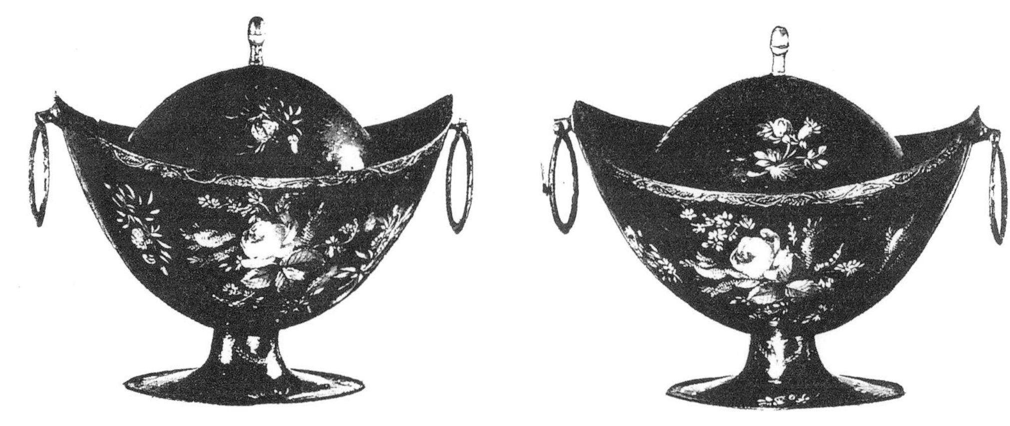

Pontypool Sauce-Tureens and Covers c.1775.

Pontypool Early Knife-Boxes c.1755-1760.

Soon after Edward's death a family quarrel resulted in two of his sons, Edward (the second) and Thomas starting up a new Japan factory in Usk, seven miles away, while John, the other brother continued the business in Pontypool under the name Allgood & Co.

William Allgood, (popularly known as 'Billy'), a grandson of the first Edward Allgood was the last male member of the family to operate the business at Pontypool. He ran it from 1790 to 1811, during which time he maintained a high standard of workmanship. He did his utmost to succeed despite the fierce competition of factories in Birmingham and Wolverhampton by continuing to introduce new designs and articles to meet the public taste and they were elaborate both in construction and decoration. Such articles included tea trays, toilet trays, tea pots, caddies, coffee urns, coffee pots, candlesticks, snuffers, cannisters and snuff boxes.

Benjamin Barker may sometimes have painted for William but he is a shaddowy figure. His son Thomas later became a famous landscape artist. Decorated with incredible detail and skill, the wares found a ready sale at home and abroad and were soon copied on a larg scale in France, Holland and the North of England.

When 'Billy' Allgood died in 1801 his widow Mary (known as the 'widow Allgood') took over the business and was assisted by her manager John Hughes. Mrs Allgood was described at the time as a 'Post Mistress, Tallow Chandler and Japanner.' This was due to the fact that she supplemented her income by keeping a general store which sold not only Japan ware but ironmongery, stationery etc and also served as a sort of post office.

She reversed her husband's policy of only producing high quality Japan ware and endeavoured to outdo her competitors by manufacturing cheap wares. When she died in 1822, the works closed and the remaining stock was dispersed, bringing to an end 162 years of enterprise.

Mary Allgood was put to rest at the little Baptist Chapel at Penygarn where many of the family were also buried. T.H. Thomas in 1905 came across her broken headstone and recorded the inscription which read:

> Here repose from the cares of Mortality the remains of Mary Allgood, Widow of the late William Allgood, who received the Reward of a Life devoted to the Retired but Active Duties of a Christian Mother in a sudden but easy dismission from this World to a better 21 August 1822 in the sixty-second year of her life. Such Honour have all His Saints.

William and Mary Allgood's daughter, also named Mary, had assisted in the running of the business and she married Dr Thomas Jones, of Trosnant. She is said to have zealously preserved the secret of the manufacture of the Pontypool Japan ware and carried it with her, undivulged, to her grave. She died on 23 January 1848 at the age of 62.

The Usk factory which had been started by Edward Allgood (the second) in 1761, was carried on until 1799 by his nephew, a Mr Hughes of Elmon Farm, Llangibby. From 1800 - 1817 it was operated by John and James Pyrke and finally taken over by Evan Jones. Techniques at the factory included the use of a chocolate-brown ground with golden varnish, and also a translucent crimson which was applied directly onto he tinned surface. One of the stock decorations consisted of butterflies and as a consequence there was a period when the inhabitants of Usk were jokingly referred to as 'butterflies.' The painting was all done by hand and the persons employed to do it were well paid and were looked upon as 'gentlemen.'

In 1840, the taste for electro-plated articles began and this spelt doom for all manufacturers of Japan ware. The Usk factory finally closed after the death of Evan Jones in 1860. The Rev Lewis Usk Jones then became the legal owner of the assets of the Usk works and the secret recipe of the process was said to be in his possession.

In 1864, Henry Bythway, a Pontypool solicitor wrote a letter to *The Free Press & Herald of the Hills* , announcing the fact that he had 'come across an old recipe containing the ingredients and quantities for making the renowned Pontypool Japan or Black varnish... I want to know if the manufacture of this ware cannot again be established in Pontypool, especially now the iron and coal trades are fluctuating.

The spirit of enterprise... leads me to think that with the addition of a little perseverance our town might again flourish in the revival of the manufacture of the old far-famed and renowned Pontypool Japan.'

When Henry Bythway's died in 1915, the secret recipe once more became lost, having presumably been put in a safe place. But it was found 64 years later by his son W. H. Bythway, when looking through the contents of an old desk in his father's office. He first found an agreement by which a Mr G. B. Jones, an old man once employed at the Japan Works, agreed to sell the recipe to Henry Bythway. The agreement was dated 14 April 1864.

On continuing his search, Mr W. H. Bythway soon came across the document in question, which fell from the leaves of his father's pocket diary for 1864. He did not reveal the contents and died in 1949. The secret recipe still remains a mystery.

The grave of Thomas Allgood (the third) at Penygarn Chapel.

**Cwmbran Ironworks**

An ironworks was established in Cwmbran by F.J. Blewitt of Llantarnam Abbey in about 1840. Its location was in the area between the Monmouthshire Canal, Clomendy Road and Commercial Street in Old Cwmbran. Some years later a new works was built on the other side of the canal and it is said that much to the consternation of the local people, a field of growing corn was cut on Clomendy Farm to make way for the new puddling furnaces and mills.

The works were acquired in the 1870s by the Patent Nut & Bolt Company of Smethwick, near Birmingham, with Arthur Keen as the managing director. Much of the output of their Cwmbran works consisted of railway items such as track chairs, bolts, fish-plates, tie bars, spikes etc. They also made cast iron sleepers for use in countries overseas where wooden sleepers would not last.

By 1879 the Patent Nut & Bolt Company had expanded their activities with the opening of Cwmbran Colliery main adit at Springvale, along with its associated coke ovens which were built to supply their furnaces.

In 1900 the firm amalgamated with Guest and Company of Dowlais to form Guest, Keen and Company. Two years later they also absorbed the business of J.S. Nettlefold of Shropshire, who had opened a wireworks at Rogerstone near Newport. The firm now became known as Guest, Keen and Nettlefolds Limited, which was usually shortened to GKN.

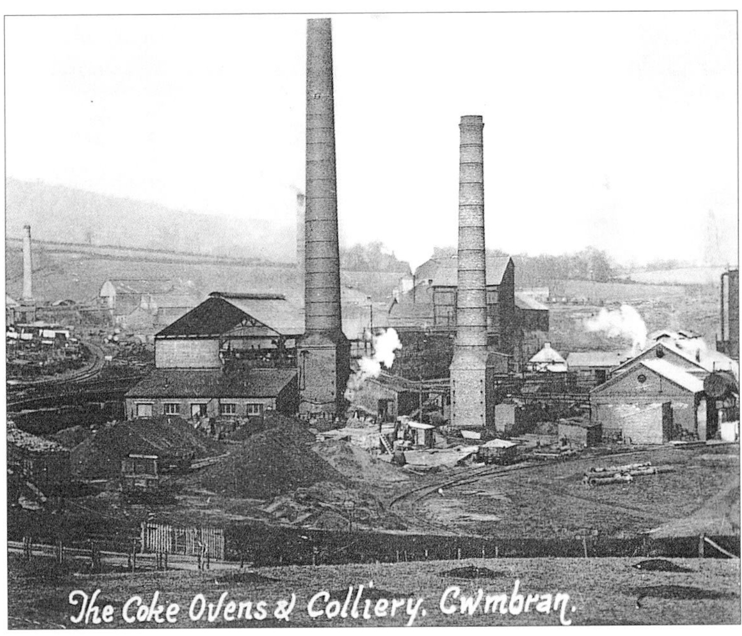


The Coke Ovens & Colliery, Cwmbran. Margaret Pead Collection.

Their large works beside the canal at Cwmbran continued to grow and produced wrought iron which was rolled into square, round and flat sections. The mills were driven by a huge beam engine. Fifty new coke ovens were added at the colliery which was now equipped with a conveyor belt feed, a washery and also a by-product plant which produced tar, benzol and ammonia.

Mild steel railway components were in great demand after the First World War and as a result the manufacture of wrought iron ceased at Cwmbran. Bolts, nuts, key and fish plates continued to be made in mild steel and were supplied to railways throughout the world.

In 1920 electricity was introduced to the colliery and works, thereby making steam and its associated buildings redundant. The blast engine house was demolished, but the blast furnace (closed in 1919) was relined with firebricks from the Henllys brickworks and extensively repaired for recommissioning, with its capacity increased from 750 to 1,000 tons per week. However, it was in fact never used again and was finally demolished in 1930.

Throughout the depression of the 1930s the foundry remained in production with its new component sleeper-plant making iron chairs cast on to steel sleepers which were brought here from the Dowlais works. These were mainly sold abroad, although the GWR did experiment with them for a short time. Two thousand chains were produced a day and also brake blocks and oil boxes. During the Second World War, small trench mortar bomb cases were produced here for use at the Glascoed Royal Ordnance Factory.

In 1951 the Cwmbran mills closed and steel rolling was transferred to GKN's Castle Works in Cardiff. Later in the 1950s railway closure, and the fact that British Railways now had their own foundries, resulted in the manufacture of all railway castings and fastenings coming to an end at Cwmbran.

It was then decided to erect a modern Automotive Cylinder Block Foundry and the old railway chair foundry was adapted to producing cylinder heads for diesel engines. Also the foundry now started producing cylinder heads, camshafts and crankshafts for various manufacturers such as Ford, BMW and Roll-Royce Marine. This resulted in a new foundry being built which was opened by Field Marshal Montgomery in 1954.

The works eventually closed in 1972 and in the following year Cwmbran Development Corporation moved into the offices and canteen block. All the factory buildings were demolished, the area was landscaped and Springvale Industrial Estate now occupies the site.

**Panteg Steel Works**

In 1871 the partnership of Davies, Pratt and Williams placed an advert in a Monmouthshire trade directory to promote their new foundry which had been established at Coed-y-gric about 2 miles from Pontypool. Their company had been set up to manufacture iron and brass castings, steam boilers, iron tanks, and colliery trams.

Within two years the name of the company had been changed to Pontypool Road Engineering Works and shortly afterwards it was sold to William Henry Osborne Taylor of Swansea. He was backed by a consortium of businessmen which included Sampson Copestake, a former Lord Mayor of London.

The works now became known as the Panteg Steel and Engineering Company Co. Ltd. and a steel works was erected on the adjacent land. It was supervised by three practical men brought over from Swansea. These were Captain Wright (later Sir J.R. Wright) as Furnace Manager, Mr Isaac Butler as Manager of the Hammering and Finishing Department, and a Mr Benjamin Smith as Mills Manager.

Specialising in the manufacture of steel rails and fishplates the steel works contained twelve melting furnaces of 10 tons capacity respectively. The ingot moulds were arranged on a moving carriage which conveyed them underneath the ladles to receive the molten metal.

Panteg Steelworks (1959) viewed from the north. The final chimney stack was demolished in 1967. Picture supplied by Avesta Sheffield Ltd.

After removal from the moulds the ingots were charged to a re-heating furnace, and afterwards hammered out before being put through the rail mill rolls and cut into rails. There were few mechanical methods in those days and most of the work was done by hand. Isaac Butler hammered out the first ingot, and Benjamin Smith rolled the first rail. However, due to economic problems, both the steel works and the foundry closed down simultaneously in 1879.

For the next three years the works remained idle and then a new company known as Wright, Butler & Co. took over the foundry and re-started the steel works for the purpose of manufacturing tin bars. The rail mill was dismantled and a new bar mill installed in its place. About this time the bar-mill process came to be generally adopted for tinplate purposes. A great change also came in the method of producing steel, and larger furnaces were erected to meet the new conditions.

Furnace charging by hand was superseded by mechanical means. The furnace-charging machine by Wellman, installed in Panteg Steel Works in 1902, was the first machine of its kind to be introduced into Wales. In the course of time, new and improved bar mills were installed to roll steel ingots direct without hammering. These mills did away with the hammers so far as tin-bar making was concerned, and the hammering process of all bar-making finally came to an end on the installation of the compound Galloway engine, later superseded by a cogging-mill driven by a Galloway reversing engine of 5,000 to 10,000 h.p., and having a crank shaft weighing 25 tons. In recent years the melting furnaces have been increased, enlarged and re-modelled to produce both acid and basic steel, and the casting pit, ladles and gas-producing machines enlarged and modernised.

Adjacent to the steel works, Alfred Baldwin Ltd. in 1885 laid down tin mills and carried on for a number of years a flourishing business in high-class tinplates made from bars manufactured in the steel works. Mutual trading connections of Alfred Baldwin Ltd. and Wright, Butler & Co. rapidly developed and, in 1902, the two firms amalgamated, and henceforward carried on business as one Company under the name of Baldwins Limited . The Tinworks were converted into sheet and galvanising works and the nucleus of the works was later known as the Panteg Sheet and Galvanising Works.

In 1935 a 5 ton capacity electric arc furnace was installed and this was added to in 1940 with 10 ton capacity furnaces and in 1944 further electrical capacity was added.

At the end of the war the works became Richard Thomas & Baldwins Ltd and Panteg became one of the foremost producers of high-grade alloy steels, including heat-resisting and stainless steels. A cold strip plant was installed in 1951 for processing steel strip and includes a continuous pickling line, and annealing furnaces for high quality steel sheets.

By the time the industry was nationalised in 1967, Panteg had become a major producer of stainless steel in coils and sheets up to 48 inches in length. Rapid steel analysis equipment was introduced in 1968, also a coil (strip) grinding line and a bright annealing plant for strip up to 48″ wide - the only wide bright annealer in Britain. A new Melting Shop was commissioned in 1971 and this became a profitable undertaking for British Steel Stainless. Additional investment in 1988 under British Steel Plc., included the introduction of a Horizontal Continuous Billet Casting Machine.

In 1992 a new company named Avesta Sheffield Ltd. was formed but an over capacity of steelmaking within the organisation resulted in the end of steel making on this site. The final furnace of cast steel was made on the 12th December 1996.

Stainless steel coil processing however continues in Coil Products where a streamlined operation produces in excess of 50,000 tonnes per annum. These products are specially developed to provide a blend of brightness, reflectivity and consistency for architectural, domestic and industrial applications world-wide.

## Blaenavon Ironworks

In 1789 an important iron works was established near the head of the Afon Lwyd by three entrepreneurs from the Midlands. Thomas Hill was a Stourbridge banker and glass maker; his brother-in-law, Thomas Hopkins had been a partner of the Kendalls in an iron and tinplate works at Aston in Shropshire and Benjamin Pratt was an ironmaster of Great Whitley in Worcestershire.

Having first carried out a detailed survey of the area, these three shrewd businessmen must have decided that it was worthwhile to invest their money in such a project, for not only was this locality rich in the basic iron ore, but it would also be able to provide coal and limestone, which were the other basic ingredients needed in the production of iron.

The Hnbury family had held a lease of Lord Abergavenny's 12,000 acres of mountain land around the future Blaenavon for 200 years when John Hanbury's widow declined to renew in 1786. The Nevill estate accordingly leased the land for 21 years at a rent of £1.300, to Messrs Hill, Hopkins and Pratt, who founded the Blenavon Ironworks to utilise the valuable reserves of iron that had for so long been brought on pack horses down to the mills at Pontypool. By now, however steam had superseded water power and works could be sited actually on the reseves of coal and iron wherever these might be.

The old charcoal process for making iron had also been largely abandoned for it had been replaced by coke as a means of fuel. The manufacture of charcoal was a slow process and, as it took something like 2,000 acres of coppice to support one average sized blast furnace, the cost was huge.

It was Abraham Darby of Coalbrookdale in Shropshire who had discovered early in the 18th century that coal when converted to coke was a far better fuel than charcoal, at least in the blast furnace. Gradually, after 1750, coke became widely used as a fuel for smelting and within the next ten years the technique spread rapidly with many new coke fired ironworks being established. For this reason the Industrial Revolution is generally dated from 1760 to 1830.

Blaenavon Ironworks began production in 1789 and it was the first multi-furnace ironworks in Wales; built at a cost of £40,000, which was a considerable sum of money at that time. A considerable part of this works has survived and today the site is regarded as the finest example of an 18th century ironworks in the world.

The three partners had chosen an ideal site that enabled their three blast furnaces to be built against a hillside, on which a ledge was formed to enable charging to take place from above. The readily available raw materials could be transported to the site by tramways leading from the mines and quarries.

Ironstone was extracted from the eastern side of the valley above Blaenavon, particularly in the Elgam Hill area. Thinly covered by soil, the ore was initially obtained by a technique known as scouring. The turf was first removed and then the top soil cleared away by releasing a surge of water over it. This was obtained by damming ponds in nearby mountain brooks, springs or drainage water. When the dam was breached, the water flowed down and scoured away the soil to reveal the iron ore. Thousands of tons of earth and stone were removed in this way with very little physical effort. It was merely a matter of watching and directing the flowing water over the various parts of the workings as required.

When the more easily extracted ironstone became exhausted it became necessary to reach greater depth by driving levels into the hillside, in order to obtain further supplies, and this of course increased the cost.

In 1800 'Welsh Mine,' which was the local name for ironstone, cost 5/- a ton. By 1830 the cost had risen to between 8/- and 9/- a ton. The cost rose to 14/- per ton or more by the mid 1850s. It then became cheaper to use imported ironstone which contained double the amount of ore in the local ironstone and the pig iron produced from it was less brittle.

Breaking up the ironstone was quite strenuous work, yet this task was undertaken by young girls employed by the Company, as well as various jobs such as filling and emptying trams. They broke up the ironstone with large heavy hammers and were paid 7/- a week for working shifts of 12 hours (6 am to 6 pm, with only a short break for lunch). It is said that the girls wore hobnail boots with 'toecaps that would pull the legs off some of the ploughmen!'

Above the Blaenavon Ironworks blast furnaces a row of calcining kilns were erected for the purpose of reducing impurities in the iron ore, such as water, carbonic acid and sulphur. It took three tons of ironstone, 8 tons of coal and half-a-ton of limestone (used as flux) to make one ton of iron and it was necessary for the raw materials to be fed into the furnaces in the proper sequence in order to obtain an even flow of liquid iron.

The molten iron sank down to the hearth at the bottom of the furnace and the slag, being lighter, floated on top of it. A stone wall at the front of the hearth had two holes, one above the other. The top hole was called a slag notch and the bottom one the tap hole. Every twelve hours a clay plug would be removed and the slag would flow out and solidify (it was found that it made excellent fertiliser). The plug would be replaced and then the lower plug knocked out of the tap hole to release the liquid iron. It flowed from the furnace along a main channel which led into the casting house and was called a trough. This fed smaller channels, dug in wet sand, which were laid at right angles and called sows. They in turn fed a series of short, end-stopped channels, in which the iron solidified into lengths of iron. The whole layout in the casting house resembled a sow feeding her piglets and this gave rise to the term 'pig iron'.

Close to the works stands a group of cottages known as Stack Square, which were built at the same time as the first furnace in 1789, in order to accommodate skilled workers who had been hired from the Midlands. The two facing rows of cottages were constructed first and at a later date the central connecting terrace was built. On the ground floor were the Company offices and the upper floor provided dormitory accommodation for single workers.

For its time this was industrial housing of high quality and the technique of brick arching over the doors and windows indicates that it was Staffordshire men who built The Square. They were indeed the key workers who had previous experience of making iron. So here resided the number one furnace men, and the engineers who looked after the blast engine. A three storey house was erected at the end of the square to accommodate the site manager. Stack Square takes its name from a 60 ft high stack which once stood on the plinth which can be seen in the centre of the square and was connected to a steam engine which supplied the blast for the furnaces. The stack was demolished in 1912.

Two more furnaces (nos 4 & 5) were added in 1810 and a second engine house was also built. Today, of the three earliest furnaces only the remains of No. 1 survive, for the other two were demolished in the late nineteenth century.

In the early days of ironmaking, the furnaces were always worked with open tops which allowed the waste gases to escape into the air and at night the whole area was illuminated, making a very impressive spectacle. The more advanced furnaces of later times enabled the gases to be collected and utilised for heating hot air stoves and steam boilers.

Blaenavon Ironworks in August 1798. Sir Richard Colt Hoare.

In 1799 William Coxe came to Blaenavon whilst gathering material for his book *An Historical Tour in Monmouthshire* . He provided us with an interesting description of the ironworks during its early years of operation and his colleague Sir Richard Colt Hoare produced a detailed engraving which has provided a useful record of how the works looked at that time:-

> 'At some distance, the works have the appearance of a small town, surrounded with heaps of ore, coal, and limestone, and enlivened with all the bustle and activity of an opulent and increasing establishment. The view of the buildings, which are constructed in the excavations of the rocks, is extremely picturesque, and heightened by the volumes of black smoke emitted by the furnaces. While my friend Sir Richard Hoare was engaged in sketching a view of this singular scene, I employed myself in examining the mines and works.
>
> This spot and its vicinity produce abundance of iron, with coal and limestone, and every article necessary for smelting the ore; the veins lie in the adjacent rocks, under strata of coal, and are from three and a half to seven or eight inches in thickness; they differ in richness, but yield, upon an average, not less than forty-four pounds of pig iron to one hundred weight of ore. The principal part of the iron, after being formed into pigs, is conveyed by means of the rail road and canal to Newport, from whence it is exported.
>
> The shafts of the mines are horizontal, penetrating one below the other, and under the coal shafts; iron rail roads are constructed to convey the coal and ore; which are pushed as far as the shafts are worked, and gradually carried on as the excavations are extended; the longest of these subterranean passages penetrates not less than three quarters of a mile. The coal is so abundant as not only to supply the fuel necessary for the works, but large quantities are sent to Abergavenny, Pont y Pool, and Usk.

Although these works were only finished in 1789, three hundred and fifty men are employed, and the population of the district exceeds a thousand souls. The hollows of the rocks and sides of the hills are strewed with numerous habitations, and the healthy ground converted into fields of corn and pasture. Such are the wonderworking powers of industry when directed by judgement!

The want of habitations for the increasing number of families, has occasioned an ingenious contrivance: a bridge being thrown across a deep dingle for the support of a railroad leading into a mine, the arches, which are ten in number, have been walled up, and formed into dwellings; the bridge is covered with a penthouse roof, and backed by perpendicular rocks, in which the mines are excavated. Numerous workmen continually pass and repass, and low cars, laden with coal or iron ore, roll along with their broad and grooved wheels; these objects, losing themselves under the roof of the bridge, again emerging, and then disappearing in the subterraneous passages of the rock, form a singular an animated picture, not unlike the moving pictures in a camera obscura. '

Benjamin Pratt had died before 1791 and when Thomas Hopkins passed away in 1789 his son Samuel Samuel took over the day to day management of the ironworks. Samuel was a very popular employer and he treated his workers reasonably well. The whole town certainly mourned his passing when he died in 1816.

By this time Blaenavon had become one of a string of ironworks established along the northern rim of the South Wales Coalfield and it was ranked as the third largest of such concerns in South Wales, surpassed only by those at Dowlais and Cyfarthfa in Merthyr Tydfil.

The products of the Blaenavon works were originally taken by tramroad to the canal terminus at Pontnewynydd (north of Pontypool) for shipment to Newport where the company had a wharf from which the goods were shipped to other parts of Britain.

In about 1817 Thomas Hill constructed a tramroad through a 1.5 mile tunnel to Pwlldu, around the head of Cwm Llanwenarth to a site on the side of the Blorenge mountain where a forge and rolling mill were established at Garnddyrys. At this subsidiary works the brittle cast iron was converted into more-easily workable wrought iron and the iron bars and rails which were produced here were then transported along the tramroad and down via steep inclines to the canal wharf at Llanfoist.

A re-construction of Garnddyrys Forge by Michael Blackmore showing how it might have looked in about 1850.

Pwlldu Tunnel which was built to link Blaenavon Ironworks with Garnddyrys Forge is the longest tramroad tunnel in Britain. Illustration by Michael Blackmore.

Garnddyrys, situated on the hillside at an altitude of 1,300 feet now seems an unlikely place to build an industrial concern, but there were in fact several reasons for this site to be chosen. The main factor being that a clause in the Brecon Canal Act compelled the Monmouthshire Canal Company to take all traffic presented to it at Pontymoel Junction, via the Brecknock & Abergavenny Canal, at the same rate of toll. As Crawshay and Joseph Bailey of Nantyglo were the principal owners and freighters of the B & A Canal, the tolls were fixed at a very low rate for iron, while the tolls on the Monmouthshire Canal via Pontnewynydd were excessive.

An added attraction was the possibility of increased trade as a result of the proposed Llanfihangel tramroad (accessed from Llanfoist) which would enable coal and lime to be sold in the agricultural markets of Herefordshire. Coal and limestone could also be transported by narrow boat on the canal to Brecon. Thomas Hill's tramroad also enabled raw materials such as coal and limestone, obtained on the Pwlldu side of the hill, to be taken through the tunnel on the return journey to Blaenavon. It was all just a question of good economics.

Thomas Hill's son, also named Thomas, now arrived in Blaenavon to assist in the running of the ironworks. Unfortunately he was very arrogant and soon made himself unpopular with the workers and the townsfolk. His extravagant lifestyle involved large amounts of drink and rich living. By 1827 both of the Thomas Hills had passed away and the business was then taken over by Thomas Hill the Third who employed Robert Wheeley the works manager as his partner. They ran the concern together until 1836, when the property was offered to a group of London bankers. One of them was Robert William Kennard and, accompanied by an engineer, he went to Blaenavon to make an exhaustive examination of the concern. The verdict proved favourable and that same year the Blaenavon Coal and Iron Company was formed to acquire the entire undertaking.

The Chairman of the Company was William Unwin Sims, a London businessman and financier. Under the management of the Kennards the Blaenavon Works developed and prospered to be favourably described in 1840 by Nicholson, in his *Tour in Wales* :-

'At the Works of the Blaenavon Iron Co. three furnaces are all in blast, blown with cold air, and others erecting. This mineral property is one of the best and most valuable in the County of Monmouth, and these Works have been distinguished for the superior strength and general excellence of their iron. These five furnaces produce about 100 tons of cast iron per week, about one-half of which is refined, and part of it made into cable iron, and the remainder is sold for tinplates and foundry work. This Company is erecting extensive forges and rolling mills.'

The iron produced in these five furnaces, operated by cold blast, had a wide reputation for its quality. But three years later the iron trade was in a state of decline and this worrying period was summed up by the following comment in the *Monmouthshire Merlin* :-

'The present state of the iron-trade annihilates hope, we see nothing but ruin before us and behind us. The trade must refine within its proper limits, but how that is to be effected - who are to stand, who are to fall - what is to become of the unemployed - how starvation is to be arrested, and the ruin of thousands averted - are questions beyond our provence to unravel, but which must be met boldly in our face because they are not to be avoided - they are already at our door.'

In 1839 James Ashwell, a young civil engineer from Nottingham, was appointed as the Managing Director of the Blaenavon Iron & Coal Company and he talked the owners into letting him build a massive water balance tower at the end of the furnace yard. The tower was built to raise one tram of pig iron up to its head, to be then taken by horse-drawn tram, through the Pwll-du tunnel and via Hill's tramroad to Garnddyrys. It was a massive structure just to raise a single tram at a time, which contained not more than one or two tons and its cost of about £22,000 at that time must have been very hard to justify.

The basic principle of its operation relied on two cages, one at the top and one at the bottom. The loaded tram was wheeled on to the bottom cage and the empty tram at the top of the tower was positioned above a tank which was then filled with water. This extra weight caused the empty tram to descend and up would rise the fully loaded tram.

This is the most perfect example of a stone balance tower in Wales and years ago local people used to call it the 'guillotine,' due to the action of the cages moving past the oval openings in the tower. Impressive as the tower may be, it certainly did not have a very long working life. James Ashwell also started building three new blast furnaces on the opposite side of the valley on land owned by the Company. But financial difficulties resulted in the suspension of this work and everything came to a stop. Ashwell then left for pastures new and the owners had to find fresh capital.

The works was then put under the management of Harry Scrivenor, but it still did not prosper and he was replaced in 1847 by Richard Johnson, a brother-in-law of William Crawshay of Merthyr Tydfil. Within a short time the works came to a stop again and fresh capital had to be raised. The management was then placed in the hands of a committee consisting of Thomas Hill (the Third), Robert Wheeley and Philip Jones, a banker who represented the Herberts of Llanarth.

The massive water balance tower built in 1839 by James Ashwell at a cost of £22,000.

Stack Square was built in 1789-92 for key workers. Before the tall chimney stack was erected this group of cottages was known as Shop Square.

This picture of Blaenavon Ironworks taken in about 1900 shows the 60ft high stack which gave its name to Stack Square and was demolished in 1912. Francis Keen Collection.

It was about this time that Thomas Dyne Steel, the son of the Blaenavon Company's first surgeon and physician, was appointed as Assistant Manager and Engineer at the Blaenavon Ironworks and Manager of the Company's Sale Coal Collieries. He resided at Pwlldu and his duties were many and various. The local collieries and quarries were under his direct control, also the tramroad to Llanfoist Wharf and the new road to Govilon. At Blaenavon, his duties were general supervision above and underground, especially to ensure that coal was brought in a clean state to the cokeyard and ironstone for the kilns was free from shale and dirt. He soon made important improvements to the transport system by converting the cast-iron tramways, which were worked by horse, into wrought-iron locomotive roads. Also he designed and organised the construction of the first locomotive engine (named 'Blaenavon') to be used at the Blaenavon Works. It was built at Newport at a cost of £825 and hauled with great difficulty via Abergavenny to Blaenavon. Dyne Steel recorded that 'it was the first locomotive of the hills and took the place of 25-30 horses.' Before long a second engine called the 'Garnero' was constructed and Steel was engaged in similar projects at neighbouring works. (He also converted the Llangattock tramway from Brynmawr to Llangattock Quarries into a locomotive line for the ironmaster Crawshay Bailey.)

Thomas Dyne Steel is best remembered for his construction of a double incline over the hill from Blaenavon to replace the Pwlldu tunnel, and provide a much improved means of transporting pig iron and minerals to the Garnddyrys Forge. This incline was successfully used until the forge and mill were removed to Forgeside and a new railway built from Pontypool. He described the incline and its operation as follows:-

> 'Each incline was half a mile long; four lines of rails were laid 4ft. 8 1/2 in. gauge. Four boiler plate trucks were constructed each of considerable strength and each capable of taking 4 trams of coal. An engine and drums with 4 wire ropes at the summit completed the plant. The mode of working was as follows:
>
> One truck was say ready loaded at the pit. Two trucks were on the summit, one with full trams and one with empties and the truck at the bottom of Pwlldu loaded with empties.
>
> In this position and on receipt of a bell signal the engine set in motion all four trucks at once. On arrival at the top the two trucks were crossed over ready to descend the inclines and those at the bottom were loaded at the pit and unloaded at Pwldu.
>
> On one occasion a truck through carelessness was allowed to slip over the top without a rope attached on the Blaenavon side. It dashed down the incline at a fearful velocity and kept the road all the way in spite of efforts made by some platelayers to throw it off by casting sleepers on the line.
>
> At the bottom it cut through an embankment 25 to 30 feet wide and 4 ft to 4ft 6in deep and half buried itself at the foot. Such was the strength of the truck. By help of a spare set of wheels and axle it was got up and at work again next day.'

In 1853 Thomas Dyne Steel resigned his position with the Blaenavon Company to become a partner in an engine and boiler works at Newport, constructing engines, boilers, pumps, iron bridges and piers. He was there for six years and then in 1859 he became the manager of Tillery Collieries and agent to Crawshay Bailey. In 1865 he became self-employed and set himself up as an independent engineer at Newport, specialising in iron bridges and roofs.

By 1860 the Ironworks at North Street, Blaenavon, had been superseded by a new plant on the other side of the valley, beneath Coity Mountain. Here there was more scope for expansion and the plant could be linked by steam railway to Pontypool and Newport.

The new plant had involved the expenditure of a vast sum of money and it comprised hot-blast furnaces, puddling furnaces, rolling mills for bar iron and rails. This relocation was incidentally responsible for the survival of the North Street remains which are so highly valued today.

Having given good service for about fifty years the old tram road /canal system now became obsolete. The Garnddyrys Forge had proved very inconvenient, being so far from the Blaenavon Company headquarters, and the journey via Hill's Tramroad, the dangerous inclines down the Blorenge and then the slow canal, was in total 26 miles. By comparison the distance from Blaenavon to Newport on the new railway down the Eastern Valley was only 16 miles.

Close to the new works, a village appropriately called Forgeside, was built to house the ironworkers and also the men employed at the nearby collieries. In due course the dwellings were complemented by shops, a school and a public house, thus making the village self-contained.

In 1861 a new mill for the exclusive manufacture of railway tyres was opened at Forgeside. The building was surrounded by a high wall except at one point where a lodge was erected and a watchman was in attendance day and night. No one but the workmen actually engaged within was permitted to enter. The reason for such secrecy was because the tyre machine was a patent and there was no other in the British Isles. It produced tyres of superior quality that were rolled out of a solid mass of iron which obviated the process of welding. Inside the iron was fibrous, while the outside was closely crystallised. They could be rolled to any section and of any diameter from 8ft down. The tyres were so even and true that turning was not required; consequently the expense of the lathe work was saved and the hard surface of the tyre was left for wear.

The impressive remains of Blaenavon Ironworks provide the finest example of a late 18th century ironworks in Western Europe. The site is now under the care of Cadw and open to the public.

Forgeside Iron and Steel Works in about 1905. Francis Keen Collection

Steel was now the material of the future and an entirely new process for its manufacture had been invented by Henry Bessemer in 1856. He had announced the previous year that he was perfecting a process which he called 'the manufacture of iron without fuel'. He did use fuel, but the oxygen in the air was added to the coal with which he had already smelted the iron. He found that by forcing hot air through the melted metal its temperature was raised sufficiently to burn up the carbon and other impurities associated with the iron and thus produce steel. This idea and the convertor he designed to make the idea practicable gave Bessemer his fame.

By this method steel could be produced at about £6 a ton. Previously it had cost about £60 a ton which was prohibitive. However, it was soon found that the steel made by the Bessemer process was often of poor quality. The reason for this was that the Bessemer process did not eliminate the phosphorus that was present in most British iron ores. The problem was eventually solved by the cousins Percy Gilchrist and Sidney Gilchrist Thomas who carried out secret experiments at the Blaenavon Works in 1878-9.

**Sidney Gilchrist Thomas**

> *'Thomas and Gilchrist of Blaenavon did more for Britain's greatness than all the Kings and Queens put together. Moses struck the rock and brought forth water. They struck the useless phosphoric ore and transformed it into steel, a far greater miracle.'*

Andrew Carnegie, 1880

Sidney Gilchrist Thomas was born in Canonbury, London on 16 April 1850. His father, William Thomas, was a Welshman employed in the solicitor's department of the Inland Revenue Office. His mother, Millicent was Scottish and was a Gilchrist before her marriage.

Sidney Gilchrist Thomas 1850 - 85.

Percy Carlyle Gilchrist 1850-1935.

From nine years of age to sixteen, Sidney was a student at Dulwich College. It was intended that he should enter Cambridge, but when he was seventeen his father died and the loss of income meant that his education at Dulwich College had to come to an end. His elder brother, Llewellyn, was commencing a medical career at St Thomas's Hospital, so Sidney now had to become a wage earner. Instead of going to university he obtained a post in the Civil Service as a clerk in the Metropolitan Police Courts at a salary of £90 per year.

In his spare time Sidney pursued an interest in science, particularly chemistry, and he attended lectures at the Birbeck Institute, where the lecturer in chemistry was George Challoner. It was a statement by Challoner which probably inspired Sidney Gilchrist to seek a solution to the problem which was to be associated with his name. George Challoner during one of his lectures commented, 'The man who eliminates phosphorus from the Bessemer convertor will make a fortune.'

From that time, in about 1870, the dephosphorisation of steel became Sidney's obsession. He set up a small laboratory at his home and also used the laboratories at Birbeck Institute. In addition he used those of Arthur Vacher of Great Marlborough Street, but it was later at the Blaenavon Company's laboratory and works that most of his experiments were carried out which led to success.

Sidney decided that the answer lay in the lining of the convertor. This had always been acid and phosphorus in its molten state would not combine with acid bricks but would do so if the lining was basic. So far he had only developed a theory and now badly needed to put his ideas into practice.

In 1875 the Blaenavon Company advertised for an analytical chemist. Sidney applied for the position, but it was his cousin Percy Gilchrist who secured the appointment. Percy was already employed as as chemist at Cwmavon, near Carmarthen, and was the preferred candidate because of his previous experience. He took up his appointment in 1876 and it was not long before his cousin Sidney was persuading him to conduct some experiments in his new laboratory. At first Percy was not enthusiastic and it was not until the summer of 1877 that experiments were started. For a long time they were carried out secretly, mostly at night and without the knowledge and consent of the manager, Mr E.P. Martin. These early experiments were carried out mainly in a blacksmith's shop where the bellows were used to supply the necessary air pressure for the blow through the molten metal. It was also necessary to obtain a vessel large enough to contain enough metal to establish results. Percy soon became infected with his brother's enthusiasm and a constant stream of correspondence began between them.

The manager caught them at their secret work in December 1877. He said to Percy, 'I have known for some time that you young men have some secret work on hand. I think it would be just as well if you took me into your confidence.' The two cousins then revealed their intentions and Mr Martin was so impressed with the results of their experiments that he at once offered the facilities of the Blaenavon Works Forgeside, for larger-scale experiments. Also, he promised similar facilities at Dowlais on terms favourable to both companies should the process succeed. In addition he undertook to purchase a share in the patent, making an offer which was very helpful to Sidney at that time, for his financial situation was not good.

The promised experiments were put in hand immediately at Blaenavon and Dowlais. At first the Dowlais experiments were unsuccessful, but at Blaenavon they proved very promising. A small Convertor holding 3-4 cwt of material was erected at the Blaenavon Works and some fifty to sixty 'blows' were made. The next step was a series of experiments in a 12cwt Convertor and gradually the essential conditions for the removal of phosperous from the molten iron were obtained.

By March 1878, Sidney was so confident of success that he decided to make a public announcement. As a visitor he attended the Spring meeting of the Iron and Steel Institute, to hear a paper read by Mr I Lowthian Bell on *the Separation of Phosphorus from Pig Iron in a furnace lined with oxide of iron.* After the resultant discussion, Sidney Gilchrist rose to his feet and commented:-

> 'It may be of interest to members to know that I have been enabled, by the assistance of Mr Martin at Blaenavon, to remove phosphorus entirely by the Bessemer convertor. Of course this statement will be met with a smile of incredulity and gentlemen will scarcely believe it, but I have the results in my pocket, of some hundred odd analyses by Mr Gilchrist, who has had almost the entire conduct of the experiments varying from the very small quantity of 6 lbs, up to 10 cwt. The results all carry out the theory with which I originally started, and also that, in the worst cases, 20 per cent of phosphorous was removed and, in the best, I must say that 99.9% was removed, and we hope that we have now overcome the practical difficulties that have hitherto stood in the way.'

Describing this occasion some years later, Mr Challoner, one of Thomas's tutors in Birbeck College, wrote, 'We well remember the sneers and smiles of incredulity which were exhibited to an unknown youth who presumed to proclaim the solution of a problem which leading metallurgists had pronounced well-nigh impossible.'

Later that year Thomas wrote a paper for the Autumn meeting of the Iron and Steel Institute. He gave it the title: *On the Elimination of Phosphorus in the Bessemer Convertor* . But the Institute foolishly failed to recognise the significance of his paper and priority was given to papers to be presented by foreign members. Discussion on Thomas's paper was thus put off until a meeting in May 1879. Now with an attentive audience, Thomas commented in his opening sentence that: 'The non-removal of phosphorous in the Bessemer convertor, owing to which the great bulk, not only of British, but of French, German and Belgian ores are still unavailable for steelmaking, is a fact too familiar to metallurgists to need insisting on.'

Describing the experiments carried out with the aid of his cousin Thomas reported as follows:-

> 'After a very extended series of trials it was found that by firing bricks made of aluminosiliceous limestone at a very intense white heat, a hard and compact basic brick is formed. These bricks, unfortunately, labour under the defect of a liability to disintegration when exposed to the action of steam. By the use of certain aluminous magnesian limestones - and equivalent combinations - this difficulty has been, after many failures, overcome. The problem is solved by substituting a reasonably durable basic lining for the former siliceous, and therefore acid, and by avoiding waste of lining by making large basic additions so as to make a highly basic slag at an early stage of the Blow.'

A paper on the subject was down for reading at the Autumn meeting of the Institute in Paris, but was never read. However, details of the process had now been published in the trade journals and Sidney wrote to his sister that, 'Great Guns from the North of England have been to see our experiments at Blaenavon.' One of these men was a Mr Steaf of Middlesborough and he was so convinced of the success of the process that he went back to Middlesborough and constructed a 30cwt convertor for large-scale operations with the Thomas Basic Process. It was not long before Middlesborough was besieged by the steel-makers of the Continent who wished to negotiate for the patent rights.

The first continental licence was granted in 1890 for £20,000 and in December of the same year the American rights were sold to Andrew Carnegie for 250,000 dollars with royalties on steel made.

Andrew Carnegie later said of Sidney Gilchrist Thomas: 'I never saw anyone so near the indescribable thing called genius. All about him was extraordinary - appearance, manner, dress, voice, gesture - all said, without saying, 'Listen to me! Attend! I am not of the routine world, I walk no beaten track. From the unexplored, the unknown, I bring you fruit.' He did not need to speak this. He had only to appear and we bowed before his power.'

It was certainly an epoch-making discovery, for geologists estimated that 90 per cent of Europe's iron ore contained more than one part of phosphorus to a thousand parts of iron and steel made from phosphoric ores was too brittle for extensive use. Britain's supplies of iron ore were limited and ironically the cousin's discovery merely served to open the doors for Andrew Carnegie in Pitsburgh USA, and Alfred Krupp of Essen, Germany to exploit their country's vast resources.

Sir Henry Bessemer, the originator of the famous Bessemer process, had confessed that any quantity of phosphorus in iron ore was fatal to his hopes, because when he and George Parry of Ebbw Vale discovered the new method of steel making, British and foreign manufacturers were vainly seeking to find new areas of the non-phosphoric ores necessary to steel making.

The discovery at Blaenavon of the process whereby phosphorus could be eliminated was a tremendous step forward and by its means phosphoric ores were brought into practical steel-making. An important by-product of the process was 'basic' or 'Thomas' slag, which is used as a fertilizer.

In 1881 Sidney Gilchrist Thomas travelled to the United States as the guest of Andrew Carnegie and toured for two months. But sadly his health started to deteriorate and four years later on 1 February, 1885, just before his thirty-fifth birthday, he died in Paris from lung trouble.

On the Continent, plaster casts of Sidney Gilchrist Thomas can be seen on the offices of nearly every steel works, yet in this country his name was virtually forgotten until the late 1950's when a fund was launched in Gwent to honour the memory of Sidney Gilchrist Thomas and his cousin Percy Gilchrist. Contributions came in from every country where basic steel is made to finance a suitable memorial which was designed and erected by H. Davies & Sons, the Newport Sculptors. It was unveiled in 1960 near the spot where the first experiments were carried out at Forgeside. The monument has since been moved to the  Ironworks car park on the opposite side of the valley..

Edward Martin's role has also been important and was recognised in 1884 when he was presented with the Bessemer Gold Medal for his part in the development of the basic Bessemer process.

This granite obelisk commemorating Sidney Gilchrist Thomas now stands in the Blaenavon Ironworks car park but it was originally erected at Forgeside.

## Final Years of the Blaenavon Company

At the end of 1879 the Blaenavon Works had been converted into a Limited Company, under the title of the Blaenavon Company, Limited. The first Chairman of the Company was Samuel Laing, then Chairman of the London, Brighton and South Coast Railway, and a prominent figure in British commerce. In 1889 he was succeeded in the Chairmanship of the Blaenavon Company by Mr. H.J. Kennard, who with his brothers Arthur and Edward Kennard had occupied seats on the Directorate since the formation of the Company.

On the death of Mr H.J. Kennard in 1896, he was succeeded on the Board by his son, Mr R.W. Kennard, who in 1903 was elected Chairman of the Blaenavon Company. For nearly three-quarters of a century, through four generations, the Kennard family were not only closely associated with, but controlled and guided the fortunes of Blaenavon.

Blaenavon became world famous for the production of steel rails for the Great Western Railway Company and also supplied other railway companies throughout the world. Also it may be claimed that the first steel tyre mills in Britain were established at Blaenavon, to make steel tyres for railway waggons and locomotive wheels.

After 1900 the old ironworks at North Street was no longer in use and permission was given for the removal of facing stones from the furnaces for the purpose of building St James Church. As a result of this demolition work the three bottle-shaped brick-built furnaces were exposed.

Blaenavon's days of ironmaking ceased when the local ore supplies became exhausted; steel markets became depressed and with the establishment of new steelworks near the coast relying totally on imported ores. The last furnace at Forgeside was closed down in 1934 and dismantled in 1938.

Removal of the facing stones of Nos 4 and 5 furnaces at Blaenavon Ironworks in 1911. The stone was used to build the new St James Church. Francis Keen Collection.

# The Establishment of more Recent Industries

## Pilkington's Glassworks

Small glass works, such as the one at Crindau in Newport ,had been in operation from 1870 until after 1920, but there was no large-scale production of glass until the arrival of Pilkington Brothers of St Helens, in 1938. It is surprising that they were the first to take advantage of the large amounts of coal, readily available in the county, that was needed for the manufacture of glass.

Pilkingtons decided to establish their new factory at Pontypool on an 11 acre site between the Turnpike and Pontypool Road Railway Station. When production started about 190 workers were taken on.

William Pilkington had been the first of his family to enter glass making in 1826. He was later joined in his St Helens Crown Glass Company by his brother Richard and by 1848 these two Lancashire men had become sole owners of their business. Later, when their two sons had also joined them, the firm adopted the family name.

The Pontypool works produced sheet window glass which was largely used for the glazing of windows in houses, schools, factories and other buildings. There was also a good horticultural market and they exported glass made in Pontypool to many parts of the world. After the Second World War, the capacity of the works was increased by the installation of a large new unit and the output of glass was more than doubled.

Glass production is an interesting process in which the raw materials consist of dolomite, limestone, sand and soda ash which at Pontypool were melted in a furnace of over 1,000 tons capacity at a temperature of around 1500 degrees centigrade. The molten glass could be seen floating in a tank resembling a swimming pool and the method of drawing it out of the pool was particularly fascinating. Like huge spoons dipping into treacle; the 'hoists' drew continuous ribbons of glass vertically, and could be adjusted to draw a variety of thicknesses. During its ascent the glass solidified and at the top was cut, trimmed and sent to the warehouse, where it was examined for faults and trimmed to stock sizes or cut to customers' requirements.

In 1959 the huge furnace was converted to oil firing and two years later a smaller furnace was also converted. This reduced coal consumption by 1,000 tons a week and by this time the factory was providing employment for about 600 people. Production ceased in 1975.

## British Nylon Spinners

British Nylon Spinners was a firm jointly sponsored by Imperial Chemical Industries and Courtalds, and a 112 acre site at Mamhilad, two miles outside Pontypool, (compulsorily acquired from the Pontypool Park Estate in 1939 for military use), was chosen for the first major British nylon factory, the result of a directive from the government about setting up businesses in the distressed areas of South-east Wales. The new factory was designed by Sir Percy Thomas who ensured that the factory administrative blocks and the Research and Development centres were carefully landscaped to blend in with the rural background. The completed factory has been described as one of the finest examples of post-war industrial architecture.

British Nylon Spinners Factory (DuPont) is a fine example of post-war industrial architecture.

Building construction began on 8th October 1945 and the first section - roughly a third of the floor space - was in operation as a training unit by February 1947. The first yarn was produced on 20th April 1948 and the factory was officially opened by HRH the Duchess of Kent on 24th June 1949.

The factory at this time was manned by a team of just over 1,000 under a 38 year old managing director and in the first few months of 1948 some £1,000,000 worth of nylon yarn was exported. With a floor space of one million square feet, this was the largest factory in Europe to be housed under one roof and it became the world's second largest producer of the nylon yarn which became the raw material of a multitude of articles. Nylon ropes, sleeping bags and other equipment assisted Hilary and Tensing to the summit of Everest; nylon transmission belts, fire hoses, tarpaulins and carpets all joined the nylon hosiery and clothing as a part of everyday life.

In January 1960, Bri-Nylon rainwear and Bri-Lon knitwear were chosen for men and women who would reprsent Britain at the Olympic Games in Rome. In addition the men would be supplied with Bri-Nylon socks and the women with Bri-Nylon gloves.

By 1962, with a capital outlay of £30,000,000 and with two auxiliary factories at Doncaster and Brockworth (Gloucester) BNS employed 10,000 in what was still the largest nylon production plant in Europe.

The partnership of ICI and Courtaulds was ended when in 1965 ICI acquired 100% ownership of the firm and merged it with its existing fibres division to form ICI FibresLtd. More extensions were begun which were intended to bring the production of nylon yarn up to 300 million pounds a year by the end of 1966 which was treble the 1962 output.

In 1971 the first Terylene yarn spun at ICI Fibres marked a new milestone in the history of the works. By 1976 the workforce had dropped to 2,700, following shock redundancies, and in 1986 just 1,000 people were employed at the Pontypool plant.

...993 by DuPont, one of the largest companies in the ...£30 bn. It was an unusual deal as DuPont exchanged ...peration plus £250m. Dupont also took over 5,200 for- ...ich included the one at Mamhilad. They stopped mak- ...soon afterwards and concentrated on the production of ...1m and a further £6m in 1996 to upgrade the spinning ...7,000 metres of polyester a minute. The factory was then ...olyester a year and among its best known brands are

**...area**

...d opened the new **Weston Biscuit Factory** at Llantarnam. ...ted enterprise which was to give work to 450 people in a

...actory at the wheel of a quaint little Morris car of pre-1914 ...t of cars each bearing on its front bumper, the slogan 'Work ...g, he gave the signal - 'Go ahead boys!' - for a battery of 30 ...eramen to go into action. Mr Garfield Weston then conduct- ...d handed him a mauve silk cushion which supported gold ...or the opening ceremony.

...the four factories operated by the Weston group in Great ...h the most modern machinery for the large scale production ...ater not only for the whole of Wales and the West Country, but ...biscuits required by the Company for their export trade. The ...n more recent years amalgamated with the Burton Company ... name to Burton's Biscuits.

...he Jospeh Lucas organisation, was started in 1938 with a new ...n designed by Captain A.H. Girling. The company expanded, ...dson Cycle Company was acquired by the Joseph Lucas Group ...and suspension manufacturers to form Girling Limited.

...0s Girling was one of the major employers in the area, manufac- ...g equipment for the motor, agricultural and railway industries. ...ment to this location was further confirmed in the mid 1960s, ...he lease of Llantarnam Grange, it constructed a purpose designed ...n side of Cwmbran. Since this time the company has developed ... a world leader in braking systems for passenger vehicles at its ...commercial vehicles at the Pontypool Works.

... company has changed ownrship, firstly merging with Varity to ...nd more recently the Cwmbran plant was taken over by Merdor of ... most local residents it is still fondly remembered as Girlings.

...Alderman Arthur Jenkins MP for Pontypool. in the presence of over ... opened a new £10,000 engineering works at Cwmbran of the ...**Ltd.** The factory was situated near Grange Road on a site of about ...the only one of its kind in South Wales.

...**Company** established a Pharmaceutical Laboratory near Pontypool in ... at Cwmoody. This base became responsible for marketing operations in the Uni...gdom, Eire, Scandinavia, Finland and Eastern Europe. The group merged with Warner-Lambert and in due course more than 1,000 persons were employed at the Pontypool factory.

Some other important companies which established factories in this area included Siebe Gorman who are world renowned for their breathing and diving equipment and Alfa-Laval which is a Marketing Company supplying the British dairy farmer with milking machines.

There is insufficient space to mention all the important industrial developments that have taken place in this area during the last two decades but it should be stressed that Cwmbran New Town has played a significant part in the growth of these new industries. The Development Corporation was particularly successful in the building of a wide range of unit factories for small and medium sized firms. The Eastern Valley, which for so long in the past had been reliant upon coal and iron production for employment now gave way to the establishment on of numerous new industrial estates on reclaimed land where the old heavy industries of the past once stood. These new estates were developed by the Borough Council and the Welsh Development Agency.

The largest and most recent development is the 110 acre Llantarnam Industrial Park where a range of well designed buildings from small advanced factory units to individual high technology premises have been establishe. Strategically placed on the southern edge of Cwmbran the Llantarnam Industrial Park is only five minutes drive from the M4 to which it is connected by expressway.

**Nimbus** is an example of a modern technology factory situated on the Llantarnam Industrial Estate, and it produces compact discs. The firm was founded by brothers Michael and Gerald Reynolds and the late Count Alexander Labinsky. Nimbus Manufacturing UK Ltd., are now the country's biggest independent CD manufacturers.

In 1992 Nimbus was bought out by American investors and the main headquarters are now in Charlottesville, Virginia. They also have factories in Sunnyvale (California) and Foetz (Luxembourg).

Cwmbran New Town has undoubtedly been the focal point of growth within Torfaen, for since its designation in 1949 and in more recent years the locality has developed into an important manufacturing, technological and service centre.

## -- 3 --

## The Hanbury Family and Pontypool Park

*'The town owes its existence to the foresight and enterprise of some members of the Hanbury family, and the head of the principal line of that family can boast that his seat - Pontypool Park - is one of the most beautiful domains that England posessses .'*

W.H. Greene 1870

Richard Hanbury was born in about 1538, the eldest son of John Hanbury of Elmley Lovett, a branch of the family known in Hanbury parish since early in the twelfth century, and possibly there before the Norman Conquest. As a young man, Richard went to London where he became a goldsmith or banker at Wood Street. In 1562 he appears in the Court Rolls of the Manor of Feckenham as 'Citizen and Goldsmith of London, son and heir of John Hanbury of Elmley Lovett, husbandman.' Seven years later he appears as one of the tenants of 'the Mayden Head, Goldsmith's Row in Chepe.'

In 1560 Richard Hanbury married Alice Fisher, the daughter of Jasper Fisher, who was also a member of the Goldsmith's Company. Also in that year Richard became connected with the Company of Mineral and Battery Works which had established an iron wire works in the Angidy Valley, near Tintern.

Within a few years Richard acquired ironworks at Monkswood near Usk and at Pontypool. These works supplied the fine Osmond iron which was needed for the wire making at Tintern. By 1570 he was employing about 180 workers and he erected a new furnace at Monkswood in 1572, and added another forge (or hammer mill) there in 1575.

After 1577 Richard Hanbury concentrated his activities at Pontypool and formed a partnership with Edmund Brode and Edmund Roberts. A furnace and forge had been established by Brode at Trevethin (probably Old Furnace) and soon after, the lease of this property, including the woods of Glyntrosnant and Wentwood (to provide charcoal) was transferred for three years to Richard Hanbury and Robert Bracebridge. In 1580 Richard Hanbury also acquired an interest in a works at Abercarn, following the death of Edmund Roberts, who for a few years had a gun foundry there.

Richard Hanbury probably spent very little time in South Wales and largely left the day to day running of his various works to his chief clerk, Bartholomew Pettingale, who was in charge of operations at Pontypool. In 1593 Richard was elected Member of Parliament for Minehead, but he served in only one Parliament. His wife Alice also died in that year at the age of 55.

When Richard Hanbury died in 1608, his holdings in Monmouthshire were valued at £5,000. His last ten years seem to have been spent in retirement at Datchet in Buckinghamshire and at the local church can be seen a fine brass commemorating him and his wife, which was apparently erected by Richard after the death of his wife.

In Richard Hanbury's lengthy will there were many bequests, including £5 to the poor of Elmley Lovett, to be employed in repairing the highways of the parish, and £66 13s 4d towards the building of a school in the parish of Feckenham. The future profits from the ironworks were to be divided between the children of his daughter Elizabeth and of his uncle Thomas Hanbury and William Hanbury.

# THE HANBURYS OF PONTYPOOL

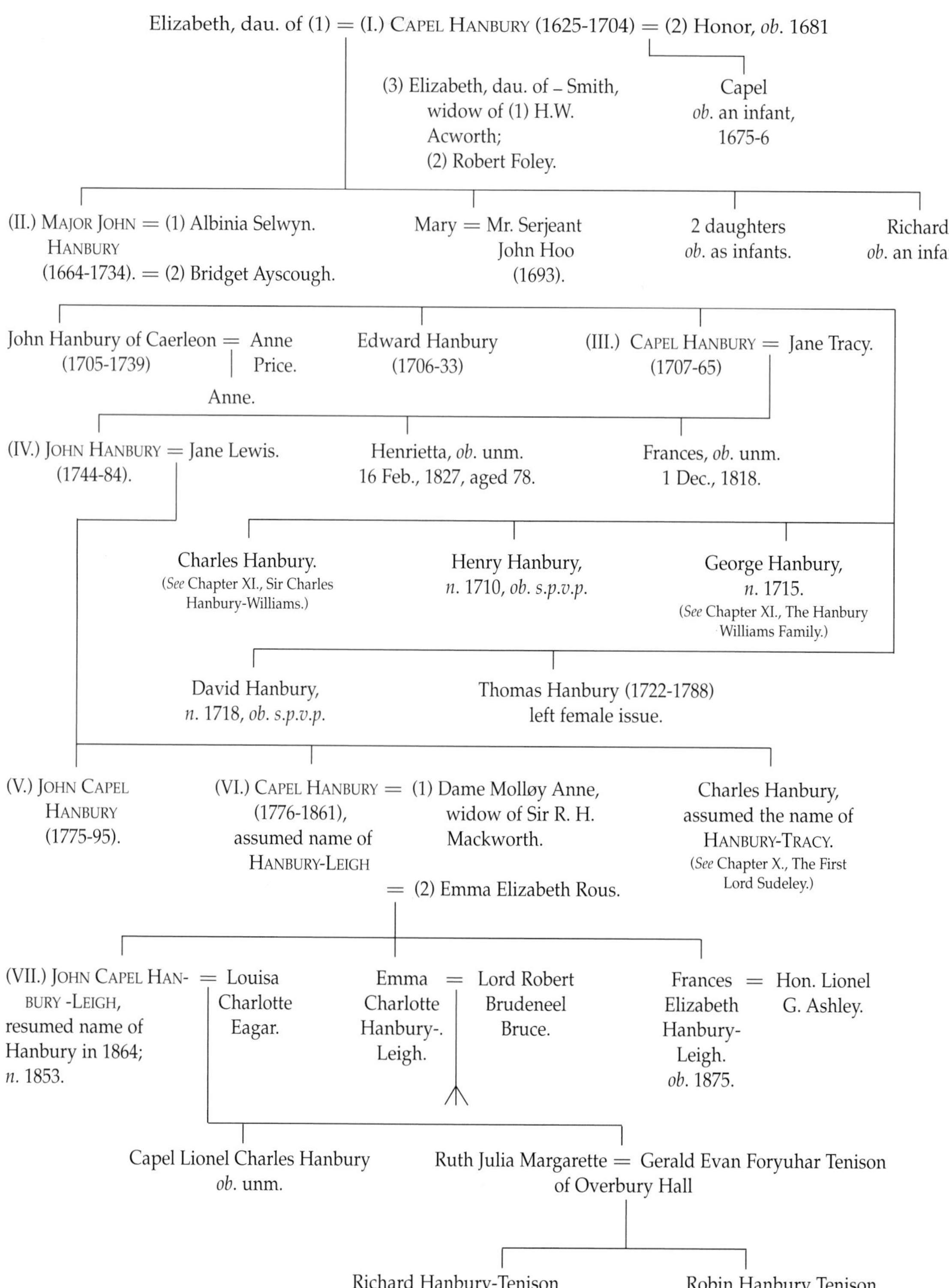

Since Richard had no son, his nephew and executor, John Hanbury of Purshall Green, Elmbridge, inherited the ironworks. On John's death in 1658, his son Capel inherited the business and greatly improved the works at Pontypool. Richard, his brother also, came into the business but died five years later in 1660. Besides the whole of the Monmouthshire properties, Capel, on the death of Richard, also acquired lands near Kidderminster where his brother had lived.

In 1677 Capel purchased for the sum of £192 an area of land on the east side of the Afon Lwyd which flowed past the hamlet of Pont y Pwll. It is recorded that twelve years later he bought a substantial area of additional land from John and Mary Waters for £860. On this land Pontypool Park House was later to be established, which became the seat of the Hanbury family for two hundred and fifty years.

Pontypool Park in 1801. Torfaen Museum Trust.

Capel normally resided at his brother's house, Hoarstone, and there he died in his 79th year on 14th January 1704. He was buried in the chancel of Kidderminster Church, within the altar rails and beneath a flat sepulchral stone. He had, however, built a new house at Pontypool in 1681 and possibly lived in it for a year or two before retiring to Worcestershire. His only son, John Hanbury (b. 1664) received a good education, proving himself a fine scholar. Best known as Major John Hanbury, he gained his military title on serving in the Militia at the age of about 21, and there is a portrait of this period showing him as a young man in an officer's coat of mail. It seemed that he was really destined to become a lawyer for he became a student of the Middle Temple, but on the suggestion of a friend that he should gain more advantage from the ironworks at Pontypool than from the profits of the bar, he turned his attention to mines and forges.

He was the first of the Hanburys to take up permanent residence at Pontypool. The main part of the house at that time faced the park with the original entrance between two short wings, to the front of which was a bowling green. Running out from this original frontage is the modern (early 50s) teaching block which was built on the site of the original stables.

At the rear of the house used to stand a small free-standing chapel in which services were held in English, rather than the Welsh language which was used at the parish church of Trevethin. There was also a dovecote nearby which supplied pigeons for the table.

The estate of Coldbrook, near Abergavenny, was purchased and settled on his son Charles, godson of Charles Williams of Caerleon. Subsequently Charles Hanbury was knighted and known as Sir Charles Hanbury Williams.

In 1701 Major Hanbury married Albinia, daughter of Major George William Selwyn, of Matson in the County of Gloucestershire, and so acquired a considerable fortune. Albina died the following year and John, largely through her family interest, became Member of Parliament for the City of Gloucester in three successive Parliaments. He subsequently represented the County of Monmouth in Parliament during the reign of Queen Anne, and the early part of the reign of George I.

In 1703 he married Bridget Ayscough, daughter of Sir Edward Ayscough of South Kelsey in Lincolnshire. She was a friend of Sarah, Duchess of Marlborough, and stood high in her favour. At the famous Duke's death in 1722 John Hanbury was appointed one of his trustees and executors and, in consequence of his services, the widowed Duchess presented him with a service of plate, and his wife a set of jewels. She also later gave the Hanburys a fine set of wrought iron gates, which accordingly became known as the 'Sally Gate.'

Major Hanbury displayed considerable skill and energy in his business affairs and is celebrated as a pioneer in methods of iron production. He was also well served by his subordinates and in particular his manager, Thomas Cooke, is said to have invented a new method of manufacturing tin plates, by rolling them between water-turned iron cylinder. Twenty years later tinning was introduced and for a generation Pontypool had the monopoly of British tinplate.

So high was John Hanbury's reputation, that, at the reconstruction of the South Sea Company after the crash in 1721, he was appointed one of the new Directors. He was chosen to represent Monmouthshire in Parliament in March 1721 and continued to act as its member until his death in 1734 at the age of 70, when he was buried at Trevethin Church.

Sarah Churchill writing to her grand-daughter, the Duchess of Bedford, on June 22nd, 1734, commented, 'I was really very sorry for the death of Mr Hanbury, for he was a very useful friend to me and mighty easy to live with.'

Major Hanbury's widow continued to reside in Pontypool Park House until her death in 1741, when Capel, the second son, inherited the estate. Seventeen years later he undertook some extensions and alterations to the house. Between 1752 and 1765 the house was extended by a bow-fronted and slightly taller addition to the rear of the original building. This included on the ground floor a new dining room with a high ceiling, to accommodate some large portraits which had formerly been in the London home of Sir Charles Hanbury Williams (brother of Capel Hanbury). The mantle piece in this room is said to have been made of Russian marble and sent to Pontypool by Sir Charles, whilst he was ambassador to the Russian Empress Catherine the Great between 1755 and 1758.

Following Capel's death in1765, he was succeeded by his son John ( born in 1744) who inherited the estate which by then amounted to 16,000 acres in the parishes of Aberystruth, Trevethin, Caerleon, Llanfrechfa, Llanthony, Llanbadoc, Llangattock near Caerleon, Llandegfedd, Llangibby, Panteg, Varteg and Tredunock. He died in 1784 and his eldest son, also named John, died in 1795 when the estate was inherited by the second son, Capel Hanbury Leigh. The name of Leigh had been adopted in hopes of inheriting the estate of the 5th Lord Leigh of Stoneleigh Abbey, which Lord Leigh had bequeathed to his next-of-kin, bearing the name and arms of Leigh.

Brass of Richard Hanbury in
Datchet parish church Berkshire

Capel Hanbury Leigh

Major John Hanbury

Sir Charles Hanbury Williams

Capel Hanbury Leigh had married well, for his wife was Molly, the 20 year old widow of Sir Robert Mackworth of Knoll Castle, Glamorgan. Her first husband had died in 1794, aged 30, bequeathing almost the whole 10,000 acres estate to her. Molly herself came from a family of Quaker ironmasters who had settled further up the Neath Valley at Melin-y-cwrt.

In 1799 Capel Hanbury Leigh was appointed High Sheriff of Monmouthshire and he and his wife soon set about improvements to Pontypool Park House and plans were made 'to improve and beautify' the place.

The building was given a new entrance with a pillared portico and the space between the wings on the ground floor was filled with a library. A new hall and staircase were built and the century-old rooms were re-decorated in the sort of neo-Louis XV style then popular, involving extensive use of gold leaf.

Filling the centre of the south-east front, the Drawing Room was a magnificent apartment with Ionic capitals. The Grand Staircase opening off the north-western end of the Hall was fitted with a metal balustrade, surmounted by a light mahogany hand rail, the whole well lit by a lofty window. The Dining Room although not large, was noted for its deep frieze, with a grape vine ornamentation, and rams' heads set at intervals. A marble mantlepiece gave added dignity to the room. Mural decorations, ceilings and cornices and the furniture throughout the house were all typical of the eighteenth century, and an extensive art collection was in keeping with the period.

In about 1830 the stables to the east of the house were demolished and new ones in the form of a quadrangle built on the west side. This involved the removal of the dovecote and chapel and the new stables were laid out around a quadrangle. These have now become the Valley Inheritance Museum.

Capel was handicapped by the surrender by his widowed mother of the lease of mineral rights on Lord Abergavenny's estates, notably the area around Blaenavon, which had been held for nearly two hundred years. But he injected new life into the Pontypool business, which included a new works at Pontyfelin, the old Osborne Forge, the Town Forge and Plating Mill, the Park Forge (still in the Park until 1830) and the Trosnant Forge, together with extensive mine workings and blast furnaces at Coed Alice and Blaendare.

In 1807, Capel entered into a partnership with the engineer Watkin George and during the Napoleonic wars the Pontypool works reached a peak of efficiency and prosperity. After the first two years of the partnership, profits of £32,000 were paid to Capel Hanbury Leigh and £8,300 to Watkin George.

By 1831, Capel Hanbury had closed the Park Forge and probably used the rubble from the demolished buildings to fill in the Forge Pond. He also erected three new buildings around this time. These were the entrance lodge, Tank Cottage (which was given this name because the man living there was responsible for controlling the sluice gates regulating the Nant y Gollen stream) and the Rustic Lodge which was constructed of large blocks of conglomerate or 'pudding stone'. The town map of 1836 shows all these changes complete and the Park Forge resited outside the Park.

Despite the fact that Pontypool iron and tinplate continued to be among the best in the world, competition increased and during the 1830s and 1840s profit margins declined. The Hanbury Leigh / Watkin George partnership was dissolved and by the 1840s the works were losing £10,000 a year. In 1851 the decision was made to lease all the business interests to a group which later became the Ebbw Vale Company, thus ending the Hanbury association with Pontypool ironmaking which had lasted for two hundred and fifty years.

John Capel Hanbury the last Squire of Pontypool.

Molly Hanbury Leigh died childless on 27th January 1846 and a year later Capel married Emma Rous of Cwrt-yr-ala, Glamorganshire. Two daughters, Emma and Frances were born of this second marriage. Emma's third and last child, named John, was born in London on 14th May 1853 and the *Monmouthsire Merlin* reported that:-

> 'The welcome news was echoed and re-echoed through the hills by the mighty booming of cannon and a Committee was formed ... for the purpose of making arrangements for the manifestation of their sincere regard for the worthy squire and his excellent lady.'

There was great rejoicing in Pontypool when the Hanbury family returned to Pontypool on the 9th June. A procession of several thousand people marched from the Blue Boar Field to Pontypool Park where an address was made by Dr Edward Phillips to which Capel Hanbury Leigh replied:-

> 'Gentlemen, the sentiments conveyed in the address you have done me the honour to present, are too flattering to allow me to express in suitable terms the sincere gratitude I feel for this generous demonstration of respect and attachment. Be assured, gentlemen, that the day will be indelibly impressed on my mind. I have not the vanity, however, to suppose that this mark of estime is unaccompanied by feelings to those of my family who have preceded me, and to whose popularity I am mainly indebted for this token of your respect. To me the pleasing task now devolves of acknowledging this tribute to their memory.
>
> I must now advert to the occasion which has given rise to the demonstration of this day, in celebration of the birth of a boy, which is indeed a source of infinite joy to Mrs Hanbury Leigh and myself. I trust he may live to merit and enjoy the goodwill of his neighbours. Be assured no exertion shall be spared to inculcate those principles which may render him worthy of the regard you have ever evinced towards his family.
>
> In commemoration of this event and in consequence of the growing importance and prosperity of this town, I am induced to hope that a hall or suitable building for public meetings and deliberations on all local requirements would be of the greatest utility and service to the inhabitants of Pontypool. I therefore beg to be allowed the gratification of erecting a hall, to obviate the inconvenience arising from the want of such accommodation which I fear has been too long felt.
>
> I will no longer detain you than to assure you from Mrs Hanbury Leigh and myself, that the anniversary of this day will ever be cherished in grateful remembrance of the honour you have done us.'

Festivities in the town to celebrate the birth of the Hanbury heir culminated in the roasting of a three-year old ox, weighing 1372 lbs, in the Vegetable Market (probably on the site of the present market). It was then taken to the park and carved and portions distributed to an estimated crowd of 20,000 people.

In 1861 Capel Hanbury Leigh passed away at the age of 85, at his summer house in Penarth, after accidently taking poison. He was ill and when he asked his valet, who had served him well for 28 years, to give him his medicine, the man accidently took the wrong bottle of two which stood on the mantlepiece in Capel's bedroom. It was the one which contained not his master's medicine, but a lethal 'Hawkins Embrocation'.

Capel Hanbury's son John, who was only six at the time of his father's death, came of age in 1874 and his birthday was celebrated throughout the town. The Town Hall was gaily decorated, and a decorative plaque placed at the front entrance, which read: 'May he tread in the footsteps of his forefathers and be beloved as they were.'

In January 1864 John Capel had resumed the family name of Hanbury by royal licence and his only changes to the family home included the demolition of some rooms at the back and the construction of a wing which opened out from the north-west side of the Dining Room and had a suite of bachelor's bedrooms above it.

To escape from the cloying atmosphere of his widowed mother and two daughters, for a few years he rented Kentchurch Court in Herefordshire from the Scudamore family, where he entertained in lavish style.

On the 8th July, 1885, he married Louisa Charlotte Tasmania Eager (better known as Elsie), daughter of Colonel Edward Hungerford Eager, in St Michael's Church, Chester Square, London. On the day of the wedding cannon, specially cast at Pontymoel Foundry, were fired in Pontypool, the loud salvos producing echoes far and wide. At Pontypool Park House firing also took place, and in the afternoon a huge bonfire was lit in the Park, and rockets and other fireworks were let off.

A son was born to the couple in London during 1893 and they named him Capel Lionel Charles. John Capel Hanbury and his wife now took a long lease of Gordonstoun House, near Elgin in Morayshire, an impressive property (now a famous school) owned at that time by Sir William Gordon Cumming. This enabled them to spend their summers in Scotland and then head down to London for the winter. However, it was also necessary for John Capel Hanbury to make regular visits to Pontypool in order to discuss the management of the family estate with his agent.

In August 1908 young Capel, the only son of John Capel Hanbury, returned home from Winchester College feeling unwell. Symptoms of appendicitis showed themselves and the development of the disease was so acute that Dr Stanley Boyd of Harley Street, London was called in by the family doctor. An operation was performed but Capel unfortunately died soon after.

Mrs and Mrs John Capel Hanbury of Pontypool Park
and their daughter Ruth Julia Margarette.

John Hanbury announced in 1912 that he would be giving up his family residence at Pontypool Park and three years later the mansion was leased for 21 years to the nuns from St Alban's Convent. The stables together with the cattle market on the other side of the road were sold to Pontypool Urban District Council.

In 1913 a conference of Pontypool, Panteg and Abersychan Councils with Mr J. O. Tyler, agent to the Pontypool Park Estate, met to discuss a scheme for setting aside part of the Pontypool Park as an area for the public to enjoy. It was decided to ask Mr Hanbury (who later agreed) to give the councils a portion of the park. They would then make a through road from the Pontymoel gates to come out at the back of Park House and continue over Park Road up to the Old Mill, Pontnewynydd. Here there would be a division into two roads, one joining Leigh Road, near the Pontypool Hospital, while the other would connect with the existing road near the Old Brewery. A new road was also proposed from the Town Hall to connect with the proposed road near the pond in Home Park. Abersychan's proportion of the cost was estimated at £8,000, Pontypool's at £5,000 and Panteg's £3,000 of which a private contribution would provide £1,500. These roads were never built.

The 158 acre Pontypool Park was transferred in 1920 to the urban district councils of Abersychan, Panteg and Pontypool as trustees of the public on generous terms and conditions for the sum of £11,000. During April of that year John Capel Hanbury (68) was taken ill with jaundice and liver failure and he died at his home in Sevenoaks, Kent on 8th May and was cremated at Golder's Green Crematorium. He left his widow, Elsie, and a 20 year old daughter, Ruth Julia Margarette.

The arms of Hanbury of Pontypool

During his life Squire Hanbury had made countless gifts to local causes. He had provided the site on which Pontypool Hospital was built and financially helped the hospital in its early days. When his son Capel L. C. Hanbury died in 1908, the Squire commemorated him by adding a wing to the hospital. He also provided sites for the West Monmouthshire School, St Hilda's Church, Griffithstown and numerous other public buildings.

A committee was now set up by the three local authorities to draw up a report on proposals for managing and improving the Park. It was stated that their aim would be:-

> ' ...to make the Park as far as possible part of the daily life of the town and not a space merely used for Sundays and holidays. With a little effort it should be possible to make it a place which would at all times attract anyone with an hour to spare for rest and recreation. For the children, a special childrens' corner will always be available, not only for small children but for those of school age. The value of an hour or so each day spent in the open air among pleasant surroundings cannot be over-estimated both for children and their elders.
>
> With so many natural features of beauty and interest and such charming viewpoints from the higher ground, it will be obvious that the upper portion of the Park, with its steep undulating slopes rising from 400 ft to over 700 ft above ordnance datum, should as far as possible be preserved in its natural state, although even here much can be done by wise and effective free planting to improve the quality of the landscape. The dead or decayed trees should also at the same time be removed.
>
> The utmost use should be made of all natural watercourses and the central valley - both above and below the reservoir - developed with a chain of cascades. It may be found possible at a later date, by constructing a dam across the valley just above the existing reservoir to form a lake of some size. The banks of the lower portion of the stream below the reservoir can readily be transformed into a rock garden, specially devoted to local ferns and flowers.
>
> At the principal viewpoints a sufficient number of seats should be provided. At present a certain number of benches have been provided in the neighbourhood of the bandstand, but these need to be largely supplemented at important points.
>
> A certain number of shelters or summer houses will be desirable at special viewpoints and if constructed in the manner of the small Grecian temples at Kew Gardens, these might add considerable architectural charm to the Park. The design and placing of these structures will need considerable thought and should be done under the direction of a qualified architect.
>
> The Grotto should form one of the Park's greatest attractions both from the quaintness of the workmanship and the curious nature of the shells, bones and stalactites used in its construction. It occupies one of the most commanding viewpoints in the whole district and a visit to the grotto enables the visitor to see the full extent and charm of the Park itself.'
>
> The proposals also included a Bowling Green, Tennis Courts and Sports Ring, Children's Playground and the siting of a Tea House 'on rising ground just above the pond beyond the Mansion, from which point are magnificent views of Cwm Lichey and the evening sun.' There would also be a New Bridge and entrance from the south - 'a light suspension bridge at a fairly high level with sloping approaches could be constructed with charming effect and thus give entrance from the Town Hall.'

A fine set of wrought iron gates at the Pontymoel entrance to Pontypool Park.

**Pontymoel Gates**

At the Pontymoel entrance to Pontypool Park can be seen an impressive set of wrought iron gates which are not only the best example of 18th and 19th century ironwork in South Wales, but also the most significant monument to the iron industry in Pontypool still standing.

The central portion was constructed in the 1720s, but the gate piers and side gates were reconstructed in 1835 by Thomas Deakin, a local mining engineer and an associate of John Vipond of Varteg Collieries. He was instructed by Capel Hanbury Leigh to produce some drawings and specification which came to light when William Webb found them among the papers of S.T. Roderick,. The works was probably done in the old Cross workshop occupied by Davies & Edwards before they moved to Crane Street, later to become Sandbrook and Dawe.

So it was in that year that the cast iron columns with grape decoration were made. These cluster of vine in beaten lead are a noteworthy example of the moulders' art, as it was practiced at Blaenavon Iron Works. Thomas Deakin's name used to be on a brass plate which was fixed to a cross-bar of the gates but was removed some years ago. In 1849 he died whilst emigrating to Australia and was buried at sea.

Beside the gates at the Pontymoel entrance used to stand Park Lodge, the home of a park keeper. But, being adjacent to the Afon Lwyd, the building suffered from frequent flooding and was demolished in 1959, having become uninhabitable.

The road on the south side of the gates passes over the river and the old bridge which once stood here gave its name to the locality. Pontymoel in English means 'the bridge by the bare mountain.'

In 1920 the Pontypool Urban District Council purchased the Park Stables from the Hanbury estate, including a pair of 19th century iron gates which filled the archway leading directly to the grounds. They served no other purpose than that of ornament and the archway was later bricked up. In 1924 these gates were brought to the Park to form part of the Joint War Memorial of the Pontypool and Abersychan Councils.

## The Stables

The existing stable block was built by Capel Hanbury Leigh in 1835 near the site of the demolished chapel and dovecote. Around the quadrangle the single storey blocks were stables and the line of double doors marks the coach-houses, with loft above. The tall arch opposite gave entry to the front of Pontypool Park House and the two-storey block adjoining it housed tack rooms. In the centre of the courtyard is a circular horse trough.

Along with Pontypool Park the stables came into the ownership of the local authorities in 1920. For some years the buildings were used for a variety of purposes which included a disinfectant factory, barracks for Indian soldiers during World War Two, housing, education centre, council depot, old age pensioners'' club and chest clinic. By 1978 the buildings had reached a poor state of repair. They were then restored and became the headquarters of the Torfaen Museum Trust. Here can be found the fascinating Valley Inheritance Museum.

The first chairman of the Trust was the well known Cwmbran magistrate Arthur Wait, who as a child lived at the old Llanyrafon watermill. The aim of the Trust is 'to protect the whole of the Eastern Valley as a living museum, preserving sites and areas of particular historical significance. The Park Museum, to be called the Valley Inheritance would provide visitors with geological, geographical, archaeological and historic background before they set out on site visits.'

## The Icehouses

Near the front of the stable block are the remains of a pair of icehouses built in 1838. These were designed to keep ice year-round which was collected in the winter from the Forge Pond and kept in layers separated by straw. The ice houses were constructed in brick and stone and on the same principle as a vacuum flask. The outer casing has been renewed, but layers of brick lining survive. A pair of ice-houses is very unusual for they were normally built in single units.

## The American Gardens

During the depression of 1841 Capel Hanbury Leigh imported a substantial cargo of foreign shrubs and engaged local unemployed men to plant the American Gardens which were watered by the mountain stream Nant-y-gollen (hazel brook). A wall was built, some large trees removed to make space for more rhododendrons and azaleas; plants from the Pacific coast of the USA and sequoias were obtained and the Rustic Lodge was built from large blocks of conglomerate (pudding stone) to house a caretaker. Capel subsequently kept fourteen gardeners maintaining the gardens and also the roads in the vicinity, along which he rode daily in his carriage.

## The Italian Gardens

This part of the Park was designed and planted with exotic trees and plants in about 1850. It was inspired by a visit to Italy on the occasion of the honeymoon of Capel Hanbury Leigh and his second wife Emma Rous.

When the Park was transferred to the three local authorities in 1920, for some reason, the Italian Gardens were not included, but four years later they were given to the town by Mrs Ruth Tenison.

The Shell Grotto in Pontypool Park was erected between 1830 and 1840.

The interior of the Shell Grotto is decorated with shells, stalactites, minerals and bones.

## The Grotto

Molly, the wife of Capel Hanbury Leigh, is credited with the idea of establishing the Grotto which stands at the top of the Park at an altitude of 700 feet above sea level. She had a similar grotto at her home in the Neath Valley and obviously decided that the Pontypool Estate should have one as well. A story is told of how she was travelling in France and came across a hermit whom she brought back to Pontypool, where he was given the task of constructing the Grotto. He is said to have spent seven years on this project, during which time he lived inside the building whilst undertaking the interior decoration.

Whether this story is true or not, the Grotto was probably designed by the Bath architect, Stephen Gunstant Tit and it was erected between 1830 and 1840. Its design reflects the 'romantic' period which also gave us the poetry of Wordsworth and Shelley and the paintings of Constable. The building is circular in shape with a conical tiled roof, fan vaulted inside and supported by six pillars. The walls and ceiling have been decorated with thousands of shells which include mussels, periwinkles, cockles and limpets, were brought mainly from the West Wales coast. In addition there are stalactites and clusters of spar and minerals. Animal bones from mainly horses, sheep and deer that used to be on the Park Estate have been arranged on the floor in geometric patterns, stars, and a ring of hearts and diamonds.

The Hanbury family used the Grotto as a summer house and for their shooting party lunches. It is of interest that he first royal visitor to the Grotto was the Prince of Wales, later crowned Edward VII, who was entertained at Pontypool by Squire John Hanbury.

On May 16, 1952 the Grotto was broken into and wrecked by hooligans. A large hole was made in the roof and entrance was apparently gained that way. Windows, shutters and chairs were broken and a cupboard forced. The interior of the building was strewn with debris from the roof. Repairs were carried out but, following further vandalism in the 1960s the Grotto was closed to the public.

In 1994, Torfaen County Borough Council decided to restore the Grotto to its former glory. Funded by the Heritage Lottery Fund (£30,000 grant), Cadw and the European Regional Development Fund, work commenced in June 1995 and the Grotto was at last reopened to the public in May 1997. The four stained glass windows were restored and even the old rustic chairs have been repaired.

The official opening of the Grotto, and also the lighting of the Folly Tower was celebrated in June 1998 with a mock 1830's picnic involving actors dressed as members of the Hanbury family. Later in the evening there was a torchlight walk to the Folly to mark the switching on of the new floodlights.

## The Folly Tower

William Coxe tells us how in the company of Mr and Mrs Hanbury Leigh, he had a pleasant ride through the Park and grounds to reach the folly, '...a summer house built by the late Mr Hanbury, near the southern extremity of the chain of hills, which stretch from Pont y Pool park and terminate in the Blorenge. From this eminence, the wild and fertile parts of Monmouthshire, the hills and dales, plains and mountains, are beautifully combined, and enriched with woodlands, which overspread the country beneath and around to a considerable extent. No traveller should quit Monmouthshire without enjoying this singular and almost boundless prospect.'

This Folly Tower was built by John Hanbury in 1765 on the supposed site of an ancient watch tower reputedly established on that spot by the Romans. There is no doubt that this story arose from the alleged Roman Road which ran from Llanhilleth through Pantygasseg and Trevethin, past the site of the Folly and then descended to Mamhilad. Historians on the other hand argue that the length of paved road that can be seen descending the hillside to Mamhilad was in fact constructed in medieval times.

John Hanbury's tower was octagonal in design, about 38 feet high and 19 feet across the base. It was positioned in an ideal position to take advantage of the extensive views. His grandson, Capel Hanbury Leigh was obviously proud of his inherited tower for he carried out renovations to it in 1831.

Most follies date from the 18th and 19th centuries and they are relics of a period when there was a new appreciation of nature and landscape. Towers of many shapes, round, triangular, octagonal etc., were set up in places where they 'commanded the prospect,' or distant view. Others took the form of a sham castle and such an example in Monmouthshire is at Clytha. Another well-known prospect tower in the same county is Kemey's Folly which stands on the edge of the Wentwood escarpment overlooking the Usk Valley.

It used to be claimed that seven counties could be seen from the top of Pontypool Folly on a clear day and years ago it was also a popular place for picnics, particularly on Bank Holidays. On the Silver Jubilee of King George V, in May 1935, an estimated 17,000 people gathered around the Folly to witness the lighting of a bonfire.

In 1931 Pontypool Council asked Panteg Council to expedite the work of repairing the Folly Tower. Mr R. S. Trump said the Folly should be one of the chief attractions of the town. He hoped to see the Folly lighted up, attracting thousands to Pontypool, the best shopping centre in Monmouthshire.

In February 1935 it was suggested by Mr. R. S. Trump that the Folly which at that time was in danger of collapse should be repaired, to commemorate the Silver Jubilee of King George V. A public fund could be set up to cover the cost.

A nearby dwelling known as 'Twr Watch Farm' (Watchtower Farm) was demolished in the 1930s, and ten years later the Folly itself was blown up by the Army on 7th July, 1940, by order of the Ministry of Defence, as a secondary measure under the Emergency Powers (Defence) Act 1939. They were concerned that it would be a useful landmark for German aircraft seeking to bomb the nearby Royal Ordnance Factory at Glascoed. It is ironic that a year or so later a stray German bomb fell onto the rubble of the Folly and would have destroyed it anyway.

A keystone over the doorway bearing the date '1831' was salvaged from the rubble and taken to the Pontypool Estate Office. It obviously related to the restoration of the tower by Capel Hanbury Leigh in that year.

Three years after the War ended, pleas were starting to be made for the Folly to be rebuilt. The following letter to the Editor of the *Free Press* is but one example:-

> 'The site of the Folly, to a home-coming exile, used to quicken the pulse as the sight of his beloved quickens the pulse of a lover. Only exiles really understand this, and as one of them, I want to add my plea for the rebuilding of the old tower.
>
> We are told that it was pulled down in the public interest. Very well, the sacrifice has been made, and now is the time to replace it.
>
> If a subscription list was opened I am convinced that the necessary money would soon be raised. The Folly was an integral part of the place we call home.'
>
> J.B. Hynam 1948.

Re-construction of the Folly Tower was commenced by Jack Everson, a local stonemason during the Autumn of 1992 and completed by Davies & Jenkins (Pontypool) Ltd in July 1994. The project was funded by ERDF, CROFT, Gwnt County Council and the Prince of Wales Committee.

But surprisingly Pontypool Council by a heavy majority voted against taking steps to rebuild the Tower. 'The best landmark we can get in our area is more houses,' said Councillor Smith, moving that the Council take no action in response to a request from the Chamber of Trade that they approach Mrs Ruth Tenison and then take the initiative in launching a public appeal for the necessary funds to rebuild the Folly.

In September 1951 Mr Protheroe wrote to the Editor of the Free Press:-

> 'I understand that there is still a body of ineffective opinion in Pontypool that would favour a re-construction of the Folly Tower. Sometime ago a rumour reached me in London that a group of youths in Pontypool had vowed never to shave again until the tower had been restored, and that they could be seen at every full-moon making incantations as they moved in be-whiskered circles around the remains of the tower.'
>
> J. Cliff Protheroe

Mr F. C. Chapman at the monthly meeting of the Pontypool Chamber of Trade in November 1958 suggested that a 'tower of glass' should be erected on the site of the folly. He considered that such an erection would advertise the town and the fact that glass was manufactured at Pilkington's Pontypool. He argued that it would be a financial asset and a great attraction to visitors as well as a good advertisement for the local glass industry.

It was not until 1990 that serious consideration was given to rebuilding the Folly. Some local men, including the authors of the book 'Pontypool's Heritage decided to take action and in March of that year held the inaugural meeting of CROFT, which is an acronym for 'Campaign to Rebuild the Old Folly Tower.' The organisation was registered as a charity and the eight founder members conveniently included an architect and a stonemason.

With full cooperation from the Pontypool Park Estate and with the consent of the Brecon Beacons National Park Authority, the group raised initial finance by holding concerts, raffles, walks and a 'Sponsor a Stone' appeal which brought enthusiastic response from locals and Pontypool exiles living as far away as America and Canada. Their names were to be recorded on a special commemorative plaque placed inside the tower.

Construction started on the site in the Autumn of 1992, with Jack Everson, a local stonemason doing the building and volunteers acting as labourers. Torfaen Borough Council assisted the project with the donation of 175 tonnes of dressed stone from the demolished Cwmffrwdoer Primary School and the old platform of Crane Street Railway Station.

In April 1993 a time-capsule was buried within the Tower cavity walls. It contains a civic message from the Mayor of Torfaen, a Torfaen Borough Council plaque, CROFT'S campaign literature, contemporary copies of the 'Free Press' and 'South Wales Argus' and a Pontypool RFC programme.

A month later the foundation stone laying ceremony was performed by Richard Hanbury Tenison, who said, 'I lay this stone for the rebuilding of this tower, a symbol of our heritage, for the benefit of the community at large.'

By September the tower had reached a height of 20 feet and towards the end of the year a financial breakthrough was made with grant aid being obtained from the Prince of Wales Trust and the European Regional Development Fund. It was stipulated, however that the remainder of the work would have to go out to tender.

In due course a contract was awarded to the local firm, Davies & Jenkins (Pontypool) Ltd., who worked hard to complete the tower by Friday, July 22nd 1994, when Prince Charles flew in by helicopter to perform the opening ceremony. He was undertaking a grand tour of the Principality to celebrate the 25th year of his investiture as Prince of Wales. The tower is 38 feet high, measures 19 feet across the base and cost an estimated £60,000 to restore.

Official opening of the new Folly Tower by Prince Charles on 2nd July 1994.

**From the Last Squire to the Present Day**

John Capel Hanbury, the last Squire of Pontypool, died on 8th May 1921, having been taken ill the previous month with jaundice and liver problems. His only son Capel Lionel Charles had died in1908. The heir to the estate was the only daughter Ruth, who married Major Gerald Tenison, and their eldest son Richard was born in 1925. MrsHanbury, the widow of John Capel Hanbury, died at Gordonstoun, Scotland in 1927 at the age of 82.

In 1946 Richard Hanbury-Tenison, celebrated his coming of age and fifty tenant farmers of the estate presented him with a water colour painting of Park House, the family ancestral home.

Richard joined the army in 1943 and after being wounded in France served as a Staff Captain.In 1953 he married Euphan Wardlaw Ramsay and they were blessed with three sons and two daughters. His later career was in the Diplomatic Service.

In 1970 the Hanbury Tenisons took over Clytha House near Abergavenny and carried out major renovations to the building. Much of the contents of Pontypool Park House were moved there and the collection of paintings includes contemporary portraits of the Duke of Marlborough and Robert Walpole, who were friends of the family.

Richard decided to retire from the Diplomatic Service in 1975 and to manage his estate full time. Two years later he was appointed High Sheriff of Gwent and in 1980 he was made Lord Lieutenant, the Queen's representative in the county. The last time the Hanbury family had supplied a Lord Lieutenant was in 1836. As the Queen's representative in the county, Sir Richard Hanbury Tenison has the responsibiliy of co-ordinating royal visits and he also represents the Queen at important events in Gwent. He received a knighthood in 1995.

Sir Richard Hanbury-Tenison laying the foundation stone of the new Folly Tower in May 1993.
*Picture supplied by Arthur Crane.*

## -- 4 --

# Coal Mining in the Eastern Valley

*'The Welsh valleys suffered to a peculiar degree the horrors of the first industrialism: the well-known abuses of child labour, excessive hours and sordid conditions for men and women, low wages and unfair methods of payment were felt to the full, and the very nature of coalmining made all this terrible in the extreme.'*

E. & P. Lewis 1937

Stretching from the Eastern Valley to St Bride's Bay in Pembrokeshire, the South Wales coalfield is over 90 miles in length and varies in width from over 16 miles in Glamorgan to about 2 miles in Pembrokeshire. Coal had been mined in the vicinity of Pontypool for centuries, but at first it was only used for domestic purposes and for the burning of limestone to provide lime for the land, a practice which started in 1615. Records are scanty, but it is known that around 1600, local tenants were working 'outcrop' or surface coal for their personal use in defiance of the Manor of Wentsland and Bryngwyn by whom the minerals were claimed.

In the first period of the Industrial Revolution, from the 16th century, timber was used for the manufacture of charcoal, then an essential ingredient in the making of iron, and the wooded slopes of the Eastern Valley were no doubt one of the main attractions for the first ironmasters who came to Pontypool. But their charcoal burning furnaces had greedy appetites which led to a scarcity of timber and a serious decline in the iron industry. Sixteen sacks of charcoal were required to produce one ton of pig iron. An acre of woodland was only sufficient to supply enough charcoal to enable a mere three tons of iron to be produced.

In the last decade of the eighteenth century coal began to play an increasingly important part in the production of iron as a result of the work of Abraham Darby, who in 1735 first succeeded using coal, converted into coke, as a fuel for his Coalbrookdale Works in Shropshire.

Ironstone mining on the hills north of Blaenavon had begun as early as the 16th century, excavating the outcrops by processes such as 'patchworking' and scouring with water released from behind a dam. Coal was gathered by similar methods and later both minerals had to be reached by small shafts known as bell pits. In these early days mineral working was usually a part time activity of local farmers. By the early 19th century the Blaenavon Company had taken charge and many levels were being driven into the hillside, with deeper shafts following in the 1840s. The landscape near Blaenavon retains valuable evidence of these early workings today.

The next development was the sinking of shallow pits known as 'Balance Pits' and it is significant that a part of old Abersychan became known as 'Balance Houses'. Coal was raised to the surface by a system of balancing in adjoining pit cages, in one of which was a full tram of coal; while to the other was attached a tank of water which could be filled or emptied as required. The ponds for filling the tanks were known as 'Balance Ponds'.

Prior to the development of the steam engine by Newcomen in 1712, mining could not be carried out below the level of natural drainage; that is below the level at which underground waters would flow away either of their own accord or by way of a narrow addit cut through to a neighbouring valley. The invention of this machine meant that at last deep mining could be undertaken for it provided a mechanical means of removing water from deep underground. New pits were sunk and old ones which had become flooded could now be re-opened. Steam operated engines (later powered by electricity) were also introduced to power winding and haulage of coal.

Another important change was that the method of working the seams by the pillar and stall system was superseded by the long-wall method which was introduced during the latter half of the 19th century. This technique enabled the coal to be removed in one continuous operation. The space from which the coal was removed, known as the 'gob,' was afterwards packed with rock and debris which took the weight of the roof strata as it settled. The main advantage of this system was that no coal was abandoned as were the pillars in the old method. It also enabled more men to be employed along a given length of face which produced a greater proportion of large coal.

Pontypool began to develop as a coal extraction area soon after the cutting of the Monmouthshire Canal. John Barnaby, a native of Herefordshire obviously realised that there was a good future in coal, for not long after acquiring the Blaendare iron furnace for £10,000 he disposed of the works in order to concentrate on coal mining. After seeking the advice of Edward Martin of Swansea on the driving of a level he spent £30,000 on developing his collieries. By 1809 he was raising over 200,000 tons of coal per annum.

In 1820 the first deep mine was sunk on the Pontypool Park Estate, at Coed Golynos above the Glyn Valley, the Balance Pit in 1832 and the Glyn Pit in 1837. At the Glyn Pit important surface buildings still remain and are some of the best of the period anywhere in the United Kingdom.

At Blaenavon, colliery workings had started in 1782 when the Bridge Level was opened by Thomas Hill, Thomas Hopkins and Benjamin Pratt. They drove two levels, one above the other and iron rails were laid to carry away the coal and iron ore. By 1799 one of the passages was three-quarters of a mile in length and it was later extended to form the Pwldu tramroad tunnel.

Other early collieries in the Blaenavon area included:-

Aaron Brute's level, near the houses of that name; Wood Level, by the riverside; Old Slope, near Engine Pit; Big Pits; Horn Coal Slope; Dodd's Slope; Coity Pits; Coity Level; Cinder Pits; Frank Reid's Level; Dick Shon's Level; Middle Level; Garn Pits; Kay's Slope; Waunavon Slope; Milfraen Pits; Grwn-chin Level; New Pit; Balance Pit; Hill Pits; Jack Bennett's Level; Moses Robin's Level; Jom Hoskin's Level; Gant's two levels; Pwldu Collieries, and Engine Coal Levels.

By now people were flocking to the Eastern Valley from all directions in search of employment or higher wages than could be earned as agricultural workers and as a result the population of Monmouthshire between 1801 and 1841 increased by 117 per cent, which was the highest rate of increase of any shire in the British Isles.

This in-rush brought with it a large non-Welsh element, particularly from the south-west of England and also a particular increase of Irish workers, driven out by recurrent famines in 1817 and 1818, culminating in the great famine of 1846. Irish families, in extreme stages of destitution were brough over as ballast by returning coal boats which landed their human cargoe on the Glamorgan coast. From there they would beg their way to the centres of industry. Many other Irishmen had come over as 'navigators' digging the Monmouthshire and Brecon Canal.

*'The boys called carters are employed in narrow seams of coal in parts of Monmouthshire. Their occupation is to drag the carts or skips of coal from the working place to the main road. In this mode of labour the leather girdle passes round the body and the chain is between the legs, attached to the cart, and the lads drag on all fours.'*

Report of the Childrens' Employment Commission of 1842.

**The Employment of Women and Children**

It is on record that in 1841 there were 2002 people employed in the underground iron and coal works at Blaenavon and included in this total were 26 female adults, 58 girls between the ages of 13 and 18; while under the age of 13 there were 36 girls and 135 boys. Statistics given for the year 1838 show that during that year 58 children under 13 and 62 between the ages of 13 and 18 were killed in the mining industry in South Wales and Monmouthshire. It was said in those days that to take the children out of the mines would ruin the industry. Also it was believed that to improve their conditions would have the same effect.

Children were sometimes carried down the mine at an early age in order that the father might claim an additional tram but they generally started work as trappers at the age of five years for sixpence to eightpence a day. Their duty consisted of opening and shutting trap doors to assist ventilation and to allow the passage of trams, a task which was a form of solitary confinement. At the age of eleven they graduated to the task of hauling and assisting in the carting of coal to the mine shaft.

Rhys William Jones and Robert Hugh Franks of the Royal Commission compiled a report in 1841 on the employment of women and children in South Wales and when it was published the following year it contained the following information regarding the employment of young people at Blaenavon:-

> 'The coals are brought from the workings to the mainways by horses, adults and children, and young persons from 12 to 18 years of age. In the mine-work there areat this employment, males 50, females 30 in number, and in the collieries 70 males from 12 years to 18 years old.
>
> Children and young persons very seldom draw by belt or girdle in the mine-works, if by chance any are so employed in air-courses or other small places, males are employed from 14 to 16 years of age; but in the collieries young persons from 12 to 18 years of age draw with a belt a carriage of the weight of about 5cwt. for a distance of from 10 to 40 yards. In some instances in the mine-works they draw 500, 600, and even 700 yards, a carriage running upon tram-plates, containing 12 cwt; 18 cwt, and sometimes one ton.

Females are employed in getting the mine (ironstone) and loading it into the trams; there are also a great number of boys under 13 years of age assisting their parents in getting coal.

The other employments for children and young persons are driving horses and tending doors for turning the current of air for ventilation, and sweeping roads. They begin work as early as nine or ten years of age.

The works do not require them so young, but the parents themselves are desirous that their children should be employed very young to tend doors or any other light work.

Girls regularly perform all the various offices of trapping, hurrying, filling, riddling, tipping and occasionally getting, just as they are performed by boys. One of the most disgusting sights I have ever seen was that of young females, dressed like boys in trousers, crawling on all-fours, with belts round their waists and chains passing between their legs.'

Employment in the mines from an early age tended to stunt a child's growth and one witness told the commissioner that 'anyone can distinguish a collier's child from the children of other working people.'

The commissioners regarded work in the ore mines as more severe than in the coal mines and more unhealthy due to the fact that the iron-ore levels were generally not so well drained and ventilated as the coal mines.

As a result of the exposures of this Report, the Coal Mines Regulation Act was passed in1842 which decreed: 'That from and after the passing of this Act it shall not be lawful for any owner of any mine or colliery whatsoever to employ any female person within any mine or colliery, or permit any female person to work or be therein, for the purpose of working therein, other than such as were at or before the passing of the Act employed within such mine of colliery.' The mine owner was given three months' grace to find new labour and replace the labour of all young women under the age of eighteen.

The Act made illegal the employment of women and children underground, and stated that children could not be employed under ten years of age. However, insufficient Inspectors were appointed to check that these rules were being observed, and the Act was frequently ignored and the practice continued. This is confirmed by the mineral agent to the Blaenavon Company in his evidence to the Commissioner of Mines inquiring into the operations of the Mines Act:-

'Hearing that women were employed underground, and being desirous to follow strictly the expressed views of the directors that it should be put to a stop, he searched the pits. Notice was, however always conveyed to them that he was coming, and they got into hiding places, so that it was not until a month after he had been there that he was able to discover them. In April he turned out 70 women and girls, as many as 20 of the latter being not more than eleven or twelve years of age. He has no doubt that since then many have gone back from time to time. He gave notice that he would fine any man whom he found employing them again, and he has fined seven or eight from 5s to 10s 6d each. He gave employment to as many as he could on the pit banks; three or four orphans were obliged at first to apply for relief from the parish, and many of the men went away to works where they could take their daughters or other females underground. These men were earning in the worst times at least 12s 6d a week clear, after deducting powder and candles, and consequently had no excuse of poverty for thus employing their children. So many of the pits being accessible by levels, it was difficult to keep them out when they chose to go in.'

The Commissioner of Mines estimated in 1850 that some 200 women (70 of them at Blaenavon) and girls were still working in the collieries of South Wales and many of them were just 11 or 12 years of age.

By the time Big Pit opened in 1860, more inspectors had been appointed and heavy fines introduced, which had the desired effect of eliminating the possibility of women and children working underground. (It is of interest that the law prohibiting women from working underground was repealed on 26th February 1990, 150 years after it was introduced).

**The Cinder Pit Disaster, 28th November 1838**

The Monmouthshire Merlin on December 1st 1838 reported:-

> 'On the 28th after 2 days incessant rain and following snow of some duration, about midday, the sky was suddenly darkened by the accumulation of dense clouds upon Wain Avon and along the Coity, in the district of the Varteg, when an immediate discharge occurred, which inundated the works and almost filled the valley, causing a sudden rise in the river of many feet additional, and bursting over an embankment which protected the mouth of an old level leading to the deep coal and ironworks of the Blaenavon Company. Messengers were dispatched to the different workings and the miners and colliers, to the extent of many hundreds, immediately came out. Every effort to divert and check the torrent was most energetically made, which from the numerous workmen in the employment of the Company, and the almost immediate cessation of the rain, was accomplished in a few hours, but melancholy to relate, not before some of the headings ( and one which has for years been worked 'under level') were filled in water. In this there is no doubt 14 lives are lost. The damage to the Works is trifling. The pumping, which alone can enable the workmen to reach the bodies of the sufferers, had been urged with every possible speed, and every means of drawing water adopted, yet it will be several days before their bodies can be obtained. - 11 men (7 unmarried), 2 girls and 1 boy. It is to be feared that some lost their lives from not feeling sufficiently alarmed to leave with the same rapidity as their fellow miners. One, an old man, returned to fetch his lantern. Another we understand would not leave his son (8) and both are missing. One true hero - brave man - seized a boy not related and put him on his shoulders and carried him above the water a considerable distance while he himself was covered by the flood.'

When the rescue party was at work, they came across eight bodies clinging to each other, and drowned in that position. The bodies recovered were: John Sutton (aged 24); Thomas Thomas (60); Edward Jones (35); James Ashman (24); John Morris (26); Philip Price 25); John Jones (39); Mary Hale (15) and Elizabeth Havard.

## Early Unrest

In January 1830 depression in the iron industry forced the price of coal down from 10/- (50p) to 8/- (40p) a ton and the owners proposed twopence (1p) per ton reduction in wages. Two months later all the Monmouthshire workers were on strike. They demanded an end to the truck system (payment by tokens to be spent at the Company shop) and requested that they should receive a weekly payment of 10/- of their wages, with any balance due to be paid fortnightly.

Following a mass meeting of Monmouthshire workers the owners agreed 'to keep coal up to a fair market price and to pay the men in money as proposed'. The strike ended on these terms, and later a slight improvement in trade allowed the owners to withdraw the notices of wage reductions. The government passed an Anti-Truck Act in 1831 but the evil practice was still continued by many ironmasters and coal owners.

This was the time of the notoroius 'Scotch Cattle' who dealt severely with any black legs who were guilty of strike breaking. On 12th May, 1832, the Monmouthshire Merlin reported such an incident: 'On Wednesday week last at midnight, about 200 of these deluded men (Scotch Cattle) visited Blaenycwm Colliery, distant from Pontypool about three miles, and acted in their usual manner, destroying furniture etc., of the colliers and otherwise injuring the houses by hurling immense stones at them. They have unfortunately succeeded in intimidating the peaceable and well-disposed from pursuing their labour. There are scarcely any collieries in the hills that have escaped their visitation, the most of which have been stopped working.'

Following a strike at Cwmbran Colliery in 1843, two of the strikers, D. Daniel and P. Evans, were sent to the house of correction for six weeks as punishment for absenting themselves from work. At the trial there were also other men before the magistrates for the same reason, but on promising the Justices that they would return to work, the summonses against them were withdrawn. By setting an example in this way strikes could be easily broken.

In order to supplement their low earnings, the workers' wives and children had to take employment in the mines, hauling trams and opening and shutting ventilation doors. Some owners even went so far as to put pressure on the men to take their children into the mine, either as a condition of employment or by allotting extra trams for filling according to the number of children taken. As described above, as late as 1850 girls in Blaenavon were employed to haul the tubs from three or four o'clock in the morning to eigh or nine in the evening.

The mine owners in 1850 made another attempt to reduce wages by two pence (1p) on a ton of coal and many collieries immediately came out on strike. They formed a committee to guarantee common action, refused all arbitration and insisted on bargaining with the masters, but in the end had to admit defeat.

## Safety Improvements

Before 1850 no systematic record of accidents was kept and nor were those concerned with the industry willing to provide information about the nature or number of accidents in their collieries. In general there was a lack of concern about individual accidents until the occurrence of catastrophic explosions involving very large numbers of deaths.

It was only after the Coal Mines Act of 1850 that any attempt was made to reduce the dangers of mining by legislative control. By this Act owners were compelled to keep accurate plans of their collieries and to inform the Home Secretary of all fatal accidents.

Coroners were also required to give two days' notice of inquests. Four inspectors were appointed for the whole of Britain with the legal right to enter any colliery and to notify owners of any defects revealed by their inspection.

The first inspector to cover the South Wales area was Kenyon Blackwell who took up his appointment in November 1850, but when he resigned in August of the following year the post was left vacant for a few months. Then on 12th November, Herbert Francis Mackworth took up his duties as inspector for the South Western district which included the whole South Wales coalfield and he held this post until his death in 1858.

The work of a single inspector for such a large area as South Wales made very little impression on the problems of safety, for to have inspected all the collieries in his very large district would have taken him between four and five years. Most of the accidents that he investigated were, he considered, 'attributable to the neglect or recklessness of the proprietors or managers of mines, whilst they generally content themselves with attributing the same faults to the men.'

A constantly recurring danger was that arising from falls of coal and stone from the roofs and sides of working places and of travelling ways. A later inspector wrote, 'We have treacherous roofs in South Wales, roofs that to look up at, and to try with a pick, sledge, or any other tool, sound like thick cast iron, or like rock of vast depth, yet they are often so complete with concealed slips or 'backs,' 'bell moulds,' joints and 'grimes' that perhaps a minute after trying or sounding, a fall, without the slightest warning in the world, will take place.'

Roof falls were almost a weekly occurrence and over a period of time caused more deaths than the occasional calamitous explosion. Skillful and careful propping was the main safeguard against roof-falls, but colliers were paid for the amount of coal they cut and not for the timber props that they erected in their stalls. As a result timbering was generally neglected, particularly when they were about to finish their shift.

During the five year period from 1851-5 there were 738 deaths from accidents in coal mines reported in South Wales and Monmouthshire. Of these 173 were caused by explosions, 300 by falls of roof and sides, 143 by accidents in shafts, 98 by miscellaneous causes and 24 by surface accidents.

Boys between nine and ten years old comprised only about one-ninth of the employees but they accounted for more than one-fifth of the deaths from accident. The youngest boys were employed in minding ventilation doors, but many of them ran along with the hauliers to open doors for them. It was very easy for the boys to miss their footing as they ran past the horse and trams to get to the next door in time to open it for the haulier.

Following the reports of two Select Committees on Accidents in 1853 and 1854, The Mines Act of 1855 was passed to amend the law for the Inspection of Coal Mines in Great Britain. It was required that each colliery should establish printed rules, a copy of which was to be displayed at the colliery and a copy handed to each workman. Seven general rules were applicable to all collieries and these stipulated that ventilation should be adequate for safety under normal conditions, that every working shaft was to be securely lined if the natural strata were not safe and that all shafts out of use were to be fenced. The other general rules dealt mainly with winding - that there should be a means of signalling in the shaft and that the engines used for winding should have a proper brake and an indicator to show the position of the cage in the shaft. In addition to these general rules each colliery was to have its own special rules, designed to cover the safety requirements arising out of local conditions.

The penalties for non-compliance with these rules were, for all workmen and officials, a fine not exceeding £2 or not more than three month's imprisonment and, for owners or principal agents, a fine not exceeding £50. To assist the enforcement of the Act the number of officials was increased to twelve and South Wales was made a separate district with Thomas Evans appointed as inspector.

When this Act expired the Mines Regulation Act of 1860 came into force and this increased the number of general rules to fifteen, while the penalty for men not observing the rules was increased to a sum not exceeding £20.

No one under the age of eighteen was to be in charge of an engine used for lowering or raising people to or from the mine. No boys under the age of twelve could be employed in the mines unless they had a certificate saying either that they could read and write or that they were attending school for at least three hours a day and two days a week, Sunday excluded.

**Owners and Unions Compete**

After 1860 the situation changed, for industrial progress on the Continent resulted in much increased markets for Welsh coal and it was able to to command a higher price. A regular export market came into being when the introduction of steamships created a demand for steam or bunker coal and South Wales coal was found to be the best in the world for this purpose.

Ironmasters who possessed collieries now began to transfer their main attention to the sale of coal and the output of the South Wales coalfield was greatly increased. The Bristol Channel soon became the busiest waterway in the world and by 1881 South Wales was the foremost coal exporting district in Britain. As the railway systems expanded, previously inaccessible collieries gained easy access to markets or ports.

In 1858 the Ebbw Vale Company sank Cwmnantddu Colliery (later named Llanerch Colliery). They sank two shafts to a depth of 750 feet to reach the Meadow Vein - a seam of coal 7′ 6″ thick. It was largely extracted by the pillar and stall method and the colliery had an output of over 70,000 tons.

Big Pit on the side of Coity Mountain was opened in 1860, the year that the Urban District of Blaenavon was created and it was also at that time that the Garnddyrys Forge and rolling mill was dismantled for re-erection near the mine. Also in 1860 the Varteg Pit was sunk by John Vipond, a Cheshire man and further new mines in the Eastern Valley followed at regular intervals.

Transport arrangements at Varteg were greatly improved in 1861 with the construction of an incline leading down the hill to Cwmavon Station. It was operated by a steam engine and enabled 3,000 tons of coal to be sent down weekly. This output was increased in 1868 with the completion of a new slope in the colliery which also improved the ventilation of the whole of the mines at Varteg. Driven from two points (from the bottom of the pit outwards and from the surface inwards) the slope was 393 yards in length, and such was the accuracy of the survey that it did not deviate a single inch from a straight line.

During 1868 coal from the celebrated Elled vein at Messrs Partridge and James' collieries at Varteg was used in the Bristol steamer Apollo when she made the passage from Cork to Bristol in the remarkably fast time of 15 hours 10 minutes. The passage normally took from 24 to 25 hours.

In 1871 the miners took advantage of the legalisation of trade unions to combine against any proposed reductions in wages. The owners, for example, in February, 1871 announced a 10% reduction in pay, but the Amalgamated Association of Miners countered this by demanding an increase of the same amount. This led to a strike which lasted

Cwmbyrgwm Water Balance Lift (now dismantled), was erected in about 1820 and until recent years was the only surviving example of such a pit-head gear on its original site, to be found in South Wales. Coal was raised by balancing a tram against a full tank of water, which was then emptied to reverse the process. Illustration by Michael Blackmore.

Lower Varteg Slope. near Talywain. David Boddington Collection.

twelve weeks and arbitration resulted in a slight increase . Soon afterwards the owners formed a Monmouthshire and South Wales Coal Owners' Association and in the following year they again announced a ten per cent reduction in wages. The men rejected the demand and another strike broke out in January 1872, which collapsed when the Miners' Union failed to give any support.

The Mines Regulation Act of 1872 improved the safety code by stipulating that the manager of all mines where more than thirty persons were involved must hold a certificate of competency. Also boys of under twelve years of age were not to be employed underground and boys of under sixteen were not to be employed at night or work more than ten hours a day.

During 1874 the price of coal fell from 22/- (£1.10) to 12/- (60p) a ton and the coal and ironmasters united in calling for another 10% reduction in wages which would have brought the miners down to 4/4d (22p) a day. The notices expired on 1st January, 1875, and then commenced the Great Strike and Lock Out that was to continue for five months, after which the owners threatened to increase the reduction to 15%.

On 31st May, the miners were compelled to accept a 12.5% reduction in wages and it was agreed that henceforth wages would be regulated by a sliding scale according to the selling price of coal. The end of the strike was celebrated on both sides, but the Amalgamated Association of Miners was now bankrupt and dissolved soon afterwards.

Many people at this time decided that the only solution was to emigrate and large numbers of workmen and their families left the Eastern Valley to start a new life in America. This caused a scarcity of hands at some collieries and the owners often had considerable difficulty in completing orders within the time agreed.

A man covered in rough sacking once had the dangerous job of exploding the dangerous fire-damp found in many mines.

Scene at the Llanerch Colliery Disaster in 1890. Illustrated London News.

**The Llanerch Colliery Disaster**

On Thursday 6th February, 1890 a terrible explosion occurred at Llanerch Colliery, Cwmnantddu, which claimed the lives of 176 miners. The explosion occurred in the Meadow Vein at a place known as 'Cook's Slope' at about 8.45 a.m. Most of the men working in this colliery used naked flames, apart from those working in an area known as the Long Slope where pockets of gas had been reported and covered lamps started to be used. Some eighty men working in the Rock and Three-Quarter veins and on the straight slope of the Meadow Vein seam escaped.

> 'The inhabitants of the district have scarcely recovered from the shock which they experienced at the recent catastrophe at the Glyn Pit, when another and more terrible accident has occurred to the profound grief and consternation of all. The Glyn Pit horror claimed but five victims - all too many - but that of the Llanerch Pit has sacrificed full 34 times that number of workers. When the news was first circulated on Thursday morning, people were at first incredulous - they could not believe that so tremendous a holocaust could have happened almost at their own doors. Confirmation came, however, and soon all knew that the most fearful of events in a mining district had occurred.
>
> Llanerch Colliery, the scene of the most appalling disaster which had ever occurred in the Pontypool district, is situated on the top of the Cwmnantddu Valley, about a mile and a half from Pontnewynydd. It was formerly the property of the Ebbw Vale Co., and was purchased some little time ago by Messrs Partridge, Jones and Co., who own six other collieries in the neighbourhood. It is about 750 feet deep at the bottom of the shaft and the daily output is computed to be about 500 tons.

The accident happened at about 8.45 a.m. on Thursday. As to how many men were in the pit at the time, we are not at present in a position to say, but it is generally thought that between 250 and 300 men must have been down at the time. A survivor, who was at work near the bottom of the shaft, and who escaped with comparatively little injury, says that without the slightest indication of impending danger, a deafening explosion occurred, the rush of air driving before it with terrific force the airway doors, coal from filled trams and anything loose, causing sad havoc amongst the unfortunate men who were struck by the whirling debris. The explosion shook the engine-house, and all the men at work on the bank were blown about, but happily received no injury. Fortunately the explosion was confined to one seam, or the loss of life would have been quite as great as, if not greater than, that of the Prince of Wales Pit, Abercarn, when 264 men and boys lost their lives.

The officials of the colliery were quickly on the spot for the purpose of rendering all assistance in their power. Mr. E. Jones, JP., Snatchwood House, managing director of the Company, who arrived within half-an-hour of the catastrophe, and Mr Joseph Morgan, manager of the Colliery (who was in the pit at the time of the explosion) were indefatigable in their efforts. Particularly valuable assistance to the officials was given by Mr D. Lougher, mining engineer, who was in charge of the night exploring party. Relief parties were speedily organised, there being no lack of volunteers eager to join in the search for friends and comrades who were in the pit. The first party were delayed for about an hour by the fact that the explosion had dislodged a quantity of brick-work near the bottom of he shaft, which prevented them from penetrating the working until a way had been cleared.

Joseph Phelps and his brother Thomas were working in the Three-quarter seam when the explosion occurred. Cramming their scarves into their mouths and holding on to each other they made their way to pit bottom. On the way they had to pass a horse which had been blown over and was lashing out in its death agony. At the pit bottom they had to wait some time before they could ascend as the cage gearing had been damaged.

By 10 p.m. all the workings except Nos. 1 and 2 heading had been explored for the purpose of discovering if any of the men were still alive, but to no purpose. As the explorers met with a considerable amount of after-damp, it is considered practically hopeless to expect that any of the men remaining in the pit can now survive. A large medical team were on the spot very shortly after the accident. Dr. Mulligan was on the ground first and went down the shaft with an early relief part. There were also Drs. Verity, J.R. Essex, W.S. Essex, E.S. Wood, Milne, Hayes, Rennett and Muir, many of whom remained on the spot until a late hour; but unfortunately, their services were not required much after he first batch of injured men were brought up, the whole of the remainder being dead.

The cause of the explosion is up to the present quite a mystery. Neither Mr J.S. Martin, HM Inspector, nor R.D. Bain, Assistant Inspector, could form any idea as to the exact spot where the fire originated. There had been rumours in circulation to the effect that the disaster was caused by the expulsion of gas from the Glyn Pit, from the action of the water when that mine was flooded, the gas so expelled being supposed to have made its way across the two miles or so of space between the two pits. This theory however, has received authorative contradiction from several experienced colliery managers.

At 11 p.m. on Friday it was reported that 163 bodies had been brought up, 77 were brought up alive, and four are still missing. Fifteen bodies are still unrecognised. The list of the deceased included men from Abersychan, Talywain, Pontnewynydd, Snatchwood, Cwmffrwdoer, Pentwyn, British, Garndiffaith, Tranch and Pontypool.

Around 30,000 mourners and spectators attended the funerals of the victims, who were laid to rest in the graveyards of Trevethin, Penygarn and Ebenezer Churches.'

The Queen sent a message of compassion and the Home Secretary ordered an enquiry. In due course a relief fund totalling £35,000 was set up for the 70 widows and their 240 dependent children. The widows received 5/- per week from this fund and there was an additional 2/6 for each child.

The trust fund raised for the benefits of the dependents of the Llanerch Colliery Explosion of 1890 was eventually closed in July 1956. The few hundred pounds left in the fund was used to purchase an annuity of £65 a year for Mrs Dina Lewis aged 91 of Ffrwyd Road, Abersychan, who was widowed by the disaster. The original fund amounted to £24,265 which was transferred to the trustees on 25th January 1892. The amount was practically doubled by investment and £47,963 had been paid out when the fund closed on 14th June 1956. An additional £1,436 was paid throughout the years in audit fees, salaries, printing and sundry expenses.

The first Workmen's Compensation Act was brought into being by Joseph Chamberlain in 1895. At that time payment of compensation was not made until the injured workman had been idle for a month. The Act was also not compulsory and many of the workmen in those days were prevailed upon by the employers to contract out of its provision.

**Output Peaks and Falls**

Coal production in South Wales reached its peak in 1913 with the Eastern Valley collieries all sharing in the boom. During the first World War the coal produced in this valley spread far and wide over the country, especially under the coal distribution order to the West of England. At this time all the iron and steel works were fully employed and traffic on the railway lines of Britain was exceedingly heavy.

Much excitement was caused in January 1914 when, after a search of twelve months, a seam of coal known as 'the Old Coal' was found at the Deep Black Vein Colliery, Garndiffaith. During the same month the Meadow Vein was struck at the new Mynydd Maen Colliery and rapid developments were anticipated.

Meanwhile, at Vipond's Varteg Hill Colliery there was considerable dissatisfaction among the men when the management began to introduce electric lamps. At a mass meeting the colliers agreed that all work at the colliery would cease until the 'new fangled' electric lamps were withdrawn.

For a few years after the end of the First World War there was a slump in the coal industry and a number of collieries such as Kay's Slope (Blaenavon) and the Elled (Pontypool) closed down because they were no longer profitable. In January 1925 the workmen of Milfraen Colliery, Blaenavon received 24 hours notice to cease work because of severe depression in sales. This meant that another 750 men were thrown out of employment. They had been on day-to-day contracts for some weeks, and even so, had been working only intermittently.

The crunch really came in 1926 when the national coal subsidy ceased and between 12,000 and 15,000 miners in the Eastern Valley received notices terminating their contracts. By 1927 there were 4,000 unemployed miners in the Eastern Valley and in November of that year this number increased when 550 men at the Cwmbran GKN Colliery and nearly 600 at Powell's Tillery Colliery at The British, Talywain were given their notice. The strength of union membership was demonstrated at the end of the year when 2,000 miners attended a meeting at Blaenavon Workmen's Hall. Then, led by their officials, they all marched to the terraced cottages of two men who had refused to join the Federation. As a result of their visit the membership was brought up to 100%!

Employment prospects began to improve in 1929 and for example, work, now resumed at Llanerch Colliery which had been closed for about eight months. The re-discovery of the 'Elled' coal seam at Big Pit in October 1931 was hoped to provide a boost to the mining industry in Blaenavon. This seam provided very high grade coal and it had been lost some years previously owing to an extended fault. At one time it had produced as much as 1,000 tons of coal a week.

Some of the country's biggest and most productive coal mines used to be within a six mile radius of Pontypool and the underground workings beneath the area of the Pontypool Urban District were of rateable value to the authority.

Nicknames of old mines in the Pontypool area have included - 'Jack Pit,' 'The Hole in the Field,' 'The Drunkard's Home' and 'The Rat Hole' the latter applying to the Glyn Level at Crumlin Road so-called because of the hundreds of rodents which infested the place. It later operated under the name of Glyntillery and was one of the oldest mines still operating in the Eastern Valley. 'Spare Coat' Colliery was the nickname of a mine at Lower Race, Pontypool. It got that name because the colliery was so wet that the miners had to carry spare coats for they were continually drenched with water.

### The Milfraen Colliery Explosion

Situated at the edge of the Coity Mountain, Milfraen Colliery was 240 yards deep. Except for a few isolated houses dotted here and there, and the well known 'Pig & Whistle Inn,' the mine stood grimly aloof about a mile from the GWR Waenavon Station, standing 1,400 feet above sea level. To reach the mine it was necessary to leave the Blaenavon-Brynmawr road and travel some distance along a deeply-furrowed cart track.

In July 1929 an explosion at the mine killed eight men and five were injured. The explosion occurred at 8.30 am, soon after the morning shift had started work. Sixty-five men were in the pit at the time, but all that was experienced by those outside the actual explosion area was a rush of wind and a cloud of dust.

The rescue party had a difficult task. They first found four bodies lying within a space of two hundred yards, about three quarters of a mile from the bottom of the shaft. They also found a pit pony which somehow had survived the explosion.

It was not until 4.30 in the afternoon that the final body (8 in total), blackened and scorched was brought up from the pit. In an official statement, Mr. F. Kemp Cartwright, the Colliery Agent said:-

> 'There has been an explosion, and as far as can be gathered at present it was a gas explosion. It was confined to a small area, eight men were killed, and the eight bodies have been recovered. A further five men were injured, suffering chiefly from burns. I cannot say what was the cause of the explosion. It occurred in the section known as Mapstones district, a small district consisting of a heading and four stalls. There is little sign of violence. In fact practically none, and no serious damage to the workings. There were 65 men altogether down the pit at the time the explosion took place.'

As soon as the accident was reported, two doctors were summoned to the colliery and they subsequently gave interviews to the waiting journalists.

Dr Crowe commented that: 'We both went down in the cage. We found four men and started working on them, but were ordered up at once by the superintendent, who was afraid of the return of gas. Rudden and I were stripped to the waist. I should think we went down some 440 yards to the bottom, and then walked through water and muck for about a mile, when we came across these four men, who were in a state of collapse against the wall. I asked that they should be removed into fresher air, but we then got the order to ascend.'

Milfraen Colliery, above Garn-yr-erw was the scene of a disaster in 1929 when an explosion caused the death of nine miners. The inquest decided that inadequate ventilation had caused the accident.. The colliery closed in 1930. Torfaen Museum Trust.

Dr Rudden remarked: 'It was the first time that I had been down a mine. I could not see anything much. It felt cold at the beginning of the journey; afterwards it became very warm and sort of stifling, and then it was cold again. I still have the smell in my nose of singed hair.' The doctors, who were both Irish, were praised by many for their heroic work.

Arthur Holder, although seriously injured, also gave an account of his experience: -

'I was working with my father a few minutes before it happened. 'Stay here for a minute father,' I said. 'I am going to fetch some wood.' I left my father and went further down the workings, and a second later the disaster occurred.

I felt my vest whipped off my body by the force of the explosion. Then there was a flash which blinded me, and I was flung to he ground. I have a vague memory of clutching hold of someone and carrying him to the shaft. One thought was in my mind - I must save my father - but I was powerless to do more than I did.'

George Jones, who was in the pit when the explosion occurred said: 'There was no noise at all. I was working close to the spot where the explosion occurred. The first I knew of it was when I felt a rush of air, and realised something was wrong. I ran to the shaft for air. Then the first man affected by the explosion came running from the scene of the tragedy. It was Arthur Holder. He was staggering along with an injured companion, Ted Weaver in his arms.

Arthur was the hero of this terrible thing. His face was burned, and blood was running from a terrible gash in his side. He laid Weaver at the shaft and ran back to try to rescue his father. It was impossible, however. The terrific heat made it impossible for him to go far, and he came back in a state of collapse.'

The inquest on the victims of the Milfraen Colliery explosion resulted in various theories being put forward to account for the incident. David Lewis Davies of Treforest, an expert in mining accidents, who had examined the pit at the request of the South Wales Miners Federation declared that quite definitely in his opinion the electrical coal-cutter had caused the explosion.

The seam of coal in which the explosion occurred was generally considered to be a non-fiery one, although quantities of gas had been discovered in it from time to time. There was a conflict of evidence between the workmen as to whether the ventilation in the mine was sufficient or not, some saying that it was 'nothing to write home about,' whilst others said it was at all times adequate.

Arthur Henry Holder was the first witness to give evidence and he described how he had heard a hissing sound, similar to the noise made by a sky rocket going out of a bottle. Then there was a gush of hot wind which came along and he saw a blue flame. He was knocked to the ground and his singlet burned off his back. He felt in a fainting condition, similar to that when he had gas administered for the purpose of removing teeth. Having lost his lamp, he tried to crawl to the side of the trams. When he had recovered a little he could hear Redvers Southcote calling for help. The voice gradually became subdued as though he was passing away.

When he got past the tram he found Edward Weaver lying on his side with his lamp nearby. He assisted Weaver up the slope. The place was dark and dust was everywhere.

The jury found that the explosion was not purely accidental; that ignition was produced by defects in the coal-cutting machine; that there was insufficient ventilation; and faulty supervision on the part of the manager or other responsible individuals. It was recommended by the jury that a better system of packing the gobs should be adopted; that one oil safety lamp should be issued for each working place; that the coal-cutting machine should be examined more frequently; and that a better method of searching men before they proceeded to their work should be adopted.

The number of men killed in the mines of Britain each year from 1923 - 1932 averaged 1,079, more than 3 per day, while more than 350 men each day left the pits having sustained injuries.

**Setbacks and Improvements**

Blaenserchan Colliery experienced a major set back in 1931 when the power house was gutted in a disastrous fire. Damage to plant and property was estimated at £20,000 and it also affected Llanerch Colliery, for the power house provided the main air drive to both collieries as well as the electricity supply for the whole of the workings. Everything came to a stop at the two collieries with the exception of the emergency fan, which was at once put into operation to prevent the suffocation of some eighty horses which were in their stables at pit bottom. A total of 1,250 men were put out of work but within three weeks both collieries were able to resume operation.

In February 1932 the 1,000 men of Garn Drift and Kay's Slope Collieries of the Blaenavon Company were provided with a pit head baths at Garn-yr-erw. They were of the latest design and, built at a cost of £23,000 they were also the largest pit head baths in Wales.

Garn Pit, near Garn-yr-erw, was sunk by the Blaenavon Ironworks Company prior to 1839. It was ventilated by a furnace and was initially sunk in order to gain access to the deeper veins of ironstone, but coal was worked soon afterwards. Francis Keen Collection.

A possible new colliery was under consideration by the Blaenavon Company in November 1933. They employed a number of men to work in the old Pwlldu tunnel, driving a heading leading out of the tunnel, a quarter of a mile from the Blaenavon end. In doing so they discovered a seam of coal two to three feet thick which was found to be workable. It was high quality steam coal and within a short time was being worked by 15 to 20 miners who brought it out in the old limestone trams. It was hoped that the Company would eventually launch the 'Tunnel Colliery' as a new undertaking which would absorb a large number of Blaenavon's unemployed miners. But there were several factors to be taken into consideration before any definite decision could be made. Faults or intervals in the coal system could exist there as they had been found in other parts of the Blaenavon coal area and the presence of water might impede the working, making it necessary to install expensive plant for pumping it away. There was also the question of the extent, if any, to which coal had been worked in the neighbourhood of the tunnel, for in the vicinity were several old, disused pits. In due course the scheme was abandoned. This coal was to be a target of unsuccessful opencast proposals nearly sixty years later.

The provision of pit head baths was really catching on and the twenty-third of such facilities to be opened in the South Wales coalfield were established by Messrs Partridge, Jones and John Paton Company Ltd for the men of Llanerch and Blaenserchan Collieries near Pontypool. Built at a cost of £14,000 they were the 140th to be opened in the British coalfield under the Mining Industry Act of 1926. The baths were situated on the Llanerch side of the valley but were easily accessible to the Blaenserchan men.

The men working at Big Pit were still waiting for their pit head baths and they were not opened until January 1939. Now at last, every miner working in the Blaenavon collieries had the opportunity of coming home from work as clean as when he left it. The Big Pit baths were of the most modern design, an improvement on the one existing at Kay's Slope and the others in the Eastern Valley. The cost of £17,000 was borne by the Miners' Welfare Association. There 792 lockers in total, separate doors for entering the baths dirty and for leaving after a bath; a boot-greasing device, first aid section, showers with large numbers of cubicles and two sets of open showers.

Mynydd Maen Colliery was provided with a canteen in 1944 which was built to serve the 176 miners employed there. Alderman Arthur Jenkins, MP for Pontypool, performed the opening ceremony and in his speech he commented that coal was one of the most vital things at this stage of the war, yet more needed to be produced. 'Steel could not be made without coal, nor aluminium, nor could huge engineering works be run. Electricity, gas, cooking and everything industry produced had its basis in coal.'

During March 1944, a strike involved all thirteen collieries in the Eastern Valley (now employing about 6,000 miners). It had started in the Western Valley and spread to 156 South Wales Collieries, having been caused by anomalies in the recent wage award. Nearly 3,000 men attended a mass meeting at the Market Hall in Pontypool and decided almost unanimously to reject the advice of their leaders to return to work.

## Post War Decline and Opencasting

Alderman Arthur Jenkins JP, Parliamentary Labour candidate, speaking at a public meeting just after the end of the war said that he was concerned that the industries of Blaenavon, particularly coal, were rapidly reaching the point of exhaustion and little or nothing had been done to prepare for a continuance of the industrial life of the town.

> 'For at least 150 years men have toiled in and on the hills of this district. Countless millions of tons of coal, ironstone and limestone have been mined. It is now estimated that at the present rate of production there are only 25 or 30 years of coal left to be worked, and then, unless new industries are located in or about the town, the industrial life of Blaenavon will be finished, and the 10,000 inhabitants will have to seek life and work elsewhere.
>
> There are roughly about 1,000 young people from this town now serving in the Forces. A large number of them will soon return, but will there be a job for each one of them? When will those who are married get a home? There is hardly a sign of a satisfactory answer. We saw a similar situation at the end of the 1914--18 war, followed by the full blast of unemployment and widespread poverty. Blaenavon had well over fifty per cent of its insured population out of work for years.
>
> It was in 1921 that the blast furnaces were closed down. One of the furnaces was new, loaded, ready to begin production, but that one, along with the others, was closed down, demolished under pressure from the combine of the big steel-producing companies. Iron and steel production was to be reduced in obedience to the combines, and Blaenavon, one of the places least able to meet the effects of the works closed, was the victim. The effect was that some hundreds of highly skilled workmen lost their jobs, and they and their families were made dependent on unemployment benefit, the means test and public assistance.
>
> The Labour party will take steps to modernise the old industries and where there is evidence of contraction or decline, to establish new industries. These are vital to the continued life of the town.'

By 1946 the number of miners employed in the Eastern Valley had been reduced to just 5,000. But life was not all doom and gloom for at Glyntillery Colliery near Pontypool the output per man-shift reached a level of double the average for the South Wales coalfields. This achievement was marked with the directors giving their officials and workmen a celebration dinner.

At the end of the year it was commented in the *Free Press* how opencast mining had reduced the stretch of mountainside between Blaenavon and Waunavon and across to Pwlldu into '...a most unsightly landscape. This once lovely area has been reduced to a desolation almost beyond belief. The gigantic mechanical navvies have wrought a havoc which will take generations to repair. The original scheme was to level off the ground as work progressed, but this has apparently been found impracticable in the race for production.'

In January 1947, the coal industry was nationalised and the National Coal Board assumed control of all the country's coal mines. At local collieries this historic event was greeted with considerable enthusiasm. The general feeling among the men was one of determination 'to make it work.' Mr Obediah Evans JP, miners' agent,said, 'This is the culmination of fifty years of propaganda by our leaders and it is up to us to prove that our demands were justified. Our men will respond, and I am sure that the improved conditions which are definitely promised will attract many more young men into the mines. The five-day week comes into operation in May and there will be social and welfare amenities. Mining will be the King-Pin industry.'

Concern was expressed by several members of Blaenavon Council when new borings for opencast coal on the Coity Mountain were carried out by the NCB. Mr W. H. Taylor in particular commented that the unspoilt open spaces on the outskirts of the town were the heritage of Blaenavon peoples' children and should be restored. He also pointed out that the amount of coal to be won by opencast mining on that side of the valley was insufficient to justify the destruction of the mountainside. It was decided to write to the Ministry of Fuel and Power drawing attention to the spoilation of the mountainside and asking that the surface be replaced.

Further upset was caused by the NCB in December 1948 when they announced their proposal to close Blaendare Colliery, Pontypool. It was one of the smallest in the area, employing 143 men, only 17 of whom were coal-getters. The NCB regarded the undertaking as uneconomic and decided to close it down and transfer the employees to neighbouring collieries. An enormous expense was entailed in the upkeep of three miles of railway track which served the mine; the haulage engine could only pull a maximum of five trams up the slope and more transformers would have to be installed to increase the power; the drift was in a terrible state of repair; pumps were working 24 hours a day pumping water to the surface; and the return airway was badly in need of repair. This was the first of many such closures under nationalisation, as coal markets became smaller and difficult seams uneconomic to work.

Blaenavon people were dumfounded in July 1949 when it was announced by the Ministry of Fuel and Power that the Blaenavon coke ovens were to close on August 27, prior to which 170 men would receive notice to terminate their employment. The Blaenavon coke ovens, built just before the first World War, had a varied experience following a successful run when the coke was a valuable supply to the Blaenavon Company's hot blast furnace. Then came a period when their by-products, tar, ammonia etc were in great demand and in the inter-war years, when the South Wales coal industry was in a bad way, Blaenavon collieries were able to keep fairly regularly at work. This was due to the fact that the Company was able to utilise the coal from their own pits at the coke ovens. Even after Blaenavon's blast furnaces were dismantled, the coke ovens functioned as a sale coke works. Just before the Second World War, Blaenavon coke ovens supplied the Pontypool area with gas. During the war the coke ovens were taken over by the Ministry of Fuel and Power and supplied a large part of Monmouthshire with gas, sometimes nearly two million cubic feet per day. With the introduction of the new gas works at Pontypool the Blaenavon plant was superseded. Many men had worked all their lives at Blaenavon coke ovens. These ovens were believed to be a primary objective in South Wales for German incendiary bombs. Though much damage was done by one such raid, the plant was again in full production within a few hours.

Six hundred men were involved in a one-day strike at Blaenserchan Colliery in October 1951, following a dispute over the introduction of steel pit-props, which the men said were too heavy to handle. New inventions were not always readily accepted by workers who had become accustomed to traditional methods.

At Kay's Slope Colliery, Blaenavon, the men were in good spirits for during 1951 they won the second prize of £250 in a competition organised by the News of the World to boost coal output. The fact that the seams at this colliery were very thin - some of them less than 2 feet thick - was taken into account by the judges.

The NCB in November 1957 adopted a £4.5 m scheme for linking the Glyntillery, Hafodyrynys and Tirpentwys collieries which enabled their coal to be brought to a common surface plant for treatment and dispatch.

Tirpentwys Colliery was in the news the following year when Mr R. Burchell, who for fifty years had been in charge of the horses at the colliery, was chosen as head keeper of the six pit ponies from the South Wales coalfield who were to take part in the Royal Show at Bristol. He recalled that in 1914 there had been more than 70,000 horses and ponies working in the collieries of South Wales, but as mechanisation was introduced this number had dropped to just 10,000 by 1958.

In March 1963 nearly 450 men at Blaenserchan Colliery, Pontypool staged a mass walk out as a protest against certain reorganisation. When the night shift reported for work on a Sunday they were told they would have to split into two teams to work two separate faces, but the miners would not agree to this and claimed that the management had ignored their seniority rules. The men then walked out and by Tuesday the whole pit was on strike. But after negoiations a temporary settlement was reached and the men returned to work the following day.

Deakin's Slope (Blaenavon) which had opened in 1899, closed down during 1963. In its heyday, it had employed 500 miners who produced up to 500 tons of coal a day. The gradual wind down of the mines had certainly started and by March 1968 the future was certainly starting to look bleak. At Big Pit over 50 men were issued with redundancy notices in an NCB attempt to make the pit viable. Yet at the same time, a new drift mine just 800 yards away stood idle because of a shortage of manpower. Known as Blaentillery Drift it was originally planned to have a workforce of 350 men taken from Big Pit. When the mine was first inaugurated in the spring of 1966, Big Pit had a labour force of 800 but that was now down to less than 500. The Coal Board decided that it was not economically viable to work the two mines with such a small labour force.

Tirpentwys Colliery closed in 1969 throwing 600 men out of work. All the men under 60 were offered jobs in other pits. In August, fears were being entertained for the jobs of 40 men employed at the Big Arch coal distribution yard at Talywain because of the NCB scheme to take coal from Blaenserchan Colliery by way of a 300 yard tunnel into the

Tirpentwys Colliery was situated to the north of Glyn Pits, across Cwm y Glyn. It was first worked in 1888 and at the end of that century it was owned by the Tirpentwys Black Vein Steam Coal & Coke Company Ltd., employing 700 men below ground, 157 above and both household and steam coal were worked here. By 1919 there were 1,365 men employed underground and 265 above. The colliery ceased production in 1969, but the NCB continued to use it for pumping and for its airway for some years after.

Hafodyrynys / Tirpentwys complex. The Coal Board said that considerable costs would be saved by taking the coal underground to the washery rather than by train on the existing roundabout route.

At Blaenserchan Colliery, eighty years of steam travel came to an end on April 4th 1970 when coal from the pit was taken underground to Hafodyrynys and transported from there. This was one of the few remaining steam-operated lines in South Wales and the main loco, No. 7754 was a former Great Western Railway engine. The line from Golynos halt had a gradient of 1 in 23 in places and previously was 1 in 14 which put it into one of the steepest categories in the country. At one time the line was used to transport colliery personnel as well as coal and in winter it was often the only link with the outside world.

A few months later 500 men at Blaenserchan downed tools, complaining that conditions underground were too warm. In the first five days of the dispute more than 2,000 tons of saleable coal were lost.

The colliery was given a new lease of life in December 1977 with the NCB's decision to invest £1.25 m in the pit which was at that time providing work for 440 men. As a result output rose from about 19 cwts a manshift to over 41 cwt. The investment involved the construction of new surface facilities at the 77 year old coking pit and linking it underground with the neighbouring Abertillery New Mine complex. This meant savings on surface operating costs and cutting out £300,000 in rail transport bills, for all Blaenserchan's output could now be conveyed underground to Abertillery.

The link-up operation itself involved tunnelling only 100 yards to join Blaenserchan with the Rose Heyworth section of the Abertillery complex. Surface improvements included the construction of a new fan house, stockyard, fitting shop, blacksmith's shop and administration block.

In October 1980 the last group of men working at Big Pit, Blaenavon, surfaced for the final time and those who did not retire, started work at other mines in the area, including Blaenserchan and Marine Colliery at Ebbw Vale. Most of the remaining reserves at Big Pit lay in the 1′ 9″ Garw seam, in which there are believed to be uncharted, possibly dangerous shafts. This was a deciding factor which caused the NCB to close the pit and allow it to become a museum.

The 380 miners at Blaenserchan Colliery downed their tools at 6 am one day in February 1981 at the start of an all out strike by South Wales miners protesting to the NCB's plan to close five pits in the area. A total of 25,000 miners at thirty four collieries throughout South Wales stopped work, following a unanimous vote at the area NUM conference in Bridgend.

But in May 1981 the future of Blaenserchan Colliery and also four other Gwent pits looked secure as a result of a deal to supply coal to Port Talbot Steel Works.

Claims by miners' leader Arthur Scargill in August 1982 that Blaenserchan Colliery was to shut down were being denied by the National Coal Board. It was one of seven South Wales mines claimed by Arthur Scargill to be about to go under the axe. The NCB area director, Philip Weekes said, 'This latest catalogue of collieries allegedly from Mr Scargill reads more like a miss list than a hit list. It includes one highly productive pit and others in which we have invested or are about to invest considerable sums of our limited available capital. Blaenserchan Colliery with its workforce of about 420 is doing reasonably well.'

It was reported in December 1982 that Blaenserchan Colliery had lost £2.2m in the six months up to September. The South Wales coalfield as a whole had made a £68m deficit over the same period. Only four pits in the thirty three strong coalfield were identified as making a profit.

Yet in December 1984 claims that the South Wales coalfield would cease to exist in five years time were dismissed as 'political bunkum' by Sid Moore, an NCB official. He was employed as the South Wales area marketing director and he stressed to a meeting of miners: 'The aim of the Coal Board in South Wales is two fold; the first to sustain our deep mined output at 7,000,000 tonnes and the second to improve financial performance achieving viability at prices the customer is prepared to pay.' He did not however, rule out some pit closures through exhaustion, but those apart the aim of the NCB was expansion in order to obtain a market share.

In August 1985 miners at Blaenserchan, the Eastern Valley's last pit, entered its shafts for the final time. As part of a link up with the Six Bells Colliery, Abertillery the Blaenserchan men would in future go underground via Six Bells. The equipment at Blaenserchan was to stay in place to pump out water and provide air and a second way out in case of emergency. A new 2,300 metres underground roadway was driven connecting Blaenserchan to Six Bells, replacing its old coal route to Abertillery via the former Cwmtillery colliery. Today, the Eastern Valley has only small privately operated drift mines, two of them at Blaenavon.

In January 1993 a massive opencast scheme proposed in 1989 to be carried out at Pwlldu by British Coal was rejected by the Welsh Secretary David Hunt, who ruled that the 'environmental objections outweigh any benefits that might accrue from the working of coal and the resultant removal of dereliction.' If the plan had gone ahead more than 500 lorries a day would have transported five million tonnes of coal out of the site over a ten year period and large areas of historic landscape would have been destroyed.

A smaller subsequent opencasting scheme enabled the creation of two attractive recreation lakes at Garn-yr-erw.

Blaenserchan Colliery opened in the latter half of the 19th century and reached a working depth of over 1,000 feet. It was the last working pit in the Eastern Valley. Torfaen Museum Trust.

The Garn Lakes have been established at the Kays and Kears reclamation site by the privatised coal mining company Celtic Energy in conjunction with the local authority. One lake provides a wildlife habitat and the other one is available for fishing and noiseless water sports.

## Glyn Pits, near Pontypool

Glyn Pits were originally sunk by Capel Hanbury Leigh in 1831 and on one of the two stone buildings that remains on the site can be seen a plaque inscribed 'CHL (Capel Hanbury Leigh) 1845'. This was one of the first coal mines in South Wales to use steam and both the two stone engine houses on the site still contain their engines which were made at the Neath Abbey works in 1845.

Inside the pumping engine house is a Cornish-type beam engine with the beam and the seventeen-foot wheel still in situ. The engine is a double acting single cylinder, 24 in. bore and 6 ft. stroke. It operated at 50 lbs pressure and pumping was carried out in two stages giving a delivery of 9,000 to 12,000 gallons per hour. The shaft depth is 186 metres and the pump delivered into a water course 85 metres from the surface. The water flowed through an underground roadway to a lower surface level in the valley by gravity.

The vertical steam engine in the other stone building was in use until 1932, although the last recorded date of working coal here is 1928. Winding was carried out in two shafts at the same time and the engine is cased between four elegant fluted Doric columns. High above are the winding wheels, each 15 ft. in diameter.

In 1855 the Glyn Pits were leased to the Ebbw Vale Company but when the company was re-formed in 1891 as the Ebbw Vale Steel, Iron & Coal Co. Ltd they sub-let their Pontypool mineral estate, including the Glyn Pits, to James and William Wood, colliery proprietors of Glasgow.

In 1928 they were leased by the Crumlin Valley Collieries Ltd., Pontypool, who also owned Hafodyrynys Colliery. The Glyn Pit stopped operation in 1932 but was later used as a pumping station for Hafodyrynys Colliery. Modern pumping equipment, used instead of the old beam engine was in operation until 1966. The shafts were filled in but the two engine houses and their machinery were left intact for preservation and future restoration.

This stone building at Glyn Pits contains a vertical steam engine which was in use until 1932.

This pumping engine house at Glyn Pits contains a Cornish-type beam engine which was made at the Neath Abbey works in 1845.

In September 1967 it was announced that the pumping and winding engine houses with their historic machinery were to be preserved and that 'either the Ancient Monuments Board or the National Trust would take them over.' This was the first time that industrial machinery had been designated as an ancient monument.

Unfortuntely the National Museum of Wales abandoned these plans in December 1971 because by that time the machinery had been very badly damaged by vandals and looters.

In April 1998, Torfaen Council officers revealed a new scheme to open up the historic Glyn Pits site to tourists. It was estimated that the scheme would cost about £950,000 and involve extensive preservation/restoration work, landscaping, provision of a new access road, footpaths and car parking. The buildings are owned by the Pontypool Park Estate, who have agreed to lease the site to the council and it is hoped that finance will become available for the scheme to be implemented in the not too distant furture for this site is unique in Wales.

**Big Pit Mining Museum, Blaenavon**

One of the oldest shaft mines in the South Wales Coalfield was sunk at Blaenavon in 1860 and named Big Pit because of the shaft was unusually wide, measuring 6 metres across. It was in fact the first shaft in the area that was large enough to wind tow trams of coal side by side.

The shaft was sunk precisely dead on a fault line, thus enabling roadways to be driven into different seams on either side. Five seams were worked by the longwall system and the sixth, the Elled seam, was worked by the pillar and stall method. The workings incorporated galleries dating from much earlier in the century.

Two pumps kept the mine clear of water; a Cameron pump with two inverted cylinders and two 6 inch single acting rams forced the water from the workings to the bottom of the pit, where another pump raised it 50 yards up the shaft to an adit through which it ran off by gravity.

This large tip, (removed in 1979), once stood near Big Pit and it was one of three, which were known collectively as 'Little Egypt'.

Big Pit is one of the oldest shaft mines in Wales, being sunk in 1860, and is now the National Mining Museum of Wales. It is one of only two former coal mines in Britain which offer visitors the opportunity to descend in a pit cage to enjoy an underground tour. Illustration by Michael Blackmore.

There were four haulage engines supplied with steam from four Cornish boilers and the winding engines which are still in use are a pair of 26 inch horizontal cylinders, raising two loaded trams per journey. Until 1953 the winding engine was powered by steam but an electrical system was then installed by the Uskside Engineering Company of Newport.

By 1958 Big Pit was employing more than 1,000 men and in 1966 it was the only deep Coal Board mine left in the Blaenavon area. Only the 2ft 6ins Garw seam of coal was being worked and the face was 2 miles from the pit head in the direction of Brynmawr. It was a hard slog to get there and the miners had to undertake this time consuming journey at the start and finish of every shift.

The pit in its latter years became very short of manpower for nobody was keen to fill the vacancies due to the difficulties of working the narrow seam. By 1979 just 250 men were employed at the pit, producing about 72,000 tons of coal per year.

Mechanisation had not been developed at Big Pit as the NCB were understandably reluctant to invest in a pit which had a limited life. The narrow seams at the Garw face were getting thinner all the time and one was down to just 1ft 7 ins, which became almost impossible to work.

On 2nd February 1980 Big Pit finally closed and the remaining miners were transferred to neighbouring collieries. The pump that had drained the lower levels 500 feet down, was stopped and they were allowed to fill with water.

Plans were then put into operation to preserve the mine as a living monument to the South Wales Coal Industry. The mine was well-suited for this purpose as, apart from the valuable underground and surface features, the shaft was not deep, upper levels drained naturally, gas was not present and ventilation was comparatively simple to maintain.

The steering committee for the £900,000 project considered that as well as giving young people an authentic impression of the development of coal mining, such a museum would also provide tourist employment for local people and possibly bring some extra revenue for businesses in the town.

On 1st April, 1983, the first tourists descended the 90m shaft by cage to experience an underground tour, led by men who once worked in the mine and were now employed as guides. During the first year 90,573 visitors were received and within the next few years this figure rose to more than 100,000.

The surface tour takes in the various buildings around the pit head, where the electricians, the carpenters and blacksmiths once worked. At one time the blacksmiths' shop had nine forges in operation producing all the equipment required by the mine and also carrying out necessary repairs.

The pithead baths are the only pre-war miners' bath building in Wales to retain its lockers and other internal fittings. Refreshments are available in the old canteen which also houses an exhibition of photographs and a re-created miner's cottage..

A surface gallery, resembling a drift mine has been constructed to complement the exhibits on the underground tour by showing how the more recent coal cutting techniques employed on more modern faces operate.

But the main attraction is of course the underground tour which enables visitors to experience a ride in the cage to the bottom of he mine shaft and walk through the upper levels where seams of exposed coal can still be seen. Air doors are passed on the way, which more than 100 years ago were operated by young children who sat long hours in the dark. Their job was to open and close the doors at the approach of men, horses and trams moving to and from the surface.

Of particular interest to modern-day children are the stalls where the ponies were stabled. At one time 82 pit ponies were working here and names such as Abbot, Eton, Essex, General, Dragon and Tiger can be seen on the front of the stalls. There are also shoeing and harness rooms, containing horseshoes and the metal pulling gear worn by the horses, while nearby are the feed stores.

The last of the Big Pit ponies was 'Welsh,' who was a main attraction to tourists until May 1992, when he went into retirement at the RSPCA Wyndham Cottle Home of Rest for Animals near Milton Keynes.

Visitors to Big Pit come from as far afield as Australia and the United States and the museum is particularly popular with parties of French schoolchildren. The 1.5 millionth visitor to Big Pit was Florence Gourbin of Lycee Les Fontenelle, Louviers, France and Fred Williams who had worked at Big Pit since it opened to visitors in 1983, presented her with a miners' lamp and certificate. There is every hope that the future of Big Pit is now assured by its transfer to the ownership of the National Museum and Galleries of Wales.

## -- 5 --

# The Chartists' Uprising

*'We were the men of the valleys three thousand strong, it was said. Over at Abersychan the men of the Lwyd valley were marching under William Jones the watchmaker, and they were twice as many, while John Frost himself was gathering an army at the Coach and Horses, Blackwood. '*

Alexander Cordell, 1959
*Rape of the Fair Country .*

Between 1799 and 1824 the Combination Laws prevented workers from forming organisations to safeguard and improve their interests, and this led to secret societies and lodges being set up. They met in the back rooms of pubs, private houses and under the cover of darkness on lonely hillsides. Unions were legal after 1824 and one of their concerns was that the plentiful supply of labour resulted in low wages, so rules were formulated by the lodges to ensure that only their own children were taught the skills of ironmaking and mining. Exceptions were only allowed for persons who satisfied the conditions laid down by the lodges:-

(i) No man was permitted to take any person, other than his own children to work inthe mines without the sanction of the members of the lodges.

(ii) Any stranger seeking work in a mine for the first time was compelled to pay a certain sum of money to the local lodge before he would be allowed to start.

(iii) Any man who infringed these rules would be warned. Should such a warning be ignored, he would be visited in the night by a gang of men who became known as the 'Scotch Cattle' and they inflicted punishment accordingly.

The notorious 'Scotch Cattle' were particularly active in the Abersychan, Varteg and Panteg areas,where they enforced their laws vigorously. When a miner or ironworker disregarded a rule, an unsigned warning was sent to him threatening violence if his rebellious attitude persisted. In particular, under the cover of darkness the sign of the red Bull's Head would be painted on the doors of the blacklegs. Tradesmen who refused credit to their members were also threatened. In each 'herd' the most powerful and pugnacious man was called the 'bull' and he was the leader of the gang. A 'herd' from one locality would receive instructions to punish a transgressor in another. On arriving at their destination, the men, with blackened faces and disguised in the skins of beasts, would make a forced entry into the house and destroy all the furniture. If the intended victim showed resistance in any way they would inflict serious physical injury on him.

One Sunday morning in April 1832, about 200 Scotch Cattle surrounded the home of one Richard Jerry, between Abersychan Ironworks and Varteg Hill. After breaking doors and smashing windows, they wrecked all the furniture in the house. Richard Jerry was working at the colliery unaware of the attack, and when his wife made a spirited defence she was threatened and pushed back into the house.

In the iron-making areas of Monmouthshire there were frequent hillside meetings at night and the discontented workers generally gave the agitators a ready hearing. The principles of a new movement called Chartism were being discussed in the lodges and possible causes of action were given long and serious consideration.

Early in 1838 a document was drawn up which became known as the*Peoples' Charter*. It was prepared as a Parliamentary Bill by William Lovett, the Secretary of the London Working Mens' Association and Francis Place, a London tailor. Their charter contained six points:-

(1) Universal Manhood Suffrage
(2) Equal Electoral Districts
(3) Annual Parliaments
(4) Vote by Ballot
(5) Abolition of the Property Qualification for Election to Parliament
(6) Payment of Members of Parliament.

The Chartists' national newspaper was the *Northern Star* which was published in Leeds and distributed all over Britain. But not many working people of this period had the ability to read so they had to be guided by their more literate associates. In Monmouthshire the followers of Chartism read the *Western Vindicator* and took their inspiration from the dramatic and fiery writings of Henry Vincent. It is on record that the ironmaster Crawshay Bailey actually sacked three of his workmen for reading this paper, which is some indication of the concern felt by the ironmasters at this time, for it must have been obvious to them that the Chartist Movement was growing in strength week by week.

Henry Vincent came to Pontnewynydd on New Year's Day in 1839 and spoke to a crowd of 7,000 people. He was a handsome fellow and twenty-five years of age. This young man, the son of a Holborn silversmith, was an eloquent speaker who rivalled all his contemporaries with his powers of speech and arousal.

On 23rd February 1839, he published the first edition of the *Western Vindicator* as a weekly paper and it had the desired effect of inspiring the workers but angering the authorities. He reported that:-

> 'Associations are forming all over the hills of Monmouthshire, Glamorganshire and Breconshire; and in a short time there will not be a village in the western part of Monmouthshire and the eastern part of Glamorganshire which will not have its association for starting the peoples' charter.'

On the 16th April of that year he made a speech in Newport which lasted two hours . He promised the gathering that:-

> 'We will assemble on a certain day in thousands and tens of thousands like the Jews at the Feast of the Passover...When the time for resistance arises, let your cry be, "To your tents O Israel!" and then with one heart, one voice and one blow perish the privileged orders! Death to the aristocracy! Up with the people, and the government they have established!'

Henry Vincent's voice boomed out to a large gathering on 24th April, informing them that:-

> 'When the signal is hoisted on the tops of your beautiful hills, flock in crowds to our standard and we will lead you to victory through oceans of fire and water and dust and smoke and thunder...we have the power to do so, - and the army will be on our side... therefore we will turn off the Queen, the Parliament, the Law, the Church - in fact everything - and everybody that dares to oppose us, for we are for universal liberty.'

Two weeks later on May 9th, Vincent was arrested for, 'having conspired to produce discontent and unlawful assembly.'

A petition of over one million signatures was presented to Parliament by the Chartist Movement in July of that year but it was rejected out of hand. The following month Henry Vincent was tried at Monmouth Assizes and sentenced to twelve months imprisonment. Demonstrations took place and demands were made for his release.

In the Eastern Valley the centre of Chartist activity was at Abersychan, where the official leader was William Lloyd Jones, who was said to be the illegitimate son of a Bristol tradesman, but his name suggests that he was of Welsh extraction. In his youth he was apprenticed as a watchmaker and then he decided to make a temporary change in his career. Blessed with a rich resonant voice, a fine physique and handsome features, he set his mind on becoming an actor. He joined a company of peripatetic players and during the next year or so learned a great deal about the social and economic conditions of the working classes during his travels from one part of the country to another. There was no doubt that he was an ideal person to sway the crowd when advocating Chartist principles.

In 1833 William Jones decided to return to his old trade and came to Pontypool in order to manage a watchmaking business for a widow named Mrs Harvey. When he later married a Miss Edwards of Abergavenny, and commenced business on his own in Pontypool, Mrs Harvey accused him of embezzlement, but in court the money was declared to be a debt and the prosecution failed.

Jones now owned the Bristol Beerhouse in Pontypool and here he started a branch of the Working Men's Association and also organised other branches in the valley. In due course his beerhouse became the local Chartist headquarters for the eastern division, where a large number of lodges existed.

At a meeting in the King Crispin Beerhouse in Brynmawr, Jones is said to have told the Chartist leader, John Frost, that, 'The Abersychan Lodge is 1,600 strong; 1,200 are old soldiers; the remaining 400 have never handled arms, but we can turn them into fighting men in no time.' One of the Abersychan leaders was David Davies, who had twenty-five years of experience in the army and had fought at the battle of Waterloo.

On New Year's Day in 1839 a meeting of 7,000 members of the Working Mens' Association at Pontnewynydd heard John Frost denounce the financial extravagance of the government, in particular the £1,000 a year paid to each of the Queen's twelve grooms of the bed chamber.

Frost was chosen by the gathering as the Pontypool delegate to attend the meeting of the National Convention of the Industrious Classes on the 4th February, 1839. His speech at Pontypool however earned him a warning from Lord Russell, the Home Secretary, that a continuance of such conduct 'would result in his name being erased from the Commission of the Peace for the County of Monmouth.'

To this warning, Frost replied with a violent denial of the Home Secretary's right to interfere with his freedom of speech or opinion and continued his agitation at public meetings held throughout the county. Lord Russell then carried out his threat and Frosts' name was struck from the roll of magistrates.

Throughout the weeks before the famous march on Newport, William Jones and the Nantyglo leader, toured the lodges 'to stir them up.' In his speeches he attacked the law because it protected money, not persons. He dwelt upon the hardships of his audience and emphasised that any collier did not know each morning whether he would return home that evening alive or dead, and as compensation, they ought to earn more than anyone else. He declared that it was the Chartists' intention to liberate Henry Vincent from gaol and put Lord Russell, the Home Secretary, in his place.

On the 1st November, 1839, a meeting at the Coach and Horses in Blackwood was attended by John Frost, Zephaniah Williams, William Lloyd Jones and delegates from all the lodges in the Heads of the Valleys area and the Eastern Valley. A total of twenty-five lodges were represented and plans were made for the big march on Newport. It was resolved by the assembled delegates that all lodge members should meet, fully armed at several vantage points on the evening of Sunday 3 November. They would then march in three separate divisions towards Newport.

The western division would advance from Blackwood and be led by John Frost himself. Zephaniah Williams would gather together his followers near Nantyglo and the third contingent led by William Jones would march from Pontypool. In due course the three groups would join forces in the vicinity of Cefn (Rogerstone), on the outskirts of Newport and then march as one body into the town, arriving at 2.00 a.m., when the inhabitants would be sound asleep and completely unaware of their presence. They would first overpower the soldiers and then demolish the bridge over the Usk and take complete control of the town. A detachment would later march to Monmouth Gaol to release Henry Vincent and his fellow prisoners.

During Sunday 3rd November a large meeting was held in William Jones's residence, the Bristol Beerhouse in Pontypool. Here he held a secret armoury and weapons were distributed by a man named Shellard to marchers who required them. But most men had come as instructed, armed with guns, pikes and any other weapons they could procure. Some who arrived without weapons were told to go to a house at the top of Trosnant where they could obtain guns, swords and pistols.

They were told to muster that evening at the Race and by 10.00 p.m. a large crowd had gathered despite the appalling weather. Jones shouted through the wind and explained that the people of Newport were expecting their arrival in three bodies, and it was essential for them to be prompt.

Just as he was finishing his speech, another contingent led by a beerhouse keeper, John Llewellyn, arrived from Pontnewynydd. Many of the men had no doubt come to the meeting merely out of curiosity and intended just to make their way home at the end of it. But this proved very difficult, for the armed men had been stationed at various points to prevent the escape of any such deserters.

At 11.00 p.m. they began the march to Newport, five abreast with men carrying spears in the front, followed by those who had firearms and the rest followed behind. Jones gave orders that any who refused to march with them were to be compelled. Placards were ready, he said, to be posted in Newport on the following day with a proclamation from the executive government of England and signed, 'John Frost, President.' Jones anticipated that by Wednesday they would either have the Charter or the government would be in their hands.

John Frost

Zephaniah Williams

William Jones

Numerous houses were broken into on the way and the male inhabitants forced to join their ranks. When the main body passed through Pontypool they stopped outside the police station and considered attacking it to release the prisoners inside. But they thought better of it and decided to press on instead to the inn at Croes-y-ceiliog. Large numbers of men, now drenched and ravenous, made their way inside. Others spent their time in the vicinity of Croes-y-ceiliog going from house to house to persuade by threats and force every man they could find to join the march.

Colonel Thomas Mitchell, whose father was manager at the British Ironworks described the passage of the Chartists down the valley to Pontypool:

> 'On the eventful Sunday night, between nine and ten o' clock while our family were comfortably and unsuspectingly seated at supper a neighbour came rushing into the house exclaiming 'Mae y Siartists wedi d'od' (The Chartists are come). All immediately came out to the front of the house whence could be distinctly seen by the light of the blast furnaces (worked then with open tops), large bodies of men moving about the works, whose shouting, blowing of horns, and discharging of fire arms could now be distinctly heard, conveying to my mind at the time the impression of something terrible and indescribable.
>
> The first act of the rioters was to cause the blast engines to be stopped, thus cutting off the blast from the furnaces, the immediate effect of which was to throw the whole place into utter darkness so that nothing could now be seen but the feeble flickering light from lanterns which many of the mob carried. The horn blowing and gun firing continued and the sounds came nearer and nearer.
>
> A large number of the workmen's cottages and agents' houses were situated on the side of the hill and for these it was evident the rioters were making. The inmates were not long left in doubt for barely had the male occupants time to escape than gangs of men armed with pikes and spears and some with fire-arms appeared at every house demanding admission and searching every room.
>
> The women and children were not molested nor was any damage done as far as I am aware but threats were made where any resistance was offered to the houses being searched. The object of the searchers was no doubt primarily to secure all the firearms they could and in the next place to compel all the male occupants of mature age upon whom they could lay hands to accompany them to Newport. And this was done in many instances though in the confusion and aided by the darkness of the night most of them I believe managed to escape before the destination was reached.
>
> After visiting all the houses and creating the greatest alarm among the inmates the gangs retraced their steps and made for Pontypool and thence to Newport, while the men for whom they had been searching returned to their homes drenched to the skin by the rain which that night descended in torrents.'

From *Monmouthshire Iron and Steel Trade* published 1904.

Armed men also entered the Varteg ironworks and at the point of a musket compelled the man in charge of the blast engine to close it down and follow them. Disaster to the works was prevented by the manager, Mr Needham, who with the help of a boy restarted the engine after the rioters had left.

At 1.00 a.m. the leading marchers led by William Jones reached the Upper Cock Inn at Croesyceiliog and here they took refreshment and even attempted to dry their damp gunpowder in an oven.

William Jones was heard to boast, 'I venture that we shall have a flag on Newport church tower before ten o' clock in the morning.' At 6.00 a.m. he gave a sword and dagger to his lieutenant and sent him forward to lead the main party of men, whilst he remained behind to bring together the stragglers. Many were by now dragging their feet and Jones persuaded them to continue by pointing a pistol at their heads and threatening to blow out their brains if they did not obey him.

The advance guard, which numbered between 2,000 and 3,000 men, reached the Green House (Y Ty Gwyrdd) at Llantarnam where another stop was made to quench their seemingly unsatiable thirst.

The Green House Inn, Llantarnam drawn by Fred Hando in 1922.

On hearing of their arrival, Mr. Blewitt, MP, who lived at Llantarnam Abbey, came out to talk to them and emphasised that, 'certain ruin awaited them if they set themselves against the authorities of the country.' But the marching men ignored him and pressed on towards Newport.

When they reached Malpas Court about one hundred and fifty men entered the stable yard and compelled the gardener and coachman to fall in with the marchers. Then on they went to the Marshes Turnpike Gate on the outskirts of Newport, where they positioned a few men with orders to direct following marchers up the lane (now known as Barrack Hill) towards Penylan.

It was 10.00 a.m. when William Jones arrived here to join his men and they were suddenly surprised to see other men rushing in large numbers from the direction of Newport. Jones grabbed one of them and asked him what had happened in Newport. Breathlessly, the man, obviously frightened and very weary, told him that an attack had been made on the Westgate Hotel...three or four men had been killed and the whole body were defeated. Jones apparently then exclaimed 'Oh! damn me; then we are done! '

The news soon spread from man to man and before long they were all making their way homewards as fast as they possibly could; the motley army of William Jones the Watchmaker scattered like leaves blown in the wind.

The marchers from the Western Valleys led by John Frost and Zephaniah Williams had boldly marched down Stow Hill in Newport to reach the Westgate Hotel. But they were not to know that inside was Thomas Phillips, the Mayor, who had occupied the premises with a detachment of twenty-eight men of the 45th regiment and a small force of special constables.

The Chartists arriving at the Westgate Inn, Newport on 4th November 1839.

It had been planned by the Chartist leaders that they would enter Newport at 2 o'clock in the morning but they did not arrive until 8.30 am and even then were short of the Eastern Valley contingent. Bedraggled and weary they marched into the square in front of the Westgate, armed with their wide assortment of weapons. The mayor appeared bravely in the doorway and demanded to know their grievances.

A Chartist then opened fire at one of the Special Constables and inspired the mob into action. The Special Constables in the Westgate panicked and hid themselves in various parts of the building. One hid inside a copper boiler and did not emerge until the riot was over, whilst others escaped from the rear of the building and ran home,

The Chartists' opening volley wounded several soldiers and Mayor Phillips received a shot in the shoulder. But the Chartists' confidence rapidly vanished, when on an order from the mayor the soldiers opened fire. After a few volleys from the windows and down the passage towards the door of the hotel the riot quickly dispersed.

The wet and weary men had little heart for a fight after their long march through the rain the previous night, and they threw their weapons on the ground and fled in all directions, leaving their wounded companions groaning, moaning and dying. It was all over in 25 minutes.

Twenty two Chartists were killed outside the Westgate Hotel that morning and many more were wounded. It is thought that many more dead were taken away by their comrades and secretly buried to protect their families.

The bodies of the fallen were subsequently moved to the stable yard and among those identified was young George Shell of Pontypool, a young cabinet maker, still in his teens and an enthusiastic supporter of the Chartists' cause. He is believed to have been shot down in the passage when levelling his musket at the mayor. In his pocket was found a letter addressed to his parents on the previous night, that read as follows:-

> Dear Parents,
>
> I hope this will find you well, as I am myself at present. I shall this night be engaged in a struggle for freedom, and should it please God to spare my life, I shall see you soon; but if not, grieve not for me, I shall fall in a noble cause. My tools are at Mr. Cecil's, and likewise my clothes.
>
> Yours truly,
> George Shell

Constable Moses Scard later commented that he had seen George Shell lying in a passage near the soldiers' room with a bad wound in his shoulder. He gave the lad some water, but he was obviously beyond aid and later his body was moved to the stable.

Among the weapons abandoned by the dispersing Chartists were guns, pistols, blunderbuses, swords, bayonets, daggers, pikes, bill-hooks, reaping-hooks, hatchets, cleavers, axes, pitchforks, blades of knives, scythes, and saws fixed in staves, pieces of iron 2 or 3 yards in length sharpened at one end, bludgeons of various lengths and sizes, hand and sledge hammers, mandrills etc.

That Monday night ten bodies were buried in an unmarked paupers' grave at the St Woolos Churchyard. On 16th November, 1839, the 'Monmouthshire Merlin' put the death toll at twenty-two.

William Jones escaped to the hills of Mynydd Maen and Cefn Crib, near Pontypool, and was taken prisoner a week later in a wood near Crumlin. At first he threatened his pursuers with a pistol, but eventually gave himself up. John Frost and Zephaniah Williams were also soon arrested and at their trial evidence was given against the prisoners by Barnabas Brough and Thomas Watkins, by James Emery, a cabinet-maker of Pontypool, (who gave details of Jones' proceedings at Abersychan); by John Parry, a labourer of Pontnewynydd, and by William Ainsell, a collier of Abersychan, who explained what happened at the Bristol Beerhouse on the Sunday night.

Christopher Kidner, a butcher from near Croesyceiliog, and John Matthews, a gardener at Malpas Court, traced the route followed by the Pontypool contingent through Malpas and up the lane to Penylan. The solicitor acting on behalf of John Frost was W.F. Geach, his step-son, of Pontypool.

The trial of John Frost, Zephaniah Williams and William Jones lasted 24 days and 250 witnesses were called. Twenty prisoners had been charged with treason and 14 were committed for trial. The national papers were full of nothing else for weeks afterwards. Lord Chief Justice Tindal pronounced their sentence of death in the following words:-

> 'That you, John Frost and you Zephaniah Williams, and you, William Jones, to be taken thence to the place from which you came, and be thence drawn on a hurdle to the place of execution, and that each of you be hanged there by the neck until you are dead, and afterwards the head of each of you be severed from his body, and the body of each divided into four quarters, shall be disposed of as Her Majesty shall think fit, and may Almighty God have mercy on your souls.'

Court Room scene at the trial of the Monmouthshire Chartists.

The *Hereford Times* on 18th January, 1840 commented on the sentences and, perhaps with some bias, reported that:-

> 'Frost still maintained his superiority although his face was ghastly pale. He sat down without a tremor. Williams hung down his head, his dark visage expressing the greatest anguish, he fell back upon the seat, dropping his head upon his hand and, resting his arms upon his knees, groaned audibly, while Jones vainly striving to mash his feelings, trembled in every limb, a deathly paleness spread over his cheeks, his lips changed to a livid hue...his whole person showed the fallen man.'

The executions of the three men were ordered by the Government to take place at Monmouth on 6 February and the executioner and a headsman travelled to Monmouth to prepare the scaffold. The Chartist leaders spent three weeks in the condemned cell.

Numerous petitions from different parts of Britain were presented to the Government on the prisoners' behalf and, in acknowledgement to this national campaign to save the lives of the Monmouthshire Chartists, a reprieve was granted just four days before their execution was due to take place. However, it was a reprieve and not a pardon and the Queen remitted the capital sentences upon the condition that the prisoners were transported for the rest of their natural lives. The Queen was about to be married and it was no doubt felt that the Royal clemency might well be exercised at such a time and would certainly be a popular move. Also, hanging the three ringleaders would no doubt have sparked more revolts, so the establishment decided to transport them to Tasmania in the hope that they would soon be forgotten.

Barnabas Brough, a Pontypool brewer, who had encountered the Eastern Valley contingent of Chartists during the night of the 3rd of November, had given evidence for the Crown at the trial in Monmouth of the three Chartist leaders and it was partly due to his intercession that the lives of the three Chartist leaders were spared. The sentence was commuted to transportation overseas for life. However, because Brough had given evidence at the trial, the colliers of the Eastern Valley boycotted all the public houses which he supplied with beer, with the result that he nearly went bankrupt.

During a stormy night on 2nd February, 1840, the prisoners were taken from Monmouth Gaol under military escort and conveyed to Chepstow where the Usk steamer took them at 6.00 a.m. the following morning to Portsmouth. Here they were transferred to the York hulk and clothed as convicts.

Three weeks later, on 24th February, Frost, Williams and Jones, with 210 other convicts, were taken on board the Mandarin convict ship at Spithead. Two days later the ship put into Falmouth having lost a topmast. When repairs had been carried out the vessel set sail on the long voyage to Tasmania.

After the victory in the Crimean War the three men, after 16 years of exile, received unconditional pardons, but only John Frost returned to this country, dying in Bristol in 1877 at the age of ninety-three. Zephaniah Williams became a successful coal owner and died at Launceston in Tasmania on 8th May 1874 at the age of 82. His son Llewellyn remained in Blaina and was for many years the landlord of the Rolling Mill inn.

William Jones served as a Hobart constable in 1844, then left to drive a stage, and later went back to work at his old trade of watchmaking. When granted a free pardon in 1854 he felt no desire to return to his homeland. He died in poverty at Launceston in December, 1873 and his obituary published in an 1874 edition of the Launceston Gazette included the following passage:

> 'Few of the younger generation as they passed his modest shop in Elizabeth Street, and saw him with a glass in his eye prying into the works of a watch, were aware that the humble operator was, about 30 years ago, an object of alarm to the English government and that with misguided judgement and ill directed zeal, he, in conjunction with Frost, ex-Mayor of Newport, and Zephaniah Williams had led a mob in the vain hope of overturning the Government of England.'

The Chartist movement revived in 1841 and intermittently continued its activities until 1855, though South Wales did not feature greatly. All but one of the Chartists' demands were met by the late 19th century; annual elections have yet to be accepted as a necessary or desirable feature of our democracy.

In 1916 when the Park House and stables were being cleared out at Pontypool, an old locked cupboard in the carpenter's shop was opened and fifty flintlock muskets with bayonets attached, one hundred spare bayonets and five swords were discovered. The weapons were all marked 'Glamorgan M' for the Glamorgan Militia and were of 1761-64 date. They had been sent down to Capel Hanbury Leigh, as Lord Lieutenant, by the Home Office in May 1839, in case it was decided to arm the Defence Association, then being formed at Pontypool. In the vent the arms seem not to have been issued and they were put away and forgotten.

Blaenavon is situated near the head of the Afon Lwyd and is built on a hillside above the river at an altitude of just over 1,000 feet above sea level.

## -- 6 --

## The Iron Town of Blaenavon

*'Blaenavon's population is rapidly increasing, and it is already about 7,500; it promises to be soon a large, prosperous and well conducted town. To have in one year, a new parish, a local government act district, a new forge and mill, a new furnace, a new blast engine, a new national school, street lamps, Volunteer rifles, is proof of no mean energy and enterprise. '*

*Pontypool Free Press* 1860

The name Blaenavon means quite literally 'the end of the Afon' and refers to the once dark torrent of the Afon Lwyd, which is very appropriate for the town is built along the hillside above the river, close to its source, at an altitude of about 1,000 feet. Prior to the Industrial Revolution there would have been just a dozen or so farms to be found at the head of this valley and Blaenavon only existed as a name, indicating the locality where the river rises.

Today, it can be said that Blaenavon is one of the few surviving examples of a South Wales valley-head town that has been left little changed by modern development. Situated in an open valley on the very edge of the old Monmouthshire coalfield, it is surrounded by open moorland and the mountain slopes of Blorenge, Coity and Mynydd-y-garn-fawr. When William Coxe visited Blaenavon Ironworks in 1799, he said that 300 men were employed there and that the district contained 1,000 inhabitants and that 'the hollows of the rocks are strewn with numerous habitations, and the healthy ground converted into fields of corn and pasture.'

Housing for the workers was obviously in very short supply and this is confirmed by the drawing which Coxe's companion, Sir Richard Colt Hoare, made showing a bridge with the five supporting arches converted into hovels for the industrial workers. Coxe described the scene as follows:-

> 'The want of habitations for the increasing number of families had occasioned an ngenious contrivance: a bridge being drawn across a steep dingle for the support of a railroad leading into a mine, the arches of which are ten in number, have been walled up and formed into dwellings.'

One of the arches formed the entrance to Bridge Level, two arches were used to enable traffic in coal and limestone to pass, while the remaining seven were converted into dwellings as observed by William Coxe, The inhabitants must have found it very noisy and unpleasant living in these temporary hovels with trams rumbling overhead, and the only outlet for the smoke from their fires was through a pipe jutting through the top of the bridge.

By contrast the key ironworkers and their families, who came with Thomas Hill and Thomas Hopkins from Staffordshire, were housed in good quality cottages such as Stack Square and Staffordshire Row, which were built in the early days of the Ironworks.

A map of 1819, drawn at a time when all five furnaces were at work, shows Stack Square much as it is today, but with one of the houses being used as a shop. On their east side ran the tramroad from the Ironworks down to the Monmouthshire canal basin at Pontnewynydd. Staffordshire Row in North Street contained the 'lock up' - a place where delinquents, usually drunks, were incarcerated to cool off, sober up or await their appearances before the justices.

From about 1817 to the mid 1830s the Blaenavon Company embarked on a programme of house building to accommodate their ever-growing workforce. Terraced cottages, consisting of about thirty dwellings were constructed in batches of five. Downstairs they had a living room, a small pantry and a back room. The first floor contained an unpartitioned bedroom.

Each row of cottages was occupied by a particular group of workers according to their trade: River Row, Quick Building and Bunker's Row were where the colliers and miners lived; cokers and coke-setters lived in Coaltar Row while Upper Stable Houses were occupied by stable-men, hauliers and coachmen; Stable Yard by ostlers. In the second half of the 19th century, drivers of steam locomotives joined the aristocrats of the labour force and occupied Engine Row.

One of the terraces built by the Company in 1839 known as Chapel Row was so-named because in the middle of the row of about forty houses stood the old Wesley Chapel, which was one of the oldest Methodist chapels in the valley. The people eventually had to leave Chapel Row when the molten slag flowing down the ladle tip began to dangerously encroach upon their cottages.

**Ty Mawr**

Samuel Hopkins, the son of Thomas Hopkins, built Ty Mawr as his Blaenavon residence during the first decade of the nineteenth century. It was generally referred to as 'Blaenavon House' to distinguish it from his second home in Nevill Street, Abergavenny, where he often stayed to enjoy the social life of the town and its milder climate. He bequeathed that property to his friend Dr Steel, the Blaenavon Company Surgeon, and the strength of their friendship is shown by the fact that the good doctor's first son was christened Samuel Hopkins Steel.

Ty Mawr was used by subsequent directors of the Blaenavon Company as their official residence and shooting parties were also accommodated there. These visiting sportsmen enjoyed their pastime on the Blorenge and Coity Mountains which thenprovided Britain's most southerly grouse moors.

In 1925 the Blaenavon Company decided that they no longer needed Blaenavon House and it was leased to the local Medical Society. They adapted it to provide hospital facilities for seventeen in-patients. There was also an out-patient department and several examination and treatment rooms.

Previously, from 1883, a row of cottages in North Street had served as a basic hospital for Company employees. This was entirely managed and supported by a local committee of the workmen and agents of the Blaenavon Company. But now for the first time in Blaenavon's history Ty Mawr provided accommodation for the sick and injured of the town as a whole. The Blaenavon Medical Scheme was so highly regarded that it was one of a few examples that provided inspiration to Aneurin Bevan in the creation of the National Health Service. In return for a small weekly contribution from employers and workers the local residents could enjoy a free medical service. Responsibility for the hospital was taken over in 1950 by the Ministry of Health as a result of the 1948 Act.

This drawing by Sir Richard Colt Hoare in 1798, shows a covered bridge supported by ten arches, which had been converted into dwellings for industrial workers.

Shepherd's Square was built some time before 1812 as an irregular quadrangle of 18 houses open on the east side to the tramway from Blaenavon Furnaces down to the Monmouthshire canal basin at Pontnewynydd. These cottages were demolished in June 1970. Francis Keen Collection.

Ty Mawr ('Big House') was built by the ironmaster Samuel Hopkins in about 1800.

Blaenavon's new health centre opened in July 1980 at a cost of £130,000 and it was designed to combine the functions of a local hospital and a health centre, thus bringing all aspects of health under one roof. In January 1981 the old hospital was put up for sale by the Gwent Health Authority at a price of £30,000. It is now a private nursing home for the elderly and has been re-named 'The Beeches'.

**Capel Newydd**

In the early days of Blaenavon the only Christian place of worship available in the locality was Capel Newydd, which was situated on the hillside just below the mountain road to Llanover, about a mile-and-a-half outside the town. It was built at an unknown date as a Chapel-of-Ease to Llanover Church, to serve the various farms and villages scattered over the slopes of the Blorenge and Coity Mountain. No stonework remains on the site, but its location is marked by an iron cross.

The chapel was certainly marked on maps published between 1600 and 1610 and there is also a record that at one time a stone bearing the date 1577 stood in the adjoining graveyard. So the chapel was certainly standing here in the middle of the reign of the first Elizabeth. Maps published between 1600 and 1610 also show that it was here at that time and according to one story it was financed by three maiden ladies, who were said to live near Varteg. These ladies are also reputed to have presented silver bells to the chapel but the truth of such a gift has always been much doubted.

It was quite a small structure and the walls, which enclosed the chapel and its burial ground formed a square with sides about fifty yards long. The congregation of hill farmers and their families would have worshiped here for the best part of three hundred years.

When the Blaenavon Ironworks was built in 1789 the population of Blaenavon substantially increased and sixteen years later the Ironmasters, Thomas Hill of Stourbridge in Worcestershire and Samuel Hopkins of Rugeley, Staffordshire, at their own expense built St Peter's Church which later became the Parish church of Blaenavon.

The future of Capel Newydd must have seemed in doubt when St Peter's Church opened, for James Jenkins the curate of St Peter's undertook to preach one sermon every week in the old chapel. No language but Welsh was ever used in Capel Newydd and the last sermon was preached there in 1861 by John Jones who had recently been appointed Vicar of the new parish of Blaenavon.

Capel Newydd, a chapel of ease attached to Llanover, was Blaenavon's first Christian Church and it was established during the sixteeth century on a hillside above the Eastern Valley. It was abandoned in 1861 and its site is now marked by a simple iron cross.

After it was abandoned, the little chapel soon fell into decay and stones were regularly taken from the site to repair buildings in Blaenavon. In 1893 the remainder of the stones were carted away to build St Paul's Church and the stone altar table from Capel Newydd was subsequently installed in the Lady Chapel at St Paul's.

**St Peter's Church, Blaenavon**

Thomas Hill and Samuel Hopkins began constructing the parish church of St Peter at their own expense in 1804. It was built of local stone in plain Gothic Revival style and completed the following year, which was marked nationally by Nelson's great victory at Trafalgar.

Before the new church could be dedicated an Act of Parliament had to be ratified to legalise matters and it is of interest that the Act made the stipulation that the wardens of the church were to be: 'Two persons, being inhabitants of the said hamlet or District of Blaenavon (not being of the people commonly called Quakers).'

In the beginning the church was just a meeting place consisting of a rectangular hall and, as an afterthought, it appears, it was decided to erect the wooden gallery on three sides and the western tower containing six bells. It was many years before the chancel was added.

Thomas Hill was so pleased with the appearance of the church that he financed the building of a Parish Church at Lye on the border of his home county of Staffordshire. It was constructed on similar lines apart from the fact that it was built in brick and later additions included a taller spire and two transepts.

The first vicar of St Peter's was the Rev James Jenkins who was in post from 1805 when the church first opened, to his resignation thirty seven years later, when he became vicar of Llanfoist, near Abergavenny. He was succeeded at St Peter's by the Rev John Jones who resided in the first vicarage which stood near Glantorfaen Terrace and he lived there for forty five years until he died at the age of seventy five. He could preach in English and Welsh and he conducted services at St Peter's at 11.00 am and 6.00 pm on Sunday in English and in-between, at 3.00 pm he was preaching in Welsh at Capel Newydd. As Chapel services were at 9.00 am many chapel folk were able to flock to the St Peter's church to hear the popular John Jones preach after their own service was over.

Samuel Hopkins died in 1815, which again was a historic year for it coincided with the defeat of Napoleon at the battle of Waterloo. He was buried in the churchyard. Thomas Hill, the other founder ironmaster, died in November 1827 at the age of 59 and was buried in a vault adjoining the church.

In 1860 an Act of Parliament resulted in the parish of Blaenavon being formed from parts of the adjacent parishes of Llanover (1,632 acres), Llanfoist (1,003 acres), Llanwenarth (96 acres) and Trevethin (631 acres). Twenty-five years later a portion of Aberystruth, in the vicinity of Milfraen, was also added.

In 1867 the Directors of the Blaenavon Company were asked to be patrons of the church and to assist in providing an organ. They also paid for new gas lighting which enabled people sitting at the inner end of the pews to read services, which they could not do by the light of candles.

The church yard was enlarged in 1882 at the expense of the Blaenavon Company, by whom the land was enclosed and presented, and a further extension was made in 1891, by courtesy of the Company. They agreed to maintain the boundary wall and the fabric of the church; to provide the surplices and the bread and wine for the Sacrement; and to contribute to the church the rent of a glebe farm. These privileges continued until the disestablishment and disendowment of the Church in Wales in 1911.

A special feature of this church that is always of interest to visitors is the amount of iron used in its construction. Not only were the window frames made of iron, but also the door sills, tomb covers and even the font was made of this durable material, that wa once produced at the local ironworks. The main gates are also of interest being supported by two cannon pillars with cannon ball tops. It may be assumed that left-over cannon moulds at the ironworks were used to cast these pillars.

The memorial stones in the graveyard indicate many Worcestershire and Staffordshire origins and of particular interest on the south side of the church is a group of five tombs that have cast iron covers. They include the graves of Thomas Deakin, surveyor to the Blaenavon Ironworks Company, and that of Samuel Hopkins, joint proprietor of the works. The lid of the latter tomb has simple decorated edging and its inscription plaque is now inside the church.

It Reads:

> 'Sacred to the memory of Samuel Hopkins, Esquire of Blaenavon,
> who in conjunction with his much respected relative and partner
> Thomas Hopkins Esquire, of Dennis, Staffordshire, He founded
> the ironworks and endowed this church. The benevolence and
> utility of his character were great and uniform, because they
> were founded on the principles of Christianity.
> He died June Vth, MDCCCXV.
>
> This tablet was placed here by his sole and truly attached
> sister Sarah Hopkins.'

St Peter's Church is unusual in that it was financed by the proprietors of the local ironworks and the window frames, tomb covers and even the font are made out of iron.

Thomas Hill is commemorated on another tablet:

> 'In a vault adjoining this church are deposited in the hopes of a joyful resurrection the remains of Thomas Hill, Esq. of Blaenavon. The kind and affectionate father of five children, who survive to lament their severe loss and by whom this tablet is erected to his revered memory.
> He died Nov 29th, 1827, Aged 59.'

The vicarage on Church Road is still the residence of the Blaenavon vicars and it superseded the former vicarage on the Forgeside road which was known as Glantorfaen House. It was here that the town's second vicar the Rev John Jones resided until 1885 and the house was later purchased by the Blaenavon Company and used by a succession of works managers.

## St Peter's School

The first school in Blaenavon was opened on Bunker's Hill by Samuel Hopkins and his sister Sarah and they put in a workman's wife to teach the little children of the neighbourhood. As the population increased the need for a better school grew accordingly. When Samuel Hopkins died in 1815, his sister Sarah resolved to build and endow a school as a memorial to him. In doing so she made history, for this was the first purpose built school in Wales to be established by an industrial employer for the benefit of the workers' children.

Designed on principles set out by The National Society in 1811, the school followed a monitorial system of education, known as the 'Madras School' of teaching. Under the supervision of the schoolmaster, or mistress, older children taught younger pupils, in a system known as mutual instruction.

The first scholars at the school were taught to write on sand, but they soon became fine penmen and one pupil was said to be able to write the Lord's Prayer in the space of a sixpence!

The lower of three buildings is the original part of the school and it opened in 1816 for 120 pupils. A tablet over the entrance, inscribed in Latin, reads:-

> 'That she might elicit the perpetual praises of God from the mouths of children, and that she might, in some measure, even when he is dead, carry into effect the benevolent institutions of her deeply lamented and most deserving brother towards the Glenanovians. Sarah Hopkins, at her own expense, caused this school to be erected and founded in the year of our Lord 1816. To her memory.'

The description of the residents of Blaenavon as Glenavonians was not an error but a 'Latinisation' of the original Welsh name, Glynavon (Glynafon), for the locality in which the local ironworks were built.

St Peter's School was built and endowed by Sarah Hopkins in 1816, in memory of her brother Samuel Hopkins. This was the first individual school in Wales to be built by an employer for the benefit of the workers' children.

James Coldwell was the first teacher to be employed at the school and, when he was appointed House Agent to the Blaenavon Company, he was succeeded as schoolmaster by Messrs Bachelor (twice) and Hodgson. By 1849 it became necessary to erect a second building to accommodate the infants. By now the total number of pupils had nearly trebled. This was not surprising for during the same period the population of the town had risen from 2,000 to 7,500.

By 1860 three separate schools had been built and for the first half of the nineteenth century these schools were the only means of education available for the children of Blaenavon. The Hill family were staunch Anglicans and conducted the schools on the National system with the clergyman as visitor.

Although the schools were called 'Blaenavon Endowed Schools' and sometimes 'Free Schools' a nominal charge for upkeep was deducted from the workmen's wages in 1856 which caused considerable friction between the proprietors and the employees, since the majority of the latter were Dissenters.

The first certified teacher was Mr T. Abraham, followed in 1862 by Mr John Thomas, who afterwards became Clerk to the Council. His son Mr. I. G. Thomas followed him as Clerk.

In August 1959 Miss May Lewis retired as head teacher of Blaenavon Endowed Girls School. She had been head teacher for 33 years and during that time over 1,200 girls had passed though the school. The grandchildren of some of those girls were now pupils at the school. May Lewis had also been a member of Blaenavon UDC since 1934 and was the oldest member of the Council. She had been Chairman and was also the first woman to serve on the Council. Following her retirement from the school it ceased to be one of the few girls' schools in the county, for it was to be combined with the boys' school to form a mixed school under the headship of Frank Hatherall.

The last meeting of Blaenavon Church Endowed Schools was held in September 1965. From that time, the management of the schools would be included in the offices of the Eastern Valley Group of managers of Endowed Schools.

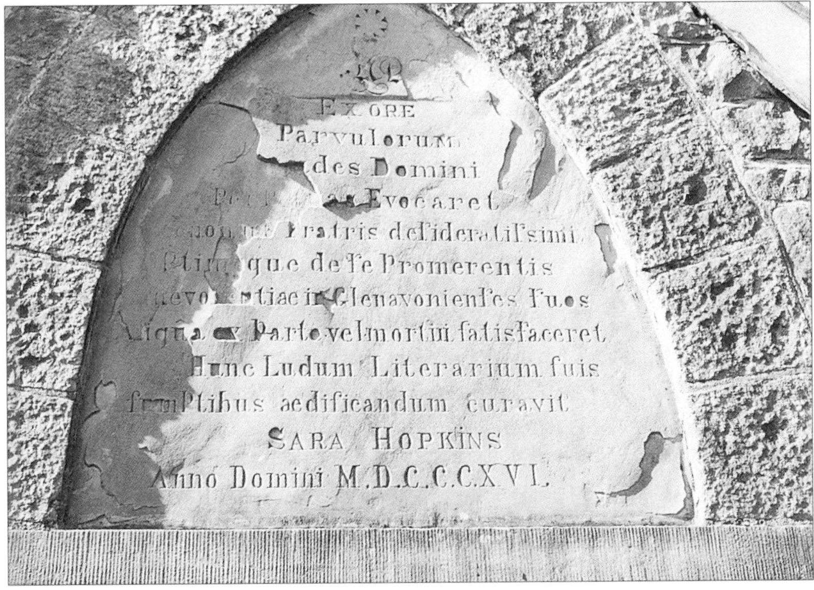


Inscription on a stone plaque above the entrance to St Peter's School.

**Other places of worship**

The establishment of chapels in Blaenavon began as a result of the Methodist Revival in the 18th century when meetings were held from about 1780 in an ancient farmhouse known as 'Y Persondy' (The Parsonage). Howell Harris, the famous Welsh Calvinistic Methodist, and Edmund Jones of the Tranch are said to have preached there. About this time the Calvinistic Methodists erected the first place of worship in the town. It was called Capel-y-graig and it existed until 1814 when owing to its close proximity to the cold blast furnaces, and being in the way of the development of the Ironworks, a new site was granted by Messrs Hill and Hopkins, on which Penuel Calvinistic Methodist Church was built in 1815.

Situated at the top of King Street this was Blaenavon's oldest Noncomformist Church and it held its last service in January 1968. Its closure was caused by the subsidence of the schoolroom which was built towards the end of the 19th century. The whole building was declared unsafe and the Monmouthshire Presbytery decided to demolish the entire property in view of the high cost of repairs. A notable member of this church at one time was Miss Hattie Harris who became Mrs Arthur Jenkins, wife of the Pontypool MP and mother of Roy Jenkins, who also entered Parliament and is now Lord Jenkins.

In 1790 the Baptist cause had its beginnings in the town with meetings held in the homes of William and Francis James, leading to the erection of the first Baptist Chapel in James Street in 1805. The building had an interesting history, for after the Baptists had finished with it, the Wesleyans made use of the building; then the Welsh Congregationalists, and finally the Salvation Army.

Following a disagreement with their brethren about a change of minister, a branch from Horeb was formed in 1825 by 81 members. They built Ebenezer Chapel the following year on land leased from Francis James, who gave his name to Old James Street.

Bethlehem Chapel, built by the Congregationalists, was so-named because it was opened on Christmas Day 1820. It stood just below the later Great Western Railway Station and was eventually abandoned in 1842, as being inconveniently situated, and the congregation moved to a new chapel in Broad Street, also called Bethlehem. Moriah Chapel which stands in the centre of Broad Street was originally known as 'Broad Street Baptist Chapel' and it was built in 1844.

In 1823 Hugh Bourne walked across the Black Mountains from Herefordshire to preach in Blaenavon and shortly afterwards a Primitive Methodist Society was formed in the town. By 1830 a Methodist chapel was opened in King Street and when the congregation became too big it was sold in 1878 to the Baptists for £500. The following year the Primitive Methodist Society opened their new church. Designed by James Hicks of Bristol it was built in the Gothic style by John Burgoyne, a Beaufort builder at a cost of £3,600. I finally closed in September 1966 when its members were unable to meet the rising costs of the maintenance of such a large building.

Prompted by the visit of John Wesley to Pontypool, the first Wesleyan Chapel in Blaenavon was built in 1837. On each side of the building were rows of houses which appropriately became known as Chapel Row. The site of these long demolished buildings is now part of the Gilchrist Thomas Industrial Estate.

The Congregational Church was founded in 1863 and its members first met in Market Street and then James Street Chapel. Lion Street Congregational Chapel was built in 1867 at a cost of £900 and it catereed for the non-Welsh speaking people who had come to Blaenavon in search of employment.

The Wesleyan Chapel in Park Street was built in 1885.

Bethlehem Chapel in Broad Street was built in 1842.

Adjoining the Workmen's Hall, is Horeb Chapel (built in 1892) with its stone portico supported by Ionic columns and with round headed side windows is a type typical of the period.

St Paul's Church in Llanover Road built of stone in 1893 from the ruins of Capel Newydd on a site which was donated by the Blaenavon Company and the Marquis of Abergavenny. The foundation stone was laid in 1893 by Mr. R.W. Kennard JP. In November 1953 the church celebrated 60 years service.

Situated beside the Abergavenny road at Cae White, St James Church was built as a replacement for the old St James 'Iron' Church, which stood near the Old Victoria Row, off the Garn Road, in the centre of a field beside a little canal which ran from Blaenavon Ironworks to Garn-yr-erw (on the site of the present-day Gilchrist Thomas Estate).

Although called the iron church, it was actually a wooden structure lined inside with matchwood and weatherproofed outside with zinc sheets. There were seats for 250 - 300 people. It eventually had to be abandoned because the tipping of molten waste from the furnaces was encroaching on the building. Before it was closed, the structure was sold to a local butcher for £20.

The decision was made to erect a new St James Church and the stone used in its construction was taken from the disused ironworks furnaces in North Street. A great deal of voluntary labour was provided by the male members of the congregation. They carried out all the excavations for the foundations and also hauled the stone to the site, which was provided by the Blaenavon Company in exchange for the site of the old church. The contract for building the new church was awarded to Isaac Edmunds, a Blaenavon man, whose tender was £1,600. He completed the work within twelve months and the new church opened in 1914, The first vicar was the Rev Watkin Edwards.

The old bell that used to hang at the iron church was installed in the new building and when that in turn became disused, it was transferred to St Paul's Church in Llanover Road. The second St James Church is currently in use as a furniture workshop.

St Paul's Church in Llanover Road was built in 1893 utilising stone taken from the ruins of Capel Newydd which was abandoned in 1861.

The Hallelujah Lampost served as a religious meeting place. Michael Blackmore.

### The Streets of Blaenavon

Many of the old streets of the town once had different names to those by which they are now known. King Street was formerly Heol-ust-tewi (Hush-silence-road); Broad Street bore the name Heol-y-nant (Brook Street), so called because a brook ran down from the Bridgend underneath the buildings down to the Afon Lwyd. It used to be a narrow lane with a house here and there and a low wall about two feet high or a shabby thorn hedge between it and the brook. Hill Street was once very stony, crooked and narrow, known by the Welsh speaking locals as Heol Garegog. Rhydnos Street, which was originally just a path across a field used by the night workers, used to be known as Llwybr Rhyd-y-nos - 'Along by night path'.

Park Street was originally called Beaufort Street and Burford Street is probably a corruption of the same name. The central streets of the town are patriotically called King, Queen and Prince Street, with a High Street slotted in amongst the royal names. A good sense of humour has always prevailed in the town and this for example resulted in the junction of Old and New William Street with Lower Hill Street, being christened 'Coffin Corner,' due to the fact that Mr Thomas the undertaker had his premises there. Likewise the Hallelujah lampost at the junction of Prince Street, Broad Street and Albert Street served as a religious meeting place and the Salvation Army band often played beneath the light. The junction of Broad Street, Commercial Street and Old William Street was known as 'The Cross'.

The main thoroughfare in the town, which is lined with shops, is Broad Street and this was laid out in 1875 as the result of the enterprise of J.G. Williams, a local businessman, who also provided Blaenavon with its first residential hotel, a gas works, paved roads, assembly rooms and a brewery. He also erected an indoor market, after which Market Street was named.

Blaenavon's first market had been in the open air opposite Engine Row, and here vegetables and fruit could be bought in abundance. Farmers and other traders also brought in butter, cheese, sheep, pigs, meat of all kinds, shoes and flannel.

Lion Square near the old Council offices used to be the venue for many of the town's open-air, public and official functions. The old Volunteers would assemble there for ceremonial parades and then return for dismissal, brightening the rather dismal surroundings with their scarlet tunics. All sorts of travelling shows also made their stand on the Square. These consisted of roundabouts, swings, side shows with fat-ladies, fire-eaters, flea circuses, cocoa-nut shies and all the fun of the fair.

Steam organs would grind out mechanical music and were replaced in later years by music blared out from loud speakers. There were wild beast shows, boxing booths, travelling theatres and quack doctors who could extract teeth or cure any complaint under the sun.

In later years the Square was used, mostly on Fridays, as an open-air market. It was purchased by the Urban Council in 1961 and the open market was no longer allowed. The Square then was used as a more or less unauthorised bus and car park, the latter now formalised.

**A pub for every week of the year!**

At one time it used to be a proud boast that Blaenavon had so many public houses that it was possible to drink in a different one every week of the year. Published in 1876, a paper entitled *Franciscan Missions among the Colliers and Ironworkers of Monmouthshire* comments:

> 'Blaenafon is completely a colony of colliers and ironmakers. No one would dream of living there unless in some way connected with the mines or works. There are many shops to supply the needs of the inhabitants and there is a vast army of publicans who profess to supply the means of quenching their thirst, but seem rather to do their best to increase it...'

The oldest tavern in the town was the old Crown Inn which stood in North Street, below Ty Mawr. A sign over the door declared that it was The Old Crown but it later became better known as 'The Drum and Monkey.' It must have been a very lively place for the furnace workers in particular drank a considerable quantity of beer and it is said that before the end of most nights there were often two or three men installed in the nearby stocks, for creating a disturbance.

Blaenavon's lost pubs include:
The Albert Inn, Alma, Belle Vue, Boot, Brittania, Brewery Vaults, Bridgend, Crown Inn, Drum and Monkey, Forge Hammer, Forresters, Globe, Greyhound, Griffin, Ivor Castle, Jolly Colliers, King's Arms, King's Head, Lamb Inn, Miner's Arms, Mount Pleasant, Nag's Head, New Inn, New King's Arms, Old Duke, Old Lion Vaults, Old Railway, Oxford, Pen Cefyl, Prnce of Wales, Railway, Rising Sun, Rock and Fountain, Royal Arms, Royal Exchange, Royal George, Royal Oak, Star, Swan, Three Cranes, Vine Tree, White Hart, White Horse, White Lion and Winning Horse.

The surviving pubs are:
The Rifleman's Arms, Lion Hotel (originally called Red Lion Hotel), Rolling Mill, The Castle Hotel, The Cambrian, The Fountain and The Queen Victoria.

The Railway Hotel in Blaenavon. Torfaen Museum Trust.

Royal Arms, Blaenavon. John Lewis collection.

The old 'Lock Up' in North Street was built in 1836. It stood just above the infamous 'Drum and Monkey' Inn which is featured in Alexander Cordell's novel *Rape of of the Fair Country.*
Francis Keen Collection.

**Keeping the peace**

The old lock-up in North Street was built in 1838 when the old stocks were done away with. These used to stand just above the old Company Shop in North Street. Blaenavon's first Policeman was Mr Hodder, whose name was appropriately changed to Mr 'Order'.

In about 1850 a building called 'The Barracks' was built in North Street to accommodate soldiers during times of unrest. A Company of the 2nd Devon Regiment was certainly stationed there at this time. It later became a public house held by a certain Shoni Bach o'r Dafarn and some years later the Blaenavon Company took the building over for use as a home for the aged and retired.

The old 'lock-up' in North Street was replaced in the late 19th century by a Police Station and Magistrates Court in Church Street. The Magistrates Court has since been demolished.

Probably the most serious disturbance in the town occurred in 1868 when riots broke out following a General Election. The unpopular Tory MPs for Monmouthshire had been challenged by Colonel Harry Clifford, who was a Liberal and regarded as a hero by the working class for daring to stand against the other candidates. The *Pontypool Free Press* reported that :-

> 'Riots broke out at various places in Monmouthshire after the declaration of the poll in the Parliamentary General Election, in which Octavius Morgan polled 3,761 votes, Poulett Somerset 3525 and Henry Morgan Clifford (Liberal) 2,338. The first two, both Conservatives, were declared elected. The valley towns voted over overwhelmingly for the Liberal candidate.'

Violence in Blaenavon started in a pub in King Street and then various shops and hotels in the town owned by Tory locals were attacked. The mob then moved on to J.G. Williams's Lion Hotel which was regarded as the Tory Party HQ in Blaenavon. A full scale siege developed with doors battered down and every window smashed. The street outside was crowded with people looking on while the rioters flung all kinds of items through windows and doorways. Costly furniture and other articles were taken into a house nearby which was being constructed and these items were set on fire. Shelves, dressers, chests of drawers, beds and bedsteads, piano, organ, tables and chairs were all destroyed. Barrels of beer were rolled outside and sent flying down the main street and containers of spirits and cider were taken away.

Moving on to the Prince of Wales, the mob smashed doors and windows, drank or destroyed all the liquor or beer, carried away all the money they could find, as well as several flitches of bacon. The looting and rioting only ended when a detachment of the 23rd Royal Welsh Fusiliers arrived to reinforce the police and numerous arrests were made. When order was at last restored the local magistrate, Mr T.W. Kennard, who lived at Ty Mawr, read the Riot Act.

The men arrested were later tried at Monmouth Assizes by Mr Justice Keating. In his summing up he said that the riots were disgraceful and that 'It was a monstrous proposition when people were not allowed to entertain and express their political opinions in a free country.' Sentences varying from four to twelve months hard labour were given to 36 men who were charged with riot and demolishing property at Abersychan and Blaenavon.

The Police Station in Church Street, Blaenavon.

## The Workmen's Institute

In 1882 a small number of working men decided to form a committee which would investigate the feasibility of providing the town with a permanent institute, where leisure time relaxation and recreation could take place. Premises suitable for this purpose were initially opened in Lion Street in 1883. The institute was financed by a halfpenny per week contribution by the members while the Blaenavon Company provided books for the library and the first billiard table. Within a few years it became apparent that a larger building was needed.

The Blaenavon Company were happy to provide a site free of charge but, due to legal problems, this was not possible so they sold the land to the Trustees for £600 and then returned £500 as a donation. The Blaenavon workers continued to contribute a halfpenny a week from their wages towards the cost of the building and in August 1893 construction began.

Councillor Robert Kennard JP., son of the Chairman of the Blaenavon Company performed the ceremony of laying the foundation stone in the presence of an estimated crowd of 7,000 people. Beneath the foundation stone a hermetically sealed box was placed, containing current copies of *The Times* , *Western Mail* , and the *South Wales Daily News* , examples of current coins of the realm minted in 1893, photographs of the Queen, the Prince and Princess of Wales, the Duke and Duchess of York, of Mr Kennard, the Chairman of the Blaenavon Company Ltd., of Mr R.W. Kennard and one of the Institute Committee.

Councillor R.W. Kennard returned on the 7th January 1895 to perform the opening ceremony following the completion of the building after seventeen months. On the ground floor the rooms consisted of library, newspaper room, magazine room, recreation room and billiard room. There were also committee rooms a Board Room and toilets. The Hall on the upper floor measured 86′ by 49′ 6″ and with the wide balcony was capable of seating 1,500 people. It was used largely for concerts, eisteddfods, tea parties, bazaars and political gatherings. Over the years many changes have been made to the interior while the exterior remains largely unaltered. In 1995 the Workmen's Hall celebrated its 100th birthday and extensive recent renovations with a gala concert.

## The Fire Station

In February 1961 a specially built fire station was opened at Cae White on the Abergavenny Road. Situated outside the town at about 1,300 feet above sea level it was built just a short distance from Blaenavon's first fire station (1886). This was considered an admirable site for the old station for the man-handled engine, known as the 'John Warton'could be easily run downhill to the town, where fires were most likely to occur. The engine was called 'John Warton' in honour of the General Manager of the Blaenavon Company.

The Company had also manufactured the engine and built the station in which it was housed, which in had even included a tower for hose drying. The engine was first used to put out a fire at a bazaar being held at the old St James' 'Iron Church'.

When the site for the new station was proposed, it was much disputed and when it was pointed out the the Council that the firemen would have have to run uphill to answer a call and would arrive breathless, it was suggested that perhaps they could be supplied with motor-scooters!

Blaenavon Workmen's Hall and Institute opened in 1894 and was one of the finest of its kind in the country. It was financed by weekly contributions from local miners and steel-workers.

## The Council Offices

Situated at the junction between Lion Street and High Street, this building was adapted in the 1930s from existing buildings for the Blaenafon Local Board by the architect I. G. Gwyn Thomas. It has been empty for a number of years but there are currently plans for it to be renovated to provide a new library for the town.

## Forgeside

The terraced cottages in Forgeside were built more than a century ago by the Blaenavon Company to house people working at their steelworks in Forge Side. The rows instead of being given names were called A Row, B Row, C Row, D Row and E Row, such uninteresting names being fairly indicative of the attitude of many 19th century employers towards their employees. A and B rows were demolished in the late 1970s.

There was no public house in Forgeside until the 'Footballers' was opened (closed at the time of writing). This was a private house once occupied by the works manager. The sale of alcohol was prohibited in Forgeside by the steelworks management. They thought that workers would leave their mills and furnaces to drink during working hours. However men used to send youngsters to bring back drink to the works.

Coity House was also once the Blaenavon Works manager's house. It is a detached 19th century Grade II listed building and is also known as The White House. The building was last used in 1990 as offices and at the time of writing is for sale as Doncasters have built replacement offices.

## Garn-yr-erw

On the north side of the Brynmawr road once stood a row of houses, built by the Blaenavon Company, that were known as the Black Ranks. Another name for them was 'Sheepshead Row' for a special feature was the stable doors in the front porches where the heads of people sitting on chairs, watching the world go by, would often be seen. The exterior walls of the houses were coated black with pitch, to protect them from the weather but at the same time giving them a very sombre appearance. The houses were demolished in 1980 after three years of uncertainty over their future, and the inhabitants moved to Council houses in Blaenavon.

Lower Garn Terrace and Upper Garn Terrace are still there, but the village school, established in 1894, closed in July 1971. There was once a chapel here called Horeb Baptist Chapel which was built in 1866 as a schoolroom. Services were also held there until a new chapel was built in 1905. The Welfare Hall was one of the first in South Wales and was erected by the old Miners' Welfare scheme.

Garn-yr-erw was once a compact little community with its own church and chapel, its own co-op shop and post office, besides the Welfare Hall. There was also a branch of the County Library in the hall at one time.

This terrace of cottages in Forgeside bears the simple name of C Row.

The 'Black Ranks' at Garn-yr-erw were coated in pitch to keep out the weather and a special feature was the stable doors which gave rise to the alternative name of 'Sheepshead Row.'

## Sweeping away the past

Numerous old buildings associated with Blaenavon's ironworks and collieries have sadly been demolished over the years and these include such historic structures as the laboratory used by the Gilchrist cousins and the mid 19th century offices of the old Blaenavon Iron & Coal Company. In 1901 there had been almost 600 cottages and houses owned by the Blaenavon Company and in the years following the Second World War these dwellings although in a poor state, were still occupied. The low rents charged by the Company no doubt made the tenants very reluctant to move out into modern houses for which they would be charged much more. But when the Coal Board took over these properties, many of which lay outside the town, the tenants were forced to leave and the cottages were gradually demolished.

Work on a new estate at Heol-y-parc was held up by the delay in a film company's arrival to shoot *Rape of the Fair Country* . For a number of sequences they wanted to use Stack and Shepherd's Squares as sets and it was from Shepherd Square that the Council intended to obtain stone for the Heol-y-parc foundations. So until the company completed their proposed filming, progress on the construction of this new estate was severely hampered. Unfortunately, the film was never made, but the delay at least resulted in the survival of Stack Square and the preservation of the old ironwork as a visitor attraction.

During his period of demolition and slum clearance many of the old terraced houses were replaced with new Council estates which included Elgam, Capel Newydd, Heol-y-parc, Hillside, Ty Fry, Avon Road, Riverside, Kennard Court and Kennard Crescent. The past was not completely ignored for the las two mentioned developments were named after the Kennard family who formed the Blaenavon Coal and Iron Company Ltd., in 1836.

Looking down North Street before some of Blaenavon's history was swept away.

In June 1986 Blaenavon Tourism Committee held their first American week with the specific aim of attracting more visitors to the town. One day during the week was designated as a special Victorian Olde Worlde daye and the centre of the town was transformed by shoppers and shopkeepers into a scene out of a Dickens novel. John Lewis Collection.

**Tourism the new industry?**

*' There are few places left in Wales where there is an opprtunity to preserve a total landscape that retains so many relevant features set in surroundings of great natural beauty, as yet relatively undeveloped in terms of indigenous and international tourism. Blaenafon is one of them.'*

Richard Keen
Welsh Landscape and Culture Advisor for the National Trust.

Blaenavon was once one of the busier towns in the Welsh coalfield and its wealth came not only from its rich coal seams but from its production of high quality steel which during the last century became famous throughout the world. The decline of Blaenavon began at the end of the First World War when it was no longer economical and practical to produce steel inland. Following the closure of the iron and steel works, the town's coal industry also declined and the character and wealth of the town began to suffer in consequence.

The local authorities have had success in attracting new employers to their industrial estates on reclaimed spoil tips west of the town and Daniel Doncaster's factory on the Blaenavon Company's Forgeside site has prospered manufacturing aircraft components. Nevertheless, like many similar settlements elsewhere, Blaenavon is now a town of declining population occupied mainly by those who work elsewhere or are inactive through age or unemployment. The shopping centre has declined dramatically as residents prefer to make their purchases elsewhere, and too many premises are derelict or in poor condition.

When Big Pit, the town's last deep mine, closed in 1980, plans were in hand to reopen the mine as a visitor attraction, the jewel in a new industry - tourism. Since 1984 Big Pit Mining Museum has attracted around 100,000 visits annually and smaller numbers have enjoyed the remains of the 18th Century Ironworks, Stack Square and a steam railway venture.

However, twenty years of tourism have not proved to be the salvation of the town. Jobs have been created but visitors have not brought their spending power into Broad Street and little overnight accomodation has been provided. Visitors have been given little reason to come into the town from the attractions on the outskirts.

The new Torfaen County Borough Council has recognised that the heritage value of the Blaenavon area, and thereby its tourism potential, has sometimes been insufficiently appreciated and, like the fabric of the town, has been inadequately resourced and managed. The Council and its partner organisations are trying to inject a new and lasting momentum into heritage tourism development at Blaenavon both as a conservation duty and in the hope of increasing community benefits.

Heritage tourism is still potentially a growth market and in the Blaenavon area there are considerable opportunities for it to develop into a major visitor attraction and an educational facility of high quality. Not only is Blaenavon an important birthplace of the Industrial Revolution but its unique features provide potential for achieving World Heritage Site Status, which could bring considerable economic benefit to the local communites.

This former ironmaking and mining town, bounded to the north west by a landscape of early iron and coal workings, forges and links to the canal below, provides a unique opportunity to tell dramatically the story of 200 years of history. As one of the most complete industrial landscapes left in Britain it has already been designated a Grade I Historic Landscape, as the result of a campaign for its preservation conducted over a number of years. Hopefully in the not too distant future Blaenavon will be added to the list of recognised World Heritage Sites and the necessary investment will be forthcoming.

Already it seems that the future of Big Pit Mining Museum will be secure with the National Museum and Galleries of Wales, and it is to be hoped that the historic landscapes will be safe from the threat of the open cast coal working.

Blaenavon in the 21st century will need much more than tourism to recover its dignity, but steps now being planned and taken can create an image of quality and desirability which should help to reverse the trends of the 20th century.

## ---7---

# The Market Town of Pontypool

*'Pontypool is a small town of Monmouthshire, which has risen up in the course of the last century. It owes its existence to the mineral treasures which lie concealed in the surrounding hills. The quantities of iron ore and coal, here dug out of the bowels of the earth are astonishing. The hammer and the pick-axe are heard to resound where used to prevail the profoundest silence; whilst the roaring furnace and the thundering forge shake the vallies through which the brooks are wont to flow with an uninterrupted placidity! '*

John Evans 1805

Pontypool is the oldest industrial towns in South Wales and for more than 200 years it was one of the most important towns in Monmouthshire. Its existence is undoubtedly owed to the foresight and enterprise of the Hanbury family who settled here in the 16th century and laid the foundations of a once important iron industry.

There is an ancient tradition that the town derives its name as the result of a local man, called Dafydd ap Howell, building a bridge across the Afon Lwyd. He was described as 'a stout, strong-shouldered parson, well fit for a tussle, fond of a bottle and a song.' After supper one night he went down to the river and met his Satanic Majesty. They had a discussion and argument as to which of the two should build a bridge over the water. It was agreed that they should join hands for a tug, and whichever should be drawn across the river, should build the bridge. The Devil was forced to yield to the superior muscles of the sturdy Welshman and in accordance with the terms of the contest was obliged to build the bridge which was named after Howell and the place accordingly became known as Pont ap Howell. But this is of course bad Welsh, for a Welshman could not have been called Ap Howell, He might be called William ap Howell or John ap Howell, but never Ap Howell. The correct name is more likely Pont y Pwll, the bridge over the pool or hollow and it is of significance that in Norman times the place was known as 'Le Pool'.

The Devil competes with Dafydd ap Howell

This 19th century engraving shows the old bridge in Pontypool and Park Cottages which were built by the Hanbury family before the stables were erected. Torfaen Museum Trust.

An alternative version of the above story is that a one-time vicar of the parish of Llanover, named Dafydd ap Howell, built the bridge in order to enable the inhabitants of the nearby village to attend services at Trevethin when the river was flooded. The bridge was named after its builder and the village on the west side of the river became known as 'Pont Dafydd ap Howell' (the bridge of David, the son of Howell). This long name over the course of time was shortened to 'Pont ap Howell,' which in turn was gradually reduced to Pontpwll. As the place became more and more under the influence of the English language, the present name of Pontypool was adopted.

Speed's map of 1600 does not even show the name so the village must have been regarded as quite insignificant at that time. It was the development of Pontypool as an industrial centre under the Hanbury family that increased its importance. William Coxe who came here in 1799 commented that, 'Before the existence of the present town, the place contained very few houses and was called from the church Trevethin.' He described the town as being 'placed on the edge of a steep cliff, overhanging the Afon Lwyd, and on the slope of a declivity under impending hills, partly bare and partly mantled with wood. The line of the canal is seen winding above the town; a rapid torrent, descending from a lake at the foot of Mynydd Maen, flows under the canal, and rushing impetuously along the outskirts of the town precipitates itself into the Afon Lwyd, which rolls in an abyss beneath.'

Pontypool is certainly very cramped for space, being wedged into the bottom of a steep valley, with the result that it has been commented that 'the town lies outside itself' and flows for example into the neighbouring parish of Panteg.

William Coxe also tells us that:

> 'Pont y Pool is a large straggling place, containing 250 houses, and 1500 souls. Several neat habitations, and numerous shops, present an appearance of thriving prosperity, notwithstanding the dusky aspect of the town, occasioned by the adjacent forges. The inhabitants derive great support from the iron works and collieries, and have been recently benefited by the trade of the canal. The place is the principal mart for the natives of the mountainous district, and the weekly market is not the least considerable, and the cheapest in Monmouthshire. It is a pleasing amusement to mix in these crowded meetings, to observe the frank and simple manners of the hardy mountaineers, and endeavour, in asking the price of their provisions, to extort a Saxon word from this British progeny. The women were mostly wrapped in long cloth cloaks of a dark blue or brown colour; all of them wore mob caps neatly plaited over the forehead and ears, and tied above the chin; several had also round felt hats like those worn by the men, or large chip hats covered with black silk, and fastened under the chin. This head-dress gives an arch and lively air to the younger part of the sex, and is not unbecoming.'

Coxe noted that the town was, 'peculiarly commodious for the establishment of iron manufactories; and perhaps another generation may see a new Birmingham start up in the wilds of Monmouthshire.'

During most of the 18th century the numbers employed by the various works in Pontypool was not huge and conditions of housing were accordingly good by the standards of the day. The diary of an unknown traveller in 1782 (in the National Library of Wales) compared 'the misery and want endured by the workmen and their families at Tintern, where the works were declining, with conditions at Pontypool where we saw one of these families sitting down to a dinner of a roasted shoulder of veal and a dish of peas, by the cheerful blaze of a fire, that might be envied by many a reputable farmer?'

But the population began to grow rapidly after 1800 and by 1841 was larger than that of Newport or Cardiff. The result of this rapid growth was a shortage of housing and the deplorable conditions in which many people lived is described in an address given on 17th March 1840 by George Kenrick, proprietor of the Varteg Ironworks, at the Mechanics' Institution, Pontypool. His lecture was entitled: *The Populations of Pontypool and the Parish of Trevthin, situated in the so-called 'Disturbed Districts:' Its Moral, Social and Intellectual Character.*

The following is an extract from this addresss:-

> 'The population of our parish, which some of you may remember as low as twelve hundred persons, chiefly employed in agriculture, has rapidly increased of late years, in consequence of the erection of iron works, which afford employment to the greater portion of the inhabitants; and the first object which engages our attention is the proportion of sleeping rooms to the population. This is important as a measure of the civilisation of the people, and of the comforts which they enjoy, and their taste and inclination for the retirements of a private life; these habits are generally accompanied, though not always, with a corresponding progress in morality. Wherever there is a large mass of persons congregated in ill-ventilated, confined premises, there misery, disease, and want, are sure to abound, with their usual attendants, vice and wickedness; for a confirmation of this we have only to look to our crowded streets and squares in large towns, which are the resort of the lowest of the population, morally and physically.
>
> The average to the whole parish is three and an eighth persons, including children, to a sleeping room, but there are some variations in different localities. In Abersychan village,

where there are several houses too much crowded; for instance there were four houses with only one sleeping room each, to accommodate seven persons, of whom in two cases, four were lodgers, and the other two houses had each two lodgers.

At Pentwyn there are some houses very much crowded, as many as twelve, fourteen, fifteen, and sixteen persons in one house, with three small sleeping rooms; in one instance there were twelve lodgers, of whom eight were married persons. In Pontypool twenty-one persons were numbered in one house, of whom thirteen were lodgers. But the Sowhill sets competition at defiance; there from thirteen to sixteen persons are in a few instances found billeted upon one sleeping room. I am ashamed to say that at the Varteg, one house shelters twenty Irish, men women and children; the inhabitants of the Sister Isle are so gregarious that it is difficult to separate them into small families. Many persons will be surprised to hear that so many persons can lodge in a house, but it must be remembered that the iron works are never idle and some men work at night and others during the day; so that when six o' clock strikes, one set of men leaves their beds, and is succeeded by those who have been working all day, and by this admirable contrivance the beds never require warming, even in the depth of winter. I need not say that this practice is very injurious to health, and as it is always discouraged, it exists to a very limited extent. '

The town had originally consisted principally of the cottages of the workers of Major Hanbury and these were scattered on the Tranch, in Cwmynyscoy and on the Upper Race. But as industry developed and prosperity increased, other settlers were attracted and the houses gradually spread up the western slope until they reached the summit of the steep ground known as 'The Sow Hill.' This name is derived from the carriers taking the sows and pigs (of iron) from the backs of their mules and horses whilst they refreshed themselves at 'The Jolly Colliers', an inn later named 'The Labour in Vain' as no one had done well while in charge of it.

Old cottages in Trosnant, Pontypool at the turn of the century. Margaret Pead Collection.

A far better site in which the town could have developed would have been the level area in the bottom of the valley, through which the road ran from Pont y Moel (anciently Rhyd y Moel) to Pontypool. However, the Hanbury family, having bought the Bell Inn and other premises for themselves, then purchased all the land they could possibly obtain on that side of the river to form the Park. Consequently, apart from Pontypool Park House, no buildings were allowed to be erected on that side of the river.

Practically all the land between the Turnpike Road and the river belonged to the Hanbury family and it effectually prevented the erection of any houses in that locality. So the only place in which Pontypool could develop was on the hillside and as a result its streets had to be kept narrow.

Before the present road from the Clarence Hotel was cut through the Graig Field in 1822, the entrances into Pontypool on that side were very dangerous, particularly the old Darren road, which overhung the Afon Lwyd and led into Trosnant. Poor old Walter Richards was making his way along this hazardous road in 1821, when his horse stumbled and he was thrown over the edge. Some men managed to rescue him and badly injured he was carried into the King's Arms, where he died a few days later.

The town is intersected by two main streets at a central point called 'The Cross' and immediately connected with it were built Commercial Street, Hanbury Road, George Street, Clarence Street, Crane Street and Osborne Road.

George Street, Pontypool in the 1920s.

Standing near The Cross for hundreds of years, the Old Bath Beerhouse was believed to be one of the oldest buildings in the area. It had been established in 1839, by Thomas Davies and was then known as the 'Ponty Pool Inn.' He left it to his daughter Martha Whitney, and to her children in perpetuity. When this family died out the property was acquired by Donald Reid, who formed the Castle Brewery, Ltd., Pontypool. It was sold in 1902 to Westlake's Brewery Ltd., who amalgamated with the Reform Brewery Co., Ltd. The firm was then taken over by Andrew Buchan Ltd., Rhymney. The pub was finally demolished in January 1951 when a start was made on widening the narrow George Street.

Another old pub was the Blue Boar Inn which stood at the corner of Crane Street, opposite the Red Lion and it was well known because it gave its name to the Blue Boar Field, which was an open space in the middle of the town. This field was bordered by the present day Market, Crane and Commercial Streets, and there was a cattle market on the fourth side. Stretching up as far as the Globe Inn, this green pasture at one time had part of its ground converted into a garden by the landlord of the Blue Boar Inn.

It was in the Blue Boar Field that traders, cheap-jacks and hawkers used to gather to sell their goods. Records show that two hundred years ago, you could buy beef on this field for 11/2 (56p) a pound and chickens 10d (5p) each. A barrel of oysters would cost you 8d (4p) and a Christmas turkey as little as 1/6 (8p). This was also a pitch for strolling players to stage their shows and local sportsmen played cricket on the field in the summertime. Pontypool Market now stands on the site.

Soon after 1840 the Blue Boar Inn was pulled down and the White Lion erected in its place.This adjoined the Red Lion in Crane Street and both inns later became the Lion House.

By 1885 there were no less than 254 licensed houses in the Pontypool area and a list of pubs in Pontypool in the year 1911 included: the Sir Garnet Wolseley Hotel, Ship, Swan, Three Cranes, Globe, White Lion, Wrington Arms. Montague, Prince of Wales, Bath Beer House, Full Moon, Crown, Castle, White Hart, Three Salmons, Alma, Fountain, Bull, Greyhound, George Hotel, Red Lion, Coach and Horses, Unicorn, Hospitality, Horseshoe, Albion, Finers Arms, Labour in Vain, Oak, Forge Hammer, Victory, Colliers Arms, Noah's Ark, Wellington, Bell, Bush, Winning Horse, Market Tavern, Wheatsheaf, New Found Out, Upper Forge Hammer, Lower Forge Hammer, Clarence Hotel, Hanbury (Hanbury Road), Hanbury (Trosnant), Star, Waterloo, Kings Arms, and Prince of Wales (Pontymoile).

The Clarence Hotel was named after the Duke of Clarence - a title bestowed in 1789 on William the third son of George III. He ascended the throne to become William IV in 1830. The handsome building was badly damaged by fire in 1987 and has now been sadly boarded up and closed for many years

Up to 1830 the only public houses between Pontypool and Blaenavon were the 'Horseshoe' at Pontnewynydd, the Fox and Hounds at Abersychan and the Rising Sun, about half-a-mile further on, and for a few years the King's Head near the Varteg Company forge at Cwmavon.

**Pontypool Market**

In addition to being an important industrial centre, Pontypool has also been a market town, and permission to hold a weekly market for the 'selling of all manner of cattle, goods and merchandise' was given as far back as 1690 by King William and Queen Mary.

Miss Francess Bray Lady of the Manor of Wentsland and Bryngwyn, built a Corn Market in Commercial Street, near the Cross in 1750. The building has been listed and it can still be seen. A tablet on the facade surmounted by the Morgan family Arms commemorates the founder:-

'Frances Bray, daughter of Sir Edward Morgan of Llantarnam,
in this County, Baronet, and relict of Edmund Bray, Barrington,
in the County's of Gloucester and Berks, Esq., deceased,
erected this Market House in the year 1750.'

Front of the old Corn Market in Commercial Street with tablets inscribed in English and Welsh commemorating the founder Frances Bray, Lady of the Manor of Wentsland and Bryngwyn.

Pontypool Market, built at a cost of £22,280 was officially opened on 1st December 1894 by John Capel Hanbury.

For almost a century the upper floor of the building, for almost a century, was used as assembly rooms for the local community and also provided a theatre which was operated by the Kemble family who had established the Brecknock and Hereford Theatre Company. In later years the building was occupied by shops and the office of the Manor of Wentsland and Bryngwyn, as the Llantarnam Abbey estate, now divided among numerous co-heirs was generally called. After that it became the stationery shop of Messrs Hughes & Son Ltd.

In 1827 another market house was erected by William and Elizabeth Watkins for the sale of butter and meat. Following their bankruptcy the premises were purchased by John Griffiths of Blaenavon. He subsequently succeeded in purchasing the market tolls from the Manor of Wentsland and Bryngwyn in 1837.

This building was replaced by a new market in 1846, which was built next to the Blue Boar Field and, even though this property proved to be inadequate in size, a market of suitable proportions was not erected until 1894. It was designed by Robert Williams ARIBA of London and D. J. Lougher of Pontypool to cover an area of 20,070 sq ft., and was built at a cost of £22,280. This was the first electrically lighted market in Wales, having the 'magic power' installed during its construction. The official opening was performed on 1st December 1894 by John Capel Hanbury. Accompanied by his wife he performed the ceremony at the Lower Crane Street entrance using a golden key. The whole town was decked with flags and banners and large crowds lined the streets to watch the procession from the Town Hall to the market.Three years later, a new entrance and arcade, from Crane Street, was added to commemorate Queen Victoria's Jubilee.

The *Pontypool Free Press* reported how in June 1897 the Queen's Jubilee was celebrated by, 'some 1,100 Pontypool children, who sat down to a spread in the Market Hall. Encouraged by their elders to eat their fill they set to work with a will.... Some of the voracious youngsters ate six pounds of cake and a like quantity of bread and butter...They drank their tea out of mugs on each of which was a likeness of Queen Victoria, whose Diamond Jubilee they were celebrating.'

Pontypool Market once had the reputation of being the cheapest market in the county for dairy and farm produce and still offers good value. Its spacious interior was even used years ago by Pontypool RFC for passing practice when the weather was too bad for training at the Recreation Ground.

**The Town Hall**

Capel Hanbury Leigh financed the building of the Town Hall to commemorate the birth of his son and heir, John Capel, who was born on 14th May 1853. At 76 years of age, the proud father was no doubt particularly pleased that the continuance of the Hanbury connection with the town was now assured.

Festivities in the town to celebrate the birth of an heir culminated in the roasting of a three-year-old ox, weighing 1372 lbs, in the Vegetable Market (probably on the site of the present market). It was then taken to the Park and carved and portions distributed to a crowd of an estimated 20,000 people.

Designs for the Town Hall, which was to be built in the Italian style at a cost of £1,500, were sought through a national competition, which resulted in thirty-nine entries. The winning design was submitted by Messrs Bidlake & Lovett of Wolverhampton.

The following year, on the first anniversary of the birth of her son, Mrs Hanbury Leigh laid the foundation stone of the new building. She and her husband had been escorted to the ceremony by the Pontymoel Brass Band playing a medley of lively airs.

Glantorfaen House in Hanbury Road was constructed in 1857 in the Italian Palazzo style to the design of T.S. Lysaght of Bristol.

Pontypool Town Hall was built for the town by Capel Hanbury Leigh. Behind it now stands a six storey Civic Centre constructed by Torfaen Borough Council.

The stone was then duly laid with the aid of a massive silver trowel which was decorated with a delicately engraved elevation of the intended building.

An account of the stone laying ceremony was published in the *Monmouthshire Merlin*, and the need for a Town Hall in Pontypool was explained:

> 'Surrounded by some of the most valuable and extensive mineral works in the Principality, and possessing various capabilities of commercial advancement, the town of Pontypool is rapidly growing in wealth, while its enterprising inhabitants have steadily pursued their active and industrious career. As the place of their abode increases in material importance they are anxious that it should also possess augmented facilities for mental cultivation, and such means of social improvement now occupy due attention in the proper quarters.
>
> Among other wants long felt has been that of a town hall in which people might assemble for the discussion of important questions - for the acquisition of knowledge, for the gratification of taste, and for the daily transaction of business... It may be that this hall at no distant period may be invested with a municipal character and that a Mayor of Pontypool, surrounded by Aldermen and Councillors, may sit there in civic state. It may echo from time to time with the stirring voice of the Christian patriot, and the eloquent appeal of the philanthropist; within its walls may science have her numerous votaries; there may sweet song entrance the listening multitude and moral conversation gladden the hearts of the toilers.'

The builder was William Prosser of Abergavenny and he completed the construction work in time for the grand opening ceremony on 1st January 1856 which was duly reported by the *Monmouthshire Merlin* :-

> 'The opening of this handsome and capacious edifice, an event which has been anticipated with great interest by the inhabitants of Pontypool, took place on Tuesday last under circumstances which cannot but prove highly satisfactory to the distinguished individual by whose munificence it has been reared as well as by the public by whom the need for such a building has long been felt. That a thriving and important town like Pontypool should be without a commodious hall for the transaction of public business and the promotion of objects of general importance, has long been considered an anomalous state of things...'

The first of many great events to be held in the Town Hall was staged on the following Tuesday when a 'Grand Concert' was attended by 400 people. In April 1866 General Tom Thumb, his wife and infant daughter appeared at the Town Hall. The event was described as the last appearance locally of the General (whose real name was Charles S. Stratton) before his retirement. The party of midgets were conveyed to the hall in a miniature carriage drawn by four of the smallest ponies in the world.

Sixteen black performers, who prior to June 1865 were held as slaves in the State of Georgia, gave an entertainment there in May 1867, which represented negro life on the plantations of America.

An exhibition held in the Town Hall in May 1872 included some rare and interesting curiosities. It consisted of hundreds of articles ranging from King Henry V's childhood cradle to the hoary head of a wild boar, captured in Ceylon by a Goytre man. There was the polished suit of armour of Henry V and a piece of bedhanging from a bed in which Mary Queen of Scots slept in 1546. There was a fine display of paintings, including many local landscapes and portraits of local personalities. Pontypool Japan Ware was well represented. Among the more unusual exhibits was the tripod on which the Chartists dried their powder in front of the fire at Croesyceiliog, a mummified frog and a tobacco pouch made from the foot of an albatross.

In November 1892 a London dentist demonstrated his novel technique of extracting teeth by electricity at the Town Hall. Many people took advantage of his offer to have teeth extracted free of charge. Entertainment was provided by a pianist, conjuror, ventriloquist and vocal soloist.

Mrs Pankhurst, the Suffragette, addressed a packed meeting at the Town Hall in October 1915. Her speech was entitled 'How to win the war.' She remarked that the Germans' attitude towards women was almost the most degrading thing in the whole world. They looked upon women as a kind of domestic animal to be used at their convenience.

In June 1948 several people narrowly escaped injury when an explosion occurred at the Town Hall under the boards of the Food Office. The problem was assumed to have been due to an accumulation of gas under the floorboards where a burst gas-pipe was later found. Someone struck a match to light a gas ring to make a cup of tea and about fifteen seconds later there was a very loud bang!

In March 1966 the old magistrates court in the Town Hall was converted into a council chamber at a cost of £20,000. It was the first council chamber that the local authority had in all its long history.

### Glantorfaen House

This fine building on the Hanbury Road was constructed in 1857 in the Italian style to the design of T.S. Lysaght of Bristol. It was erected by local builder John Farrant Williams for Richard Greenway an eminent Pontypool solicitor. In later years it became the home of Mr W. H. V. Bythway who for many years was clerk to Pontypool Urban District Council.

In June 1953 the property was acquired by Pontypool Council at a negotiated cost of £7,775, and the members all agreed that it was certainly 'a fine captive,' particularly as it was so close to the Town Hall. Today, it is occupied by a firm of local solicitors, Messrs Watkins and Gunn.

### Maesderwyn House

Built in 1830, this was the home of the Agent for the Hanbury estates. On the front of the adjoining estate office can be seen the monogram of John Hanbury, the last Squire of Pontypool. During the mid nineteenth century the estate yard was moved here from nar the river. It is the nerve centre of the Pontypool Park estate.

### Local Chapels

One of the earliest Non-conformist chapels in the district is the New Inn Congregational Church which was founded in 1710. An altar tomb in the burial ground preserves the memory of the founder of Wrench's Charity which was attached to the church.

In 1727 the Baptist movement erected their first chapel at Penygarn and four years later Pontypool became an important centre for the movement with the construction, at Trosnant, of an academy for the training of Baptist ministers. In 1770 it was transferred to Abergavenny and then a new Baptist College was opened at Penygarn in 1837. This continued to be used until 1893. Many other Baptist chapels were built in the Valley including one at Abersychan which was erected in 1846 and catered for Welsh speakers. At this time the language was being replaced by English in Established churches throughout South Wales.

John Wesley visited Pontypool on three occasions and this sketch by Ken Haynes shows the famous preacher, astride his horse preaching to the people of Trosnant. Picture supplied by Arthur Crane.

Following several visits by John Wesley during 1739-41, the Welsh Methodists in 1813 built Rehobeth chapel in High Street, Pontypool and it subsequently became a Calvinistic Methodist Chapel. A Wesleyan Chapel was erected in 1814 in Crumlin Street but in 1853 a larger chapel was erected in High Street and the reformed Wesleyans occupied the original. The Welsh Wesleyans of Pontypool worshipped in the house called 'The Old Japan' until the erection of their chapel in 1839. In Pontnewynydd the Methodists occupied the club room of the Horseshoe Hotel until their chapel was opened in 1849.

Other Independent chapels in the area included the Sardis Chapel at Varteg, founded in 1827; another established in 1832 at Cefn-y-crib and Siloah at Abersychan which started in 1837. The Mount Pleasant Congregational Church in Pontypool dates from 1855.

Zion Baptist Church was founded at Lower Trosnant in 1844 and united with Crane Street Church in 1878. At Noddfa Chapel which was established in Abersychan in 1846 services were conducted in Welsh.

One of the oldest places of worship in the area is Ebenezer Chapel in Cwmffrwdoer, which was opened by the Rev Edmund Jones in 1742. Today it is known as the Ebenezer United Reformed Church.

**Early Pontypool Printers**

The story of the Welsh Press is among the most interesting features of Welsh history. The first Welsh book, Sir John Price's *Yn y Lhyfyr hwnn* , was published in 1546, but it was not until 1718 that a purely Welsh Press was established in Wales. In that year one Isaac Carter set up a press in Trehedyn in Cardiganshire. He was followed in 1721 by Nicholas Thomas, who set up another press at Carmarthen.

St James Church was built in 1821 for the benefit of English people who had settled in Pontypool and were unable to understand the Welsh services.

St Alban's Church was built in 1846 to accomodate the large numbers of Irish Catholics in the town. It was extensively modernised in 1890.

In 1740 the first printing press in Monmouthshire was set up at Pontypool on the instigation of Miles Harri, the minister of Penygarn Baptist Church. This press owed its establishment to the great religious revival inaugurated by Howell Harris in Wales and by John and Charles Wesley and George Whitefield in England.

The first printed book from the press, (like the six that succeeded it) was in Welsh, being a version of John Gammon's 'Christ, a Christian's Life.' But this first Monmouthshire press was only in operation for two years for it appears to have ceased production sometime in 1742. As far as records go, its output consists of a bookplate and seven small books, five of which were first described by Rowlands in his 'Cambrian Bibliography' (1853). In a later edition (1869) a description of the sixth book is added, while the seventh is recorded by *The Gloucester Journal* of July 29th 1740

Pontypool's first press and type later came into the possession of Thomas Henry Thomas and when seen in 1907 it was described as 'an old oak press standing five feet high and two feet wide on a pair of three-inch pillars, and having two cypress-wood rollers similar to those of a domestic mangle.' The owner stated that he had been given the press by Charles Conway, the Proprietor of the Pontnewydd tinworks.

In 1825 William Rowlands, who was born in London in 1807 of Welsh parents, came to live in Pontypool, where he began preaching with the Calvinistic Methodists. He was a good Latin scholar and at Pontypool he acted as co-master of a day-school with the Rev Evan Evans of Nantyglo. He then spent three years as a travelling missionary. In 1829 he gave up missionary work and, using his inheritance from his parents, he bought a printing press and type (from Richard Jones) and set himself up in Pontypool as a 'printer, book binder and bookseller.'

He knew nothing about printing, but by August of that year he had issued his first number of the Welsh Sunday School monthly entitled *Yr Athroaw*. He also printed several booklets, pamphlets and ballads. But by 1831, he had tired of the printing business and sold it so that he could sink all his capital into a coal pit at Blackwood.

Evan Prosser, using the press of William Rowlands, commenced printing at his office in Commercial Street in 1831 and one of his apprentices later became the eminent Baptist minister, the Rev John Jenkyn Brown, who was born in Pontypool in 1817. The business ran successfully until the autumn of 1842 when Evan Prosser suffered a mental breakdown and took his own life. He was succeeded in the business by his cousin Henry Hughes who was later to become Editor of The Pontypool Free Press.

### The Birth of the *Pontypool Free Press*

In 1858 David Walkinshaw, an experienced journalist, set up as a jobbing printer in the Corn Market House and on March 5th 1859, he issued the first number of *The Pontypool Free Press and Herald of the Hills* . The first issue consisted of four pages measuring 23 ins by 17 ins. Three of the pages were printed in London so only the front page at his time was the true local portion of the paper.

David Walkinshaw was born on June 18th 1817 in the Forest of Dean and was of Scottish descent. In early life he had received his training as a journalist on one of the weekly papers in Newport. He then joined the *Sheffield Free Press* and worked his way up to a responsible position on the staff of that journal. In 1855 he left Sheffield and spent four years in the Forest of Dean, before moving to Pontypool. His father, John Weir Walkinshaw (d.1863) had resided for some years at Abersychan where he was associated with David Mushet the eminent metallurgist, in the erection (1826) and the subsequent management of the ironworks there.

In June 1871, David Walkinshaw removed his printing and publishing office from the Corn Market House to the old Assembly Room over the Butter Market. Six years later, after eighteen years of successful proprietorship, he sold the paper to Henry Hughes (junior) and retired with his wife to Bristol, where he died at the age of 83 on July 13th 1899. His body was brought back to Monmouthshire and buried in Llanfihangel Pontymoel Churchyard, where his only child (a son who had died at the age of 9) had been laid to rest. His widow Elizabeth Walkinshaw died on December 24th 1906 at the age of 85 and was buried with her husband.

Henry Hughes, the new proprietor of the paper, came from a long line of printers and publishers and served with his father as a journeyman at various newspapers and printers. He then set up his own printing business and was so successful that in 1841 he was awarded the Freedom of the City of London. The following year he sold his plant to Messrs Waterlow and returned to Pontypool, his home town, to succeed his deceased cousin, Evan Prosser as a local printer.

In July 1877 Henry Hughes moved his machinery and type from 6, Commercial Street to workrooms over the old Corn Market House, which was David Walkinshaw's old printing office. Two years later he took his second son David into partnership, and traded henceforth as Hughes & Son.

In 1891 Henry Hughes doubled the size of the *Pontypool Free Press* to eight pages and also moved to a new and commodious premises in Osborne Road. When he had taken over the paper, only two of its four pages were printed in Pontypool on a hand press, entailing a long and laborious process, for each sheet had to be inked and printed by hand.

Henry Hughes died on March 20th 1892 and was buried in Trevethin Churchyard. His eldest son also named Henry, continued the business which by now also included a stationery shop at 6, Commercial Street. In April 1909 the size of the paper was increased to 16 pages and its name changed to *The Free Press of Monmouthshire* . Henry Junior's health had been failing for a number of years and he died at his residence, 'Honddu,' 72, Osborne Road, Pontypool, on February 3rd 1912 at the age of 73. After his death *The Free Press of Monmouthshire* became the property of his widow Rebecca. Assisted by her eldest son, Henry Hughes, she continued to publish the paper, every Friday morning, the firm now trading as Henry Hughes Newspapers, Ltd.

The paper was printed at Osborne Road for over 32 years but in 1927 the firm moved to an office at Clarence Corner and on June 22nd of that year the first edition to be printed in the new building appeared a week before the proclamation ceremony of the Royal National Eisteddfod which was held in Pontypool.

In December 1994 The Press moved from their office on Pontymoile Corner to new premises, equipped with the latest computer technology, on the Pavilion Estate, Pontnewynydd. The Pontymoile office was then demolished to make way for the new gyratory road system.

**Railway Stations**

Crane Street Station (demolished), close to the middle of the town, connected Blaenavon in the north with Newport to the south of the Valley. It also connected through Brynmawr to the principal towns of West and Mid-Wales.

Clarence Street Station (demolished), a little to the south of the town, was on the Pontypool-Road - Crumlin line, giving access to the heart of the Valleys and Swansea to the west and to the Ross line via Usk and Monmouth to the east.

Pontypool Road Station (existing) about 1.5 miles south east of the town on the main line from South Wales to the North. Forty years ago it was the site of extensive marshalling yards where coal and other freight was organised and dispatched to ports and inland destinations. (The railway system in Torfaen is dealt with fully in Chapter 9).

### The National School at Pontymoel

In 1859 a school was built at Pontymoel for the 'National Society for the Education of the Poor in the Principles of the Established Church' which was a pioneer organisation sponsored by the Church of England. Construction of the building was funded by the Ebbw Vale Company (which took over the local ironworks in 1856) and it was built specifically for local children whose parents were employees of the Company.

Records of 1863 show that apart from the headmaster the staff consisted of a pupil teacher, two paid monitors and five fourth grade monitors. Walter Williams, the pupil teacher was paid 10s a month, Frederick Davey and Siddy Powell, the 'paid monitors,' received 23s 6d each per month; Sarah Ann Coleman and Elizabeth Morgan, the 'fourth grade monitors' received one shilling a month.

The pupil teachers certainly earned their ten bob a month, for they had to be at the school by seven o'clock in the morning to help clean the classrooms, and then between eight and nine they themselves had instruction from the headmaster. From nine o'clock onwards they helped in the education of the children.

By 1928 the old school building had become a training centre where young boys were taught practical skills such as woodwork and metalwork. It was later used for a variety of purposes including a Sunday School, shooting range etc. but has since been demolished.

Pupils at Pontymoel School in 1923. Torfaen Museum Trust.

Pontypool Road Station, New Inn. Torfaen Musem Trust.

Clarence Road Station, Pontypool. Torfaen Museum Trust.

West Monmouthshire Grammar School stands on a hillside overlooking Pontypool.

**West Monmouthshire Grammar School**

Overlooking Pontypool from the south, this imposing building was erected as a Grammar School for boys in 1897 at a cost of about £27,000, which was defrayed from the legacy of William Jones of Monmouth who died in 1615. His fortune of £40,000 was made in the London clothing trade and he left it to the Worshipful Company of Haberdashers with instructions that the money was to be used for educational purposes. It was his wish, '...that there should be for ever in the town of Monmouth an almshouse for the maintenance of poor people and also one *Free Grammar School* for the instruction and education of boys and youths.' Astute investment by the Haberdashers enabled Monmouth to have two schools - one each for boys and girls.

Money was also available by 1890 to build another school in the more populous part of the County and Newport, Tredegar and Pontypool were considered as possible sites. The choice was simplified when John Capel Hanbury of Pontypool Park offered six acres of prime land to the Haberdashers, free of charge as a site for the school. The foundation stone was laid on 27 July 1896, and two years later on 1st December, West Monmouthshire School (so named because it was west of the original Haberdashers' schools in Monmouth) was declared open.

The buildings of red brick and Bath stone dressing stand in grounds of six acres and initially provided accommodation for 200 boys, including 70 boarders. There was a large house for the headmaster, large hall, classrooms, chemical and physical laboratories, lecture room, art room, gymnasium and covered swimming bath. Over the front porch of the main building are carved the arms of the Haberdashers' Company, with their motto, 'Serve and Obey.'

Up until 1957 the school remained independent, but it was then taken over by Monmouthshire County Council and it was a Grammar School for Boys until 1982. Girls were then admitted for the first time and it became a mixed comprehensive school. On 19th January 1998 the school celebrated its centenary on the anniversary of the date when it had welcomed its first pupil.

Pontypool Baptist College Became the County School for Girls in 1850, but is now part of Trevethin Comprehensive School

**The County School for Girls at Penygarn**

The Welsh and English Baptist Education Institution, established at Abergavenny in 1807 removed to Pontypool in 1836. The object of the institution was to provide young students with a suitable education for the Christian ministry.

Following the removal of the Baptist College to Cardiff, the building at Penygarn above Church Wood at Trevethin, and overlooking Pontypool, was transformed into a County School for girls under the provisions of the Welsh Intermediate Education Act. It was opened by Mrs Hanbury of Pontypool Park on January 13th 1897. The building had been extensively repaired and enlarged to accommodate 120 pupils by Messrs Morgan and Evans at a cost of £1,600. Forty rather nervous youngsters took their places at the desks and became the first of many thousands who spent happy years at this famous school.

A beautiful stained-glass memorial window in the school hall, is dedicated to the memory of the first Head Mistress, Miss A.M. Dobell.

In 1997 Trevethin Comprehensive School celebrated a centenary of education on its Penygarn site (the former Pontypool Girls Grammar School site) with a week of celebrations. The Grammar School for Girls had joined with Trevethin Secondary School to form Trevethin Comprehensive School in September 1982.

**St Alban's Convent School**

In 1903 three Roman Catholic sisters of the Congregation of the Daughters of the Holy Ghost, who had been driven from Brittany by political persecution, arrived in Pontypool and rented a cottage in Waenfelin. Their Order had been founded in 1706 by a compassionate priest, Father John Leudager, and it was dedicated to the service of the poor, the orphaned, the sick and the ignorant. As a result, schools, hospitals and orphanages were established in many parts of the world. Pontypool had no doubt been identified as a place in need of such assistance. In 1905 the sisters opened a small school in Osborne Road which was initially attended by four pupils. Then in 1907 the sisters acquired Glanwern House as a boarding school for girls, with their first pupil being a young French girl.

Early in 1914, Park House, the home of the Squires of Pontypool, was available and the sisters took a lease to found St Alban's Convent School for girls. The billiards room was converted into a school hall, the servants' quarters into a science laboratory and the drawing-room into an oratory. After they had acquired the freehold further improvements were undertaken; central heating and electricity were installed and an art studio and natural history museum added.

In 1954 the school was extended with the erection of a £50,000 building which was officially opened by Archbishop McGrath of Cardiff. Three years later the school was reorganised and it became the St Alban's Roman Catholic Secondary School with 400 - 500 pupils. Twenty-five years later, in 1982, the name was changed to St Alban's Comprehensive Roman Catholic School.

**Pontypool Hospital**

This impressive building, situated in Leigh Road was constructed of local materials by the Pontnewynydd firm of Bailey Brothers at an initial cost of £6,384. The land was given by John Capel Hanbury and the building financed by the people of Pontypool. When it was officially opened by Mrs Hanbury on 19th October 1903 it had just 19 beds and 3 cots. Over the years the hospital was improved and extended many times:-

1908 A new wing was added at John Capel Hanbury's expense as a memorial to his son Capel, who died that year.

1910 The 'Capel Wing' was completed, providing 10 extra beds.

1915 A nurses' home was opened and this enabled the accommodation for patients to be increased to 47 beds.

1920 The conversion of a convalescent room into a ward enabled a further 10 beds to be added. A £900 ambulance was donated by Garndiffaith Workmen's Hall & Institute.

1925 The gift of the house called Cefn Ila, near Usk added to the bed spaces and provided a convalescent home for 24 women and children.

1928 Construction of a £200,000 extension provided one of the best operatiing theatres in the country.

1929 Pontypool Chamber of Trade organised a hospital carnival and fete, raising the sum of £3,211 4s. 3d., and this popular fund raising event continued until 1942.

1931 A further extension to the building provided an additional 21 beds.

1934 The hospital was recognised as a training school for nurses.

1939 Captain Geoffrey Crawshay, the District Commissioner for Special Areas performed the official opening of a £17,000 outpatients department. It had all the latest equipment, including two iron lungs which were donated by Lord Nuffield.

1946 A gymnasium was opened at the hospital to assist with muscular therapy in the rehabilation of patients and outpatients.

1948 The hospital was absorbed into the National Health Service on 5th July.

1987 The first threat of closure came at a time when the hospital was being used by 8,000 patients a year.

1993 Closure of the hospital at the end of July, following a plan to move community services to the County Hospital. The building was put up for sale.

1997 A local campaign was started for the still empty building to be re-opened as a Community Hospital. It was rightly argued that it had been built by and for the community and it was only right that it should be returned to the community.

St Alban's Convent, The Park, Pontypool. Torfaen Museum Trust.

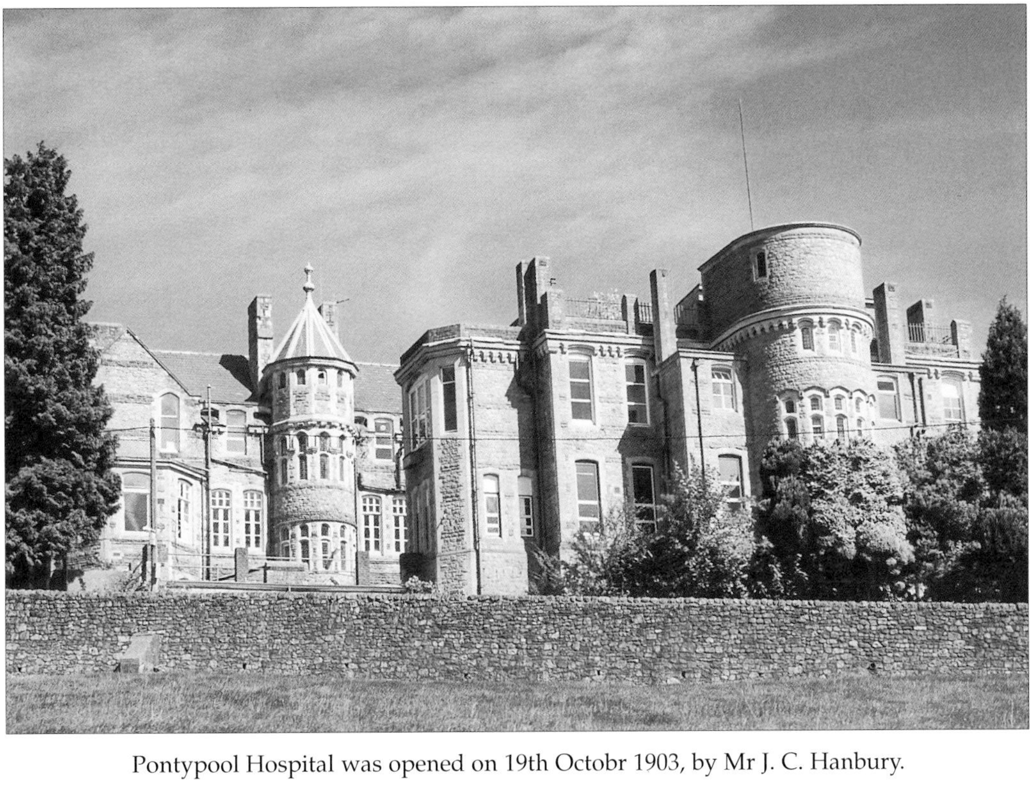

Pontypool Hospital was opened on 19th Octobr 1903, by Mr J. C. Hanbury.

## The Town Murals

In the subways created by the Pontypool western bypass can be seen three colourful mosaic murals completed by father and son Kent artists Ken and Oliver Budd in 1993. The head wall of the George Street Subway depicts 125 years of Pontypool Rugby Club. It shows some great sporting moments: Robin Williams is taking a conversion, Chris Huish scoring a try and among the sporting heroes commemorated are Terry Cobner, David Bishop, John Perkins and Graham Price.

On the wing wall a mural shows the Town Bridge (c.1760) and washing day in the Afon Lwyd.

The mural in the Crane Street underpass shows scenes from Pontypool, including the Folly Tower, local Japan Ware, the Grotto, Baptist Church and College and the Town Hall. Of particular interest is the fact that this mural tells the story of Japanning, a process which was developed in the early 18th century, only a short distance from this site.

## -- 8 --

# Old, Upper and New Cwmbran

*'The word Cwmbran as indicating a built-up area is of comparatively recent origin, though, oddly enough, long before 1946 'Old Cwmbran' included a district known as Newtown.'*

Reginald Nichols 1972

Two explanations have been given for the origin of the name Cwmbran. According to tradition the name is derived from Brân, the 1st century local chieftain reputed to be the father of Caradoc (Caractacus) the famous warrior who led the Silures in battle against the Romans. We are told that Bran either lived in this valley or was buried here. However, it is more likely that the name is just descriptive for the literal translation is 'Valley of the Crow.'

The first Ordnance Survey map of Monmouthshire, published in 1833, based on a survey made some years earlier, shows the name 'Cwmbran' a little to the north of 'Five Locks Bridge'(on the Monmouthshire Canal). It was in the district now known as Pontnewydd, which at that time was of so little consequence that it was not shown. This 'Cwmbran' was in fact merely the name of a farm lying to the east of the stream 'Bran' running down from 'Blaen Bran' on Mynydd Maen. It runs through the valley marked 'Cwm Bran' to join the Afon Lwyd below the Tin Works at 'Pont Rhyd yr Un'.

### Old Cwmbran

Cwmbran as a settlement originated as a result of the industrial works that were established there after the mid-nineteenth century. Up to the year 1860 there were only a few scattered mountain farms in this locality but by 1865 the iron works of Messrs James Charles Hill & Co. had been established as well as brickworks by Cyrus Hanson, nut and bolt works by James Gibbs and iron works by Messrs Roper.

The village that grew here was situated partly in the parish of Llantarnam and partly in that of Llanfrechfa. By 1909 it was an important industrial centre, described in that year by G.W. Wade in his guidebook to South Wales, as 'a grimy place, abounding in factories, furnaces and rolling mills.' By this time the extensive works of Messrs Guest, Keen & Nettlefolds were providing employment for a large number of workers in the manufacture of patent nuts, iron chains and wire nails. The Henllys Firebrick Works, collieries and a tin plate work were also to be found in this locality.

Cwmbran Iron Company was producing iron from a furnace established in the 1840s by R.J. Blewitt of Llantarnam Abbey. The works were acquired in the 1870s by the Patent Nut & Bolt Company of Smethwick, near Birmingham. Arthur Keen was the managing director and he later formed a partnership with Guest and Nettlefolds. G K & N was to become a famous name for iron and steel in South Wales. The works closed in 1972 with the loss of 800 jobs. Cwmbran Development Corporation acquired the site and developed it for light industry and is now known as Springvale Industrial Estate.

James Hill established the Oakfield Wire Works in the late 1850s and by the 1870s it had some twenty-five puddling furnaces and nine mills. Later, steel wire replaced iron, puddling was given up, and steel billets were rolled down to rod at the works, then drawn into wire and galvanised. In 1925 the works was acquired by the Whitehead Iron & Steel Co. Ltd., and rolling was given up as the rod could be supplied by the parent Company.

The Nut & Bolt Works, Cwmbran. Torfaen Museum Trust

Commercial Street in Old Cwmbran. Margaret Pead Collection.

In 1860 James Gibbs established a Vitriol Works on a site in Old Cwmbran. It was taken over by the Cwmbran Chemical Company in 1911 and merged into the Imperial Chemical Industries Group in 1926. At its peak the works employed about 100 people and produced 450 tons of heavy sulphuric acid per week.

By 1937 it was clear that the business had outgrown its Wolverhampton factory. Under the Special Areas (Amendment) Act, 1937, the Government had powers to invest in new industry in areas where it was needed. With great foresight the Government and the Nuffield Trust laid the foundations for a flourishing business at Cwmbran.

Weston Biscuits, now Burtons was the first factory to be built under the Act and it opened in 1938. This was followed by Girlings and then Saunders Valves.

**Upper Cwmbran**

The village of Upper Cwmbran was so-named to distinguish it from the 'lower' village which had developed as the result of the iron industry and the Monmouthshire Canal which was built to pass through it.

A cluster of houses known as The Square was built high up on the slopes of Mynydd Maen at an altitude of 700 feet to house colliers employed in the nearby Porthmawr Colliery which had been established in 1833 by Reginald James Blewitt of Llantarnam Abbey. This group of dwellings, built in the form of a square, was first shown on the tithe map published in 1840 and were probably constructed soon after Porthmawr Colliery opened in 1837. The sloping land resulted in the cottages being stepped one above the other and originally they numbered from 1 to 29. Sadly, cottages Nos 1 and 2 and half of the row at the back of the Square have been demolished and it is much to be hoped that they can one day be rebuilt. Of the Squirrel Inn which once stood here, only the end wall and foundations can now be seen.

In 1852 a school was established by local people in a room above this inn. It was large enough to accommodate 100 children but they must have been packed together like sardines. Thomas Lewis of Goytre, who had previously taught at Llandovery, was the first headmaster and he was followed in 1862 by David Morgan whose log book has survived. It tells of life in The Square during the 1860s and his disciplinary problems due to the overcrowding. The delay in building a new school got him down so much that he resigned his position in December 1866. Two years later a new building, designed for use as a school, measuring 84 feet by 36 feet was erected further down the hillside. It was built by Mr Parfitt, mason and Mr Hugh Thomas, carpenter of Cwmbran. The foundation stone was laid by John Lawrence who donated a sovereign towards the cost of the building.

In addition to the Squirrel Inn there were once three other pubs and three chapels in Upper Cwmbran and the locals who enjoyed a drink used to have a saying: 'The Queen lost The Crown in The Bush.' Unfortunately, The Crown, like the Squirrel Inn is now lost and gone forever, but The Queen and The Bush, situated below The Square are still flourishing.

Near the present-day bus terminus stands the Siloam Baptist Chapel, which was built in 1838. There are some interesting tombstones in the graveyard with the oldest dating back to 1849. One stone commemorates John Jones who died at the age of 61 in 1871, whilst visiting friends in the village. He had travelled here all the way from Newburgh, in Ohio, America, having spent twenty years in the USA.

A moving inscription on another stone records the deaths of two small brothers, Llewellin and Thomas Williams, in 1870. The first died at he age of 2 years 8 months and his brother passed away ten days later, aged 7 years. The inscription is in Welsh: 'Nac Ymffrostia or dydd y fory canys ni wyddost beth addigwdd mewn diwrnod,' which translates: 'Do not boast of tomorrow because you do not know what will happen within the day.'

Victims of industrial accidents can also be found here, such as 40 year old Thomas Morgan, who was killed at Upper Cwmbran Colliery on 18th January 1858. Another stone commemorates local mason Isaac Maynard, who died suddenly in 1866, at the age of 39 years:-

'Death to me no warning gave But took me sudden to my grave,
To meet my Lord without delay For sudden death took me away.'

Close to The Square stands the Ebenezer Chapel which strangely is not shown on the tithe map of 1840 but it is said to have been built in 1811. It was enlarged in 1863 when the gallery was added.

A boundary stone within the chapel enclosure is of interest. One side bears the letters 'J.C.H.' and the other, the letters 'M.de S.' They mark the boundary between land belonging to John Capel Hanbury on the one side and to Madame de Solignac on the other. This lady was formerly Jane Griffiths who was married to Charles Griffiths of Llanyrafon Farm. He died in 1836 and four years later she married a Frenchman to become Madame de Solignac and went to live in France.

The Square, Old Cwmbran before the top row of cottage was demolished.
Drawn by Fred Hando in 1955.

Bethel Congregational Chapel in Upper Cwmbran, celebrated its centenary on Easter Sunday and Monday 1937. Originally the building was intended to be a public house but while it was being erected the minister at New Inn Congregational Church launched a public protest, and when a vote was taken on the need for a pub or a chapel, only one vote was cast in favour of a pub. The owner swallowed his rebuff and offered the house to the minister as a chapel for the sum of £190. As a religious and social centre the new chapel flourished until Cwmbran Colliery closed in 1927, and many of the inhabitants moved away to seek work elsewhere.

Nonconformity was spreading its influence. A Methodist chapel had already been formed in the hillside hamlet, and Baptist churches were firmly established at Pontrhydyrun and Henllys. The nearest Congregational Church was at New Inn and its minister paid frequent visits to the faithful at Upper Cwmbran, and in this way New Inn Chapel became the Mother Church of Bethel.

Other buildings of interest in Upper Cwmbran include Glyn Bran house which was built in the 16th century of local sandstone and with a stone tiled roof. A curious feature is the bread oven which projects into the adjoining road and was so built in order to give it extra depth.

Below the present day bus terminus a water powered woollen factory was built in 1822. Flannel shirts were once manufactured here for the local miners, until it was forced to close in 1901.

**Coal mining in Upper Cwmbran**

The first record of coal mining in Upper Cwmbran was a deed of Thomas Arnold's 'cole-work' in 1698 which was sold to Major John Hanbury of Pontypool. By the middle of the 18th century this mine was supplying coal to the Tin Works in Caerleon and Ponthir. In 1793 Thomas Stoughton (a member of the Hanbury family by marriage) invested in the small scale mining activities and leased additional land from Mr. Jones of Glyn Bran Farm 'For the purpose of mining coal and iron ore'. Further investment was made by. R.J. Blewitt who opened the 'Fire Clay Level' or 'Porthmawr Colliery' in 1837. Porthmawr means 'The Great Gate' and the name perpetuates the Cistercian Abbey of Llantarnam from which the Manor took its name. A Tudor style mansion which stands on the site of the old abbey was at one time the home of mine owner Reginald Blewitt.

It was due to Blewitt that Upper Cwmbran made rapid development as a mining centre and the various levels driven into the hillside were to provide employment to a large numbers of miners. As a result, this once agricultural district, scantily populated by Welsh speaking locals, attracted an influx of people from such places as Bristol, and English became the common tongue.

In 1843 Blewitt's colliers went on strike following his announcement that he and other South Wales mine owners were going to make a reduction of 5d (2p) a ton in their pay. Some of the strikers were sentenced to one month's hard labour for breaking their contract and this had the desired result that their colleagues then agreed to return to work.

After a few years R. J. Blewitt ran into financial difficulties and in 1852 he sold all his mining interests. The mines at Upper Cwmbran were then taken over by John Lawrence who opened up the new Mine Slope. The stone used in its construction was probably quarried from the land close by, which is shown as 'old Quarry ' on the 1880 Ordnance Survey map. The Patent Nut & Bolt Company took over the Mine Slope in about 1879 and the final owners were Guest, Keen & Nettlefolds who acquired the mine in 1900.

All the remaining buildings on this site were demolished in the late 1970s. They had originally consisted of a large Fan House which had a steam driven fan for extracting foul air from the mine. A small building near the mine entrance contained a stable housing two horses, a changing room for the miners and a lamp house where they could light their lamps in safety before starting their shift underground. Gas was not such a problem here as in other areas, but even so all precautions were taken.

There was also an Engine House which accommodated the winding gear, a boiler to make steam to drive the fan and a blacksmith's forge. The engine within hauled trams out of the mine and also those on the Upper Incline. This was constructed by Reginald Blewitt and was initially single track with a brake-house at the top to control the speed of the descending trams. During the 1850s it was made double track and a balance system put into operation with loaded trams pulling up empty ones. A row of houses beside the incline is still known as Incline Row and they were probably built in the mid 1850s.

A map drawn by John Prujean in 1843 shows a tunnel which ran through the mountain to Pontypool and there is a local tradition that the ladies of Upper Cwmbran used to ride through it in the trams to do their shopping in Pontypool and thus avoid the long walk over the mountain.

The Mine Slope, Clay Level and the nearby brickworks were all connected by tramroad and a main line, known as the Porthmawr Tramroad, which ran from Upper Cwmbran down to the canal at Old Cwmbran by the 'Halfway House'. This tramroad then continued to Ponthir and Caerleon where it ended at the old quay.

Situated at the top of the incline on the site of the later filter beds for the reservoirs was a brickworks, which was certainly in existence in 1839 for Reginald Blewitt agreed to deliver fireclay there, 'unless he was prevented from doing so by faults, failure of clay or coal, or any general strike or combination among the Colliers or Miners.' The brickworks is clearly shown on John Prujean's map of the county and according to the *Monmouthshire Merlin* in 1845, production by then had risen to 100,000 firebricks per week. John Lawrence took the works over in that year and in 1847 leased them to Henry Parfitt, a local builder, 'with Stoves, Kilns, Smith's shop and cottages.'

The main adit at the top of Clomendy Road was opened in 1879 by the Patent Nut and Bolt Co. Ltd. This adit ran into the mountain for about one and a quarter miles to a point where stables accommodating about 120 pit ponies were situated. From this point workings branched out in various directions. The coal produced was a steam coal mainly from the Meadow Vein and Black Vein seams. The majority of it was exported but considerable quantities were supplied to the Railway Companies and also to Gas Works and similar undertakings.

The celebrated Black Vein Coal (also called the Rock Vein) was reached 2,100 yards from the entrance and for the greater part of its length the tunnel was brick-arched. For a short distance after reaching the coal a drivage was turned to the left and became known as the Hanbury Slope and dipped about 1 in 12 for about 250 yards and then at less gradient. In due course there were four districts in production, the Abercarn section, the Hanbury section and the Pontypool section on the Black Vein and a section in the Meadow Vein which was developed off a drivage to the left of the Hanbury Slope.

Guest Keen & Nettlefolds purchased the colliery in about 1902 and at its peak employed about 1,200 men, whose output was 5,000 to 6,000 tons per week. By 1913 a total of 1,490 men were employed at the Cwmbran and Henllys collieries and this number went down to 1175 by 1925 and reduced further until economic conditions forced their closure in 1927.

### Proposed demolition of The Square

For over a century the small community living in The Square had lived a contented existence. But in January 1964, they were threatened by a 'slum clearance' programme devised by the local council. The sturdy stone cottages, by now all owner occupied, were to be demolished and their occupants moved to a new council house estate in Cwmbran New Town.

It was stated in the official report that with one exception none of the 29 dwellings comprising The Square came up to the rigid standard set by modern regulations. Only one had a bathroom and in others the bedroom ceilings were lower than they should be and failed to provide the minimum seven-foot headroom.

Apart from these problems, the sewerage system for Cwmbran stopped four or five hundred yards short of The Square. For tmore than a century the householders had been burying their sewage in their gardens or somewhere on the mountainside, whilst others made do with a septic tank system, which discharged its contents into an open brook lower down the hill. The Council argued that it would cost as much as £1,000 to extend the sewer as far as The Square. At that time, as elsewhere in the Valley, the option of improving the homes and their services, and saving the community, was scarcely considered by the local authorities even though it would probably have been much cheaper.

The Square at Upper Cwmbran is the oldest community in the area and hundreds of people protested at the threatened demolition. A petition was carried around Cwmbran New Town and vigorous support was given by the trades people who served the folk living on the mountain and would 'trust them with anything.'

Councillor O.J.R. Pruden, who was the Council's public health inspector for ten years was against the demolition proposal. 'My memory of Upper Cwmbran goes back fifty years,' he said, 'and during that time there has never been an epidemic at The Square. I would have thought this conclusive proof that the houses are certainly not unhealthy.'

He added that the air at Upper Cwmbran was like wine; the houses were not overcrowded and they were occupied chiefly by old age pensioners whose parents and grand parents were there before them. The community was held together by a spirit of neighbourliness all too rare in modern times. 'The aim should be to improve this attractive place, not to destroy it,' he declared.

Fortunately Cwmbran Council decided to reprieve The Square and the motion to rescind a minute recommending a Clearance Order for the Square was carried by 12 votes to two. The hillside community breathed a sigh of relief and has since benefited from various improvement grants.

### The Upper Cwmbran Reservoirs

Nestling in the shadow of the hill above The Square are two reservoirs which were built to supply water to the local communities. The lower reservoir was constructed in 1884 by the Llanfrechfa Upper Local Board on land owned by John Capel Hanbury. Originally it had a capacity of just 5 million gallons but was enlarged in 1930 to hold over 11 million gallons. The upper pool situated at an altitude of 950 feet above sea level, was built at the start of World War I and has a dam 23 feet high and 215 feet long.

In 1930 the filtration plant was installed, and later a storage service reservoir, filled by water pumped up from a connection with Newport's Talybont pipe near the Upper Cock inn at Croesyceiliog. The Newport waterworks authority took over the reservoir in 1930 and it is now empty.

Towards the end of the war the Government appointed a committee under the chairmanship of Lord Reith to consider the implications of building New Towns. The result of the deliberations of this committee was the passing of the New Towns Act in 1946. Mr Lewis Silkin, Minister of Town and Country Planning in February 1949 announced that the first New Town to be built in Wales would be established in the lower part of the Eastern Valley.

Several possible sites were considered by the planners and the area around Pontypool Road Station was initially at the top of their list. They had to take into account the workforce which would be coming into the area for employment at the new British Nylon Spinners factory. Also to be considered was the large workforce at the Royal Ordnance Factory at Glascoed, between Usk and Pontypool, which it had been announced would be retained after the war.

The argument against the Pontypool site was that it occupied prime agricultural land which was badly needed at that time. Eventually the Ministry of Agriculture stepped in and said that the planners would not be allowed to build on that site.

Amongst local people there was widespread conjecture as to the likely location of the new town but in August 1949 it was revealed that it would be sited in and around the existing villages of Cwmbran, Pontnewydd and Croesyceiliog. The total area comprised 3,160 acres of which 2,550 acres were in Cwmbran Urban District and 610 acres in Pontypool Rural District. The vicinity of Cwmbran had been finally chosen because of its pleasant situation and existing facilities, such as good communications and ample supplies of water, gas and electricity.

Post Office Croesyceiliog in 1930's

One of the objectives in building the new town was to provide homes for the thousands of workers who were travelling daily to work in the vicinity of Cwmbran from the adjoining towns and valleys, as a result of the rapid growth of new industries in the area.

Although the principle of establishing a new town in Monmouthshire was generally welcomed there was some criticism of the site chosen. At the public enquiry Newport County Borough Council objected because of its close proximity, and the main alternative was to situate it further to the north east. Whilst this would have moved it further from the concentration of industry in the Afon Lwyd valley it would have put it nearer to the British Nylon Spinners plant (later ICI) at Mamhilad, the Royal Ordnance Factory at Glascoed and the Panteg steel works, all of which it was intended to serve. But this proposal was rejected because the nylon works were deliberately established in the clean air of open country for the benefit of the manufacturing processes, and there were obvious objections to the placing of any large scale development close to the Royal Ordnance Factory. Also such a location would have taken up more valuable agricultural land.

The site chosen in fact offered the opportunity to create a rationally organised development out of a somewhat unsightly and unplanned area. There was plenty of space for expansion and it was also more suitable for further industrial development.

In 1949 the Cwmbran area consisted of three villages and some twenty firms employing almost 7,000 people. The Glascoed ROF, British Nylon Spinners at Mamhilad and the Panteg steelworks employed a further 7,500 people. These three works were outside the designated area but it was intended that Cwmbran should provide much of the housing needs of their employees.

On 4th November 1949 Cwmbran New Town was designated to be administered by Cwmbran Development Corporation (CDC) for the purpose of developing the town for a population of 35,000 and providing housing and social facilities for the benefit of people who were employed in the various industries (present and future) which were situated in the valley between Newport and Pontypool. The Chairman of the CDC was to receive a salary of £1,500 a year, the Vice-Chairman £750 and each of the five members £400 a year and the appointments were all part-time. Major General Wynford Rees who lived at Goytre Hall near Abergavenny, was appointed as the first General Manager on 3rd March 1950.

Shortly afterwards, the London firm of Minoprio and Spenceley and P.W. Macfarlane were appointed as planning consultants to compile a Master Plan which would outline their proposals for the area. During the compilation of the Plan a series of public meetings were held to obtain the views of local people which were in due course given full consideration.

It was decided that the new town would consist of seven residential neighbourhoods and a town centre. The seven neighbourhoods proposed and their future populations were: Coedeva 5,450, Croesyceiliog (North) 5,040, Croesyceiliog (South) 5,000, Greenmeado, 3,640, Oakfield 4,175, Pontnewydd 6,680, and St Dials 4,310. Each neighbourhood would have its own recreational, shopping and educational facilities. Particular attention would be given to landscaping and to the preservation of existing trees, but one tree would also be planted for every house built. The town centre would be right in the middle of the designated area with the main road which was also the shopping street running north and south through the middle with plenty of car parking. There would be several new schools, facilities for further education, homes for the elderly, clinics and health services, all designed to give the new town of Cwmbran the modern facilities of urban life.

One of the first major tasks of the CDC was to clean up the large areas of industrial dereliction that were scattered throughout the district. These included the abandoned sites of the Cwmbran Chemical Company (the Vitriol Works) and Cwmbran Brickworks near the old village. A particularly large area of derelict land stretched from Victoria Street to Oakfield Road and to a point beyond Llantarnam Road. It included the remains of two works and the deep scars left by the extraction of clay from the brickworks. The ground was pitted with holes which filled with water and was littered with areas of shale which was unsuitable for brick making. A very polluted acid stream ran through the site and a small lake was even known as the Acid Pond.

There were other clay pits at Woodside Road and Ty Coch which all had to be filled in. Deposits of ash and other waste from various works scarred the area around Avondale Road and there was a disused brickworks at Croesyceiliog. Overall it was a typical landscape of dereliction that could be found in so many parts of South Wales at this time.

Unfortunately the building of the new town resulted in the destruction of many ancient buildings which today would have been considered worthy of preservation. These included Court Farm; Tyn-y-pwll, built in the reign of the first Elizabeth and a good example of a regional house of that period; and Little Pontrhydrun Farm, a complete Tudor house.

Other buildings which fell victim to the bulldozer were examples of industrial beginnings in the locality, such as the early 19th century Pontnewydd House, once the home of the Conway family who were pioneers of the tin-plate industry. Some 18th century lock keepers cottages on the Monmouthshire Canal were also demolished.

In 1951 the CDC moved into their headquarters in Victoria Street in old Cwmbran and by the end of the year had published the Master Plan which was set out in a 47 page booklet.

The first two houses built by the Corporation were completed on 2nd February 1952 and occupied at the provisional rents of 36/6 (£1.82) a week. It was expected that 18 houses would be completed by the end of March.

Mr Harold Macmillan, Minister of Local Government and Housing, visited the New Town in June 1952, walked around the new houses at West Pontnewydd and inspected the interior of the home of Mr and Mrs Davies at Ty Pwcca, the rent of which was £1 19s 10d a week.

Not everyone was happy with all the changes that were proposed for the area. In October 1952 every householder in Croesyceiliog signed a petition against plans for the development of their village. During a two-day public enquiry, the petition was described as 'a vote against the new town of Cwmbran.' The Croesyceiliog folk were unhappy because of the prediction that their picturesque village of 1,200 people would in time grow into a busy urban unit with a population of 10,000, as indeed it did.

By 1955 the population of the new town had reached 16,000 and the Corporation were confident of attaining their target of building a further 700 - 800 houses during that year. Their plans for Llanyrafon even included the possible construction of a helidrome, should such a service be required in the future.

Mr Duncan Sandys, Minister of Housing and Local Government, toured Cwmbran New Town in September 1955 and refuted charges made by Pontypool RDC members and local tenants that sub-standard houses were being built. 'I have seen absolutely nothing,' he said, 'to justify statements that the new housing is being jerry-built.'

Work began in May 1956 on the first public building in the town centre with the laying of the foundations for the £54,000 post office and by the end of the year the CDC had built a total of 2,417 houses, 18 miles of road and 54 miles of sewer. A £76,000 scheme to improve the Afon Lwyd on its course through the new town was also under consideration. Its subsequent construction was to involve the building of eight weirs and the cutting of a new channel at Llantarnam.

View across the Water Gardens to Monmouth House in Cwmbran Town Centre.

This large canopy erected over Monmouth Walk at a cost of £1.5m is one of the largest unsupported span structures in Europe.

Developments at Llanyrafon were also by now rapidly taking shape with 350 houses completed and eight businesses were operating from temporary premises by August 1958. The following year Cwmbran's new Post Office was officially opened by Lady Rhys Williams, Chairman of the CDC, who marked the first purchase by buying a book of stamps. Shops at North Walk were also completed and work commenced on the Electricity Board's offices.

In October 1959 Major General Rees, General Manager of the CDC, collapsed and died whilst visiting the offices of the Ministry of Housing and Local Government in London. During the war he had commanded the 19th Indian Dagger Division in Burma which in 1945 captured Mandalay from the Japanese. This distinguished soldier was a small and stocky man who claimed to be the general with the most nicknames!

The area in front of the Post Office was later named 'General Rees Square' to honour the man who had been the CDC's first manager and served ten years in the post. The ceremony was performed by Dame Evelyn Sharpe, Permanent Secretary to the Minister of Housing. Major General Rees was succeeded, as General Manager in November, by Mr. W. K. Morris the chief legal and administrative officer to the CDC.

One of the community's vital services is education and the Monmouthshire County Council, as the Local Education Authority, was responsible for schools in the new town. Much thought was given to the provision of new buildings on the most appropriate sites for the various neighbourhoods as they were established. Mr T. M. Morgan the Director of Education for Monmouthshire, opened Coed Eva Secondary School in February 1961. It was the fourth new secondary school to be opened in Cwmbran during the past six years. The others were Llantarnam (1954) and the Croesyceiliog Secondary Schools (1957 & 1959). The new school cost £161,000; furniture and equipment a further £13,500 and when developed to its full capacity it would enrol 600 pupils. Mr T.M. Morgan commented: 'Children in this school will have opportunities to equip them for jobs in all walks of life. They will be able to take the Monmouthshire and the General Certificate of Education and from there get to any type of college or university in the country.' Nursery, Infants and Junior schools were also established at places within easy reach of all parts of the new town.

The first new public house to be built in the town centre was 'The Moonraker' and it opened in March 1964 with the CDC Chairman, Rear Admiral St. J. A. Micklethwait, pulling the first pint. This was the largest of the five new public houses to be built in Cwmbran to cater for the rapidly rising population.

Mr. Edward Heath, Secretary of State for Industry, Trade and Regional Development, was the chief guest at a luncheon given to several hundred people by Saunders Valve Company Ltd. in May 1964. The ceremony was held to mark the 25th anniversary of the factory being established at Cwmbran and the fact that it was one of the first new industries to come to the locality.

Later that year Lady Brecon opened the David Evans Department store. With a frontage of 210 feet facing Gwent Square it was to date the largest store in the new town. David Evans was a very reputable firm established in Swansea in 1900. It was hoped to attract every type of trader to the Town Centre, from the smallest local shop to the largest type of multiple store. The aim was to provide Cwmbran with a shopping centre second to none, for a town of its size, with adequate space reserved for all the civic, social and cultural development of a modern town. Cwmbran's first multi-storey car park was formally opened by Sir Miles Thomas, Chairman of the Development Corporation of Wales, in December 1964.

There seemed no end to the official openings and celebrity visits and in June 1965 Mr James Griffiths, the first Secretary of State for Wales, came to Cwmbran to lay the foundation stone for Block Seven, subsequently named Monmouth House. This was one of the largest single shopping developments ever undertaken in Wales at that time and it cost three quarters of a million pounds. The building provides 63,500 sq ft of sales area and includes 56 luxury flats. A large underground service yard in the centre of the building is accessed by vehicles from the nearest road and large commercial lifts were installed to take goods up to shop level. Monmouth House was officially opened in 1967 by James Callaghan MP, when Chancellor of the Exchequer.

One of the most easily noticed buildings, which indeed was designed to pinpoint the new town, is the 210 feet high, 22 storey block of flats which was completed in 1967 and claimed to be the tallest residential building in Wales. Built at a cost of £385,269 it contains 81 flats comprising 20 bed-sitters, 40 one-bedroom, and 20 two-bedroom flats and a flat for the caretaker. From the enclosed viewing platform at the top of the escape staircase it is possible to see the Somerset coast, a considerable stretch of the Bristol Channel and a vast area of countryside around Cwmbran.

In May 1966 Leo Abse MP officially opened Llantarnam Grange which had been renovated to provide a social meeting place and arts centre for Cwmbran. A few years earlier this historic building had been threatened with demolition but was fortunately reprieved.

By 1968 the CDC had completed their 7,000th house and the new town had almost reached the new population ceiling of 45,000 which had been set in 1967. The Welsh Office therefore on 18th December 1968, instructed the Corporation to continue its activities towards the figure of 55,000. It was also in that month that Glyndwr House in the town centre was opened by the new Secretary of State for Wales, Mr George Thomas. He unveiled a commemorative plaque above the northern staircase entrance near the door of Boots and commented, 'I need no convincing that the Cwmbran Development Corporation has done a fine job here. I congratulate them and their staff on what they have achieved. They have made Cwmbran one of the principle towns of Wales. It is now the seventh largest town in Wales with a population of some 43,000. Only twenty years ago it was a scattering of large and small villages with a population of just over 12,000. Now there are well laid out estates, modern homes, neighbouring shopping centres - a boon to busy wives and mothers - and this magnificent town centre which many older towns would envy.'

The pedestrianised precinct was an important design characteristic of the town centre. In its time this was an unusual concept but proved to be an innovation which had all the advantages of traffic-free shopping. Extensive and free car parking was also an enlightened decision which undoubtedly continues to prove an enormous attraction to shoppers from well outside the surrounding area.

Work was started in 1972 on a new police training centre at Greenmeadow. It was designed by the Chief Architect's Department of the Corporation for the Home Office to meet the training needs of police forces throughout Wales. It was during this year that the CDC's industrial promotion campaign named Cwmbran 'The Garden City of Wales,' a term which was prompted by the English new town of Welwyn Garden City.

Opposite Monmouth House, another large commercial building named Glyndwr House was also constructed to provides more shops and 18,000 sq ft of lettable offices. Under the building is a car park with a capacity of about 400 cars.

Gwent House, the largest commercial development to be built in the town centre was completed in 1972. It cost in excess of £800,000 and comprises 25 shops, County Library, a

This 22-storey block of flats is the tallest residential building in Wales.

theatre /concert hall, licensed entertainment centre and six floors of lettable offices. Enclosing Gwent Square along its eastern boundary, the building effectively knits together earlier developments in the town centre.

Outdoor recreation was not being ignored and it was also in 1972 that the Cwmbran boating lake came into use. The charges introduced at that time for the half-hour were 15p for large boats, 10p for smaller ones and 5p for paddle boats in the small children's pool.

An important watershed was when Marks & Spencers Ltd signed an agreement with the CDC in August 1973 to lease a site in the town centre. The company announced that they would build a store of around 28,000 sq ft sales area. Also in that year the first Job Centre in Wales opened in the town centre and Lord Raglan, Chairman of the CDC, performed the opening ceremony of a £58,000 social centre in Llanyrafon. It was erected at the junction of Llanfrechfa Way with Llanyrafon Way on the site of an old orchard at the derelict Llanyrafon Mill.

In March 1974 murals depicting the history of the area, designed by Henry and Joyce Collins on the front of Gwent House, were unveiled by Sir William Crawshay DSO, Chairman of the Welsh Arts Council.

The new swimming pool at Cwmbran Stadium Sports Centre was opened to the public in September 1974. The official opening wasperformed by Brian Clough, the manager of Leeds United.

Cwmbran's new open-air market, sited in a car park between the Moonraker public house and the North Walk shopping area in the town centre, opened for trade in December.

In April 1975 Mr. John Morris, the Secretary of State for Wales, gave his blessing to plans by Cwmbran Development Corporation to extend the designated area of the new town to Henllys, where they proposed to build some 2,300 homes to enable the required population of 55,000 to be achieved.

The official opening of Fairwater Leisure Centre was performed in November of that year, jointly by the Mayor of Torfaen, Mrs M.L. Lee, and the Chairman of Gwent County Council, Mr D. J. Williams. It was built at a cost of £300,000 by the former Monmouthshire County Council and Cwmbran Urban Council.

In June 1976 Councillor Dennis Puddle, Mayor of Torfaen, pulled the first pint at the official opening of Cwmbran's newest public house, the Golden Harvest in Greenmeadow. A few months later Sainsbury's opened their first supermarket in Wales at Cwmbran. The new store was among the largest of the firm's 178 supermarkets.

Improvements were carried out to the David Evans department store and a new look ground floor was officially opened by disc jockey Noel Edmunds in November 1978. Thousands of people, mostly women and children gathered around to watch him arrive. Renowned for his sense of humour, he did not disappoint the crowd for as he cut the ceremonial tape, he quipped, 'God bless this store and all who sell in her.'

Some new arrivals in Cwmbran in September 1979 were the Lu family from Saigon. They were the first of five families of Vietnamese 'boat people' who were offered homes in the Eastern Valley. After escaping from their troubled country by boat they had been rescued from the sea and taken to Hong Kong. From there the family was flown to London, where they lived for about 3 months. When they arrived in Cwmbran they first attended a small welcome reception in the town centre and were then taken to lunch at the Nam Kwok Restaurant. Afterwards they were driven to Coed Eva to see their new house, which had been decorated by members of Ebenezer Church, Pontnewydd.

By 1980 the CDC had completed 9,602 dwellings. Also during that year they provided 18 extra factory units covering 13.846 square metres. Springvale Industrial Estate, for example, now accommodated 115 Corporation built factories. It was hoped that the arrival of Ferranti Computer Systems Ltd would encourage other high technology firms to follow.

Nicholas Edwards, Secretary of State for Wales, in April 1980 accepted the £13,544,348 tender of Cementation / Costain Joint Venture for the construction of the New Inn by-pass. The scheme was to provide a six kilometre (3.8 miles) long dual carriageway from the end of the Croesyceiliog by-pass of the 1960s to the existing dual carriageway near the new Parke Davis factory next to ICI east of Pontypool. It was also to provide a dual carriageway link to Cwmbran.

Plans to build a road from the dual carriageway at Malpas to the heart of Cwmbran were finally approved by Nicholas Edwards, the Secretary of State for Wales, in March 1981.

Llantarnam Grange Arts Centre has an interesting history dating back to the 12th century when a farmhouse called Gelli Las (Green Grove) stood on the site. By the 1530s' it had become part of the estate belonging to Llantarnam Abbey which was then owned by William Morgan. The estate passed through his descendants until it was sold to Alfred Pilliner in 1871 and he converted the old farmhouse into a small stately home which became known as Llantarnam Grange.

William Jones the managing director of Avondale Tinplate Works bought the Grange in 1932 and it remained in his family until his death in 1951, after which his children put the property on the market. At a public auction on 21st October 1952, it was bought by Cwmbran Development Corporation who then let it to the GPO as a sorting office.

In 1958 the lease was taken over by Lucas Girling who used the building as a drawing office. Six years later they had to vacate the premises following a decision by Cwmbran Development Corporation to demolish the building to create a park. But fortunately the General Manager of the Corporation reversed this decision, having decided that the Grange would make an excellent meeting place for local societies.

The trustees of Llantarnam Grange took over the running of the centre in 1983 and Sarah Bowie was appointed as its first director. It is now a well known arts centre with three galleries, an artists' studio and a craft shop. More than 30,000 visitors a year are attracted to the centre and it has become the focal point in South Wales for all kinds of artistic activities. There is a strong community involvement in the centre and classes and courses are held there for both children and adults. The current director is Hywel Pontin.

Greenmeadow Community Farm is a popular tourist attraction which was set up in 1983 by a group of volunteers who included Torfen MP Paul Murphy and Councillor Bob Wellington. Their aim was to protect one of the last remaining green spaces in the area to form a 'green wedge' between housing estates and industrial development. The farmland stretches from St Dials to Thornhill and provides an attractive backdrop to the town centre as well as an educational facility for the children of the area.

The old farmhouse dates back to the 17th century and it has been completely refurbished to provide a cafe, a restaurant and a number of function rooms which cater for conferences and childrens' parties.

It is a thriving working farm with more than 600 animals which include cows, sheep, pigs, goats, rabbits, guinea pigs, geese, ducks, deer, while a special attraction is a herd of lamas. There is also a childrens' play area, woodland walk, picnic area, adventure playground and a huge water dragon (made of fibreglass) which provides a soaking for the children on a hot day.

The New Inn by-pass, built at a cost of £17m, was opened in June 1982 by Michael Roberts MP, Parliamentary Under-Secretary of State for Wales.

In October 1982 Lord Raglan opened a hotel in the former CDC offices in Victoria Street. The Corporation had moved into Gwent House, along with some departments of Torfaen Borough Council in 1972.

The Government shortly announced that the CDC would be wound up and the premises of the new town put on the market within a few years. By then the remaining tasks of the Corporation, which included the Llantarnam Industrial Park development and Cwmbran Drive, would be completed. Since its creation the CDC had provided almost 10,000 new homes and 141,500 square feet of factory space employing no less than 3,300 people.

Cwmbran Town Centre was put on the market in May 1984 at £13m. The sale included three supermarkets, a superstore, 150 shops and 115,000 square feet of office space. The buyer would also take possession of over 3,000 car parking spaces. The final selling price was £11m and in November it was announced that the purchaser was the City and County Land Company Limited, which was part of the giant leisure chain Ladbrokes. The new owners rebranded the town 'Cwmbran Shopping.'

In April 1988 the £11m Cwmbran Drive, a dual carriageway from Malpas to Pontypool built along the line of the disused Eastern Valley Railway Line, was officially opened by Welsh Secretary, Peter Walker. The ceremony was held at the end of the £2.5m (1.25miles) final stretch. It was an appropriate end to the working life of the Cwmbran Development Corporation who had planned the road back in 1971 and was wound up in the same week. As well as routing traffic around the new town centre the road serves the industrial estates at Springvale, Llantarnam Park and Ty Coch.

The first phase of the Parkway Hotel opened in 1988 near the Llantarnam Industrial Estate. This prestigious new hotel was designed to offer 148 bedrooms, private and public bars, conference facilities for about 600 people and leisure facilities such as a jacuzzi, gymnasium, swimming pool and sauna.

Ladbrokes now undertook a modernisation of Cwmbran town centre, which included the erection of a large canopy over Monmouth Walk at a cost of £1.5 million and it is one of the widest unsupported span structures in Europe. This was the first stage in a £5m improvement scheme.

The town centre was bought by its current owners, the Prudential Assurance Company, in 1994 for £73.5m, an increase in its value over ten years of £62m. The new owners installed a 24 hour CCTV system, costing £200,000 to improve security in the town centre. Prudential's future plans include the re-development of the north-west quarter of the centre and to increase parking spaces. The population of Cwmbran New Town by now had reached more than 47,000 and it had become the largest centre of population in Torfaen.

Plans for the 50th anniversary of Cwmbran's designation as a New Town were launched during 1998. Three local councils combined to organise the birthday celebrations which took place in June 1999. One event marking the anniversary was a parade from General Rees Square in Cwmbran town centre which finished with the unveiling and rededication of the re-furbished war memorial at Cocker Avenue Park. An engraved Welsh slate plaque was unveiled by Armed Forces Minister Douglas Henderson and the Lord Lieutenant of Gwent, Sir Richard Hanbury Tenison.

A floral display at the roundabout next to the Homebase store, featuring emblems of Cwmbran, the three community councils and Torfaen Council, was officially completed by Torfaen Mayor, Councillor Barbara Ryan.

Alun Michael, Wales Secretary, unveiled a clourful new mural in Monmouth Square, Cwmbran. It features landmarks and places of interest in the locality and was made by local school children to celebrate Cwmbran's 50th birthday.

Despite the end of Cwmbran's new town status, the pressure for growth continues. Expansion to the south west was ruled out in the 1980s and controversial plans for development between Cwmbran and Sebastapol are unresolved at the time of writing.

## -- 9 --

# Communications

*'The world wanted iron, iron needed transport, railways and ships needed iron. Soon, too, coal was added to the merry-go-round: iron needed coal, coal wanted railways and ships, railways and ships wanted coal and iron, and South Wales had them both.. '*

E & P Lewis 1937

Roads at one time were virtually non-existent in this area and to make matters worse there was also no system of maintenance for the routes that were available. An attempt to rectify this situation resulted from an Act passed in 1555 which ordered each Parish to appoint a surveyor who would have the power to compel parishioners to assist in the repair of a road. The Parish was permitted as an alternative to levy a rate for road improvement but as parish groups objected to any expense the roads generally remained as eroded tracks with high banks on each side.

Account books of the Surveyor of roads for the Panteg parish are still extant for 1736 and for Trevethin from 1767. The Trevethin registers tell us that after a flood at Trosnant in 1773 Walter Joshua and Thomas Jayne were paid 5s 10d (29p) for seven days' work in clearing away the gravel after it. We also learn that at a vestry meeting held on December 12th, 1782, it was decided to offer a reward of 10s 6d (52p) for the discovery of anyone throwing stones off bridges or weirs or destroying water courses in the district.

As a better means of maintaining main roads, Turnpike Trusts were created by two Acts of Parliament passed in 1755 and 1758, and the tolls levied on road users were used to fund repairs to the roads. Increasing use of the roads and the competition to purchase the right to collect tolls are illustrated by the prices paid.

A turnpike road was so-called because at frequent intervals a gate or bar was placed across the road which would only be opened when the traveller paid the toll. 'Pike' is an old word meaning to 'go' or to 'turn quickly.' The person who looked after the gate and collected the tolls was called a pike man and he lived in a toll house beside the gate. In particular, turnpike gates were placed at strategic points along roads leading into market towns.

Until 1825 there was no carriage road from Blaenavon to Abergavenny and people travelling between the two towns followed a lane over the side of the Blorenge (past the Foxhunter Car Park) by the Ninfa Farms, (through Llanelen) and Llanfoist. It was the Blaenavon Company who constructed the road to Abergavenny past Keeper's Pond and down the west side of the Blorenge. It became a turnpike road with a toll gate half way down and also one at the bottom. In 1847 a Turnpike road was made from Pontypool through Abersychan and over Varteg Hill to Blaenavon.

The Pontypool Turnpike Trust built an early tollhouse at the junction of Usk Road and The Highway so that tolls could be collected from travellers passing to and from Pontypool, Abergavenny and Usk. Near the tollhouse is an ancient milestone. This was sadly defaced rather than removed in 1940 during the threat of a German invasion.

Fortunately a photograph enabled restoration in 1946. The 'New Passage' referred to on the stone was near Beachley, where travellers to London embarked in a boat for the other side of the Severn before continuing their journey by road.

The Turnpike at this junction was certainly a key location at one time, for nearly to the turn of the century the 'Mail' left Abergavenny every evening about 8pm for Newport in a box-van drawn by two horses. It travelled via Llanover and Goytre to the Turnpike where the Blaenavon 'Mail' a smaller van drawn by one horse, would be waiting. This vehicle, starting from Blaenavon, picked up mail as it progressed down the valley, including Pontypool and conveyed it to the Turnpike. Here the bags were transferred to the Abergavenny van which then proceeded to Newport. After a rest and a feed for man and horses, the mail returned by the same route, the Blaenavon van picking up the bags for Pontypool and elsewhere at the Turnpike.

In May 1864 eleven strong horses were hauling a large wagon which was being used to transport a huge driving wheel that had been cast by Thomas Spittle of Newport. It was destined for the Pontnewynydd Works to replace one which was broken, and its dimensions were so large that some of the toll-gates on the route had to be removed to enable the heavy load to pass.

Collections of tolls were abolished in 1875 and the bow-fronted toll-house residence became a private residence until 1963 when it was demolished as part of a road improvement scheme. It was not until the Local Government Act of 1888 that a definite county council responsibility for roads was established and improvements and extensions began to be made.

Turnpike House (in 1960) at the junction of The Highway and Usk Road. Torfaen Museum Trust.

For centuries, laden pack-horses jogged along the bridle-path from Elgam Hill to Pontypool. providing a primitive form of transport. Illustration by Michael Blackmore.

### Industrial Transport

Transport to and from the early ironworks in the Eastern Valley initially involved the use of packhorses and mules, operating in teams of twelve along parish roads and hillside tracks, such as one between Blaenavon and Pontypool. Mules were generally preferred for they could carry loads of three hundredweight (151 kilos) in panniers without difficulty and compared to the horse their working life of 25 years was generally five years longer. But this was obviously a very slow and costly method of transport and hardly suitable for the rapidly expanding iron industry.

The ironmasters of the time decided that the key to providing a more efficient form of transport would be the construction of a canal linking Pontnewynydd with Newport. A Parliamentary bill for the construction of the 'Monmouthshire Canal' was first proposed in 1791 and the assent was received during the following year. Construction started in 1793, which was the year that the Brecknock & Abergavenny Canal, received its assent.

Shareholders of the Monmouthshire Canal Company were mainly local landowners, industrialists and bankers who were all interested in improving communications in the area. This would increase the scope for development and at the same time raise the value of their land or industrial concerns.

Sir Charles Morgan of Tredegar, William Esdail, the London banker, Josiah Wedgewood, the 1st Duke of Beaufort, and Thomas Hill the ironmaster, were the main promoters of the scheme. An initial estimate of the cost of the canal construction was £108,000, but the final figure was nearer £220,000.

The Canal Act also provided for the building of tramways from the canal to the ironworks, quarries and coal mines within a distance from it of eight miles; the wording being as follows:-

> '... for making and maintaining a navigable Cut or Canal from, or from some place near, Pontnewynydd, into the River Usk at or near the town of Newport ... and for making and maintaining Rail Ways or Stone Roads from such Cuts or Canals to several Iron Works and Mines in (the County) of Monmouthshire.'

It was a unique development because prior to this date there is no record of any rail or waggonway in Wales. Unfortunately, very little record of the actual construction of the canal is available, but we do know that the engineer appointed by the Company was Thomas Dadford Jnr. He was the son of an experienced canal builder and he had previously assisted his father in the construction of the Glamorganshire Canal. Thomas Dadford Senior had been apprenticed to James Brindley, the first canal engineer who had been employed by the Duke of Bridgewater to build the Bridgewater Canal, Manchester. Brindley had also invented the puddle-clay bottom which Dadford used on the Monmouthshire Canal to conserve water.

The thousands of canal labourers were known as navigators, presumably because they were employed on a water transport project, but subsequently this name was shortened to 'navvies,' a term which is still in use as an alternative to the word labourers. These men were employed to excavate 'the cut' and they were paid about 2/- (10p) a week. This was more money than they could earn on the local farms, but the catch was that the Canal Company paid them in tokens which could only be spent in the Company shops. It was a policy which ensured that the navigators stayed with the Company until the job was finished.

Between Newport and Pontymoel the canal is 8. 5 miles in length, with the substantial height difference requiring the construction of 31 locks. Near the '5 Locks' at Pontrhydyrhun a 260 feet long tunnel was constructed. No towpath was included, so when it came into operation the horse had to be led over the top and the boatmen 'walked' their narrow boats through by side-stepping with their feet on the tunnel walls.

From the Basin at Pontymoel to the canal head at Pontnewynydd it was a distance of approximately three miles with a height difference of 110 feet, which required eleven locks. The total distance from Pontnewynydd to Newport was thus 11. 5 miles and the distance in altitude 447 feet (138 metres), requiring no less than 42 locks. These were all about 10 feet in width and long enough to take the narrow boats which were 64 feet long and 9 feet 2 inches wide. The average depth of water in the canal was 3.5 feet.

In 1794, John Fox, writing for *The General View of the Agriculture of the County of Monmouth* forecast that the Monmouthshire Canal would bring the following benefits to the county:-

> 'It will bring down coal in such abundance from Pontypool, etc., of so excellent a quality, to the seaport of Newport and the neighbouring country, as will in a short time after the canal is finished, and the veins are properly opened, become a great object of export from hence to different parts (probably even to the metropolis) if the canal from Bridgewater through Somersetshire and Dorsetshire, designed for vessels of 300 tons berth, should be carried into execution.
>
> This canal will also supply the internal part of the country with this necessary article of comfort. Each of the two branches extends more than two miles, and the whole of the railroads are upwards of twenty-four miles. The iron-works of Blaenavon, consisting of three furnaces, are carried on with great spirit by Messrs Hill and Co., and have a railroad of more than five miles to bring the iron down to the head of the canal. For this and for other works carried on by different proprietors, there is much merit due to them, they having expended very large sums in the establishment of these capital works, which will produce many thousands of tons annually, for the consumption of this country, and assist much in preventing the importance of such immense quantities of iron as we have been obliged to introduce from Sweden and Russia, to the prejudice of that balance of trade, which it is the dignity and interest of Great Britain to preserve.'

Locks and lengthman's cottage on the former Pontnewynydd arm of the Monmouthshire Canal. Illustration by Michael Blackmore.

In February 1796 the Monmouthshire Canal was opened for navigation and it is said that the old folk of Pontypool immediately declared: 'Now is the prophecy of poor old Morgan Davy brought to pass.' It would seem that Morgan Davy was an old Welsh bard or prophet who had died many years before, in a time when canals were not even a gleam in an engineer's eye. His prophecy was that the time would come when Pontypool would be surrounded by water, and that there would be no access to it except by bridge or by ford. No doubt in those days very little of the town existed on the north side of the Afon Lwyd except Trevethin Church and the Bell Inn, which stood where the Park House was built.

Blaenavon Ironworks was linked with the canal head at Pontnewynydd by a rail-road constructed by Thomas Dadford Jnr. in 1795. It was five miles in length and descended a total height of 600 feet (186 metres). The iron rails were bolted to large stones weighing from 3 to 4 cwts which served as sleepers. The rails were four feet long, three inches deep, two inches at the top and set forty inches apart (rebuilt to a 4′ 2″ gauge in 1829). The driver, when descending the track, would hitch his horse to the rear of the wagon in places where the gradient allowed, enabling the tram to run under its own steam. On the return journey the horse pulled the empty trams back up the track.

These early tramroads followed the contours of the ground and required as little embankment as possible. In 1800 as the result of a recommendation from the engineer Benjamin Outram, the old rails were replaced with flanged iron plates and it was then no longer necessary for the wagons to have grooved rims on their wheels.

A branch from Varteg of 1.5 miles was also built to link up with the Blaenavon tramroad at Cwmavon, while another one from the 'Old Furnace' (Trosnant Furnace) in the Glyn Valley was built to meet the canal. The Trosnant tramroad left 'The Old Furnace' and ran nearly straight for a hundred yards. It then turned slightly to the left, skirted the lower edge of Coed Alice Wood and continued until it met the canal near the later Clarence Hotel. It hugged the canal to a point just above the brook from Cwmynyscoy and then crossed over via a stone bridge to the north bank to terminate at 'The New Coal Yard.' When the Taff Vale Extension to the Newport & Abergavenny Railway was built in 1857 a tunnel was constructed under the railway to maintain access for the tramroad to the coal yard. The Blaendare Tramroad left the Blaendare Furnace and passed down what is now Blaendare Road to meet the canal a little lower down than the Trosnant tramroad. Because the canal was so slow and needed so much water a survey was made in 1825 to explore the possibilities of the Blaenavon Tramroad being extended from Pontnewynydd to link up with the tramroads at Pontypool. The route was eventually opened in June 1829. It was known as the Pontypool Tramroad and extended from the termination of the Blaenavon Tramroad at Pontnewynydd along the north bank of the canal i.e. between the canal and the Afon Lwyd, through Pontnewynydd and past 'Canal Bank Row,' off Osborne Road, and 'Canal Parade,' at the top of George Street.

The tramroad crossed 'Pound Lane' (later named Lower Bridge Street) above the Baptist Chapel before making a wide sweep around a 'coal yard' where the Clarence Bus Station later stood. It then linked up with the Trosnant Tramroad below the bottom of Albion Road. The 1836 Town Plan of Pontypool shows the route from that point as 'Monmouthshire Tramroad.' It then kept close to the canal for some distance and suddenly made a wide sweep up the lower Cwmynyscoy valley to nearly encircle 'The Boat Dock' and, keeping to the Maesderwyn bank finally reached the canal at the Basin. The construction of the Pontypool Tramroad, by ensuring the avoidance of use of the canal and its time consuming eleven locks, sounded the death knell of this section of waterway.

During 1798-9 the canal carried 28,091 tons of coal, 11,159 tons of pig iron, 32 tons of bar iron, 573 tons of blooms, 288 tons of timber, 153 tons of lime, and 1,748 tons of sundry other goods. Fourteen narrow boats carrying loads of 25 - 28 tons were working between Pontnewynydd and Newport. It took a day for them to reach Cwmbran and a further day to complete the journey to Newport. On the return journeys from Newport the narrow boats brought back ale and porter, ironstone, castings, iron ore, bark, slate and manure.

The above figures certainly fell short of the original estimates of the Monmouthshire Canal Company who had calculated that 156, 000 tons of coal would be carried annually and that the various ironworks would provide another 334,000 tons of cargo. However, trade did increase considerably during the next four decades, for by 1845, the Monmouthshire Canal was carrying over half a million tons of goods a year.

In 1797 a further Act authorised a link between the Monmouthshire Canal at Pontymoel and the Brecknock and Abergavenny Canal, which was completed in 1812. These two canals now connected the industrial hills of Monmouthshire and the agricultural lowlands of Brecknockshire with the rapidly expanding town of Newport.

But within a short time thelink between the two canals resulted in a reduction of use on the Pontymoel to Pontnewynydd waterway, for the Blaenavon Ironworks Company now sent their iron via Garnddyrys, along Hill's Tramroad to Llanfoist Wharf. This route was economically preferable because the Monmouthshire Canal Company were compelled to accept traffic at the Pontymoel junction at the same rates as those charged by the B&A Canal Company, on which the Baileys, who were the principal shareholders had fixed a low toll for iron.

The canal between Pontnewynydd and Pontymoel was a difficult route to operate for it often suffered from a shortage of water and the eleven locks were very time consuming.

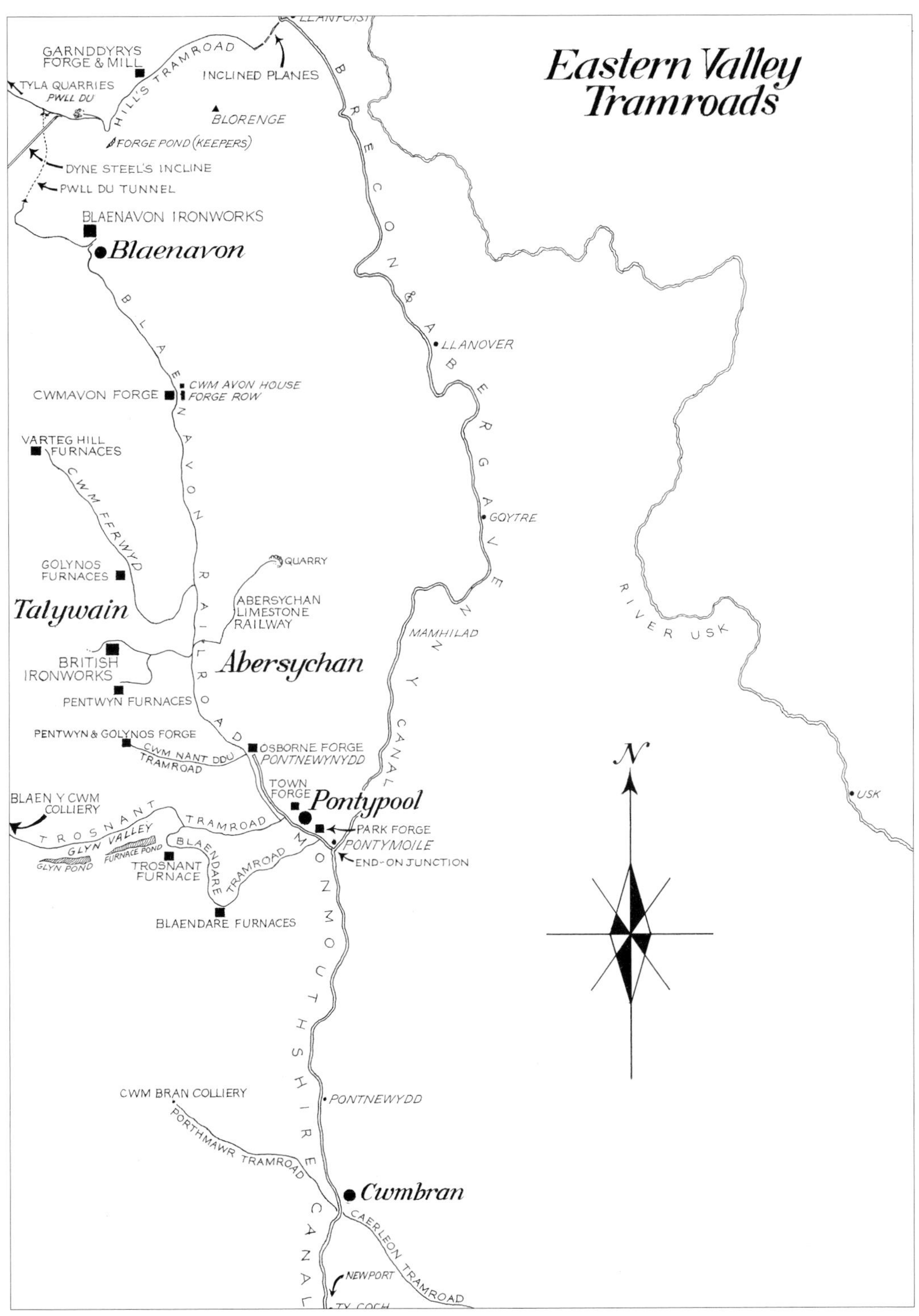

Eastern Valley Tramroads
LLANFOIST
GARNDDYRYS FORGE & MILL
HILL'S TRAMROAD
INCLINED PLANES
TYLA QUARRIES
PWLL DU
BLORENGE
FORGE POND (KEEPERS)
DYNE STEEL'S INCLINE
PWLL DU TUNNEL
BLAENAVON IRONWORKS
Blaenavon
BRECON & ABERGAVENNY CANAL
BLAENAVON RAILROAD
LLANOVER
CWMAVON FORGE
CWM AVON HOUSE
FORGE ROW
VARTEG HILL FURNACES
CWM FFRWYD
GOYTRE
GOLYNOS FURNACES
QUARRY
Talywain
ABERSYCHAN LIMESTONE RAILWAY
RIVER USK
MAMHILAD
BRITISH IRONWORKS
Abersychan
PENTWYN FURNACES
PENTWYN & GOLYNOS FORGE
CWM NANT DDU TRAMROAD
OSBORNE FORGE
PONTNEWYNYDD
N
BLAEN Y CWM COLLIERY
TOWN FORGE
Pontypool
USK
TROSNANT TRAMROAD
PARK FORGE
GLYN VALLEY
PONTYMOILE
FURNACE POND
BLAENDARE TRAMROAD
GLYN POND
TROSNANT FURNACE
END-ON JUNCTION
MONMOUTHSHIRE CANAL
BLAENDARE FURNACES
CWM BRAN COLLIERY
PONTNEWYDD
PORTHMAWR TRAMROAD
Cwmbran
CAERLEON TRAMROAD
NEWPORT
TY COCH

In order to increase the water supply, the Monmouthshire Canal Company in 1803 enlarged the ponds in Cwm Glyn (between Pontypool and Hafodyrynys), which impounded the waters of the Trosnant Brook. These ponds also supplied the Glyn Furnace and the Town Forge with water.

The Glyn Ponds lay midway between Pontypool and Crumlin and were known as the Upper, Middle and Lower Ponds. When the ponds were enlarged by the Monmouthshire Canal Company for the purpose of topping up the canal they paid Capel Hanbury £50 for the privilege. He had hoped that the enlarged capacity would be able to supply his works at Pontymoel, but the canal drew off ever increasing amounts of water and even the operation of the nearby Trosnant Forge was put into jeopardy.

Inevitably, the ponds became popular for boating and fishing and they are sadly remembered for a tragedy which occurred there on 23rd July, 1868 when eight young people and a boatman lost their lives. The boat struck a stake which made a hole in its side and it very shortly turned over. A rescue bid was made in a punt by Dr James Essex and Luke Sanger (boatman) who also ended up in the water when their craft was overturned by those they were trying to save. Dr Essex managed to save six of the children, but eight of them and Luke Sanger were drowned. (The Glyn Ponds were later drained and covered over by the Lower Race to Hafodyrynys by-pass, which opened in 1988).

Gradually the Pontnewynydd branch of the canal became redundant. As we have seen, by June 1829 the Blaenavon tramroad had been extended from Pontnewynydd to link up with the Trosnant tramroad which led to Pontymoel, thus avoiding the laborious lock section altogether.

Pontymoel by this time had become a hive of activity with wharves, warehouses, tramroads and storage yards on each bank. A toll house known as Junction Cottage had been built in 1814 at the junction of the Brecknock & Abergavenny Canal and the Monmouthshire Canal. It was erected for the Brecknock & Abergavenny Canal Company by William Jones, a local mason and its shape allowed the canal to be viewed from both directions, which is a feature of the traditional design of all toll houses.

Junction Cottage at Pontymoel was built in1814 at the junction of the Brecknock & Abergavenny Canal and the Monmouthshire Canal. Illustration by Michael Blackmore.

The towpath-level ground floor was probably an office which contained the various documentation, charts and equipment relevant to the duties of a water tender (toll and lock keeper). A spiral staircase led down to the lower floor which provided a kitchen and day time living accommodation. The first floor, also reached by a spiral stairway was used as a bedroom. It was the job of the man who occupied the cottage to look after the locks, keep the waterways clear and gauge the weight of the narrow boats. These duties were carried out seven days a week and 52 weeks a year.

Load tonnage was determined by making measurements between the water line and the top of the vessel's bargeboards to thus identify the 'displacement' of the craft. These measurements were usually taken in four places; fore and aft, port and starboard. The average figure was then calculated and reference made to a chart which related specifically to each craft at the time that it was built. In this way the weight of cargo that was being carried could be determined and according to the nature of the goods (coal, iron, limestone, agricultural products, livestock etc.), a charge would be levied relevant to the Company's schedule.

The Act of Parliament permitting the building of the Brecknock & Abergavenny Canal authorised tolls to be charged at the following rates:-

| | |
|---|---|
| Iron ore, coal and coal products | 2d (1p) per ton per mile |
| Lime, limestone, quarry products | 1d (1/2p) per ton per mile |
| Iron and lead | 3d (1 1/2p) per ton per mile |
| Timber and general merchandise | 4d (2p) per ton per mile |
| Cattle, sheep and swine | 4d (2p) per ton per mile |

The canal proprietors also built warehouses on the land adjoining the Cottage during the 1820s to provide storage facilities for goods to be transported or distributed.

The lock near Junction Cottage was at one time protected by gates, two at each end, and it was another of the water tender's duties to operate them. They were designed to hold back the water so that in the event of drainage of the canal a total loss of water could be prevented. These gates were probably removed after the B&A Canal navigation was absorbed in to the Monmouthshire Railway and Canal Company in 1866.

To the east of Junction Cottage, the Brecknock & Abergavenny Canal crosses an impressive aqueduct built over the Afon Lwyd. The original stone structure was built in 1810 by the engineer William Crosley, but within a few years it was found that the fast-flowing river was beginning to undermine the foundations.

William Crossley and another engineer, John Hodgkinson, carried out a survey and recommended that the aqueduct should be demolished and a good foundation excavated for a new one. This drastic step was taken and in additio the river bank to the north of the structure was given a stone facing which extends into the river bed. Cast iron plates were also driven into these revetments to divert the flow of water away from the aqueduct abutments.

In 1880 canal was acquired by the Great Western Railway Company who erected boundary posts that can be seen to this day and the joint canal became known as the Monmouthshire & Brecon Canal.

In 1843 Reginald Blewitt MP, who resided at Llantarnam Abbey, was so dissatisfied with the Monmouthshire Canal that he submitted a paper which put forward a proposal for a 'New Monmouthshire Railway from Newport Dock to Nanty-glo and Blaenavon through Pontypool.' He emphasised the need of such a scheme by stressing the many problems that were associated with the existing canals and tramroad system, which was now considered to be a poor and outdated means of transport. A number of landowners, iron masters and others had in 1842 formed themselves into a company for the purpose of building such a railway. It was argued that Newport, the port of shipment for the whole of the minerals of the Monmouthshire iron and coal districts, possessed 'no safe or commodious means of access for travellers to any part of such districts.'

For several weeks during the summer of that year, two or three miles of the Pontypool cut had been without water, 'and that part of the traffic almost entirely suspended, to the great injury of every freighter. This canal is, indeed, at all times, a most defective means of transit. In consequence of the numerous locks and continual impediments of one kind or other, a boat from the Pontypool works can only make five journeys in a fortnight between that town and Newport, although the distance is not more than ten miles. Coal taken down the same canal, from a point not much exceeding five and a half miles, does not, on the average, reach its destination in less than eight hours.'

Blewitt pointed out that the main part of the Blaenavon iron was being sent, 'at a ruinous expense,' by tramroad and incline planes via Abergavenny to Newport, a distance of twenty-eight miles, due to the heavy tolls demanded by the Canal Company at Pontnewynydd.

He commented that the coal transported on the tramroads and canals of the Monmouthshire Company was exposed to considerable opportunities for theft, for these routes were:

> '...unfenced and accessible to every idle trespasser. In consequence, the coal of the freighters is stolen to an enormous extent, and principally by women and young children, the latter of whom are instructed in the practice, and thus brought up from their earliest infancy in a system of vice and immorality which must necessarily lead to other and greater crimes. It is a notorious fact, that few, if any, of the cottagers living near the canals and tram-roads ever buy coal from the coal-owners: what they use is stolen by themselves or bought from others who make their livelihood by a regular system of pilfering it.
>
> The state of the poor collier during a stoppage of the canal from any cause is most pitiable. He is paid only according to the number of tons he gets from the mine; and when the coal can no longer be sent regularly to market, he is thrown out of work, and exposed very often, in the depth of winter, to the most afflicting privatations.'

Blewitt stressed that the line of the proposed railway would not be a competing route with that of the Canal Company for it left them nearly the whole of their red-ash coal trade. It would enter Newport by a different route from that of either of the Company's canals and roads, and at a different part of the town. It would ascend the Pontypool valley in a direct line towards Nantyglo, pass through a mountain tunnel, traverse the Nantyglo valley on a higher level and by easy curves and gradient.

Above Pontypool the proposed railway would be connected with a number of ironworks which were operated by the following concerns: 'The Pontypool Company, the Pentwyn and Golynos Company, the British Iron Company at Abersychan, the Varteg Company (not at present in operation), the Blaenavon Company, the Cwm Celyn and

Blaina Company, the Coalbrook Vale Company, and the Nant-y-glo Company of Messrs. J and C. Bailey. These works have produced and sent to Newport, for shipment in the course of one year, the following quantities of iron:-

| | |
|---|---|
| Pontypool Company | 9,584 tons |
| Pentwyn and Golynos Company | 28,640 |
| Abersychan Company | 12,482 |
| Varteg Company | 14,953 |
| Blaenavon Company | 14,889 |
| Cwm Celyn and Blaina Company | 16,430 |
| Coalbrook Vale Company | 9.701 |
| Nant-y-Glo Company | 39,159 |
| | 145,838 tons |

In 1845 the Monmouthshire Canal Company, which had been jolted into action by this potential threat by a new rival company, took positive action by obtaining an Act of Parliament which gave them permission to improve their tramroad and to build a 4′ 8.5″ gauge railway from Newport to the head of the canal at Pontnewynydd, with a branch line to the docks in Newport. Also they planned to improve all their existing tramroads (with the exception of the Rassa and Cwmffrwyd railroads which had gradients that were too steep), so that they could be adapted for locomotive engines.

By 1847 nearly all the Newport and Pontypool Railway shares had been allocated, but since work had not seriously begun and a mere four miles let to 'a highly reputable contractor,' it became necessary to ask for an extension of time for building the line. But the Company were unable to raise the necessary capital and the contract was annulled. In 1848 a new Act was passed and the name of the Company was changed to the Monmouthshire Railway and Canal Company. They took over the operation of the former Canal Company and appointed Thomas March to survey the line of their proposed railway. According to his estimates the cost of the line would average £10,000 per mile. The cost of land purchase came to £8,600 and the necessary earthworks were assessed at £28,000 which included the construction of a 110 yard tunnel at Malpas, near Newport.

The line was subdivided into nine separate contracts and put out to tender. There were only two major engineering features of note - the short tunnel at Malpas (Contract No.3., let to Benjamin Farmer) and the seven arch viaduct at Cwmynyscoy (let to Stephen Thomas), to carry the line over the Dane Brook, the road to Cwmynyscoy and the tramroad from Race Ironworks to the canal at Pontymoel. The whole of the ballasting and laying of the lines from Pontypool Crane Street to The Marshes Foundry at Newport (Contract No.9), was let to the firm Giles and Morgan for £2,935. It was proposed that the canal be closed from Pontnewynydd to Pontypool, and the new railway built on the bed of the cut.

In preparation for an extension of the railway to Blaenavon, the original tramroad plateway from Pontnewynydd to Blaenavon was lifted and replaced with wrought iron tramplates on wooden sleepers. This was in fact just a temporary measure and the line between Pontypool and Blaenavon was still only suitable for horse traffic and totally unfit for locomotives. Nothing could be done to rectify the situation until the canal from Pontymoel Basin to Pontnewynydd, could be closed.

During the construction of the Malpas Tunnel an accident occurred when the roof fell in and forty men were buried by about 100 tons of earth. Rescuers managed to dig them out and surprisingly they all survived, but not without injury.

At Skew Bridge, where the railway crossed the canal at Coed-y-gric Farm, near Pontypool, a technical problem added to the cost of the scheme. The embankments on either side of the bridge had been completed by William Fleetwood in August 1851 and had required some 35,000 tons of infill. The bridge was calculated to have a span of 52 feet, with the line rising on a gradient of 1 : 56. However, when the four wrought iron girders were transported from the Pillgwenlly Iron Foundry at Newport, and placed in position, it was found that an allowance had not been made for the 1 : 56 gradient, which meant that one of the piers was too low and as a result the contract had to be re-assigned.

But at last the day of the grand opening of the Newport and Pontypool Railway finally arrived. On Wednesday 30th June, 1852, the event was celebrated by the Monmouthshire Railway & Canal Company with a well publicised inauguration ceremony. The first train departed at 2.30pm from the temporary terminus at the Marshes Gate, Newport, to the sound of cannons and the band of the 48th Regiment. The six stations on the line were all decorated with flags and the following technical description of the line was given in the local papers:-

> 'The extent of the railway is 8 miles - single track - the rails 'Double T.' weight 70lbs to the yard, on transverse sleepers 9 ft long x 5 ins deep x 10 ins wide, spaced 2ft to 2ft 6ins apart. Gradients are as follows - the first 5 miles, 1:25: 1 mile 1:90: and the last 2 miles 1:56. There are 26 bridges, representing fine and substantial masonry; there is sidings accommodation at Cwmbran, Pontnewydd, Pontrhydyrun and Pontypool.'

William Fleetwood undertook the completion of the line from the temporary terminus to Great Dock Street and the work was finished according to the contract within three months. Three passenger trains in each direction were initially programmed, starting at 7 am, 12 noon and 4 pm from Newport and returning from Pontypool at 10 am, 2 pm and 6 pm.

After the opening to Pontypool, doubling of the line was started as further traffic from northern lines was expected. In1854, a delivery of 14 new locomotives and 18 carriages was made while a new station at Pontypool was built for the start of through traffic.

Meanwhile, work had also been proceeding on constructing a railway between Pontypool and Blaenavon. In his last report to the directors on 20th May, 1853, David Jones the Chief Engineer announced that he had reconstructed and permanently laid the railway between the canal head and Blaenavon; formed and ballasted the incline connecting Varteg and Golynos Tram lines with the the Blaenavon Railroad; purchased rails necessary to double the line on the Pontypool Railway and was able to report that the canal closure from Crane Street to Pontnewynydd was imminent.

In January 1854, the *Monmouthshire Merlin* reported:-

> 'The canal (Pontnewynydd branch) is now empty. The water has been let out nearly a fortnight and the bed of the canal is now dry from Pontnewynydd to Trosnant locks. At Pontnewynydd a great number of labourers are employed in levelling the bottom and laying a temporary line of rails, the object being to furnish sufficient room for an engine to go under the bridges; and thus to apply steam-power instead of horse-power, in the transition of trams between Pontnewynydd and Pontypool. In two or three weeks this will be accomplished and then the permanent line will be begun, and, we sincerely hope, speedily completed.'

On 1st January, 1854 the railway from Hereford to the junction with the Monmouthshire line at Cod-y-gric was opened to traffic and trains commenced to run between Hereford and Newport (Mill Street) Station. This new railway was called the 'Newport, Abergavenny and Hereford Railway,' but Parliament decreed that it should commence not at Newport, but at the junction with the Monmouthshire Railway which was soon to be known as Coed-y-gric Junction.

Coed-y-gric Farm had lost land when the canal was being constructed and the building of the railway had resulted in the erection of an embankment in front of the main windows of the old farmhouse, thus cutting off the view of the lush meadows and woodlands stretching down to the river-side. Joseph Cowles, the owner of the farm at the time when the canal was built, had fought hard to receive compensation for his lost amenities, but he did not live long enough to suffer the sight of his land invaded by the steam locomotive. As the years went by, more and more of Coed-y-gric's lands were taken, to be covered with railway lines and sidings, to eventually become one of the largest traffic marshalling yards in South East Wales.

On 20th August, 1855 the section from Pontypool Road to Crumlin Junction came into use and it was extended in October of that year to Llanhilleth Junction with the Western Valley Railways. The Crumlin Viaduct was brought into operation on 1st July, 1857 and trains ran over it to Pontllanfraith, or Tredegar Junction as it was then known.

Trains began to run between Pontypool and Merthyr from 11th January, 1858 when the section from Pontllanfraith to Quakers Yard Junction with the Taff Vale Railway was finished. This new railway was extremely important for it provided rail contact with the important coal mining and iron smelting areas of Blaenavon, Ebbw Vale, Beaufort, Brynmawr, Blaina, Tredegar and Rhymney and by its junction at Quakers Yard, with Merthyr, Aberdare and later with the Rhondda Valleys.

By 1859, it was possible to travel by train the whole length of the Eastern Valley, i.e. from Blaenavon to Newport, Mill Street, with three services in each direction being provided. They started from Blaenavon at about 6.30 am and finished from Newport at 6.00 pm. The service was soon increased (on the doubling of the line) by a similar set of trains from the Newport end and the last 'up train' was arranged to leave Newport at 9.15 pm, an arrangement which continued for many years.

The railway had three-class trains which allowed the rich to ride in comfortable and uncrowded first-class carriages; second-class carriages were cheaper but crowded while third-class passengers travelled at a cheap rate but suffered draughty compartments and sat on wooden benches.

> 'The liberality of the Monmouthshire Railway Company, in providing third-class accomodation for the working class popular of our district, is a fact that all must acknowledge. Every train that runs on the line comprises: first, second and third-class carriages. Most of the second-class carriages are provided with stuffed seats.'
>
> *Pontypool Free Press* 1859

By 1864 the canal was very little used and in fact the tolls yielded just £1,222, which was less than the maintenance figure. In 1865 the Brecknock & Abergavenny Canal Company sold out to the Monmouthshire Railway & Canal Company for £25,000 plus debts of £36,000. Inadequate water supplies for the Monmouthshire Canal had been a constant problem, with it sometimes being obtained from streams as much as 1,000 yards away and the embankments were very expensive to maintain. It would seem that the chief reason for the purchase was that the Monmouthshire Company wished to make use of the B & A water which was virtually trouble free.

**Railway Growth**

An Act of 16th July, 1866, gave permission for the Brynmawr & Blaenavon Railway to be built, linking Brynmawr Station on the Merthyr, Tredegar & Abergavenny line with Blaenavon. The line was to be just over four miles in length and capital of £80,000 was required. It was stated that the line would be completed in four years from the passing of the Act. The railway accordingly opened for mineral traffic on 1st November, 1869 and for passenger traffic on 1st January, 1870, which was just within the set time limit.

Brynmawr Station was at an altitude of 1,160 ft above sea level, and the line was constructed on a gradient of 1 in 41 on the two miles to Waunavon Station which, at 1,400 ft above sea level, became the highest standard gauge railway station in England and Wales.

A branch line from Pontypool (Trevethin Junction) to Talywain was opened on 18th September, 1879 and as a result the incline between Varteg and Cwmffrwd was no longer required. The London and North Western Railway Company then extended the Brynmawr and Blaenavon railway to Talywain through Blaenavon (High Level) and thus providedanother through route between Newport, Pontypool, Blaenavon and Brynmawr. This line united what was then a terminus of the LNWR line at Blaenavon with the GWR's Monmouthshire Railway at Talywain Junction. In detail the 'top' route was from Blaenavon, through Garndiffaith, Talywain, Pentwyn, Pentrepiod, Cwmffrwdoer, Cwmnantddu, Pontnewynydd, Trevethin Junction and into Pontypool (Crane Street), where it joined the Monmouthshire Railway above the Fountain Bridge in George Street.

The engineering works included a cutting at Garndiffaith, some 90 yards in length and 60 feet deep, and this was followed by an impressive railway viaduct spanning the steep sided valley of the river Ffrwd. Constructed by John Gardner, consultant engineer to the London and North Western Railway for this area, it is supported by nine semi-circular arches and is built on a gentle curve.

Pontypool was by now served directly by two stations which were known as Crane Street (on the Eastern Valley line)and Clarence Street (on the Swansea line). A third station was built at Pontypool Road, about 1.5 miles east of the town. It served a junction between the Swansea line and the Ross branch and the main line to Hereford and the midlands and the north of England.

From 1859 the 'yard' at Pontypool Road continued to expand as the flow of traffic to Birmingham and the North of England began to develop. Manufacturers in the Midlands and the North were quick to realise that new markets for their goods had been opened for them in South Wales. Pontypool Road thus became the collecting and distributing centre for all rail borne traffic from and to the whole of South Wales. Trains with wagons for ten or a dozen destinations in South Wales arrived daily and were sorted out and sent away on appropriate trains. To deal with these 'transfer' wagons a shed was erected in the middle of the yard and here the contents of the wagons were sorted and then sent forward with other similar consignments to their destination.

The impressive viaduct at Garndiffaith was constructed by the engineer John Gardner in 1878.

Abersychan Station on the 'Low Level' line. John Lewis Collection.

Varteg Station on the extension from Blaenavon to Talywain Junction. John Lewis Collection.

The Great Western Railway Station which opened at Blaenavon in 1854, later became known as the Low Level Station. It used to stand at the bottom of Bridge Street and the line was closed by Dr Beeching in 1961. John Lewis Collection.

In 1870 the Cwmffrwdoer and Cwmnantddu branch lines from Pontnewynydd were constructed to serve the Blaenserychan and Llanerch collieries on one side and the Tirpentwys colliery on the other. The former had a gradient of 1 in 22 and the other 1 in 19 was so steep that the engine always remained at the lower end of the train to prevent a 'run away.' It was believed to be one of the steepest railways worked by locomotives with ordinary adhesion in Britain.

A new line via Caerleon to Newport was opened in 1874 and also a new passenger line between Pontypool Road Station and Coedygric Junction, which enabled the sidings to be re-organised to better advantage. It was also decided to build a stone viaduct to span the whole yard.

In 1878 the engine-shed was entirely re-conditioned and a new elevated coaling-stage erected. A few years later a piece of spare land lying between the yard and the Caerleon line was laid out as sidings to deal with the freight trains. Also in that year a short branch was opened between Llantarnam Junction on the Pontypool Road - Caerleon line and Cwmbran Junction on the Monmouthshire line.

The London & North Western and remaining Great Western trains ceased to pass over the old Monmouthshire route via Malpas in 1879 and the passenger stations at Mill Street, Llantarnam and Cwmbran (Oakfield) were closed. A new station was provided at Cwmbran, near the junction with the branch line into Llantarnam.

An amalgamation of the Monmouthshire Railway and Canal Company with the Great Western system took effect from 1st August 1880. The Great Western Company then gradually set about standardising its various equipment. The track was improved, new signalling installed, the old Monmouthshire engines were withdrawn and replaced by new standard types built at Swindon and Wolverhampton. Passenger and freight services were increased according to the growing demands of industry with the result that the Eastern Valley lines became intensely occupied.

As the train traffic increased more and more men were required to work on the railways, driving locomotives and also doing maintenance work. Experienced engine drivers and mechanics were recruited from the Midlands and North country, where there were a greater number of locomotives in use. Guards and shunters were recruited from the Great Western and South Wales Railways and demands on accommodation in Pontypool increased accordingly.

This influx of additional railway workers also resulted in Pontypool Road becoming recognised as the spring-board of the Associated Society of Locomotive Engineers and Firemen which was founded in 1880 by a young Irishman named Charles H. Parry, who was a driver at Pontypool Road. Members of this new Trade Union drove trains to places such as London, Oxford, Birmingham, Woverhampton and Birkenhead, and drivers or firemen of other railways that they met in those places were encouraged to join.

The opening of the Severn Tunnel in 1886 brought new trains to and from Bristol and Exeter, mainly with traffic for the North of England, and the development of local industry, particularly iron and steel, brought even more traffic into the yard for distribution. A revision of passenger services brought by the introduction of the North and West Express services between Manchester and Plymouth, gave Pontypool and District a rail service with a range that was seldom enjoyed by a town of its size.

In about 1908, there was considerable public demand for more frequent passenger trains, particularly in the upper part of the Eastern Valley, and in response to these demands the Great Western Company introduced a frequent service of 'auto-trains,' based on Pontypool Road depot, between Panteg, Pontypool (Crane Street) and Blaenavon (Low

Level); also over the 'top' line to Talywain, Blaenavon (High Level) and Brynmawr. Additional 'halts' were provided at Snatchwood and Cwmffrwd on the lower level line and at Wainfelin, Cwmffrwdoer, Pentrepiod, Pentwyn and Garndiffaith on the high level line. By 1936 eighteen trains worked to and from Blaenavon (low level) per day and seven over the high level line to Brynmawr.

The yard at Pontypool played an important role during the Great War and Mr E. A. Pratt, the author of *Railways and the Great War* , wrote:

> 'Generally speaking the time taken on the journey from Pontypool Road to Grangemouth (on the Firth of Forth) was less than 48 hours. The fact that so great a traffic was run day by day at practically time-table timing and for more than four years might be regarded as establishing in itself the efficiency of the British railway system. Yet that efficiency becomes still more pronounced when one learns the specials were run without any serious interruption on any one occasion. The British Fleet never once had to wait for its coal.'

World War Two did not call for such intensive transport arrangements but the yard played an important part in that crisis too. A dramatic change to the site took place in November 1993 when the remaining building at Pontypool Road Station was demolished as part of an ambitious scheme to improve the facilities at a cost of £150,000. The work included installing a bus turning area, a public address system and provision of a platform shelter.

**The End of the Line**

The high level railway between Newport and Brynmawr via Pontypool was built primarily as a mineral line and the passenger service was only briefly well patronised. As a wartime economy measure it was suspended on 5th May 1941 but never reinstated. From that time the only traffic to run on this line was exclusively carrying coal.

In February 1961 the track between Blaenavon and Brynmawr was lifted and it was commented in the *Free Press* that 'another step in the isolation of the town (Blaenavon) has been achieved.' This single-track line had been in existence for nearly a century and when Blaenavon was a prosperous industrial town, much of its coal, steel and coke was carried on this line.

Passenger services were withdrawn on the bottom line during the following year, when the last passenger train left Blaenavon for Newport on 29th April. Crane Street Railway Station in Pontypool closed the following day. Two years later the infamous axe of Dr Beeching struck in the Pontypool area when it was announced that the Pontypool Road - Vale of Neath line was to close on 15th January and this meant that many local railway workers would have to face redundancy or regrading.

Pontypool Road Station, which for more than a century had been a major passenger and freight junction, was largely demolished in December 1970. The platform, almost a quarter of a mile in length, with its huge Victorian ornamental ironwork canopy was dismantled and reduced to scrap.

Blaenavon Town Council in 1979 requested that the old top level line should be reopened to passengers. It was stressed that even if a passenger service was only operated in the holidays it would be a worthwhile asset to the people of Blaenavon. Torfaen Museum Trust and some railway societies also expressed an interest in the idea, for they considered that if the line was developed along with other tourist plans it would be an excellent tourist attraction.

Nevertheless the high level line to Big Pit closed at the same time as the colliery in 1980 and the last train ran on April 13th. Christened the 'Welsh Colliery Rambler,' this special train with 650 people aboard made its way up the Eastern Valley and took its place in history as the last passenger train to be seen on the line.

In November 1980 the local Railway Society endeavoured to purchase the line between Crane Street, Pontypool and Furnace Sidings, Blaenavon from British Rail. They were given just five weeks to come up with the £140,000 asking price. If they failed to meet the deadline British Rail firmly stated that they would tear up the track and sell it for scrap.

In October of 1982 the Society, now to be reformed as a charitable company, were given one last chance by British Rail to either 'pay up or give up' on their proposed purchase of the line. Unless there was a firm commitment in the next two months work would commence on recovering the whole of the track, including a section previously offered to the Society.

British Rail then began removing the track from the junction with the main line at Llantarnam up the valley, leaving only a 2.5 mile section from Gallows Green, mid-way between Blaenavon and Varteg, to Garn-yr-erw. The trackbed was subsequently used in the construction of Cwmbran Drive and Pontypool Bypass with other small sections becoming industrial and housing estates.

In 1983 the Pontypool and Blaenavon Railway Co. Ltd. (a preservation society) was formed with the object of purchasing the remainder of the line from Cwmbran to Big Pit, Blaenavon and to run it as a special attraction for tourists visiting the Eastern Valley. The following year they began operating a short passenger carrying steam service between Furnace Sidings and the Whistle Inn, but without a platform it was not possible for the passengers to disembark at the inn. This platform was constructed four years later and officially opened by Paul Murphy the MP for Torfaen and Company President. An extension to Forgeside Bridge was opened in 1990.

The Pontypool & Blaenavon Railway can boast to have the highest standard gauge railway in preservation in England and Wales. It also has a steeper continuous gradient that any other line. Trains run every Sunday and Bank Holidays during the summer from the Furnace Sidings platform near Big Pit to the Whistle Inn at Garn-yr-erw. Martin Herbert Collection.

In November 1998 agreement was reached by the Company to lease land as far as the High Level Station on Varteg Road. The 25 year lease would enable them to extend the line to run for two miles by the year 2000. Their ultimate dream is to one day extend the line for over 8 miles from Talywain to Brynmawr., the latter town having replaced Pontypool as a realistic goal.

Entirely manned by volunteers, the Company provides its members the opportunity to train and act as drivers, firemen, guards and station, sales and refreshment staff. Other members are more concerned with restoration of locomotives, coaches and the track itself.

**Demise and Restoration of the Monmouthshire Canal**

The Monmouthshire Railway & Canal Company's policy of encouraging traffic onto its railway had an obvious effect on the commercial use of the canal. This situation continued after the Great Western Railway took over the concern in 1880. By 1900 the canal was carrying very little traffic and in 1915 the last market boat made its nostalgic way from Brecon to Newport, The Monmouthshire & Brecon Canal now became little more than a supplier of water to industry and to Newport Town Dock in particular. It proved, however, to be the last of the South Wales canals to survive as a navigable waterway.

The last revenue earning journey was made in 1933 and in subsequent years the only use of the waterway was for leisure purposes such as school outings, while the canal water continued to be taken for industrial purposes.

On January 1st 1948, ownership of canals passed to the British Transport Commission and then to the British Waterways Board in 1963. Five years later the Board, in conjunction with the Breconshire and Monmouthshire County Councils, through their Brecon Beacons National Park Committee, began a reclamation programme on the canal from Brecon to the National Park boundary north of Pontypool to allow pleasure craft to use the waterway. Southward to Sebastapol the canal was termed 'remainder' water and was only maintained to provide a source of water to canal-side industries.

Navigation on the Monmouthshire & Brecon Canal was restricted at Crown Bridge, Sebastapol, in the 1960's when the local council rebuilt the old hump-backed bridge at South Street in order to improve the main Pontypool to Cwmbran road. The carriageway was lowered and a corrugated steel lined culvert placed beneath the bridge. It was also very difficult for a boat to turn near that location. The canal between Pontymoel and Crown Bridge gradually silted up and was little used.

Cwmbran Urban District Council in 1972 obtained outline planning permission for a marina at Five Locks but it was not realistic to build such a facility because of the problem at Crown Bridge, which was in the area of Pontypool Urban Council.

A public meeting was held at St Hilda's Hall, Griffithstown in 1975 to inaugurate Torfaen Canal Society. Nearly seventy people attended the meeting and it was agreed that the new Society would press for public ownership of the canal. Also they would assist with working parties to help clear the canal of weed and rubbish etc., and to act as an organising body for all water-orientated sports.

In May of the following year, a scheme to clean up the Monmouthshire & Brecon Canal from Jockey Bridge, Llanfihangel Pontymoile, to Crown Bridge, Sebastapol was approved under the Government's Job Creation programme.

It was proposed in 1982 that the provision of a winding hole (turning area) near Crown Bridge would encourage boaters to venture further and this would help to keep the recently dredged length of canal between Jockey Bridge and Crown Bridge clear of weed.

It was commented that the raising of head room under Crown Bridge would allow further restoration of the waterway. If this was carried out the terminus could be just above Five Locks where the provision of facilities for informal recreation and boating could be carried out.

A project at Five Locks was undertaken in 1984 by the Gwent Land Reclamation Joint Committee with the assistance of Torfaen Borough Council. No longer navigable, the flight of locks was dredged and re-built with imitation lock gates made out of concrete.

In June 1993 a report to the Newport Borough Council Leisure Services committee on the proposed restoration of the Monmouthshire & Brecon Canal between Cwmbran and Newport, stated that benefits from economic growth could be approximately £390k - £500,000per annum. It was suggested that a Trust Company should be set up to carry out the restoration. The study considered that the restoration of the canal to a navigable standard of cruising waterway was technically feasible, at an estimated cost of £11.15m.

Torfaen Borough Council in October 1993 announced that £350,000 would be spent to reconstruct Crown Bridge in Sebastapol to enable canal boats to travel all the way to Five Locks in Cwmbran.

In 1996 as part of the 200th birthday celebrations of the Monmouthshire Canal, the redeveloped Five Locks Wharf at Pontnewydd was officially opened. The cost of the development was £258,000 and it was financed by the Welsh Development Agency.

Exciting proposals were revealed in 1997 for a £42m scheme (rather more than the 1993 estimate of £11m) to restore the nine mile section of canal between Newport and Cwmbran to enable a navigable waterway from Newport to Brecon. It would be nearly 50 miles in length and would undoubtedly add to the tourist appeal of the Cwmbran - Brecon section, bringing significant economic benefits to the area. Included in the scheme was the creation of a marina development at Crindau in Newport. Construction of a £3.5 million aqueduct to span Greenforge Way in Cwmbran to take the canal over a busy road, behind the B& Q superstore, thus linking two truncated sections of the waterway, is a key part of the project. Funding is currently being sought.

**Modern Highways and Traffic Congestion**

It is interesting that Pontymoel was experiencing traffic problems as early as 1900 for Adolphe George Jones wrote, ' An awkward corner had to be negotiated at Pontymoel, where the road forms a right angle; cyclists returning this way should exhibit caution, mishaps otherwise being frequent here.'

An alarming forecast of the traffic situation in Pontypool by the end of the decade was provided in January 1964 by Mr W. L. Sambrook who told the Chamber of Trade that there would be as many cars in the area as houses. If trends continued, then by 1970 there would be 9,000 vehicles in the urban district of Pontypool which was an increase of 75 per cent on the present figures. By that date the population of the area would be in the region of 37,000 - a drop of over 2,500 - but the number of cars in the district would be 6,000, as well as 3,000 other vehicles. At peak periods there would be something like 2,000 cars an hour passing through the town which was equal to 35 cars a minute. Mr Sambrook added, 'If nothing is done then Pontypool will be completely blocked and if the population increases then the situation will be even worse.'

In the 1970s a new road was built on the floor of the valley to relieve Commercial Street and Osborne Road of through traffic but this did nothing for Pontypool's main shopping street, Hanbury Road, which was also part of the main route to the north of the valley. In 1988 this road was being used by some 19,000 vehicles a day and a Pontypool by-pass was long overdue. The town had become one of Gwent's worst traffic bottlenecks, for the through traffic was having to contend with service vehicles and shoppers in the town, while two bus stops and three busy pelican crossings also helped to increase the problems.

Proposals were put forward to build a single carriageway, 24 feet wide and three-quarters of a mile in length, from a new roundabout on the A472 Usk - Crumlin road south of Pontypool, around the west side of the town to the existing Riverside/Osborne Road roundabout north of the town centre. Most of the road would follow a long tradition of transport routes, the old Pontnewynydd arm of the Monmouthshire Canal which had been superseded by the now disused Pontypool to Blaenavon railway, and this meant that only nine properties would need to be demolished.

Work began in March 1992 on this new by-pass which was expected to relieve the existing A4043 route through the town centre of 60 per cent of its existing traffic. Eighteen months later, Paul Murphy, Torfaen's MP, formally opened the 1.7 km Pontypool western relief road (A4043) and dedicated it to the memory of the late Councillor Jim Mullin, who as Gwent's highways chairman had been a driving force behind the scheme, but had died earlier in the year.

It was hoped that the new road would promote growth in the upper part of the Eastern Valley by acting as a spur to important commercial and residential development and relieve chronic congestion in Pontypool town centre.

The road building of Cwmbran has been dealt with in Chapter 8 but mention should be made of the Valley's latest, and perhaps last, major road scheme. Work started on the A4042 Llantarnam bypass in 1994 and this £9m dual carriage way, 3.2km in length, was constructed to connect the Newport section of this road with the Croesyceiliog bypass. The road opened in April 1996 and its completion restored a feeling of comparative tranquility to the village of Llantarnam.

### The Cycle Route

In recent years Torfaen Council has been gradually implementing a Newport - Abergavenny (via Brynmawr) cycleway proposal conceived in 1982, now part of the National Cycle Network. The route follows the canal towpath in the south of the county borough and the old high level minerals railway line between Griffithstown and Waunavon in the north. More cycling, walking and use of public transport is hoped to stem the relentless growth of road traffic.

It has been recognised in the Local Plan for Torfaen that:-

'An effective transport system, including roads, public transport, cycling and pedestrian links, is essential to the economic and social well being of the County Borough.'

# -- 10 --

## People of the Valley

*'The natives of these districts speak the Welsh language, and few of them even understand English. They wear white or red flannel shirts. This custom is well adapted to mountainous countries, which are subject to sudden changes of weather...'*

M. Willett, 1825

Lewis Browning, a native of Blaenavon, writing in 1906, expressed his pride in the fact that the Eastern Valley had given birth to so many 'intelligent, eloquent and able people'. The range of professions, skills, trades and talents that have flourished in this valley is quite amazing and these pioneers of industry - preachers, puddlers, colliers, quarrymen, furnacemen, doctors, artists, poets, musicians, shopkeepers and numerous others - have all contributed to the social history of this locality.

Even today, most people of the Eastern Valley still have pride in their heritage and the achievements of their ancestors and the following random selection of people of past and present times has been included to portray the vast range of expertise, colourful characters and respected members of society, who have all made some contribution to the social history of the communities to be found in the valley from Garn-yr-erw to Cwmbran.

### Men of Industry

In December 1865, the black flag was hung out at the Hanbury Arms, Garndiffaith, as a sign of mourning for the sudden death of John Vipond Esq. (59), who had established the Varteg Hill Colliery. He died at Cwmavon House and his funeral was attended by some 2,000 people.

Employees of the Blaenavon Iron Company with their wives, in June 1866, were conveyed by rail to Raglan where they spent a day of jollity and fun amid the ruins of the castle. Also in the party were members of the seventeen friendly societies of the town. The total number of people involved was about 3,500 and the entire cost of engaging four special trains comprising more than a hundred carriages was generously defrayed by the directors of the Company.

Later, at the Prince of Wales Inn, Blaenavon, a substantial dinner and a quart of ale each was given to the furnacemen and others, whose duties prevented them from participating in the excursion.

Ironworker, Hugh John of Baker Street, Blaenavon, died in January 1870 at the age of 95. As a young man he had been employed as a roller and was said to have rolled the first bar of iron at Dowlais Works, Merthyr Tydfil. In later years he had kept the Queen Inn at Garnddyrus.

Mr R.W. Kennard, Chairman of the directors and one of the principal proprietors of the Blaenavon Works, also passed away in January 1870 at his London residence. In

August of that year the people of Blaenavon turned out in large numbers to welcome home Mr E. Kennard (son of R.W. Kennard) and his bride. The town was decorated with banners and flags. There were horse and foot races, rustic sports, acrobatic performances and evening fireworks. Music was provided by the Cyfarthfa and Blaenavon Bands and about 12,000 people were present to enjoy the fun.

Isaac Butler, who had assisted Sieman in his experiments which revolutionised the steel industry died in 1917. He is largely remembered for his connection with Panteg Steelworks where in 1873 he had been appointed manager of the Hammering and Finishing Department. When the works closed down he formed a new company in 1892 which ten years later amalgamated with that of Alfred Baldwin Ltd. In 1911 Isaac Butler served as High Sheriff of Monmouthshire. His family residence for many years was Panteg House and there is a memorial tablet to him in St Hilda's Church, Griffithstown.

Joseph Morgan of Talywain retired in 1922 after 54 years service with Messrs Partridge Jones and Co Ltd. He had begun his working life at the age of 12 as a pit boy and finally ended up as the agent of Llanerch, Blaenserchan and Gwenallt Collieries. After being presented with a miniature grandfather clock, Joseph recalled, 'I went down the pit as a boy of 12 and the usual wage was 2s. 6d (13p), but as I was a big strong boy I was given 1s. (5p) a day.'

A notable figure in the industrial life of Pontypool who died in 1923 at the age of 83 was George Fisher. His family's association with the district went back about 200 years to the time when a Mr Fisher came to Pontypool to manage the ironworks for the Hanbury family at Old Furnace. It was his son Ishmael, born in 1750, who superintended the erection of the Blaendare Ironworks which began to operate in 1756. When Ishmael died in 1811, Squire Hanbury presented the Fisher family with a vault at Trevethin. George Fisher was a clever engineer and inventor. He devised a method of using waste gasses from blast furnaces to fire boilers and also pioneered a new process of annealing steel sheets, which he introduced at Lower Mills. He made a sewing machine for his wife and was the first person to ride a bicycle in Pontypool.

Thomas Challenger of Holly Tree, Tranch, claimed in October 1927, to be the oldest working miner in South Wales. At the age of 77 he was still employed as a shot-firer at Tirpentwys Colliery, after a total of 68 years underground.

A Blaenavon man, born on Christmas Day 1862, was named Christmas James and in January 1937, he was still strong and upright at seventy five. Talking with great nostalgia about the old days, he recalled how he had been one of the young and vigorous strikers employed by the Blaenavon Company.

'I knew Gilchrist and Thomas quite well,' he said. 'They used to carry out their experiments in a little machine shop over there.' He pointed to a spot across the valley, where a heap of debris could be seen. 'They had a small cupola furnace specially set up for them, and they used to make small quantities of steel.

I was striking then for David Thomas, the blacksmith, and we used to go to work on Saturday afternoons for Gilchrist and Thomas. We used to test the steel they made while they and their wives and Mr E.P. Martin, the works manager, looked on. We heated it, twisted it and hammered it until finally it was all right. The first steel tyre made from that steel was made in the old tyre mill close by.'

John Hunt Lones (69), managing director of the Blaenavon Company for 21 years retired in January 1939. He served first as General Manager and then as Managing Director. Mr I. G. Gwyn Thomas commented that 'Mr Lones has never made the mistake of standing still, but has persevered and made his *footprints* in the sands of time.'

James Thomas Morgan (90), a well known citizen of Blaenavon died in 1974. He had been born in 1883, the youngest of seven children in a family which had been connected with the town since 1794. At the age of 12 he had left school to work as a colliery weighman, first for the Blaenavon Company and then for the NCB. During his 57 years in the job he had estimated that he personally weighed over 17 million tons of coal from Kay's Slope and Garn Drift. He had reluctantly retired in 1953 at the age of 70, when the local union suggested that he stood down and made way for a younger man.

**Popular Doctors**

Blaenavon people in July 1897, were mourning the death of Samuel Elmes Steel MD., who had been called to see a patient during the night of July 29th. On his return to Abergavenny, he accidently fell from his horse and died within a few hours. He was buried in Llanfoist Churchyard. The following year a tablet in his memory was erected by Mr W. Burgoyne, builder and sculptor, at St. Peter's Church, Blaenavon.

The Steel family had provided the first medical men in Blaenavon and Drs Thomas, William and Christopher Steel, living in Abergavenny, had visited Blaenavon on three times a week and more often in cases of emergency. These visits had continued for a number of years and their surgery was just below the Company stables. Medicines such as salts, senna, plasters, oils etc., were also left in the care of a few old women in the neighbourhood in case of urgent need.

Dr Richard Steel was the first resident medical man in Blaenavon and he had four sons, three of whom, Samuel, Richard and William also practised medicine. The other son, Henry was for many years the land and house agent for the Blaenavon Company.

On one occasion one of the doctors was called to attend a man whose arm had been cut off. He had been sitting asleep, and probably drunk, on the seat in front of the starting handles of a blast engine. The air pump rod passed through the iron floor plates and a projecting cotter pin also passed through a slot just large enough to take it. The man fell off the bench on the upstroke of the engine with his arm across the slot and the descent of the cotter pin cut it off just above the wrist. He struggled forward and the descending cotter cut off another length.

The doctor had to amputate the limb a third time and the unfortunate patient was ordered to bed on which he said, 'Oh Dr Steel, let me sit up and have my pipe first.'

Dr Steel in February 1871 had to deal with four broken legs, three broken arms, three broken shoulders and one detached shoulder as a result of falls on the steep icy streets of Blaenavon. He called upon residents to put ashes down to try and reduce the number of accidents.

**Those who lived to a ripe old age!**

Mrs Margaret Lewis of Blaenavon reached the age of 100 years and one month and lived in the same house for seventy years until her death in March 1869. Also in that year an 80 year old lady of Blaenavon was mentioned in the local paper for having married her fifth husband, 'a smart young man of nearly 60.'

A familiar Pontypool figure in 1900 was William Rogers of George Street, one of the town's oldest inhabitants. He trundled a parcel-laden barrow through the principal streets of the town and at one time was the sole letter deliverer in the district, covering the ground from Pontypool to Blaenavon. This meant a tramp of not less than 20 miles a day.

Two of Varteg's oldest inhabitants, Joshua Jeffries and 'Granny' Morris died in January 1922. Joshua, aged 80, had been an overman at Messrs John Vipond Collieries and Mrs Morris, who was 90, for over fifty years had been the only available maternity nurse in Varteg. She herself had a family of 10 sons, 5 daughters, 86 grand children and 41 great-grandchildren - a total of 142 descendants!

In June 1930, Mrs Hannah Maria Matthews of Cwmavon Road, Blaenavon, died at the age of 96. She was the town's oldest inhabitant. Her father, J.G. Williams was a distinguished son of Blaenavon. He provided the town with its first reservoir, its public market, its first brewery, its first licensed house and its Town Hall. He also obtained an order for the manufacture of gas prior to the formation of the Blaenavon Gas and Water Company under an Act of 1872.

Mrs Elizabeth ('Grannie') Fisher of Hill Street, Blaenavon, celebrated her 93rd birthday in December 1933. She had come to Blaenavon when she was 3 years old and had lived there ever since. When she was a young girl she used to sell milk around the town. She would walk to Llanover in the small hours and get back with her cans of milk by eight o'clock to retail it from house to house. 'Blaenavon was different then,' she said. 'The top of the town was all fields and I well remember most of the houses being built. Also I remember Hill Street being built.' The Ironworks, she said, was a hive of activity at that time and she would frequently go there to watch the molten iron being tapped from the furnaces. Only a month before her death she had walked to Abergavenny Market and back with her basket and she proudly claimed that she had never used a bottle of medicine in her life.

In February, 1934, Mrs Elizabeth Thomas of Chapel Street, Pontnewydd, celebrated her 100th birthday. She was born at Nantyglo where her father was a puddler in the ironworks. While she was a little girl her father died of cholera and she then came to live in Blaenavon. She had memories of her mother being baptised in the brook where King Street Baptist Church was later built. High Street and all the environs of St Peter's Church were still meadows and countryside. She married James Thomas, foreman moulder at Blaenavon Iron Works foundry, and could recall every detail of his tragic death. He was crossing the works yard one day in 1889 when he was run over and killed by an engine. She talked of the Chartist riots at Newport and of the terror of the people when it was announced by astronomers that Halley's Comet would burn up the world in it's passing.

When Mrs Sarah Davies of Penrhwyd Farm, Cefn-y-crib, Pontnewynydd, died in April 1935 her correct age was not known but she was thought to be over 100 years. Her father had fought in the battle of Trafalgar and he too had lived to nearly a hundred. She possessed a wonderful memory and could recite poetry which she had learned as a child. Her eyesight was excellent and she had never worn spectacles.

In January 1937, Mr Evan Powell of Pontnewynydd Works, believed to be the oldest locomotive driver in the country, decided to retire. He was 78 and had been employed at the works for 55 years.

May of that year saw the death of Mr Enoch Evans of Forgeside who played in the Blaenavon Colliery Band on the occasion of the Coronation of George VI. He had also played with the band during the celebrations of Queen Victoria's Golden and Diamond Jubilees (1887 and 1897), the Coronation of Edward VII (1901), of George V (1911) and King George V's Silver Jubilee (1935).

In 1938, the oldest inhabitant of Australia was said to be George Brown, aged 107, who had left Talywaun in 1857 to take part in the Australian gold rush.

Mrs Mary Jane Harris the oldest inhabitant of Griffithstown died in February 1940 at the grand old age of 97. She used to relate how long years ago she had travelled on the old stage coach which used to run from Abersychan to Newport and she had also made the trip to Newport by canal.

Thomas Stone of Middle Farm, Griffithstown, celebrated his birthday in February 1940. It was officially his 23rd birthday, but having been a leap year baby of 1848, he was really 92 years of age!

John Taylor of Pontypool was once a collier at the "Clog and Legging" Pit. He died in 1947 at the age of 92 and was survived by five sons, two daughters, 56 grandchildren and 57 great-grandchildren.

A Blaenavon lady who gave long service to her customers was Mrs E.J. Morris of the Alma Inn, Blaenavon ( 89), believed at that time to be the oldest licensee in Wales. She had vivid memories of polling day riots at Blaenavon in 1868 when soldiers were called to keep the crowd back while the Riot Act was read. (She died in March 1950).

Miss Ellen Allen of Abersychan celebrated her 100th birthday in 1949. She told the Mayor of Newport: 'I always knew I would live to be 100 and I am just as sure that I will reach 110. Then you can really make a fuss!' Miss Allen lived at Garndiffaith until 1933 and from the age of nine until she was in her twenties had worked with her father in the furnaces at the old British Iron Works, Abersychan. After wheeling heavy barrow-loads all day she earned a little extra money by fetching beer for the men on the night shift.

William Jacob of Victoria Row, Blaenavon, became a centenarian in May 1952. He was serenaded by the choir of Blaenavon OAP Association and congratulated by his neighbour, Edmund Lewis, who was a mere 96.

Mr and Mrs Cobner of Park Street, Blaenavon, on the day of Stephen's 90th birthday in 1959, recalled their long years together. He had started work at the age of 11 at Big Pit Colliery, where he worked ten hours a day, except Saturdays (a short day), as a 'doorboy'. It was his job to open and shut a ventilation door for the horses and trams of coal to pass from the coal face to the turn-out. When asked if he was frightened being alone in the dark, he replied, 'No, I amused myself catching rats in a trap.' Mrs Cobner talked of how she used to walk over the mountain to enjoy a day at Abergavenny May Fair. 'With threepence in my pocket, I would be rich and walk to and from Abergavenny on a bottle of pop and a penny bun.'

William Hughes, (92) of Hawthorn's, Llanover Road, Blaenavon died in January 1958. He was one of Blaenavon's oldest inhabitants and a well known local personality. He had been an undertaker and a master carpenter in the town. He was the last surviving craftsman who had worked on the building of the Blaenavon Workmen's Hall.

In August 1959 Mrs Sarah Jane Jenkins, Blaenavon's oldest inhabitant celebrated her 99th birthday. Following a bad fall at her home in Hill Street, she became one of the first patients of Blaenavon Hospital's beds for the chronic sick.

A celebration in July 1960 for the 100th birthday of Mrs Sarah Jane Jenkins, a patient at Blaenavon Hospital, had to be postponed when it was found out that she was two years younger than she had previously thought and would not become a centenarian until 1962. 'I don't want to be 100,' she said. 'I have lived long enough, it is time for me to go.'

In January 1990, Mrs Eliza Ann Evans (103) of New Inn died at the County Hospital, Griffithstown. She was born in Fowler Street, Wainfelin in 1886 and had thirteen children and the eldest son Bill was now 78. Altogether she had 24 grandchildren and 37 great-grandchildren with the sum of their ages totalling 826 years !

Mrs Bertha Jenkins, residing at the Ty Bryn Residential hom in Abersychan, celebrated her 100th birthday in September 1999.

## Leader of the band

Gwilym Gwent, the well known Blaenavon band leader decided to emigrate to America in 1872 and he was to be sorely missed. His real name was William Aubrey Williams and he had been born in Tredegar in 1834. On becoming a traffic manager at the Blaenavon Ironworks he had taken charge in 1850 of the Garnddyrus Brass Band which was formed under his conductorship. This band was in great demand for the processions and fetes of the various friendly societies which were held annually in those days.

On settling in America, Gwilym set up two fine brass bands in 1875 at Wilkesburg. He later moved to Plymouth, Pennsylvania, where he died in 1891. Gwylim had become so popular and distinguished as a composer and conductor in his adopted town, that 2,000 people followed his coffin to the graveside and a Welsh choir of 400 sang the old hymn 'Bydd Myrdd o Rhyfeddoau.'

## A night to remember

Six Blaenavon people were injured and a number of others cut and bruised when the entire floor of a room at the Queen Victoria Inn, Garnddyrys, collapsed at about 10.15 pm on Saturday night in August 1946. About thirty people in the room were precipitated nine feet into the cellar of the inn. The majority of the customers were unhurt and sustained only bruises and scratches, but six of them were conveyed to Blaenavon Hospital, where they were treated by Dr Frumin and later sent home. The Queen Victoria Inn was owned at this time by Messrs Facey's Brewery Co., Abergavenny, and the licensee was Mr E. Lewis.

## The first ones

One of the leading Irish citizens in Pontypool at the turn of the century was R.W. Fynn. In 1902 he became the first man in Pontypool to drive a hansom cab and a few years later the first to own a motorised taxi. He ran his business from the Crown Stables (later called the Crown Garage), at the bottom of George Street. He also drove the Pontypool Fire Engine and the Pontypool Hospital ambulance.

In February 1915 Henry Griffiths passed away in his 91st year. He had been the first stationmaster at Pontypool Road and subsequently gave his name to Griffithstown. He could also claim that his father had fought at the battle of Corunna, and his uncle was commander of a frigate at the Battle of Trafalgar.

William Barnett and his brother Harry started the Eastern Valley Motor Service in 1921. Their solitary vehicle was a chain-driven 332 seater Commer and it did sterling service for a number of years. The firm grew steadily until 1929, by which time the Barnett brothers had 25 buses in their garage at Pontnewynydd, but in that year the company merged with the Western Welsh Company.

The first journey made by Blaenavon's new fire engine was made in June 1939, to carry the body of Chief Officer F.D. Willis to St Peter's Churchyard. Mr Willis had received the engine when it had been handed over to the town's Fire Brigade. His helmet and axe rested on the coffin.

During July 1946 Pontypool's first policewoman, Miss Verlie Edwards of Newbridge was appointed. She was a slim, attractive brunette, 5ft 8ins in height, who during the war had served for three years as a volunteer telephonist with the National Fire Service.

Mr I.G. Thomas of Blaenavon was appointed in that year to succeed Canon A.A. Matthews as a foundation trustee of Blaenavon Endowed Schools. He was the first layman to act in this capacity since the erection of the schools in 1816.

April 1947 saw the death of the Reverend Mother Celinia Cadio (83), at Pontypool Convent. She was the first Daughter of the Holy Ghost to come to this country from Pontivy, Brittany in 1902. Twenty two years later she came to Pontypool and was the Reverend Mother at the Convent from 1926 to 1938, when she became a semi-invalid and retired.

In 1949 Blaenavon's first postman, Mr. James Smith, died at the age of 84. He had been appointed in 1885 at a wage of 15s 10d (80p) a week. At that time he could carry the whole of Blaenavon's correspondence in one hand! Few of the older folk could read and he often had to read their letters to them and explain the contents.

Ted Wilson of Lower Waun Street, Blaenavon, reached the age of 92 in 1950. He was the first Eastern Valley man to kick a football. This was at Pwlldu in 1871, when the recently arrived English school-master had a ball made to his specification in Abergavenny. This was the year when the Rugby Society (afterwards the Rugby Union) was formed.

Miss Jean Williams was appointed in June 1954, by the Blaenavon Male Voice Choir as their new conductress. She was the first woman to hold that position and it was under her baton that in October of that year the choir won first prize at Talybont Eisteddfod.

Blaenavon's first woman pastor was 24 years old Nanett Lewis-Thomas and she took up her duties at Lion Street Congregational Church in 1965. She was the third woman to be ordained into the Congregational Church in Wales.

The Eastern Valley's first ever Mayor was William Henry Arnold, a local businessman and chairman of Blaenavon Rent and Ratepayers' Association. He was elected in February 1974 at the first meeting of the town's new Community Council.

In September 1996, Peter and Susan Knight were the first ever couple to be married at St Paul's church in Blaenavon. This was the first marriage ceremony to be licensed at the church.

**The last ones**

With the death of Mrs Alice Preece, aged 65 in January 1935, passed the last surviving member of the Allgood family, the pioneers of the Pontypool Japan industry.

On June 8th 1939, Mrs R.J.M. Tenison, daughter of the late John Capel Hanbury, returned to Pontypool to visit her family home for the first time since she was six years old. It was the 25th anniversary of St Alban's Convent, which used to be the Hanbury family residence. Celebrations included a garden party in the beautiful grounds and the grand opening ceremony, presided over by the Rev Mother Superior, took place in front of the main entrance to the school.

Mrs Minnie Flora (81) of Pontypool died at the local hospital in July 1946. Her passing severed a link with the Chartist movement in Monmouthshire, for she was one of the two remaining grand-daughters of the Newport livery man, Henry Gwyther, who was so prominently connected with the riots that he lost his business.

Robert Trump, Pontypool's last town crier before the advent of loudspeakers, died in November 1956. He had spent many years tramping the district posting bills and 'crying' meetings and public announcements. In addition he had served on the Pontypool Council for 27 years and was Chairman in 1923-24, the year before the Royal National Eisteddfod was held in the town.

In October 1957, Mrs Dinah Lewis of Abersychan the last surviving widow of the Llanerch Colliery disaster died on her 93rd birthday. She was known as 'Aunty Dinah' to generations of Abersychan people - having lived there all her life. When her husband was killed, she was just 25 years old, but never re-married. She was the last of the 259 dependents (including 72 widows and 166 orphans) of the explosion victims to benefit from the trust fund set up for their relief.

Thomas Harvey, licensee of the Panteg Hotel, Sebastapol, passed away in May 1966. He was one of 'The Few' who saved this country during the Battle of Britain and served in Squadron Leader Bader's squadron and had thirteen 'kills' to his credit.

**Service to the Community**

Pontypool people in May 1921, were saddened to hear that Squire John Capel Hanbury JP DL, died at his home in Sevenoaks, Kent, at the age of 68. During his life he had generously made countless gifts to local causes. In particular he provided the site on which Pontypool Hospital was built and financially helped the hospital in its early days. When his son Capel L.C. Hanbury died in 1908, the Squire added a wing to the hospital to commemorate him. He also provided sites for the West Mon School, St Hilda's Church, Griffithstown, and numerous other local buildings. John Hanbury was cremated at Golder's Green Crematorium. He left a widow, Louisa Charlotte Hanbury, and a twenty-year old daughter, Ruth Julia Margaret.

Blaenavon Council's first chairman, Mr Henry Morgan Davies JP of Broad Street, died in June 1934, at the age of 85. He became Chairman of the Council in 1894 when the old Local Board, of which he was a member, became defunct.

Mr John Morgan, surveyor to Blaenavon Council from 1914 to 1932, died in 1935 at the age of 91. He went to Blaenavon as foreman of the building department of the Blaenavon Company, and later set up in business on his own account. Among the buildings he erected were the Workmen's Hall, the Co-operative Society building in Ivor Street and the reconstruction of Blaenavon Council offices.

In 1941 Arthur James JP, of Griffithstown, was appointed by the King as High Sheriff of Monmouthshire. He was formerly general manager of Messrs Baldwin's Panteg Steelworks and had served on a number of local government bodies, including the Monmouthshire County Council and Pontypool Council. He was also a past chairman of Pontypool Rugby Club.

Another local man who had served as High Sheriff of the County (in 1916) was John Paton, managing director of Partridge Jones and John Paton Ltd. of Pontnewynydd. He was a member of the old Abersychan Council and Monmouthshire County Council. In addition he became President of Pontypool RFC, Pontypool Golf Club and Pontypool Cricket Club. He died in February 1943 at the age of eighty.

In April 1946, Mr William Henry Vipond Bythway, clerk to Pontypool Council announced at the last meeting of the old Council, his intention to resign his position on June 30th, thus ending an unbroken period of service of fifty years to public authorities in the Eastern Valley. He said, 'For the whole of that period I have tried to do my best for the district. I have been criticised I know, but fortunately or unfortunately I never took the slightest notice of that criticism. If I had done so I should have been dead long ago.'

Mr Bythway died on 20th November 1949 at his home, Glantorfaen, Pontypool, at the age of 82. This native of Pontrhydyrun was a son of the late Henry Bythway, solicitor of Pontypool, a grandson of a former Wesleyan Circuit minister, and a great-nephew of the late John Vipond, founder of the Varteg firm of that name and one of the oldest colliery proprietors in South Wales. Wiliam Bythway became the first clerk of the new Pontypool Council in 1935 and continued to hold that office until his resignation in 1946.

In July 1970 nurse Catherine Maud Carson of Pontypool died at the age of 80. She had been a midwife in Pontypool for nearly fifty years and during that time had brought at least 4,000 babies into the world.

Fred Percy, one of Blaenavon's best known and respected citizens, retired in September 1975, after 60 years of living up to his own personal motto ' Greater love hath no man than that he liveth his life in the service of his fellow men.' He was manager of Fowlers, the town's main drapers for over a quarter of a century. He was an honorary life member of the local Chamber of Trade, a vice-president and life member of Blaenavon Bowls Club, a founder member of the town's OAP Christmas fund which was set up in the 1920's, and Chairman of the Torfaen Community Savings Society. At one time he was a keen sportsman, playing rugby and soccer with a little boxing in between.

Jack Salter, in January 1976, retired as editor of the 'Free Press' having been responsible for 2,000 weekly issues of the paper. He had been associated with the paper for over 56 years, from 1919 to 1928 on a part-time basis and since 1928 as editor. He was succeeded by Mr Don Touhig.

Councillor Dennis Wynham Puddle was installed as the fourth Mayor of Torfaen in a ceremony at Pontypool Town Hall in June 1976. He was born in Garn-yr-erw and worked for 20 years from the age of 15 as a miner. He joined the Labour Party at 16, following in the footsteps of his grandfather, Mr Arthur Evans, a founder member of that Party. Mr Puddle, a plant attendant at Big Pit, was awarded the BEM in 1962 for his services to mining.

In April 1988, a plaque to mark the birthplace of the former leader of London County Council, Sir Isaac Hayward, was unveiled at Blaenavon by Eric Robinson, Chairman of Blaenavon Town Council. He was born at 13 King Street in 1884. His trade union activities led him into local government and he was elected to Blaenavon Urban and Monmouthshire County Councils. In 1928 he was elected a member of the London County Council for Rotherhithe and remained a member of the authority until 1965. He was leader of the Council - London's 'Prime Minister' - from 1947 until his retirement from local government in 1965 and he was given the Freedom of the boroughs of Bermondsey and Deptford. He was knighted in 1959 and died in 1976.

The death occurred in August 1977 of Hugh Llewellyn Hughes MBE, proprietor of the Griffin Press, Pontypool, at the age of 82. The Griffin Press was founded by his father David W. Hughes, a brother of Henry Hughes, who at the same time acquired the Pontypool Free Press from its founder David Walkinshaw, who started the paper in 1859.

Fred Gifford, Torfaen's first Freeman of the Borough and a former member of the Borough Council, received the MBE from the Queen at Buckingham Palace in March 1981. He was given the award in recognition of his endeavours on behalf of the community.

In April 1989 Adrian Babbidge, who had been director of the Torfaen Museum Trust since it was formed in 1978, left the Eastern Valley to take up a new post based in Nottingham, as Director of the East Midlands Area Museum Service. He had worked hard during the previous ten years developing and implementing the work of the Trust.

Fred Gifford, Torfaen's first Freeman of the Borough and a former member of the Borough Council received the MBE from the Queen at Buckingham Palace in March 1981. He was given the honour for his endeavours on behalf of the community.

Local historian and author Reginald Nichols (75) died in July 1986. He was born in 1910 in Pontypool and educated at West Mon School. He spent most of his career working as a civil servant until his retirement in 1975. Reg was the first chairman of the Pontypool Local History Society and one of the prime movers for the establishment of a museum at Pontypool. He also edited four volumes of the *Monmouthshire Medley*, and wrote an interesting little book entitled *Pontypool and Usk Japanware* .

Jean Williams the well known musical director of Blaenavon Male Voice Choir died in 1996 and a memorial concert was held in September at the Blaenavon Workmen's Hall, the proceeds of which went to cancer research. At the time of her death she was musical director of the Blaenavon Ladies Choir which she had founded in 1974. In her teens she was a fine singer herself and won hundreds of prizes at eisteddfodau. Unfortunately the war prevented her from going to London to train as an opera singer. Instead she·became a teacher and in 1954 was invited to take the baton with the Blaenavon Male Voice Choir, a position which she held for more than 30 years. During this period the choir won many prizes in eisteddfodau, took part in the world famous 1,000 voices concert in the Royal Albert Hall and made concert tours in Norway and Israel.

In June 1999 Dennis Puddle, now aged 81 and recently retired as Deputy Leader of Torfaen Council, received news that he had been awarded the OBE in recognition for his services to local government over a period of five decades. He had been a Labour Councillor for 49 years and was still the Chairman of Big Pit Mining Museum Trust. During his local government career he had served on Blaenavon Urban District Council, Blaenavon and Torfaen Councils, Monmouthshire County Council and Torfaen County Borough Council, where he had been deputy leader and Chairman of Planning for fifteen years.

Another Eastern Valley man to be honoured in the Queen's birthday list was Roy Orringe (76) of Greenmeadow, Cwmbran, who was awarded an MBE in recognition of his work with the National Association of Retired Fire Fighters. He had served as a fireman from 1950 to 1981, during which time he was deputy chief fire officer for Monmouthshire and later Gwent.

**Popular Politicians**

Alderman Arthur Jenkins, born at Varteg in 1884, was the son of a collier and had himself, from the age of 12, worked underground at Viponds Colliery and later at Tirpentwys and Blaenserchan. But all the time he was continuing his education by attending night schools and discussion groups and at the age of 18 he won an Eastern Valley Miners' Scholarship of £30 a year to Ruskin College, Oxford, where he studied economics, political history and social subjects.

On the completion of his Ruskin course, Arthur went to France, where he lived for ten months, learning the language, attending public lectures at the Sorbonne and studying the French political system. He then returned to Wales to work once more in the mines and in 1911 married Miss Hattie M. Harris, daughter of William Harris, Bessemer works manager for the Blaenavon Co. Ltd. Arthur and Hattie had one son, Roy Harris Jenkins, who was educated initially at Pentwyn elementary school. It was here that this small boy declared his ambition by stating, 'I want to be Chancellor of the Exchequer,' when asked to write an essay on 'What I want to be when I grow up.' From Pentwyn he went to Abersychan Secondary School and then on to Balliol College Oxford.

After acting as Secretary of Pontypool Trades Council, Arthur was appointed in 1918, Deputy Miners Agent for the Eastern Valleys District to Mr James Winstone, whom he succeeded as Agent in 1921.

In August 1926 Arthur was found guilty of inciting men employed at Quarry Level to riot and was sentenced by Mr Justice Swift to nine months imprisonment.This brought a great outcry by the Labour Party and Trade Union Movement and he was released after serving 13 weeks of his sentence at Cardiff Prison.

From 1922 to 1936 Arthur was a member of the Labour Party National Executive, and also for a time Secretary of the SWMF. He was elected to Monmouthshire County Council in 1918 and was elected an Alderman in 1926 and Chairman of the Council in 1932.

When Tom Griffiths MP for Pontypool (since 1918) retired in 1935, Arthur Jenkins was the natural successor to the Labour candidature, and he won the seat convincingly against Leonard Capian, a brilliant young barrister whose father was at one time in practice at Abersychan as a dentist. Arthur obtained a record majority of 11,791. His son Roy, in that same year passed the CWB examination at Abersychan Secondary School with six credits and one exemption from matriculation at the age of 14. He too was of course destined to become a well known Member of Parliament.

In May 1936 Arthur Jenkins made a telling speech in the House of Commons in which he appealed to the Government to take steps towards industrial planning by which new industries would be established in Wales. The following year he advocated the immediate erection of a Severn Bridge to help save the depressed areas of Wales. He was appointed in December 1937, Parliamentary Private Secretary to Mr Clement Atlee, Leader of the Opposition.

Roy Jenkins in 1941 obtained a first in Modern Greats at the end of his third year at Balliol College, Oxford, and then entered the Royal Artillery, in which he reached the rank of Captain. In 1945 he married Miss Margaret Jennifer Morris, daughter of Sir Parker Morris, then clerk to Westminster City Council.

Alderman Arthur Jenkins MP was appointed Parliamentary Secretary to the Ministry of Education in August 1945, but three months later had to resign from this position due to ill health and, on his death the following year, he was buried at Trevethin Church.

In 1948 Roy Jenkins, now a 27 year old economist, was elected MP for Central Southwark. When he took his place in the House of Commons, he had the rare honour of being sponsored by the Prime Minister, Mr Atlee (to whom his father had been Parliamentary Private Secretary during the War). Roy Jenkins was appointed by Harold Wilson in October 1964 as his Minister of Aviation at a salary of £5,750 and subsequently became Home Secretary and then Chancellor of the Exchequer, thus achieving his boyhood ambition. He was the first Welshman to hold this position since Lloyd George and in 1968 Roy recalled his boyhood days in the Eastern Valley when he spoke at the prize-giving of the College of Further Education at Pontypool.

In 1970 Roy performed the opening ceremony of a County Council old peoples' home at Blaenavon which was named the Arthur Jenkins Home in honour of his very popular and much respected father. The building was designed to give 35 old people as much independence as possible, being built on one level, without stairs, and was completed within 18 months at a cost of £73,000.

Roy Jenkins the former Abersychan schoolboy who became a Labour Chancellor of the Exchequer and later launched the Social Democrats Party as part of the 'Gang of Four' was given a life peerage in 1987. He maintains a connection with Pontypool through his role as President of the Torfaen Museum Trust.

Daniel Granville West, solicitor of Newbridge, was selected as Labour candidate for the by-election caused by the death of Alderman Arthur Jenkins MP for Pontypool. In the final ballot he received 134 votes to 76 for Mr Roy Harris Jenkins, son of the late Member.

Leo Abse (41) a Cardiff solicitor and former factory worker was chosen in October 1958, from a short list of five, as Pontypool's Labour candidate for the forthcoming election. He received the unanimous approval of the 136 delegates at the divisional management committee meeting. During his election campaign he was heard to comment that the Torys were bringing economic stagnation to the Eastern Valley and that 'their rule resembled a car that lacked a steering wheel!' The following month Leo Abse was elected to Parliament with a majority of 13,727.

He made his maiden speech in the House of Commons when he took part in a debate on the Government's White Paper on 'Secondary Education for All.' He commented that in his constituency there was at Blaenavon one primary school with classes of upwards of fifty children in one room.

In April 1966, Leo Abse was fighting his fourth election at Pontypool and increased his majority for the third time to make it 20,491. His poll of 27,904 votes represented 77 per cent of the total votes cast.

Don Touhig (25) in April 1973 began his journey towards becoming a future MP for the neighbouring authority of Islwyn, by winning the Panteg East seat with a majority of 751. He became the youngest member of the new Gwent County Council.

In 1985 Leo Abse by now 68, the Eastern Valley MP since 1958, announced that he was stepping down at the next election. He told a meeting of Torfaen Labour Party's general management that he had no intention of joining the ranks of ancient politicians who tried to duck the ageing process.

Torfaen MP, Paul Murphy, when Minister of State for Northern Ireland in January 1999, was sworn in as a member of the Privy Council. He joined this ancient body of government ministers, senior members of the House of Lords and senior judges after a ceremony at Buckingham Palace. As a member of the Privy Council he was awarded the life long right to be addressed as 'Right Honourable'. He was awarded this honour in recognition of the work that he had done in the peace negotiations in Northern Ireland. During 1999 he was appointed Secretary of State for Wales.

**Famous Actors**

A one-time Pontypool tinplate-worker became a naturalised American citizen in October 1937. Reg Jones had been born at Neath but was brought up by an aunt in Pontymoile. He worked for six years at Lower Mill before joining the Horse Guards. Later, he bought himself out of the Army and went to America, where he became a Hollywood actor and changed his name to Ray Milland. This name was chosen because he had been born in a house near some mill land - Milland! When he was living and working at Pontypool, his fine upright bearing and distinguished appearance had earned him the nickname of "The Rajah," so it was not surprising that he became an actor. In 1946 he won a Hollywood Oscar for Best Actor for his role in 'The Lost Weekend.'

During May 1948, Anthony Oliver, the Abersychan born actor, was presented to Queen Mary after she had seen a performance of 'The Hidden Years' at the Fortune Theatre, London, in which he took a leading part. In November 1959 Anthony Oliver joined the cast of the Agatha Christie play, 'The Mouse Trap' at the Ambassadors Theatre, London. The play was in its eighth year with 2,903 performances to date and had been seen by nearly a million people.

William Henry Vipond Bythway
Clerk to Pontypool Council

Isaac Butler
Pioneer Industrialist

John Paton
High Sheriff of Monmouthshire

Alderman Arthur Jenkins
MP for Pontypool

Robert John Crump
Pontypool's last Town Crier

Myfanwy Haycock
Pontnewynydd Poet

Gwilym Gwent
Blaenavon Band Leader

David Walkinshaw
Founder of the *Pontypool Free Press*

## Talented Artists

Benjamin Barker the son of a barrister came to Pontypool from Ruthin in Denbighshire in 1750 and became the foreman and enamel painter at the Pontypool japan works. He lived and worked in the town until 1781, occupying a house near the Trosnant factory. He was particularly expert at painting sporting and animal figures, the works being commissioned by proud owners. Also according to the Trevethin church register, he was paid six guineas in 1774 for painting a royal coat of arms. A sporting scene painted by him on japan ware is in the National Museum of Wales. He and his family later moved to Bath where he died in 1793, having been supported in his later years by his son Thomas, the true artist of the family.

Thomas Barker was born at Trosnant in 1769 and it is said that when he was christened in Panteg Church, one of his godfathers, a local eccentric known as 'Mad Tom', insisted on riding into the church on horseback with the child perched in front of him. Thomas displayed a talent for drawing when he was very young. Although he received no formal art training he copied the work of the Italian and Spanish schools to learn and develop his potential. His first exhibition had buyers paying from 50 to 500 guineas for each work at a time when a skilled stonemason was paid the equivalent of 14p a day. He used the money realised from the sale of his early paintings to finance a three year period of study in Rome from 1791 - 94.

He made a considerable amount of money from his work, and erected a house at Sion Hill, Bath, upon the walls of which he painted a fresco 30 feet in length and 12 feet in height, representing 'The Inroad of the Turks upon Scio, in April 1822.' This was his most remarkable work.

Many of Thomas Barker's pictures were landscapes with rustic figures and his best known work of this period, *The Woodman and his dog* was reproduced on Manchester cottons and used as a model for Staffordshire pottery figures, Worcester china and an engraving by Bartolozzi. His painting of 'The Woodman' was presented to Pontypool Urban District Council by Richard Hanbury-Tenison many years ago and can be seen at the Valley Inheritance Museum.

A collection of Thomas Barker's lithographs was issued in 1813 and another appeared the following year. He exhibited at the Royal Academy, the British Institution and elsewhere. His own self-portrait was exhibited in the National Portrait Exhibition of 1868. But after 1820 his popularity as a painter declined, leading to a loss of income accompanied by failing health. By the time he died at the age of 80 in 1847 he was living off a government pension of £100 a year.

## A famous Singer

Gwyneth Jones was born in Pontnewynydd and at 17 years of age in 1953, she won a cup for singing at Cwmfelinfach Eisteddfod. By December 1959 she was one of four soloists who sang in Handel's 'Messiah' at the Royal Festival Hall in the London Welsh Autumn Festival Concert.

This former pupil of Twmpath Secondary School began work as a clerk with the Pontypool Foundry & Engineering Company Ltd., but it was not long before she won a scholarship to the Royal College of Music. In 1960 she received three top awards from the Queen Mother at the College: the Clara Butt Award, the Henry Leslie Prize and the Agnes Nicholls Trophy.

In December 1964 the biggest chance in her operatic career to date, came when she took over the principal role in Verdi's *La Trouvatore* at Covent Garden. Two years later, Pontypool Council cabled their congratulations to this remarkable contralto when she won acclaim for her performance at the Carnegie Hall, New York, in the part of Medea in the American Opera Sociey's Cherubini revival. In 1976 Gwyneth Jones was made a CBE in the Queen's Birthday Honours List.

**A famous Poet**

Myfanwy Haycock was born at Pontnewynydd in 1913. She was educated at Cwmffrwdoer Primary School and Pontypool Girls' School, after which she trained as an artist at the Cardiff School of Art.

Since the age of six she had been writing verse and later turned her attention to short stories and plays. Her first play entitled *Queen Mab's Party* was performed at Bethany Church, Pontnewynydd, when she was just fourteen years of age.

Myfanwy was the chaired bard at the 1932 Ebbw Vale semi-National Eisteddfod and, at the Port Talbot National Eisteddfod in the same year, her lyric entry entitled 'Hill of Dreams' won first prize, which was presented to her by Newport's tramp poet W.H. Davies. A number of her plays and poems were broadcast on the radio and she also made a few television appearances reading her poems.

During her life she worked as a teacher, a wages clerk in a munitions factory, publicity officer in an Agricultural College and a Welfare Officer in a barrage balloon factory. She spent the last years of the Second World War working for the BBC in London.

Over the years she had numerous drawings, articles and poems published in the Western Mail, the Daily Sketch, the Daily Graphic, the Daily Herald, the Free Press of Monmouthshire and the South Wales Argus. Her first volume of poetry entitled 'Fantasy' was published in 1938 and this was followed by two further volumes, 'Poems' and 'More Poems,' which were published during the War.

She moved to Surrey with her husband in 1947 and, some years later, tragically developed a crippling illness and died at the age of 50 in 1963. Her final book 'Mountain over Paddington' was published posthumously the following year.

**Famous Authors**

**Jack Jones**, the well known author was born in 1884 at Tai-Harri-Blawd in Merthyr Tydfil, and he left school at the age of 12 to work in the coal industry. It is of interest that before he became famous as a novelist Jack Jones worked during the 1900s at Llanerch Colliery. A period of unemployment led him at the age of 50 to start his autobiography, 'just for something to do.' He called it *Unfinished Journey* and when it was published in 1934 it had an enthusiastic reception by the reviewers. A preface to the book was written by the Rt Hon David Lloyd George, who commented:'No one can rise from reading this book without a kindlier understanding for the lives of these humble people of the Welsh Valleys, and a profounder admiration for their silent heroism.'

J. B. Priestley said that the book provided, 'A blazingly honest and vivid picture of a period, a class and a man.' It was published on both sides of the Atlantic and was favourably compared with the best autobiographies of all time.

Jack Jones followed this work with a novel, a play, a biography of Lloyd George and then further novels which include *Rhondda Roundabout* , *Black Parade*, *Bidden to the Feast* , *Lily of the Valley* and *Come Night; End Day* .

He was working at Pentrepiod when he was called up as a reservist on 4th August 1914. He later wrote:-

> 'Just when we were settling down nicely in our new home near Pontypool, the War came. My army reserve pay of six-pence per day, paid quarterly, had come in most useful during the years of struggle at Builth Wells, but I never dreamt that I would be called upon to do something for it. Furthermore, I was under the impression that I had drawn my last penny of reserve pay, and that I was free, which evidently was not the case, for I was called to the colours with all the other reservists.
> At Pontypool railway station I helped to crowd the platform. Reservists, scores of 'em, waiting for the Newport train. Women and children seeing them off, a jolly crowd, with an anxious face here and there. Couldn't see any of my old comrades, most of whom would no doubt be boarding trains in the adjoining county of Glamorganshire.'

After the war Jack Jones became the Llanerch Lodge's conference delegate. He finally left the Eastern Valley in 1921 to become the Secretary of the International Lodge at Nantgarw. In July 1940 he returned to Pontypool to give an address entitled 'Wales in Action' to Pontypool Rotary Club at their weekly luncheon at the Clarence Hotel.

For his services to the community and to literature, Jack Jones was awarded the Order of Commander of the British Empire. He died in 1970.

The most famous writer associated with Blaenavon and the surrounding area is **Alexander Cordell** (George Alexander Graber), who was born in 1914 in Columbia, Ceylon. His father was a professional soldier and in due course Alex followed in his footsteps by joining the Royal Engineers in 1932. He served in the ranks until 1936 and was then commissioned, attaining the rank of Major during the Second World War.

Seriously injured during the British Expeditionary Force's retreat from Boulogne in 1940, he spent his convalescence in Wales and developed a love and fascination for the country and its people. As a result, after being demobolised in 1950, he went to live in Llanelen, near Abergavenny in Monmouthshire.

In his spare time, he began to write short stories and his first novel, *A Thought of Honour* was published in 1954. Unfortunately, it was not very successful, but his second novel *Rape of the Fair Country* became an international best seller when it was first published in 1959. Millions of copies have been sold and the book at that time was translated into no less than seventeen languages, thus launching Alexander Cordell's long and successful career as a novelist.

Set in the turbulent times of the Industrial Revolution in 19th century Monmouthshire, the book tells the story of the fictitious Mortymer family and the iron-making communities of Blaenavon, Garnddyrys and Nantyglo. It culminates in the Chartist uprising and their historic march on Newport in November 1839.

Alexander Cordell undertook meticulous research before writing his many novels and many people would agree that no other writer has managed to capture the atmosphere and spirit of 19th century industrial Wales so well.

In July 1977, Alexander Cordell died of a heart attack near Llangollen, North Wales. The following year, in frustration that all his early novels had been out of print for a number of years, Blorenge Books of Abergavenny, obtained the rights to publish editions of Cordell's first Welsh trilogy and as a result special editions of *Rape of the Fair Country* , *Hosts of Rebecca* , *Song of the Earth* , once more came back onto the shelves of the bookshops. (*This Proud and Savage Land* will be published by Blorenge Books during 2000).

Alexander Cordell's *Rape of the Fair Country* and *This Proud and Savage Land* are particularly important to Torfaen for they are both set in the locality of Blaenavon and provide an important stimulus to the tourist industry in this area. People, from many parts of the country and even other countries, who have read and enjoyed the books continue to come here to seek out the places in which Cordell's characters would have lived and worked. The area has thus become a literary landscape, peopled by the larger than life characters of famous novels, for which Alexander Cordell will always be remembered.

**A new Novelist in the Eastern Valley**

Born in north Lincolnshire, **Marguerite Shaw**, a graduate of Sheffield University and a former junior school teacher, settled with her family in the Eastern Valley in 1978. She and her husband Gordon came here, tired of city life, in search of a more peaceful existence in a place where they could enjoy the surrounding countryside.

On joining the local W.I., Marguerite attended a creative writers' course and initially produced short stories and articles. She also compiled three volumes of *Scrapbooks* on the history of Abersychan, Talywain and Garndiffaith. Her first novel *We Shall Sing Again* was published in 1991 and the idea for it came from the words of a song which was said to have been passed on by a survivor of the Llanerch Pit disaster of 1890. the song tells of a little boy who had a nightmare and then begged his father not to go down the pit for he was convinced that there would be a disaster.

Set in Garndiffaith around the turn of the century, the novel tells the story of the fictitious Watkins family, through the eyes of young Robbie and the colliery disaster provides a background to the events which follow. Marguerite's portrait of life in this part of the Eastern Valley at the turn of the century is very moving and through her intensive research, factually accurate.

This first novel touched the hearts of thousands of readers who clamoured for more information about the Watkins family and in due course *Shall We Meet Again* was published. It traces the lives of Robbie and his family through World War I, its effects on the neighbourhood and the eventual emigration to America of part of the family.

Marguerite completed her trilogy with *Love Will Come Again* , which was published in 1996. The story begins in a distant corner of the USA and continues the story of her fictitious characters who left the Eastern Valley during the 1920s in search of a new life. It links the valley communities of Talywain, Garndiffaith and Cwmavon with the inhabitants of the Pend Oreille County in America's Washington state.

In 1996 Marguerite Shaw was appointed Writer in Residence at Cwmbran Library on a project jointly funded by Torfaen Libraries and the Arts Council for Wales. It resulted in residents compiling a written history of life in Cwmbran New Town, which was published in time for the Golden Jubilee of Cwmbran New Town in 1999.

**Ken Jones OBE, Athlete and Rugby Player**

One of the greatest sportsmen that the Eastern Valley has ever known is Ken Jones, who was born at Greenfield Place, Blaenavon, on 30th December 1921. He began his education at Blaenavon Endowed School and then became a pupil at West Mon School, Pontypool. When war broke out in 1939, he was the school Victor Ludorum and also during that year won the Monmouthshire Secondary Schools hop, step and jump title with a record 41ft 7 ins. He won his first track event in 1932.

In August 1935, Ken at the age of 13 was the only Blaenavon competitor at the Abertillery Police Sports and on winning the county boys' scratch championship shield for the 100 yards, a great future was predicted for him.

He then spent two years at St Paul's College, Cheltenham, where in July 1941, he took part in a triangular match between Cheltenham, Birmingham and Bristol. He won the 100 yards, the 220 yards and the long jump and was carried shoulder high around the arena. A period of study at the Loughborough Training College gained him a Physical Education Diploma and he also became the 100 yards and 200 yards Champion.

On joining the RAF his war service included time in India and Burma. Whilst in India in 1945, he won the United Provinces Championship 100 and 200 metres, setting new records, and also won the long jump. Then a year later he represented the provinces at the All-India Bangalore Olympics and his remarkable sprinting performances were compared with those of Jesse Owen, the coloured American Olympic sprinter.

Ken reached the rank of Sergeant and after his demob won the Welsh championship for the 100 and 220 yards in 1946-7-8-9 and also in 1948 won the Southern Counties 100 yards championship in 9.8 seconds. He later on two occasions accomplished this feat, thus becoming the only British athlete to have done so on three occasions. Ken won the Welsh 100 yards and 220 yards championship at Sloper Road, Cardiff, in July 1946, when the Welsh AAA senior meeting was held for the first time since 1939.

In January 1948, Ken married Miss Irene Edmunds, only daughter of Mr and Mrs A.T. Edmunds of Blaenavon at St Peter's Church. Both bride and groom at this time held chief appointments in Bath and Ken was certainly having a good year for he was chosen to represent Great Britain in the Olympic Games at Wembley in London. Wearing a pair of spikes that had been presented to him by Blaenavon Athletic Club Ken ran in the second leg in the 4 x 100 metres in which Britain was placed second to the USA.

For twelve years Ken was also one of Rugby's greatest personalities and he first played for Blaenavon, where in two games he scored 15 points. Commenting on this performance the *Free Press of Monmouthshire* said: 'He has the attributes of a perfect wing - exceptional speed, determination and deadly tackling. He has a bright future.'

Ken certainly played his rugby hard but his opponents always regarded him as the perfect gentleman on and off the field and in November 1946, during his first season for Newport, he was strongly tipped for a Welsh cap.

In 1950 Ken was a member of the British team which toured Australia and New Zealand and he played in all four test matches. His 18 tries on the tour put him at the top of the try scorers' list and his eventual record of 17 tries in Welsh international matches was more than any other player had scored at that time.

A portrait in oils of Ken Jones was presented and unveiled at the Blaenavon Workmen's Hall, in February 1951, by Captain Geoffrey Crawshay, Chairman of the Welsh Board of Health and one of Ken's personal friends. The painting depicts Ken in running kit and was painted by Ifor Williams of Cardiff. It was hung in the main room of the Workmen's Hall as a reminder of this great athlete and as an inspiration to other local boys who might endeavour to follow in his footsteps.

Ken on this occasion was also presented with a bureau-bookcase by Councillor Harry Watkin who was Chairman of the Council at the time when the presentation fund had been started two years previously.

In his reply speech, Ken laughingly recalled his failure as a boy to get into the Blaenavon Church School Rugby Team because he was too small. He then went on to give a word of advice to young athletes.

'Too many people have considered that Wales is backward in athletics because of a lack of facilities. I know there are boys in the valleys who can do as I have done. All they have to do is to grit their teeth and have a real go. Get down to it and put Wales in the forefront of the athletic world.'

He added, 'I have derived a lot of pleasure from doing what I have done, and even more pleasure from the knowledge that Blaenavon has gained a certain amount of good publicity.'

In May 1953 Ken was saddened by the news that Robert Barwell of Blaenavon had died at the age of 74. He was one of the town's best known sportsmen and for several years had been trainer of the Blaenavon RFC. His chief delight was in track runners and such athletes as Billy Witchell and Ken himself had received early tuition from him.

Ken captained the British team in the 1954 Berne European Games and in the same year represented Wales in the Empire and Commonwealth Games at Vancouver, where he gained a bronze medal in the 220 yards. At the end of that year Ken was honoured by Newport Athletic Club who presented him with a handsome framed photograph of himself. The presentation was made in the club's gymnasium and was attended by several hundred people. Lord Aberdare, President of the British Empire and Commonwealth Games Council for Wales, was the principal speaker. He and five other speakers proceeded to heap praise on Ken's head, while the modest sporting idol sat there trying to hide his embarrassment.

When it was Ken's turn to speak, he began, 'What can I say? My past has been revealed, my present laid bare - only my future I can keep to myself.'

After stressing that he had never regretted his choice of clubs, Ken ended, ' I am proud to have been born in Blaenavon, I am proud to be born a Welshman, and I am very proud to be a member of Newport Athletic Club.'

Ken, in May 1955, the year after he had captained the British athletics team at Berne, Switzerland, announced that he was to retire from competitive athletics. He was now 33 and would continue to play rugby in order to make a bid for the four caps in the 1955-56 season which would enable him to beat the 25 year old record of 42 appearances for Ireland by George Stephenson. The following year, Ken resigned his post as sports master at Newport High School and took a job with a motor tyre firm.

Ken finally hung up his rugby boots in April 1958 when he played for Newport against the Barbarians and bid farewell to the game which he had graced so magnificently. In the summer of that year, Ken, now aged 36, had the honour of running into the stadium at Cardiff at the opening of The Commonwealth and European Games. He was the final runner of 600 who had carried the silver-gilt baton containing the message from Buckingham Palace. It had been handed to Roger Bannister on the first leg and he had been escorted by Chris Chataway and Peter Driver.

The 40,000 crowd roared as the name of the runner was announced and Ken, in scarlet vest with the Welsh badge and white shorts, appeared in the entrance to the arena holding the baton high above his head. His mother and father, Mr and Mrs John Jones of Lower Hill Street, Blaenavon, were in the arena and they must have felt very proud of their son that day for this was indeed a fitting honour to such a fine sportsman, who had so often appeared in the scarlet jersey of Wales.

In 1960 Ken Jones was awarded the OBE in recognition of his many sporting achievements. He had won 16 Welsh Championship Gold Medals and 44 International Caps, playing for Wales.

Ken Jones running into the Cardiff Arms Park on the occasion
of the 1958 Empire and Commonwealth Games.

The famous Pontypool Front Row: Graham Price, Bobby Windsor and Charlie Faulkner.
Picture supplied by Pontypool RFC.

Pontypool RFC - Schweppes Cup Winners 1982-83.

A. Richards, S. Rogers, M. Crowley, H. Moreton, C. Huish, G. Price, M. Brown, J. Perkins, M. Jones, G. Davies, S. Jones, P. Lewis, S. O'Donoghue, C. Jones, D. Hussey, C. Norling, W. Jones D. Bishop, L. Jones, L. Faulkner, J. Squire, R. Windsor, M. Goldsworthy, B. Taylor.
Picture supplied by Pontypool RFC.

## Some Sporting Memories

*'Few districts of its size can boast of greater sporting records than Pontypool. Its sportsmen have earned it fame in many parts of the world. It has provided champions in many parts of the world and helped considerably to enhance national prestige.'*

Arthur Clark, 1958

1866 John Capel Hanbury (aged 13) became Patron of the Pontypool Cricket Club.

1877 Madame Richards walked 1,000 miles in 1,000 hours at Cwmbran Gardens.

1891 At a meeting held at the Crown Hotel, Pontypool, it was decided to form a club to be called 'The Pontypool Football Club.' The colours selected were dark blue jersey with light blue sashes and caps and stockings to match.

1893 Blaenavon Wanderers RFC amalgamated with the Athletic Club under the title 'Blaenavon Wanderers Athletic Club'. This name was later dropped in favour of Blaenavon RFC.

1901 Formation of Pontypool RFC.

1901 Formation of Pontnewynydd Cricket Club.

1902 Pontypool Bowls Club was founded at Hillgrove in George Street.

1903 Pontypool Golf Club was formed and a nine-hole course was established at Cock-y-north above the Tranch. The pavilion was formally opened by Reginald McKenna MP, who then played the first round of golf on the course with Mr Lloyd George.

1904 Cliff Pritchard was the first Pontypool man to gain international honours when he was capped against England and Ireland. He was subsequently visited at his home by a Northern Union agent who offered him £150 and good employment if he would become a professional. He refused to be bought over and resolved to remain loyal to Pontypool.

1907 Mr W.I. Thomas of Cwmbran, the well-known rugby full-back became Welsh high-jump champion.

1907 Panteg House Bowling Club was formed at Griffithstown.

1913 David Billington broke the world record for 500 yards at the annual gala of the Abersychan Amateur Swimming Club, completing the twenty lengths of the bath in 6 mins. 27 and two-fifths seconds. This was two and three-fifths seconds inside the world record.

1924 Mr. Tom Mainey made a record billiards break of 124 without a fluke at Blaenavon Liberal Club.

1924 Arthur 'Candy' Evans of Pontypool won the Welsh Amateur Heavyweight Boxing Championships.

1926 Edward Jones (13) of Cwmffrwdoer won the 5 - stone Schoolboy Boxing Championship of Great Britain at the Stadium Club, London.

1927 Pontypool RFC's most memorable season ended. They were the only side to beat the Maoris (by 6 points to 5) and for the first time they beat Newport twice in a season. They also defeated them for a third time in an unofficial match.

1928 David Charles, Blaenavon Workmens' Institute champion billiards player, won the Sunday Express competition for the highest break in England & Wales. In a game which broke all local records he scored breaks of 40, 50, 176, 54, 76 and 134, a total of 530 in 40 minutes.

1931 Flying Officer Douglas Bader the famous Hurricane pilot (who lost his legs in a pre-war crash) played a game of rugby between Pontypool and the RAF in March of that year. He played at outside-half. It was the first visit of the RAF Fifteen to Pontypool, and it produced one of the best games ever seen on the local ground. The Airmen won on a bitterly cold day by two goals, four tries (22pts) to three tries (9 pts.) It was in the summer after this game that Bader had both his legs amputated following a crash. He was only 21 when his accident occurred 12 months after he received his commission in the Royal Air Force.Before his accident he was an aerobatics ace in the Royal London Air Force display at Hendon. He was invalided out of the Royal Air Force, but became so skillful in the use of his metal legs that at the outbreak of war, he passed a flying test when he wished to enlist in theVolunteer Reserve. He was posted to the Fighter Command, and was soon leading a squadron of Canadians.

1932 William Herbert Witchell of Blaenavon became the quarter-mile champion runner of Wales.

1934 Cricketer, Cliff Lloyd scored 143 for Pontypool at the Park on Whit Monday - the highest individual score ever made there. He reached his century in 75 minutes and added the other 43 in less than 20 minutes. He scored 98 in boundaries - three sixes and twenty fours. Pontypool declared at 212 for 7 and dismissed the Newport side for 84.

1935 Harry Gallivan of Cwmbran won the Senior Welsh Cross-Country Championship at Llantarnam by the biggest margin ever recorded for this event. He covered the nine mile course - part of it water logged - in 50 mins 29 secs and finished 1 min 10 secs in front of L.W. Tongue of Newport.

1936 Thomas Jones, an Abersychan billiard player, scored 751 in half-an-hour at the Independents Club, Ludgate Circus, London. A man 'fielded out' at each of the six pockets and threw the ball back to Jones to save time. Potting was his favourite shot. This rate of scoring was claimed to be a world record.

Mervyn Thomas (14) became the first Pontypool boy ever to wear a Welsh schoolboy cap. He was selected as a prop against England at Cardiff.

1938 George Wetton, who retired as a rugby referee at the age of 67, was believed to be the smallest man who ever played for Talywain. At the age of 20, he stood 5ft 2 ins, and weighed only eight stone.

1946 Formation of Forgeside Rugby Club.

1947 Ken Jones of Blaenavon won his first Welsh cap against England.
Also in that year Ken became the first Blaenavon rugby player to be capped for Wales, and turned down an offer of £1,500 by Leeds Rugby League Club. This was said to be the highest bait ever held out to an amateur Rugby player up to then.

1948 A crowd of 14,000 in Pontypool Park, at the Monmouthshire County AAA Championships, saw Ken Jones of Blaenavon, a possible for the Olympic Games, win the 100 yards title in 9.9 seconds, after having registered an even 10 seconds in his heat. His time for the 220 yards was 22.4 seconds, a fifth of-a-second outside the Welsh record.

1948 Tom Richards, 38 years old British Olympic star, finished second in the 26 mile Marathon at Wembley Stadium. He finished 16 seconds behind the winner, 32 years old G. Caberna of the Argentine. He was born and bred at Garnwen Farm, Upper Cwmbran, where he lived until 1935.

Ernie Hopkins, Blaenavon rugby forward was in his 20th season with the club. This was believed to be a record for any Monmouthshire club. He captained Blaenavon in the season1937-38.

1949 Tom Richards, 38 years old Upper Cwmbran runner, finished second in the 26 mile Olympic Marathon.

1950 Ray Cale, Pontypool's Welsh international wing forward joined St Helen's Rugby League Club for a record fee of £2,500, the highest ever paid to a forward from the amateur code.

1952 In Pontypool's last game of the season at Blaenavon, scrum-half Allan Smith created a post-war record. It was his 235th game for the club, which beat the record of Ray Flowers, who played 234 games for Pontypool.

1953 William Thatcher of Pontnewydd, one of the well-known pioneers of rugby football in the lower part of the Eastern Valley died at his home in Cwmbran at the age of 73. He was one of the biggest men to play the game for he weighed nearly 20 stone even in his seventies. At first he played as a forward for Upper Cwmbran, the village of his birth, and he later joined Pontnewydd.

1954 Ritchie Jenkins of Griffithstown, the former Welsh amateur flyweight champion won his eighth successive fight at the Royal Albert Hall, London, where he fought for the first time as a featherweight, beating Peter Mahoney in the third round.

1960 David Jones of Blaenavon set up a new Welsh all-comers weight lifting record with a dead weight lift of 548.5 lbs, beating the previous best by seven-and-a-half pounds. He performed this feat of strength at Blaenavon where the Monmouthshire set weight-lifting championships, organised by the Welsh AWA were held.

1961 Death of Edwin Beddoe Thomas of Pontnewydd at 83. He was a former Welsh rugby international forward who played for Newport more than 300 times. He began his long rugby career with his home team Pontnewydd and was later made a life member of the club (then called Cwmbran). He was a member of the famous Welsh team of 1908-9 who were particularly memorable because they won all their four home international matches and also beat Australia.

1964 Selwyn Griffiths, 22 years old Pontypool motor-mechanic, reached the climax of his short motor-cycling career by winning the Senior Manx Grand Prix at only his second attempt. Riding his Matchless 500 c.c. machine, he covered the six laps of the tricky 38 mile circuit at an record average speed of 96.27 mph.

1966 Clive Rowlands who joined Pontypool RFC in 1961 was voted Welsh Sports Personality of the year for 1965, in a contest organised by the Western Mail. He became the third rugby player to win this, the highest accolade of his country's sportsmen, since its inception in 1954, and all three first found fame in the Eastern Valley. In 1954 Ken Jones, record holder of Welsh caps was its first holder and seven years later Bryn Meredith emulated his feat. Both these world-famous sportsmen first began on the playing fields of West Mon School and then travelled to Newport to make their mark in international rugby.

1967 Four Croesyceiliog Grammar School boys broke the world non-stop table tennis record. They played in the David Evans department store display window at Cwmbran town centre for 205 hours.

1970 Veteran fly-half, Goff Trenchard, probably the oldest man playing rugby in Wales, reached his century of points for the season when he kicked four penalty goals for ICI Fibres Seconds against Blaenavon Harlequins. Goff was 50 years old and a grandfather.

1971 Peter Ratcliffe, an 18 year old Blaenavon athlete was chosen to represent Britain at the 1972 Olympic Games.

1972 Students from Barry Training College broke the world dart record at a darts marathon at the Mall in Cwmbran New Town. They gained 1,300,000 points in 24 hours, breaking the previous world record of 1,000,000 points.

1973 PC Keith Davies, an Old Boy of West Mon. School, became the new British Police weight-lifting champion in the heavyweight division.

1974 Terry Cobner (28), Captain of Pontypool RFC for the sixth successive year, was named Welsh player of the year.

1975 Pontypool's four international forwards, Graham Price, Bobby Windsor, 'Charlie' Faulkner and Terry Cobner were chosen to play for Wales against France.

1975 Robin Williams of Pontypool RFC became the undisputed holder of the Welsh individual scoring record. His total of 373 points put him eleven points ahead of Andy Hill's previous record total of 362.

1975 Eastern Valley top athlete, ex-Twmpath schoolboy Mickey Morris, was ranked Europe's number one 2,000 metre steeplechaser. He was chosen to run at the European Junior Championships in Athens.

The first full international decathlon and pentathlon ever staged in Wales was held at Cwmbran Stadium with Daley Thompson of Essex Beagles taking part.

1977 The world's best hooker, the world's best tight head prop and the world's best flanker (in the opinion of Pontypool) would be facing the All Blacks. Bobby Windsor, Graham Price and Terry Cobner had been chosen to go to New Zealand with the British Lions in May.

1982 Rugby scrum-half David Bishop made a triumphant return to Pontypool after a miracle recovery from a broken neck.

1983/84 Pontypool RFC set a new world points scoring record for one season of 1,607 and 249 tries were scored in the same campaign. Full-back Peter Lewis claimed 472 points - the second highest total ever recorded by a Welsh player in one season.

1986 Graham Price made his 500th appearance in Pontypool colours. He was the most capped Welsh forward of all time.

1987 In May, Chris Hallam, the first man across the line in the London Marathon, received a hero's welcome when he returned home to Cwmbran. The wheelchair athlete had notched up his second triumph in the London event in three years. His time of 2 hours 8 minutes took a massive 11 minutes off his best time, but it was the first time that a wheelchair athlete had actually crossed the finishing line first. Fellow disabled athlete, John Harris fromSebastapol, made it a spectacular Torfaen double by coming fifth in the marathon.

1988 David Bishop of Pontypool RFC signed for Hull Kingston Rovers for £100,000.

1989 Chris Hallam, the well known disabled athlete was awarded the MBE in the 1989 New Years Honours List on the day he celebrated his 26th birthday. He broke his back in a motor cycle accident when he was 17 but his disablement opened up new horizons in paraplegic sports. He achieved a world record in the 50 metre breastroke and has won many awards in wheelchair marathons.

1991 Chris Hallam broke two world records in the wheelchair track championships held at Cwmbran Stadium. He recorded 16.23 seconds for the 100 metres event and shaved almost a second off the existing 200m record, clocking in at 29.20.

1998 Torfaen athletes won 16 gold medals and 3 bronze at the Welsh Schools Championships held in Deeside and Brecon.

Clive Rowlands
Welsh Sports Personality of the Year - 1965.

## WOULD YOU BELIEVE IT?

1859 An instance of the disgraceful practice of wife-selling occurred during a scene of drunkenness and debauchery at Pontnewynydd when a man disposed of his amiable spouse for the valuable consideration of a shilling and a quart of beer.

1859 A 'blind' man called upon a gentleman of Pontypool stating that he was only 5/- short of the amount necessary to get him into the asylum, and the gentleman contributed the required sum. Later the gentleman (a magistrate) entering the Town Hall, was asked for assistance by the same man, but on this occasion the 'blind' man saw that he was recognised and immediately ran off at full speed!

1865 A sheep which had been missing from a Blaenavon farm since the first heavy snowfall of the winter was found under a deep snowdrift, having been there 31 days. When found, it was too weak to stand but careful nursing brought it round and it became quite strong again.

1866 A miner named Henry Williams of Blaenavon, who emigrated from that place in May of the previous year, in hopes of bettering his condition, suddenly arrived home by the 6pm train to the great surprise of his wife and family. The whole family repaired to the Sun Inn to celebrate the happy event, the traveller saying that he was resolved never to set foot on American or any foreign soil again.

1888 A Blaenavon man who visited the Bath & West of England Show imbibed rather too freely, but was helped into a train at Newport, and arrived at Blaenavon in the brake van labelled on his back 'This side up - drunk.'

1909 On Boxing Day afternoon a Christmas party was held at The Hendre, the country seat of Lord Llangattock. A balloon called 'The Mercury' with the Hon C.S. Rolls in charge made an ascent from the grounds of The Hendre and a fair wind took the occupants of the basket to Blaenavon, 25 miles away. They landed safely and then motored back to The Hendre. The passengers included Lady Llangattock, the Hon Mrs Asheton Harbord, Mr Compton and another gentleman.

1912 No local passenger had booked for the passage of the ill-fated White Star liner Titanic. Mr A.R Beynon of Griffithstown, had an application from Crumlin to book two men by this steamer, but owing to a family bereavement the booking was cancelled and he sailed later. Memorial services were held for victims of the Titanic disaster in many local churches.

1914 A rumour was circulating in the valley that a suspicious person thought to be a German spy was asking numerous questions in Pontnewynydd district and the police were informed. The subject was detained in Newport and found to be the advance agent of a circus!

1924 A hen, belonging to Tom Edwards of Pentwyn laid one three-yolked egg and six double yoked.

1929 A donkey straying on the road in Griffithstown was knocked down by a heavy petrol lorry which passed right over him. Horrified spectators were relieved to see the donkey get up and walk calmly away unscathed.

1930 A cow on Ty Poeth Farm, Pontymoel, gave birth to a calf with five legs. The fifth leg protruded from near its front leg but was not so well developed as the others.

1932 'Major', a prize-winning cocker spaniel owned by George Broom of King Street, Blaenavon, was a sire of many famous dogs, but apart from carrying off five premier awards at an Abergavenny dog show, his chief claim to fame was that he once owned a car. He won it in the Pontypool Car Ballot of 1932. The draw took place at St James Hall in Pontypool. The Carnival Queen put her hand into the drum and a man won a joint of meat. She drew out another counterfoil and to everyone's amazement a dog had won a motor-car! It was a great joke and the only one who failed to appreciate it was Major!

1936 A postcard posted early in December in London addressed to a tradesman in Sebastapol arrived at its destination having gone to the Crimea. The sender had omitted to add the all-important word 'Mon'. The card bore a variety of French and Russian words and place-names. One of the places it visited was Moscow. At length it fell into the hands of a post office employee who had a proper appreciation of the importance of the Monmouthshire Sebastapol. In a bold hand he wrote across the only unoccupied space he could find, the word 'Pontypool', and so came the journey's end.

1939 A Talywain man was accosted during the blackout on his way home by a trio of small boys who asked him if he could change a threepenny bit for them and he duly obliged. But when he got home he found the 'coin' was just a neatly filed piece of tin!

1939 A local mathematician estimated that the men using the new pithead baths at Big Pit, Blaenavon, would have to walk 150 miles a year further than they used to. The bath had been built about two hundred yards from the pithead, and that distance had to be covered four times a day - to the baths to get into working clothes, down again to the pit, - up again to bath and change into clean clothes, and then home.

1946 Every morning at the crack of dawn a swan with a broken wing walked up to the front door of a house in Nightingale Row, Pontnewynydd, and tapped confidently on the door with its beak. Experience had taught the bird that this was the way to get a good square breakfast which was duly provided by the occupants of the house, Mr and Mrs Alfred Carr and their two young daughters.

1946 A Cwmavon miner made a statement to Blaenavon police that on his way home from work in the early hours he was confronted by a man with a horse's head and a flowing mane. The police who were bound to investigate his story, kept a close watch between midnight and dawn for a few days, but saw nothing out of the ordinary.

1947 A Llantarnam farmer chartered a special train to convey himself and his family, furniture, cattle and farming machinery, lock, stock and barrel from Llantarnam Station to a farm which he had bought at West Grinstead, Sussex. He travelled with his wife and two children in a saloon coach while the cattle, machinery and the rest of their belongings were carried in about 20 trucks. Thirty cows were among the animals and they were milked in the evening at Llantarnam and in the morning in Sussex.

1948 A cow named Mannington Frankincense aged 11 had a remarkable yearly output of milk for three years which averaged over 2,000 gallons - enough to supply 44 people with a pint each day! Never failing to beat her target, she was milked every six hours during her peak production period, putting 12 gallons into the pail each day. She was one of 65 head of cattle in the Ty Coch (lower New Inn) herd.

1948 An Eastern Valley man looked for a gas leak with a naked light and found it! Fortunately the explosion caused no serious damage.

1950 History was made at Llanfrechfa Church when for the first time in the records of Llandaff and Monmouth Diocesan Association of Change-ringers, six clergymen rang a complete peal of Grandsire Doubles, 5040 changes. It took two hours 52 minutes to ring. The peal marked the ordination of the Rev Roy Hallet, curate of Llantarnam.

1951 Four West Mon schoolboys going home to lunch at ten past one on Wednesday January 19, saw rushing through the sky a disc-shaped object trailing a greenish smoke. Said 13 year old Colin Price, who lived at the Tranch: 'It was the size of a star and spinning round, then it vanished just as suddenly as it appeared. It was visible for about 17 seconds.'

1952 Rainfall started a fire at Ty Pwca housing estate, Upper Cwmbran. A pile of lime began smouldering in a heavy shower and ignited a tarpaulin sheet which in turn set fire to roof timbers and window frames in two partly-completed houses, causing £100 worth of damage.

1954 While cleaning out the lockers at Big Pit Colliery pithead baths during the miners' annual holiday, the attendants were intrigued to find a pair of nylon stockings.

1968 A 124 years old Blaenavon man who had died 94 years previously still had six years to live according to a gravestone in St Peter's Churchyard, Blaenavon. Mr Walter Pearson Follet died in 1874 at the age of 30, but instead of that date appearing on the gravestone, a mistake was made and 1974 was inscribed.

1970 A bible reading marathon which started at Cwmbran town centre ended after 90 hours and 40 minutes of non-stop reading by the 30 youngsters taking part. The youngsters of all denominations read in relays for about half-an-hour at a time.

1975 A Pontypool man who had two ferrets in his pocket and rabbits hanging from his belt claimed that he was Harry Secombe when he was arrested by police officers for poaching.

1976 Pontypool police forwarded details of a reported sighting of Lord Lucan in Blaenavon, to the central office in London which was recording all reports on the missing Earl. A man resembling Lord Lucan was seen driving towards Brynmawr from the Racehorse public house on a Saturday evening in a white Vauxhall Viva.

1977 A mysterious star-like object was seen hovering over Twm Barlwm. An observer remarked, 'It was a clear night and all the stars were out. I suddenly noticed this star-like thing hovering over the mountain. It was not like any of the other stars - a lot bigger in fact - and it was flashing red, green and white. I thought that i must be a plane, but when it failed to move I began to think differently about it. There was an eerie presence about it - as if it was watching Cwmbran. I kept an eye on it while I walked and I noticed that very slowly it was descending. The object continued to fall until it was nearly on the mountain and then suddenly disappeared. I did not see it again - in fact I did not want to see it, for it made me feel uncomfortable.

1985 Bomb disposal experts from Hereford were called to the giant Cwmbran Tower Block in the early hours of Tuesday morning to detonate what police described as an 'elaborate hoax.' The device in question was a gas cylinder with a clock and wires attached to it and was placed at the bottom of the stairs leading to the car park under the flats. The device was spotted by police officers checking the flues after an anonymous phone call to Newport police station revealed that a bomb was to go off in 'a tower block.'

## -- 11 --

## Celebrations and Royal Visits

*'Pontypool has been the first town to celebrate the Queen's Jubilee. On Easter Monday a grand fete was held in Pontypool Park, the owner of which, Mr J. C. Hanbury, a descendant of the founder of the Pontypool iron industry, kindly placed both Home and Deer Park at the service of the public.'*

*Illustrated London News* 1887

People of the Eastern Valley have always been very enthusiastic about celebrating any event that was of local or national importance, and the Hanbury family kindly allowed their extensive grounds to be used for many a public occasion such as a local fete or a royal celebration.

The coronation of Queen Victoria in July 1838 provided an ideal opportunity for a very special celebration that would be remembered by people of the Valley for many years to come and the festivities at Pontypool were recorded by the *Monmouthshire Merlin* as follows:-

> By break of day the inhabitants of the town and neighbourhood were awoke from slumber by a salute of twenty-one cannons from the banks of the canal and the town fortifications, which were answered from the batteries on the heights of Cae Brest, and Blaendare, and which reverberated their inspiring echoes from hill to hill incessantly during the day. The royal standard of immense size and beautifully executed, waved magnificently on the ramparts of the extensive mansion of the respected Lord Lieutenant of the County, Capel Hanbury Leigh, Esq., whilst triumphal arches, flags, banners, colours etc. with V.R. crowns, etc. adorned the dwellings of the inhabitants of the town. The Bronzed Gate - which for chasteness of design and excellence of workmanship, cannot be excelled - at the entrance to the park at Pont-y-moile, was most tastefully decorated with laurels, flowers, evergreens, etc and a semi-circle with VICTORIA in letters of two feet, formed of white rosettes, surmounted with a splendid crown of six feet in height, and proportionate width.
>
> The whole of the men employed at the works in Pontypool were, by the generosity of C.H. Leigh Esq., supplied with one quart each of strong beer, and never was a day passed with greater harmony and comfort than that of the Coronation of her most gracious Majesty.
>
> A bonfire at the Race Works with about six tons of wood and coals, and one in the Blue Boar Field which continued burning all night, and shone resplendently on the distant country, with several fire balloons which were let off at intervals, concluded the festivities of the day.

In May 1853, the birth of John Capel Hanbury (who was to be the last Squire of Pontypool) was celebrated by his proud father, Capel Hanbury Leigh on a grand scale. He arranged for an ox to be roasted in the Vegetable Market and then carried in state to the Park, where some 20,000 people gathered.

Blaenavon in September 1859, celebrated the opening of a new puddling forge and the festivities in the town on that day were reported in the *Pontypool Free Press*:-

> 'After the opening of the new puddling forge at Blaenavon, a monster procession of 3,000 was formed and a volley of cannons fired. The tradesmen then proceeded to the market tavern to partake of a dinner consisting of a fat sheep (which had been roasted whole) provided gratis by the worthy landlord Mr D. Eley.
>
> Mr Eley had erected near his house a greasy pole, on the top of which was a large shoulder of mutton, which was to become the prize of anyone who succeeded in obtaining it by climbing the pole. It was eventually reached late in the evening by a person who got up by the aid of a couple of ropes. A number of barrels of beer were subscribed by the tradesmen and publicans, and distributed among the workmen, each man receiving one quart.'

In 1863 the marriage of Prince Albert Edward and Princess Alexandra was celebrated at Pontypool by the distribution of meat to about 1,000 poor persons. A public luncheon was held at the Clarence Hotel, and at night a ball at the Town Hall was attended by 35 gentlemen and 29 ladies. Streets and businesses were brilliantly lit with gas jets, arches were lit with small lamps, and fireworks were let off.

Pontypool Park Fete in June 1867, featured Menotti, the 'Stockholm Wonder,' who was reputed to be more daring than the famous Blondin. It was advertised that he would walk, skate and ride a bicycle across a wire three-eighths of an inch thick.

On Easter Monday, 1887, Pontypool became the first town in Britain to celebrate the Golden Jubilee of Queen Victoria. A grand fete was held in Pontypool Park, by kind permission of John Capel Hanbury. It was organised by Captain Gus Bevan of the Pontypool Fire Brigade, the proceeds, with the exception of a small quota for the Fire Brigade, being put towards the erection of a Free Library.

Special trains were run to Pontypool from all parts of Wales and the West of England and as a result some 80,000 people were present at the fete. The chief feature of the day was the Eisteddfod, in which some of the finest choirs in England and Wales competed for prizes amounting to £200. The test piece selected was 'Wretched Lovers' from *Acts and Galatea*. This was also the piece chosen for the National Eisteddfod to be held in London during that summer. The first prize was awarded to Dowlais, and the second to Llanelly, while Burslem was honourably mentioned.

The Ox Procession, 1853.

A fine Devon ox purchased from the Queen was led in procession round the town and then slaughtered, under the direction of a committee of butchers, and carefully prepared and roasted, as the central part of a feast for 3,000 poor people. It was intended that a hoof of the ox would be mounted in gold and presented to the Queen in the form of an inkstand as a momento of the occasion. The head of the ox was later mounted and hung in the Fire Station on Osborne Road.

The Pontypool Fire Brigade steam engine, which had been purchased the previous year, pumped water to form ornamental fountains. Later in this Jubilee year of 1887, the Pontypool Brigade were invited to take part in a Royal review of firemen at Windsor Castle, where Captain Gus Bevan was to drive the Brigade steam engine which had been christened 'John Hanbury'.

Among other entertainments during the fete was an exhibition by Chevallier Blondin who skillfully performed on the high wire. His act included carrying his son across the rope, and riding along the wire on a penny-farthing bicycle. The climax of his performance was reached in the evening when he appeared surrounded by fireworks, which were supplied by Messrs Brocks of London and featured a fire-portrait of the Queen.

Blondin's real name was Jean Francois Gravelet and he was born in France in 1824. He thrilled thousands of people at the Pontypool fetes in 1886, 87, 90 and 95, while his most famous feat was to cross a wire above the Niagra Falls. He died in London in 1897.

In July 1898 the people of Torfaen, along with the rest of the country mourned the passing of one of the greatest commoners that England had ever known. William Ewart Gladstone had been a leading figure in the political history of the country and a popular Prime Minister for many years. Memorial Services were held in various chapels throughout the Eastern Valley.

On 28th January 1901, King Edward VII was proclaimed at Pontypool by Surgeon-Major Essex, Vice- Chairman of the Council and in August of the following year, a great many festivities were held throughout the Eastern Valley to celebrate the Coronation. It was commented in the Free Press that the 'Illuminations were resplendent and there was a lavish display of flags and bunting.'

Garndiffaith celebrated King Edward's coronation by staging the first carnival to be held in the Eastern Valley. The parade was headed by the Garn Band and during the occasion watches were presented to three soldiers who had just returned from the Boer War.

A vast crowd were horrified to witness a serious accident which befell Captain Arthur Spencer, the intrepid parachute jumper. After he had jumped from his balloon a sudden change of wind carried his parachute into Trevethin Churchyard. It collapsed among the trees and Captain Spencer was flung against a tombstone. The cross on the stone was broken off and he suffered a fractured thigh.

In May 1907 the star attraction at the Whitsun fete held at the Polo Ground was the dare-devil Schreyer, whose novel aerial acrobatics were quite alarming to watch. His idea of fun was to propel himself down a specially constructed gradient, then leave the machine in mid-air and fly with the greatest of ease to land in a small tank of water. His performance at the 1907 fete may easily have been his last for he misjudged the distance and scraped the side of the tank as he landed, hurting himself quite badly.

The Whitsuntide fete at Pontypool Park in 1909 featured the appearance of H.P. Ponchery, who was featured as 'Blondin's Successor.' His act was described as follows:-

> ' He walks the rope 60 or 70 feet high, in a suit of armour carrying his balancing pole, and then having divested himself of the armour, lies on his back on the rope, turns a somersault and stands on his head. He next stands and sits in a chair placed on the rope, and afterwards he and two assistants, one a lady, form a 'living wheelbarrow'. His concluding item is an 'elephant' on the rope. Ponchery forms the head and forefeet in the 'property' elephant skin, with the balancing pole apparently in his trunk; a second man makes the hind quarters and a third rides on Ponchery's shoulders.'

In May 1910, King George V was proclaimed at Pontypool by Mr Probyn, the Council Chairman. His reading of the proclamation outside the Town Hall was preceded by a fanfare of trumpets. The coronation of King George V and Queen Mary took place on Thursday June 22 1911, and was marked by celebrations throughout the Eastern Valley. All the schoolchildren of Pontypool took part in a mammoth parade through the town and this was followed by afternoon sports in the Park. Thousands of gas-filled Coronation balloons were let off and as darkness fell, many beacons, set up by local bonfire committees were lit on the surrounding hills.

August 1924 is well remembered as the occasion when the Royal National Eisteddfod of Wales was held in Pontypool Park. The outstanding event was undoubtedly the visit of the Prince of Wales ('Iorweth Dywysog'). Between 20,000 and 30,000 people lined the road from Pontypool Road Station to the Park on Tuesday 5th August to welcome the very first Royal visitor to Pontypool.

Inside the main pavillion at the 1924 National Eisteddfod in Pontypool Park.
Torfaen Museum Trust.

The Prince was received in the Park by Mr. D.C. Udell, Chairman of the Council, who read a civic address of welcome. The Chairman of the Eisteddfod Committee, Mr Benjamin Nicholas JP., also received the Royal visitor on behalf of the Eisteddfod Committee, and the Archdruid 'Elfed' read the Gorsedd address of welcome.

Accompanied by Lord Treowen (Lord Lieutenant of Monmouthshire), Commandant J. O. Tyler JP (in charge of the parade) and others, the Prince inspected the ex-servicemen's Guard of Honour and chatted with a number of old soldiers and sailors.

Unfortunately the weather was somewhat blustery for the Gorsedd ceremony and one writer described it as follows: 'The clouds hung heavily over Mynydd Maen that morning, and the mists gave a hint of possible rain. At Penygarn a strong breeze - a bardic breeze I might call it, with appropriate poetic licence - blew across the Gorsedd circle, fresh and invigorating.'

In the afternoon the Prince was invited into the Bardic Circle by the Archdruid before a packed pavilion, and thus followed in the footsteps of his father and grandfather, both of whom were Welsh Bards. The Archdruid mounted the Loganstone and the trumpeteer having sounded the summons, east, west, north and south, the Gorsedd prayer was offered and the ceremony began.

The Prince was invested by the Archdruid, who tied the green ribbon of an ovate to his left arm. Lord Treowen, the Lord Lieutenant of Monmouthshire, then invested the Royal Bard with his bardic robes.

The Prince stated that he hoped that he might inherit some of the poetic spirit of the ancient people who for centuries had delighted in 'heroic story, and far-descended song,' and that, like those around him, he might be stirred by 'skilful rhyme and soaring music,' to contemplate and practise the higher things. During the Crowning of the Bard ceremony the Prince himself placed the crown on the head of the victor and helped him to hold the Great Sword above his head. After the ceremony, the Prince took tea in one of the anterooms with Lady Treowen and Mrs Paton.

In October 1924 the Urban District of Pontypool adopted the suggestion of Lord Treowen to designate the re-constructed Town Bridge as 'Pont Iorwerth Dywysog' in commemoration of the visit of the Prince of Wales to the Royal National Eisteddfod of Wales at Pontypool, and of his assumption of the Bardic title of 'Iorwerth Dywysog' on his admission to the Gorsedd of Bards. A commemorative plaque would be placed on the bridge and in time the structure would be known as Prince Edward's Bridge. It also had the distinction of being one of the first bridges in the whole country to be built of reinforced concrete!

During the 1930s, Pontypool Park became the venue for the Pontypool Hospital Fete, the proceeds of which were used to help run the town's hospital. Many famous celebrities visited Pontypool during this period as special guests, to help the worthy cause. They included Amy Johnson, the first woman to fly solo from Britain to Australia, and Johnny Weissmuller, the cinema's best known Tarzan. When Tommy Farr the Welsh heavyweight boxer visited the fete in June 1937 he attracted the biggest crowd the event had seen since it was inaugurated in 1929.

The Royal Silver Jubilee was celebrated in May 1935 with the planting of a Jubilee oak in the Italian Gardens. Alderman W.C. Watkins JP, the first Chairman of the new Pontypool Council performed the ceremony which had a dual purpose, for it also celebrated the amalgamation of the three urban areas of Pontypool, Abersychan and Panteg.

Sir Alan Cobham's great Air Display held in August 1935 at Race Farm, Pontypool, was a memorable event and his team of aviators gave thrilling displays to thousands of enthralled spectators. There were six craft at the display, four two-seater planes, an airliner and a wingless autogyro. A massed formation flight of these machines formed the opening manoeuvre of each afternoon's programme. One particularly clever stunt was that of looping by three aircraft tied with ribbon. They executed a number of perfect loops and finally landed with the ribbons unbroken.

Ten local people enjoyed free rides which they won in a competition organised by the Free Press. Mr W. J. Uphill, aged 81, of Trosnant, looped the loop six times and enjoyed every minute of it!

The sky 'Traffic Cop,' the wingless autogyro, was an object of wonder and its evolutions produced gasps of amazement from the crowd. It flew with its engine roaring at 140 miles an hour and at three miles an hour; it could hover motionless in the face of the slightest breeze, or could go straight up or straight down. The pilots called it the 'performing flea.'

Miss Joan Meakin, the 'gliding girl' with her new 'Wolf' glider, was towed up to 1,000 feet or so by an aeroplane and cast adrift. She looped and rolled her glider providing a marvellous demonstration of the thrills and delights of engine-less flight and was given a tremendous reception when she landed. The display concluded with a parachute descent by Mr Ivor Price. He leapt from the aircraft and landed perfectly, right in the centre of the playing field.

Between 15,000 and 20,000 people walked up to the Folly Tower for the lighting of the Silver Jubilee bonfire. Mr W. J. Everett, Pontypool solicitor, lit the fire and flames quickly ran up to the top of the 20ft beacon which contained nine tons of material. Other fires were also lit on hill tops on both sides of the valley.

In February 1936, the proclamation of His Majesty King Edward VIII was made outside the Pontypool Town Hall by Alderman W.C. Watkins, Chairman of the Council. King Edward was succeeding his father, King George V, who had died two days previously at Sandringham.

Memorial services were held throughout the Eastern Valley on the day when King George V was buried in St George's Chapel, Windsor. For the first time in history a Royal funeral was broadcast and, as all the shops, public houses, and most places of business were closed, the people of the Eastern Valley were able to follow on wireless the procession from Westminster Hall, where the king had lain in state, to Paddington Station, and the solemn beauty of the last rites at Windsor. The service at Windsor ended at 2.30 pm. At most of the local churches, memorial services followed at 3 o' clock, though some had been arranged for the evening and there was a crowded congregation at every church.

Later that year in November, King Edward VIII announced that he would visit the depressed areas of the South Wales Valleys. He asked that there should be as little ceremony as possible because he wished 'to devote the whole of the time available to studying the conditions of the unemployed, and the plans to aid them in obtaining work.'

His Eastern Valley tour started at Cwmbran on November 19th and the whole town turned out to meet him. The Royal train had been driven from Usk by Mr Hathaway of Griffithstown, who was believed to be one of the youngest men ever to drive a Royal train.

A group of unemployed men in Cwmbran presented a petition to the king, which had been signed by many of the out of work men of that locality and it informed him of their desperate plight. He was urged to use his influence with his Ministers to foster the introduction of new industries in the district.

The petition included a brief summary of the loss of employment in the Cwmbran area and ended with the statement:-

> 'Thus with the closing of these works in Cwmbran and Pontnewydd your Majesty will see that 2,250 men have been put out of work. We, the unemployed of Cwmbran, have been looking forward to your Majesty's visit with the hope that some tangible improvement and benefit will result.'

The King was heard to say, 'I am really here to help you all I can, you know, and you may be sure that I will do all I can. We certainly want better times brought to these Valleys.'

At Pontypool the King entered No 54 Folly View, Penygarn, the home of Alfred and Mary Morgan and their children, Dorien (aged 12) and Ronald (3). 'Terrible! Terrible!' he said when told that 35 per cent of the tenants of the Penygarn council houses were unemployed.

H.M. King Edward VII talking to ex-serviceman Charles Heare at Penygarn.

The Royal itinerary had not originally included a stop at Blaenavon, but almost at the last minute the plans were altered to allow the King to spend some time there. People crowded the streets of the town, eagerly awaiting his arrival and as the time drew near, the bell ringers of St Peter's Church rang peals of welcome, with great enthusiasm.

As the King's Humber car came into sight he was given the loudest cheer ever heard in the town and the Blaenavon Colliery Workmen's Band, led by Mr W. Ireland, struck up the National Anthem. Among those present to greet the King were Mr A.H. Holder JP., Chairman of Blaenavon Council, Mr I.G. Gwyn Thomas, Clerk and Financial Officer to the Council (as a result of whose untiring efforts the King's stay at Blaenavon had been arranged), Major John Lones, managing director of the Blaenavon Company Ltd., the town's chief industrial concern.

The King  was told by Councillor Holder that in this town, 'We have many willing hands to toil, but there is nothing for them to do.' His Majesty replied, 'I very much regret that it is so. Something must be done for you.'

The Blaenavon contingent of the Monmouthshire hunger marchers - who had just spent three weeks tramping to London to protest against the Means Test - were distributing an open letter, addressed to the King in the street. The King asked for a copy, was given one and he put it in his pocket. The letter read as follows:-

'Your Majesty.

To-day you will be visiting the towns and villages of our valley. It is a stricken valley; a valley blighted by the dead hand of poverty. We regret your tour has been planned in such a way that the terrible effects of this poverty will not be seen by Your Majesty.

In these towns and villages of ours, live men who have been continuously unemployed for twelve and ten year periods. Young men up to 25 years of age who have been denied the chance of ever getting a day's work. Our women grow prematurely old, and many are broken in the unequal fight against the consequences of unending penury. The bodies of our children are stunted and frail, because adequate nourishment cannot be obtained.

Up and down the valley are hundreds of dilapidated houses. An open sewer runs through thickly populated areas; many of our schools are ancient and inadequate. Yet no money is forthcoming to maintain and develop the social services.

Family life is being shattered by the cruel Means Test; the poorest of the poor are now to be subjected by your Government to another vicious attack. Our sons and daughters are being driven away to find their bread where they can. This is the truth of the present situation in our valley.

This tragic picture remains entirely unaltered by the pitiful and puny efforts of various voluntary social centres etc.

As unemployed men who had the honour of representing the people of our valley in the recent great National Protest March, we say that our economic and social plight is the result of the policy pursued by your Ministers and Government.

The poverty conditions our people suffer are known and admitted by most people. Action to alter this is what is now necessary.

We would respectfully ask Your Majesty, how can a suffering people believe talk of prosperity? Will an impoverished people be able to joyfully celebrate Your Majesty's Coronation?

As unemployed marchers we earnestly appeal to Your Majesty to indicate to your Ministers your sympathy with demands that the Means Test must go. That the unemployed shall enjoy a higher living standard. That work and wages shall be given to the thousands of willing hands so eagerly awaiting.

These were the demands we carried from Wales to Westminster. The granting of them would give new life and hope to a long suffering people.'

(The names of 31 marchers were appended)

King Edward VII arriving in Blaenavon on 19th November 1936.
Torfaen Museum Trust.

The King then proceeded along the Brynmawr road to reach Garn-yr-erw where he stopped for lunch in the Welfare Hall. It was here that he asked Mr I.G. Gwyn Thomas, 'How long have the steel works been closed? Is there any prospect of new industries being introduced in Blaenavon?'

Mr Thomas replied, ' We are hoping that Your Majesty's ministers will be able to bring about the resuscitation of trade in Blaenavon.'

The King then commented, 'My ministers are giving serious consideration to such projects as the introduction of new industries in these areas which were formerly such busy places.' From Garn-yr-erw the Royal party proceeded to Abertillery.

During this Royal tour of South Wales, King Edward was heard several times to utter his memorable statement, 'Something must be done,' on hearing of the distress and hardships that were being suffered by the people living in these depressed areas. These words echoed round the world as signifying a king's deep feelings for the common people in the want and distress which prevailed in South Wales at this time. News of his projected marriage and the difficulties it was causing had not at that time been broken to the general public. But this tour of the depressed areas of Monmouthshire was his last public appearance before his abdication on December 11. His reign had lasted less than eleven months, and he left the country immediately after his abdication. He was succeeded on the throne by his brother the Duke of York, who became George VI.

The proclamation of King George VI was read to the people of Blaenavon by Councillor A.H. Holder, from the balcony of the Council offices. But before doing so he commented:-

> 'This is by no means a pleasant duty; rather it is sad and sensational. Four weeks to-morrow the Clerk and I were presented to the ex-king. We shook hands with him, explained and conversed with him. I deeply regret the issue, that we are all familiar with, which caused him to abdicate, and while disagreeing with him I sympathise. A democratic Monarch has renounced his Kingdom. He possessed profound qualities of understanding for his people. He realised we are all human. He spoke to the unemployed of our town; he cheered them; lifted their spirits, gave them new hope and declared that 'something must be done.'
>
> Now it is my duty to proclaim a new King. Before I do so, let me pay tribute to Queen Mary. She has faced this ordeal with courage, coolness, and, I believe, motherly love. God Bless her.'

Eastern Valley folk celebrated the Coronation of King George VI later in 1937 in their usual joyful way. Scores of street parties were held and the churches were packed for special services. Chairmen and clerks of local authorities received medals, every child received a souvenir at school and babies born on Coronation Day were given money gifts from Pontypool Council. The Italian Gardens at Pontypool were illuminated with coloured lights and the Park Gates and Town Hall were floodlit.

King George VI and Queen Elizabeth paid a visit to Pontypool in December 1941. Crowds of flag waving people lined the streets of the town as the Royal party drove to the Town Forge. Here they were introduced to the directors of Partridge, Jones and John Paton Ltd., company officials and workers. It was the first time the King and the Queen had seen a tinplate works and both listened with interest as the various processes were explained by the works general manager, Mr Reg Powell.

Numerous babies born in the Eastern Valley were to be named Charles, after the Prince born to Princess Elizabeth and the Duke of Edinburgh in December 1948.

King George VI and Queen Elizabeth visited Pontypool in December 1941. Torfaen Museum Trust.

Pontypool Chamber of Trade, who had sent a telegram of congratulations to Princess Elizabeth, complained that otherwise Pontypool had done nothing to celebrate the great event. 'There wasn't even a flag out,' said Mr E. Warton Fowler. Other members said two flags were hoisted on Park Terrace School, and someone fired two rockets when the news came over the wireless.

Two Royal visits to the Eastern Valley took place in 1949. In August, the Duchess of Kent visited the BNS factory at Mamhilad and was given a warm welcome by hundreds of employees. The Duke of Gloucester visited Blaenavon Boys' Club in November where he shook hands and exchanged a few words with Ken Jones, the Olympic runner and Welsh international and founder member of the club. The Duke commented, 'It is obvious that the premises are quite inadequate for the number of people using them, and it is time something was done about it.'

Varteg staged its Festival of Britain carnival in July 1951 and practically the whole population of 500 turned out to watch the procession. Thousands of people defied pouring rain in August to watch the £200 fireworks display planned as a climax to Pontypool's Festival of Britain week. It was estimated that about five thousand people attended the Festival thanksgiving service which was held in Pontypool Park.

In February 1952, memorial services were held throughout the Eastern Valley, following the death of King George VI. Among the first of the local organisations to offer a formal pledge of loyalty to the new Queen were members of Pontypool Gas and Water Welfare Scheme, at their annual dinner at the Town Hall.

The Coronation of Queen Elizabeth II was celebrated throughout the valley in June 1953 and for the first time the event could be watched on television. Hundreds of Eastern Valley homes were converted into little theatres, thus enabling as many people as possible to watch the television broadcast covering the crowning and enthronement of the Queen at Westminster Abbey. Every home possessing a television set was crowded to capacity. Relations and friends sat on the floor or stood shoulder to shoulder to view the historic scenes.

Mr Page Stedman, a Garndiffaith shopkeeper, was heard to comment, 'There were six women in the audience in which I sat, and five of them cried continuously for an hour-and-a-half.' Another man said, 'We saw for the first time what royalty really means. Through this television broadcast the British people have become one family in the fullest sense of the word.'

The isolated mountain-top village of Pantygasseg had a memorable day of festivity. Ten of the sixty odd homes had TV sets and hardly one person failed to watch the Coronation. 'Reception is always good up here, but to-day it could not have been more perfect,' one villager said. The village's 107 children had tea and games in the village institute, together with souvenir cups, saucers, plates, a bonfire and fireworks. A gift of 5s was presented to each old age pensioner.

In the bleak and windswept village of Varteg, a specially hired TV set was placed in the Memorial Hall where 220 children, 50 old age pensioners and scores of in-betweens assembled to watch the Coronation.

At Garndiffaith, billowing winds drove all the street parties indoors. Before switching on the TV set at their hall, the old-age pensioners held a devotional service during which prayers were offered for the Queen by lay preacher Dan Fry.

The highlight of Cwmffrwdoer's celebrations was a women's comic football match on the local soccer ground between teams captained by Mrs Cecelia Shaw and Mrs Elizabeth Richards, with Mr Redvers Lewis as referee. The fete was opened by Mrs Jane Griffiths (66), a retired school-teacher, who had spent 40 years on the staff of Cwmffrwdoer Infant's School and was regarded with affection by hundreds of parents and children who passed through her hands.

In Pontypool every single street made some practical demonstration of loyalty and patriotism and the main thoroughfare of the town was a splash of colour. Pontypool Council were responsible for the lavish decorations of the Town Hall and the Clarence Corner and whose Parks Department spared no effort in adorning the focal points with flower boxes, baskets and gardens.

The festivities in Pontypool urban area reached a grand climax when, in fine weather, over 20,000 people at the Park enjoyed the £1,000 fete staged by Pontypool Council out of the fourpenny Coronation rate. In the centre of the sports ring an 80 foot mast was erected. It was topped by a revolving platform from which the Wirenguard ariel trapezists (mother, father, son and daughter) - from Sweden - provided the crowd with breathtaking thrills.

The Council had purchased a total of 6,166 souvenir crown brooches, pins, pennants and Union Jacks for the children, but these were insufficient to go round and it had to be a case of first come first served. It was long after the National Anthem had been played and the lights extinguished that the last of the merry-makers went home.

Fowlers of Pontypool, boasted that they had served the town during eight reigns:- King George IV (1820-30), King William IV (1830-37), Queen Victoria (1837-1901), King Edward VII (1901-10), King George V (1910-36), King Edward VIII (1936), King George VI (1936-52) and Queen Elizabeth (1952-). The firm was founded, one hundred and twenty five years previously, in 1828 when King George the Fourth was on the throne

At Blaenavon all the main buildings were floodlit. Miles of bunting, thousands of flags (some 60 years old), emblems and pictures of the Royal family decked streets and houses; there was scarcely a dwelling without its Coronation token. Blaenavon Collier Band headed the parade of the full Coronation Committee, children of the respective schools, Red Cross and St John Ambulance Brigade.

The 1,800 children in Blaenavon's Urban Area were guests of Blaenavon Council, who entertained them to tea. A huge army of women had to be recruited to do the catering. These came voluntarily from religious organisations to feed children in various schools in the area. Blaenavon's oldest inhabitant, Mrs. T. Griffiths, (97) of Charles Street, spent several hours watching the Coronation and it was her very first experience of television.

Two huge bonfires, one on the Coity Mountain, and one between the Keeper's Cottage and Pwlldu were built by the National Coal Board and were fired at dusk. Fireworks costing £100 at the Blaenavon Recreation Ground ended the day in a spectacular fashion.

Queen Elizabeth and the Duke of Edinburgh paid a visit to the Eastern Valley on Friday 10th May 1963. After visiting Abergavenny and the Welsh Brigade at Cwrt y Gollen Camp, Crickhowell, they arrived at the Blaenavon Council Office just before 3.00 pm.

Despite the wet weather the crowds were in good spirits and gave the Queen a great ovation. She was met at the entrance to the Council Office by Lord and Lady Raglan, the Council Chairman Miss Lewis and her young nephew Mr Neil Lewis. Inside the freshly painted council chamber the members of the council were presented to the Queen and Duke. After she had gone inside the building, the crowd chanted, 'We want the Queen,' until Her Majesty and the Duke of Edinburgh, together with Miss May Lewis and Mr Sid Banks, Chairman and Vice-Chairman of the Council appeared on the balcony. Smiling and waving, the Queen stayed several minutes on the balcony, despite the rain, before leaving for Pontypool.

Shops and other buildings along the route through Pontypool were gaily decorated with bunting, flags and hundreds of Union Jacks. The Town Hall had recently been given a face lift and re-decorated specially for the occasion. Lining the route to its entrance were parties of scouts, sea scouts and girl guides.

A reception for the Royal couple was held in the Assembly Rooms of the Town Hall and each member of the Pontypool Council was presented to them. Shortage of space and time meant that it was not possible to invite wives and husbands of the councillors.

Rare specimens of Pontypool Japanware were put on display in the Town Hall. It was the largest single collection of Japanware that had ever been put on show in the town and one set alone was worth about £1,500. The items included coffee pots, trays, urns and fruit baskets. Fourteen of the pieces belonged to the Council and ten had been loaned by the National Museum of Wales. Mr. J. Kyrle Fletcher of Newport had supplied a rare set of yellow Japanware and Major Lloyd-Johnes an unusual set of cut-out figures.

The Queen was very interested in the display and the history of the pieces was explained to her by Mr C.J. Irving, Chairman of the council. Prince Philip commented to Mrs Irving, 'So this is the famous Pontypool Japanware.'

From there the Royal couple made their way to the British Nylon Spinners factory at Mamhilad and when the visit drew to a close, the Royal party drove to Pontypool Road Station, which was decorated with some three hundred pots of flowers. A one hundred yard length of red carpet, stretched to the Royal train which was waiting to take the visitors back to London. Hundreds of people packed the station approach and many were on the platform to say farewell. As the train pulled out at 5.00 pm the Queen stood at a window, which the Duke then opened, to wave to the still cheering crowds in the station approach.

In November 1971, Princess Anne visited Cwmbran to open the new Gwent Police Headquarters and the Cwmbran boating lake. She also visited Fairwater shopping centre and Llantarnam Grange. It was the first time that she had come to Monmouthshire.

Queen Elizabeth II on the balcony of the Council offices in Blaenavon acknowledging the cheers of the crowd which had assembled in Lion Street on 10th May 1963. Standing beside her is Miss May Lewis, the Council's first lady chairman.

Princess Alexandra was to have opened Pontypool Council's £600,000 Sports Centre in Pontypool Park, during May 1974, but her visit was cancelled due to a bout of influenza. The Lord Lieutenant of Monmouthshire, Colonel Roderick Hill, performed the ceremony instead.

However, Princess Alexandra kept her promise and came to Pontypool in May of that year. She first visited the new Parke Davis pharmaceutical factory, which had won the 1973 Architecture Award. Then she inspected the Pontypool Leisure Centre where she was presented to the architect, Mr Alan Pitts, Torfaen's Chief Technical Officer.

In April 1975, Prince Richard, Duke of Gloucester, visited Cwmbran to open the £51,000 indoor swimming pool at Llanfrechfa Grange Hospital. Measuring 50 feet long and 20 feet wide, this pool was the brainchild of the hospital's League of Friends, who financed it with a public appeal.

The Prince of Wales also visited Cwmbran in the July of that year, to officially open the police training centre for the Principality. He said, 'It is the first purpose built establishment of its kind and there is no doubt it will successfully produce purpose-built young men and women dedicated to the fight of crime in the Principality.' The Prince unveiled a Welsh slate plaque depicting a dragon and commemorating the occasion. He then left Cwmbran and made his way to Pontypool and, travelling through the main street, he was greeted by flags at the Free Press building and also one on the Town Hall.

Two years later in June, 1977, the Eastern Valley celebrated the Queen's Silver Jubilee. The new Mayor of Torfaen, Mr Graham Powell, sent loyal greetings to the Queen on behalf of the citizens of Torfaen. A replica of the Crown Jewels was a special attraction at the Pontypool Ideal Homes and Trades Exhibition at the Leisure Centre. On the 18th April, 1978, the Queen Mother came to Croesyceiliog to officially open the new County Hall building of Gwent County Council.

Queen Elizabeth II accompanied by Mr J. C. Irving, Chairman of Pontypool Council, descending the steps of Pontypool Town Hall on Friday 10th May 1963. Behind them is the Duke of Edinburgh and Mrs Irving.

Prince Charles paid his first visit to Blaenavon in July 1981, just a few weeks before his wedding. The visit was part of a two-day tour of South Wales during which he visited projects being carried out by voluntary groups and assisted by the Prince of Wales Committee. At the Valley Inheritance Museum, Pontypool, he was shown around by Adrian Babbidge the Trust Director, and in particular showed great interest in the old Blaenavon fire engine. The party then moved on to Forge Row, where the Prince was shown around the terrace of twelve cottages originally built for the workers of the long vanished Varteg Forge.

Prince Charles was greeted in Blaenavon by crowds of cheering, flag waving people, who lined the streets of the town along his route. He donned a helmet for his tour of the ironworks which was fortunate for he managed to bang his head on some scaffolding as be bent to avoid it. Finally he paid a visit to Wales' first coal mining museum at Big Pit.

The Royal Wedding was later celebrated throughout the Eastern Valley in the usual fashion and Pontypool in particular transformed itself into a decorative feast of red, white and blue. Miles of bunting adorned the streets and the smiling faces of Prince Charles and Lady Diana Spencer appeared in every window as shopkeepers competed for the most attractive display of patriotism.

Two years later in November 1984, HRH Prince Charles visited County Hall to present Prince of Wales Committee Awards to groups which had completed environmental projects of benefit to the community. Among the twenty two winners was the Big Pit Museum Trust and their award was received by the Chairman, Dennis Puddle.

In October 1986, HRH the Duke of Gloucester visited Torfaen for a service to rededicate the restored chapel of the 2nd Monmouthshire Regiment in Trevethin Church. He flew from Kensington Palace in a bright red Wessex helicopter which landed on Pontypool rugby ground. As he emerged from the helicopter he was greeted by the Lord Lieutenant of Gwent, Richard Hanbury-Tenison and John Over the Chief Constable of the county.

At Trevethin Church the Prince was warmly welcomed by war veterans and British Legion standard bearers who formed a guard of honour as he was introduced to Lt. Col. David Morgan, Commanding Officer, 3rd Battalion of the Royal Regiment of Wales, Col. Kenneth Morgan, OBE, holder of the Military Cross, who was the second officer to have commanded the 2nd Monmouthshire Regiment, and trustees of the chapel restoration appeal.

The Duke of Gloucester returned to the Eastern Valley in June 1989 when he visited the Free Press offices at Pontymoile Corner as part of the paper's 130th birthday celebrations. He was shown the new computer-setting technology which had recently been installed in the building.

On July 22nd, 1994, Prince Charles opened the rebuilt Folly Tower during a tour of Wales to celebrate the 25th year of his investiture. It was 45 years to the month that the folly was demolished. Hundreds of local people turned out for the occasion and while they awaited the arrival of the Prince, they were entertained by the Pontypool Brass Band, Pontypool & District Male Choir, the Betty Eyeless Singers and Uned Cymraeg.

In August 1997 Torfaen County Borough Council extended their condolences to the Royal Family on the tragic death of the princess of Wales. Books of remembrance were made available at the Civic Centre in Pontypool, County Hall, Cwmbran and Blaenavon Libraries. Flags at the Civic Centre in Pontypool and County Hall, Croesyceiliog, were flown at half mast and all around Torfaen tributes to the 'People's Princess' were to be seen.

The Duke of Kent visited Blaenavon in April 1998 during a tour of Newport and Torfaen's industrial heritage. The visit coincided with Torfaen County Borough Council's bid for World Heritage status for Blaenavon and its surrounding area. He also unveiled a plaque at DuPont's Pontypool site to commemorate the company's 50th anniversary.

In December, Princess Anne paid a visit to the Cwmbran factory of Frank Theak and Roskilly which claims to be Europe's largest tie manufacturer. She came in her capacity as president of the British Knitting and Clothing Export Council. The Company had organised a competition in which local schools were asked to design a tie in aid of the Save the Children Fund, which is one of the main charities supported by the Princess and the winner was presented to her.

In June 1998, Llantarnam Abbey was the starting point for a 550 mile pilgrimage around Wales by a group of historians and walkers celebrating the 900th anniversary of the Cistercian Order in Wales and their modern successors. The walk finished back at Llantarnam in September.

Prince Charles talking to Bernard Derrick, Chairman of Croft on top of the Folly Tower.
Arthur Crane Collection.

## -- 12 --

# Waterloo to the Second World War

*'Pontypool Road Station was the point where soldiers from the upper Eastern Valley embarked on their war service and many will have memories of the scenes at the station as loved ones were parted - many never to meet again.'*

W. L. Sambrook 1973

In the early years of the nineteenth century the Eastern Valley iron industry undoubtedly did its bit for the Napoleonic Wars by working hard to satisfy the need for heavy artillery and cannon balls. The military campaigns caused the demand for iron to soar and during that period a considerable number of pits and levels were opened up in the vicinity of Blaenavon to enable greater quantities of ironstone and coal to be extracted.

The Battle of Waterloo in 1815 ended the Napoleonic Wars but once peace returned, the price of iron came tumbling down, for the ironworks had now lost their best customers ( the army and the navy) and a slump in the iron trade immediately followed. Local Ironmasters attempted to compete with those in the Midlands by reducing wages and this caused a widespread strike which continued until the threat of wage reduction was withdrawn.

The termination of the wars also brought about the passing by Parliament of the notorious Corn Law of 1815 which sought to continue the high prices of corn (which were established during the wars) by the prohibition of the importation of foreign supplies of corn except where the price should be 80 shillings per quarter or above.

In spite of this measure, the peace of 1815 brought about a fall in the prices of agricultural products, but as this ruined many farmers the labourer received no relief. The wages of agricultural workers were soon depressed to 6 shillings per week and under such conditions they were only too glad of the opportunity of migrating to the new industrial districts, where, in comparison with their meagre earnings on the land, wages were much higher.

### The Zulu War

One of the most famous of the local heroes who fought in the Zulu War of 1879 was Private John Williams of Cwmbran. His real name was Fielding and it has been said that he adopted the name Williams because when he joined the British Army in 1877 as a private in the 24th Regiment of Foot he was really under age. However, this could not be so, for this gardener's son was born in Abergavenny on 24th May 1857. The family moved to Cwmbran five years later and, at the age of eight, the youngster went to work at the Patent Nut & Bolt Works in Cwmbran. He was in fact 20 years of age when he joined The Monmouthshire Militia and the reason why he used a false name is because he had run away from home and did not want his family to know that he had joined the army. Three months later he enlisted in the old 24th Foot (which in 1881 became known as the South Wales Borderers and was later absorbed into the present day Royal Regiment of Wales).

During the following year, John Williams and his unit were posted to Pietermaritzburg in South Africa, where they were given orders to guard the hospital and supply depot at Rorke's Drift. This was originally a farm established by a man named Rorke on the Natal side of the Buffalo River. It was commandeered as a supply depot and base hospital by the British Army some time before the main forces under Lord Chelmsford crossed into Zululand to attack King Cetawayo at the start of the Zulu War. The post was defended by 95 men of B Company 2nd Battalion under the command of Lieutenants G. Broomhead and John Chard (of the Royal Engineers).

John William Fielding VC
(Alias John Williams)
1857-1932

John Williams was one of eleven men who won the Victoria Cross in this famous battle which took place on 22nd January 1879. Seven went to the men of the 24th, and this was the greatest number of VCs ever awarded to one regiment in one action. The VC is the highest military award for gallantry and these men were awarded the honour in view of their stubborn resistance to the force of between 3,000 and 4,000 Zulu warriors who attacked Rorke's Drift with such bravery.

The *London Gazette* of 2nd May 1879, provides the following description of the part played by John Williams in this famous incident:-

> 'Private John Williams was posted with Private Joseph Williams and Private William Horrigan in a distant room of the hospital which they had held for more than an hour - until they had no ammunition left.
>
> As communication was for a time cut off, the Zulus were able to advance and burst open the door. They dragged out Private Joseph Williams and two patients and later killed them. While they were occupied with this slaughter Private John Williams, with two patients - these were now the only men left alive in the ward - succeeded in knocking a hole through the partition, and in taking the two patients into the next ward he found Private H. Hook (of Monmouth).
>
> These two men together - one man working while the other fought and held the enemy at bay with his bayonet - broke through three more partitions and were enabled to bring eight patients through a small window and into the rear line of defence. It took Private Williams an hour to hack one hole through with his pickaxe, and when the action ended he had just two rounds of ammunition.'

The grave of John William Fielding VC at Llanfihangel Llantarnam.

Private William's time expired in 1883, after he had seen service in India and he returned to Cwmbran where he joined the 3rd Volunteer Battalion of the South Wales Borderers and held the rank of sergeant. In 1915, he was appointed as an orderly to Sir George Forestier-Walker at the recruiting office. For the rest of his life John Williams lived in Cocker Avenue. His eldest son, Tom Fielding, also joined the South Wales Borderers and was killed on September 26th, 1914, during the retreat from Mons.

John Williams was interviewed in 1929 and he re-called, 'We first heard of the disaster at Isandhlwana from Colonel Groom, and we knew that 3,000 Zulus would be mad for slaughter and would soon be upon us. We just had time to improve the barricades with mealie sacks and biscuit tins before the Zulus were upon us. The attack started at 3.30 pm and for the next 18 hours we knew all about it.'

Following a seizure, John Williams died at Ty Coch in November 1937 at the age of 75 and was given a military funeral with full honours. He was indeed a locally famous and popular man for the procession was a mile and a quarter in length and even after he was interred in Llantarnam graveyard, people were still arriving to pay their respects. He had been one of the last survivors of the Rorke's Drift epic of 1879 and also one of the oldest holders of the Victoria Cross.

William Osborne of Blaenavon was another Eastern Valley man who fought with great distinction in both Zulu Wars (1878 and 79) and was present at the battle of Rorke's Drift. He also participated in the Kaffir War of 1877.

Born at Duke's Street in Blaenavon, William was the son of Thomas Osborne who worked for the Blaenavon Company. He was still a youngster when he took the Queen's shilling at Pontypool. After a period at Brecon Barracks he was sent to Chatham and soon after embarked for South Africa. He described the incident at Rorke's Drift as follows:-

> 'We had seventeen hours of hand fighting. And if we had all been third-class shots, it would have been all over for us. They came at us in wave after wave, but we made them jump. We took six or seven prisoners, but we set 'em out in the open. If you didn't catch 'em smart as they put their hands up, they were gone like a dart. Jack Lines and me were firing together with our ammunition on the wall beside us, the corporal was in the act of raising his rifle when his arms dropped to his side from a wound to the neck. The enemy set the thatched roof afire, but we pulled the roof off during the night to stop that little game.'

From Africa William Osborne was sent to Gibraltar and then to India where he completed his six years service. He returned home to Blaenavon in 1883 at the age of 26 and began working underground for the Blaenavon Company.

Private John Jobbins was another local participant in the famous stand at Rorke's Drift and he too lived a long life, dying in September 1934 at the age of 79. He died at his house at Machine Meadow, Pontnewynydd, after an illness lasting several weeks. He had served 19 years in the Army, 16 of them with the old 24th Foot Regiment. To his great pride he was the possessor of the Zulu War Medal with three clasps, also long service and good conduct medals.

On the day of his funeral, hundreds of people assembled in the vicinity of Machine Meadow and blinds were drawn in all the houses as a mark of respect. The long funeral procession would in all probability have been even longer, but for the pouring rain. The coffin, covered with the Union Jack on which was placed Private Jobbins's Zulu medal and bars, was borne in a motor hearse decorated with floral tokens. The firing party, bearers and bugler were supplied from the Depot of the South Wales Borderers. A short service at the house was conducted by the Rev H. Sproule Jones, curate of All Saints Church, Pontnewynydd, and the burial took place at Trevethin Cemetery with full military honours.

In 1931, 76 year old George Purnell of Bridge Street, Pontypool, described his experiences in the Zulu War. He had joined the 24th Foot at Newport in January 1878 and sailed to Durban from Portsmouth in a boat called *The Tyne* . The voyage took sixty days.

> 'We made a forced march to Isandhlwana where the great disaster took place. From a hilltop we could see the enemy robbing the dead, and we charged them at the point of a bayonet. Three men were sent down to look for food and returned with a box of biscuits which Lord Chelmsford ordered to be distributed. Each man had two-and-a-half biscuits, but Lord Chelmsford refused to take his share.
>
> At break of day we set off on another 21 miles trek to Rorke's Drift, where a handful of the 24th Regiment had made a great stand against the blacks. This had happened on January 22nd. We arrived the next day, and set about burying the dead. We buried 300 in one hole.
>
> I took part in the Ulandai battle on July 4th, when Lord Chelmsford decisively defeated the Zulus in the last battle of the campaign. It lasted two hours and twenty minutes. We had two gatling guns, which were being worked by blue jackets, and so strong were the Zulu reserves that as soon as one body of them was mowed down there was another one there to take their place.
>
> At length the Zulus tied bits of white rag to the ends of their assegais and gave in. Lord Chelmsford ordered them to bring their cattle into the camp. This was done, the cattle were sold, and each man's share of the prize money was 11s 8d (59p); officers had double shares.'

Following his return to Pontypool in 1884, George spent 46 years as a boiler maker at Panteg Works and he retired at Christmas 1929. He and his wife were now living (in 1931) on his Army pension of 9 shillings per week.

George Purnell, also a veteran of the Zulu War, died at Bridge Street, Pontypool, at the age of 80 in 1934. He had been in the column which relieved the Rorke's Drift heroes on the morning after their famous stand.

Another local man who was involved in the battle at Rorke's Drift was James Fronwen Williams of Abersychan. At the age of eight, he had started work as a collier's helper and twelve years later, he enlisted in the Monmouthshire Militia, together with his friend John Rosser. They joined up at the Full Moon Hotel, Pontypool, and were sworn in by the Rev J.C. Llewellin, Vicar of Trevethin.

J.F. Williams was afterwards transferred to the 24th Regiment of Foot and sailed with them to East London, South Africa. The regiment was then taken in waggons to King Williams Town, capital of the old province of British Kaffaria. J.F.W. was one of the three hundred men who kept the large force of Zulus a bay during the defence of Rorke's Drift. He had also fought in the Kaffarian War of 1878 at Peary Bush, where the Kaffir chief was killed. In 1882 J.F.W. returned to Wales after three years with the Colours. Three of his sons were to serve in the Great War in which one of them, George Williams, was killed.

For many years before his retirement James Fronwen Williams worked at a local colliery. He had the misfortune to lose the sight of an eye as the result of an accident. and his right leg still bore marks of injuries sustained in the Zulu War.

In December 1937, when J.F.W. was interviewed at his home, 10, Dents Buildings, Abersychan, he was in good health and keen to talk about his experiences. He could sing in a voice tremulous with age, but still tuneful, a little ditty descriptive of the heroic stand of a handful of men against the Zulus on January 22nd, 1879. He was a member of the Regiment that hastened to Rorke's Drift on the Tugela River, Natal, where the gallant soldiers were making an heroic stand against tremendous odds. James was very proud of the fact that he was a member of the relief party and that he had won a Zulu War medal. He died in January 1938 at the age of 83.

Other Eastern Valley men who were also involved in the battle of Rorke's Drift included: Private John Jobbins of Pontypool, Corporal Charles Jones of Pontypool, Alfred Farr, Charley Long and William Rees from the Race, Harry Smith from Sowhill, Private John James of Blaenavon, Corporal John Lyons of Pontypool and Private George Weeks of Pontnewynydd. Corporal Patrick Lyons of Pontypool was seriously injured in the action but duly recovered and wrote a letter to his mother describing the battle as follows:-

> 'We did the best in our power to make a laager to defend ourselves. There were about 80 of us all told and we all fought like men and kept 4,000 of them at bay until the morning. Dear mother, I do not know all the boys that got killed from Pontypool but I know that Farr, the butcher and young Harry Smith were killed.'

Private John James of Blaenavon wrote to his parents:-

> 'They (the Zulus) set fire to the commissary but our boys had the best of it, they killed about 1,000 of them and our side had only eleven killed. They had to fight hard for their lives that night.
>
> Will Osborne had a very narrow escape. He sends his love to you; also Ed. Murray, S. Parry, William Davies send their love to you and all friends. George Slasher was killed in the battle. I am still alive and kicking.'

## The Great War (1914-18)

For the second time since the Battle of Waterloo, Great Britain was again at war with a major power and on the outbreak of hostilities the *Free Press* commented:-

> 'With grave and anxious feelings we have entered upon the grim encounter which has been forced upon us. There are dark days in front of us. We must expect disasters as well as victories, but calm and determined we shall win through the crisis by united efforts.'

Lord Kitchener was appointed Secretary of State for War in place of Mr Asquith and mobilisation was soon proceeding smoothly and rapidly. At Pontypool a small staff at the Drill Hall were busy enlisting recruits. During the first two days there were just fifteen rejections as a result of the medical examination.

There were more recruits per head of population from Wales than from England, Scotland or Ireland. Over 1,000 men were enrolled in South Wales and Monmouthshire for the Welsh Regiment of Horse. Eleven Pontypool St John Ambulance men who volunteered their services were sent to Aldershot and from there to the front.

Early in August 1914, Mrs Edith George, the wife of an engine driver, who lived in Stafford Road, Griffthstown, made a number of toy flags to amuse her young twin sons, and shortly afterwards it was announced that Edward, Prince of Wales, had been asked to open a relief fund for the dependents of soldiers and sailors.

It was suggested to Mrs George, by her milkman, that she could raise money for the Prince of Wales Fund by making lots of flags and selling them for a penny each. She liked the idea and wrote to Mr John O Tyle, the Chairman of Panteg Urban District Council, asking for permission to sell flags to help the fund. It was duly given and she went into production making flags of red, white and blue on matchsticks. Before long they were selling like hot cakes and Mrs George worked in the evenings making the flags to sell in the daytime. Virtually everyone in Griffithstown bought one and her noble efforts raised the sum of £10 (a large amount in those days).

Gradually other places took up the idea and it quickly spread to London and eventually all over England. It was reported by the press, that, Her Majesty the Queen was graciously pleased to accept one of the first batch of flags that Mrs George made. Sir Arthur Pearson then wrote to Mrs George on behalf of the Prince of Wales Fund, congratulating her on such enterprise. By the end of the war £35 million was raised from the selling of flags and the concept of 'Flag Days' was firmly established.

It was reported in May 1915 that 8,000 men from the Eastern Valley had joined the Forces. In connection with a great recruiting rally, eight meetings were held on the first Sunday in May at various points in the Valley. The anniversary of the declaration of war by the British Empire was marked in August with a mass meeting held at Pontypool Market Hall at which many patriotic speeches were made.

Military officers inspected the Coedygric Institution with a view to taking it over as a military hospital and Mr John Capel Hanbury, Squire of Pontypool, thoughtfully sent 100 pairs of rubber waders for the use of the 2nd Mons on duty in the trenches.

The mines and ironworks in the Eastern Valley were all fully extended to assist in the war effort. War munition volunteers were being enrolled and there was a very good response by Eastern Valley people who were all issued with badges.

In October 1915 Cwmbran residents, 2,000 in number gathered outside the council offices to greet Sergt. Cornelius Love, who had been awarded the Distinguished Conduct Medal for conspicuous bravery.

Eastern Valley soldiers departing from Crane Street Station, Pontypool during the Great War.

The *Lusitania* was torpedoed by the Germans on her way to Liverpool from New York, and sank in about 15 minutes with 1,125 of the 1,906 persons on board. Of the passengers 505 and of the crew 276 were saved. Isaac Jenkins (28) of Pontnewydd, who had been touring America with the Gwent Male Voice Party (Choir) for two years, was drowned in a remarkable act of heroism and self-sacrifice. He jumped into the sea from a crowded life-boat to give his place to a woman who was struggling in the water.

The King signed a proclamation in February 1916 for the Military Service Act to come into operation. All British subjects who on 15th August 1915, had attained 18 years and had not reached 41 and who on that day were unmarried or widowers with no dependent children, were deemed to have enlisted for the duration of the war.

Pontypool residents, in February 1916, had their first opportunity of seeing in the town a captured German gun, which had been taken in battle by the 44th Brigade, 15th Division British Expeditionary Force. The gun remained in Pontypool for a fortnight and was then taken to another district.

The following month, Blaenavon Council were asked to secure shovels and a quantity of sand and make arrangements with local builders for the use of ladders in the event of fires resulting from possible Zeppelin raids. Pontypool Council were informed that under the Government scheme, the cost of insuring their property against such raids would be £40 14s 9d (£40. 74p). Mr W. H. V. Bythway moved that all the council buildings be insured. However, it was decided by six votes to five not to take out any insurance for the time being.

In May 1916 Sergeant Drummer White, who had been awarded the Distiniguished Conduct Medal and the French Military Cross for conspicuous bravery, received a hero's welcome when he returned to Blaenavon on leave. He was met at the railway station by Mr George Dando, chairman of the council, and others who made speeches were Messrs

H.M. Davies, Tom Ruther and the Rev J. G. Mathias. A procession was formed, and headed by the Blaenavon Silver Band and escorted by the local troup of Boy Scouts and the Cadet Corps, Sergeant White was driven to his home.

There was great excitement in the Eastern Valley on Thursday November 7th 1918, on the publication of a report - unfortunately premature - that Germany had signed an Armistice and the war was at an end. In actual fact it was officially signed at 11 am on the following Monday (Nov 11). On this day blasts of hooters and whistles just after 11.00 am was the signal amongst the people of the Eastern Valley fheralded an outburst of wild excitement. The Armistice had now been signed and hostilities had ceased. It had been a period of four and a quarter years in which millions of the country's manhood had died. At last it was all over. Flags suddenly sprouted from windows and before noon all the streets of the locality, by a blaze of colour, bore witness to the fact that the wonderful news had spread like wildfire.

That same day, Abersychan Urban District Council marked the occasion by sending a telegram to Mr Lloyd George congratulating him and the Government on the successful termination of the war.

Lance Corporal George Onions, son of Mr W Onions, for many years master of Pontnewynydd Works, was invested in 1919 with the Victoria Cross at Buckingham Palace. He and a comrade on 22nd August 1918, took 200 of the enemy prisoner at Achiet-le-Petit in France and marched them back to their company commander.

Philip Morgan, a veteran of the First World War, serving with the 2nd Monmouthshire Regiment at the battle of Ypres celebrated his 100th birthday in February 1996. He was spending his remaining years at the Wentsland Residential Home at Tranch, Pontypool. In the Second World War he had served as a fireman in Pontypool and later worked at Panteg Steel Works.

### The Second World War (1939-45)

Following the Prime Minister's solemn declaration of war in September 1939, war clouds seemed to gather very slowly, for life in the Eastern Valley continued largely as before. For many of the residents it was hard for a while to accept that their country was really at war, except perhaps at night, when search light beams relentlessly probed the inky blackness. The black out in the intimate streets of a small town like Pontypool was irritating rather than gloomy, and as yet the possibility of an air-raid was regarded with little apprehension.

Humour was ever present and a local gent and his landlady are said to have had the following conversation:-

Landlady: 'Who started this war? - Hitler?'
Gent: 'Yes.'
Landlady: 'He was a painter and decorator, wasn't he?'
Gent: 'Yes.'
Landlady (grimly): 'Ah my husband was a painter and decorator - They are all the same!'

Throughout the country, cinemas and dance-halls were closed and this action enforced by the government was described by the famous playwright, George Bernard Shaw, as 'a stroke of unimaginative stupidity.' He wrote a letter to *The Time s* in protest, commenting that:-

> 'During the last war, we had 80,000 soldiers on leave to amuse every night. Now we have hundreds of thousands of evacuated children to keep out of mischief and traffic dangers. Are there to be no pictures for them? The authorities should at once set to work to provide new theatres and picture houses where these are lacking.
>
> All actors, variety artists and musicians and entertainers of all sorts should be exempted from every form of service except their own all-important one.
>
> What agent of Chancellor Hitler is it who suggested that we should all cower in darkness and terror for the duration of the war?'

The closing of places of entertainment certainly meant that there were few ways for people to spend an evening, except to talk at considerable length about war. Life in Pontypool was summed up by one man who commented: 'Riding on the buses seems strange. The faint, foggy blue lights are somewhat depressing, and fractious travellers who never have less than half-a-crown are a sore trial to conductors. One must admire the skill with which the drivers overcome the difficulty of driving with masked lights... The sand-bagging of Pontypool Police Station has given people waiting for their buses something to stare at. The Town Hall is over-run with industrious National Service workers, and a long line of cars stands outside like a rank of unofficial taxis...Very few people carry their gas masks with them, and those who do, do so consciously, almost furtively.

Brown paper and drawing pins are in demand by those householders whose war budget does not stretch to Italian cloth for black-out purposes... Policemen in tin hats with gas masks slung over their shoulders, arouse curious, half amused glances.'

Youngsters thought the gas masks were great fun, but they were fortunately too young to realise their full significance. One little Pontypool boy even refused to try on his mask until his father had bought him a water pistol. This was obviously a vital piece of equipment which had been unwittingly overlooked by the authorities.

Someone writing to the *Free Press* jokingly remarked:

> 'The practice of wearing your gas mask to avoid being recognised by your tailor or the income tax collector is greatly to be deplored. It is felt in official quarters that this degrades the high purpose for which it was developed.'

By March 1939, enough gas masks to supply the whole of the Eastern Valley had arrived and these were stored in three places ready for the emergency. In August a consignment of the new model gas masks for young babies arrived in Blaenavon. The design consisted of a bell-shaped headpiece with a skirt which had to be tied at the waist to form an air-tight bag. The air supply was controlled by the parents by means of an apparatus attached to the side of the suit. It was intended for infants up to the age of two-ad-a-half years.

During August a scheme for the reception of possible evacuees was being prepared in Pontypool and 2,608 people volunteered to take mothers and children. Mr G.T. Dixon was appointed chief billeting officer.

In September, the first prosecutions for offences against the black-out regulations were brought before Pontypool magistrate the main purpose being to ensure that people fully appreciated the importance of such precautions being taken. The problem of blacking-out St James' Church at Blaenavon was overcome by some members of the congregation who each presented the church with a curtain.

An electric light left on in an Abersychan hairdresser's shop in contravention of the blackout regulations was put out by a shot gun fired through an open fanlight window. The apprentice who left the light on was finedtwenty shillings.

One quarter of the Eastern Valley young men between the ages of twenty and twenty-five, who registered for military service on October 21st, 1939, expressed a preference for the Royal Air Force, while just over 13 per cent stated their desire to serve in the Royal Navy.

When *HMS Courageous*, the aircraft carrier, was torpedoed and sunk by a German submarine, the youngest survivor was a Pontymoile lad. He was Stanley Donoghue, aged 16, a boy seaman. His only injury was a grazed side, received when sliding down the side of the ship, but he was in the sea for two hours before being rescued.

In October, news of the Valley's first war dead was received. Marine Herbert Ronald Davies of Penygarn and First-Class Stoker, Ronald George of Griffithstown, were two ratings who were among the 800 officers and men lost when the battleship *Royal Oak* was torpedoed while at anchor in Scapa Flow at 1.30 am on October 14th.

A veterans' battalion for home service was formed in Pontypool that November and of the twenty members of the Pontypool and District Branch of the South African War Veteran's Association, one man aged 76 had fought in the Boer War. The youngest man to volunteer was aged 56.

By now the Pontypool Urban Area War Comforts Fund had been set up and the first parcels were being sent to sailors, soldiers and airmen serving overseas. The much welcomed packages contained cigarettes or tobacco worth 2s, six razor blades (6d), soap (3d), shaving soap (6d), chewing gum (3d), chocolate (1s) and a pair of insoles (6d) - total value 5 shillings.

Within a few minutes of the broadcast appeal made by Anthony Eden MP for men to enlist in the new Local Defence Volunteer Corps (the name was afterwards changed to 'Home Guard'), the first man had volunteered in the Eastern valley. Further enrolments followed rapidly and within three days 331 men had come forward: Pontypool 82, Pontnewynydd 28, Abersychan 25, Cwmbran 98, Blaenavon 56, Griffithstown 42, and Usk 39. The Germans had invaded Holland and Belgium and Winston Churchill, in his first speech as Prime Minister, told the country that the war had begun in deadly earnest, and that we must equip ourselves for 'an ordeal of the most grievous kind.'

In April 1940, Blaenavon people gave a warm welcome to a returning war hero. He was Petty Officer Pilot Reg Richards of *HMS Exete*r , which had born the brunt of the early exchanges of the German pocket battleship, *Admiral Graf Spee* , in the Battle of the River Plate.

Heavier fines were by now being put into force for black-out offences and, in June, no less than twenty-six offenders appeared at Pontypool magistrates' court. Cwmbran Council decided to erect twenty-two public air raid shelters, with the cost met by the County Council. In Blaenavon the local council agreed that three cells of the old 'lock up' would be used as air raid shelters. They were situated beneath Staffordshire Row, behind a wall which had been bricked up for many years.

WRVS women began collecting aluminium, brass and copper articles for use in the manufacture of much needed Spitfires. The *Free Press* then launched a special 'Spitfire Fund' with the contribution of £50 to assist in the provision of more fighter planes. In aid of this fund, the first Pontypool sheep-dog trials were held at Twyn Gwyn, Trevethin, in which 30 dogs participated and £12 12s 9d was raised.

People were badly shaken one evening in August when a lone Heinkel bomber, flown from a base at Rennes in Northern France, dropped approximately 250 incendiary bombs in and around Blaenavon Iron and Steel Works causing a fire at the Napthalene Plant and at a nearby house. Considerable damage to the works was undoubtedly prevented by the quick response and work of the Forge Side Air Raid Precautions Post. It had been started on a voluntary basis in 1938 and was manned day and night during the war.

A group of Eastern Valley Air Raid Wardens in 1940. David Boddington Collection.

The Blaenavon Company were working hard to assist the war effort and the coke ovens not only supplied coke for essential work, but also provided by-products, including TNT. A large quantity of Blaenavon steel was sent to the East Coast and other places for war purpose. In the tyre mill, apart from tyres, they also made parts for guns and tanks.

In September Pontypool had its first experience of bombs when a single German raider dropped a medium-calibre bomb almost in the centre of the town. Fortunately it fell one one of the few open spaces, with an air raid shelter on one side and the wall of an hotel on the other. The only casualties were seven dozen bottles of beer which were thrown from a shelf and smashed. A piece of paving stone weighing at least 20 lbs came through the roof of an hotel, crashed through a spare bedroom above and landed in another bedroom striking Mrs George James, wife of the licensee on the leg and grazing the skin. Mr John Kilgathan, who was sleeping in the adjoining room, flung himself out of bed as another piece of stone came through the ceiling and smashed the head of the bed.

In September, an RAF Blenheim twin engined light bomber based at Upwood in Huntingdonshire was on a training flight when it crashed into the summit of Garn Wen and burst into flames, breaking into two sections. The three man crew were killed instantly. They were Pilot Officer A. Coplestone, Observer, Sergeant J. November Gunner / Wireless Operator and the pilot Sergeant H. Wilson.

Mr Clement Atlee, Lord Privy Seal and a member of the War Cabinet came to Pontypool and inspected the Home Guards who were training in Pontypool Park. He afterwards spoke to an audience of 2,000 people in the Pavilion, Pontnewynydd, and emphasised that despite the heavy bombing, neither government nor parliament were going to run away from London. He said, 'I have never been more proud of being a Londoner than during the last few weeks. I believe that we, who bear the sword of the spirit, will conquer.'

By December the *Free Press* Spitfire Fund was well past its second thousand pounds. There had even been contributions from the toddlers of George Street Infants' School who sent ten shillings - all in farthings - 480 of them. Later that month an enemy aircraft flying low over Abersychan first dripped a flare and then two bombs which hit the schoolroom of the English Congregational Church and the local fire station which was a total wreck. The fire engine was damaged and one trailer pump was thrown on top of another. Mr Tom Edwards, whose house adjoined the fire station, was the only casualty. When the bombs fell he threw himself to the floor, and hit his head against a grandfather clock! The heavier bomb fell in the garden adjoining the Manse and caused a crater between 30 and 40 feet across and 20 feet deep. The bomb made a direct hit on a garage containing a car which was found piled on top of a heap of mud and stone with its engine blown out, its axles broken, but with its tyres and body still in good order. About a mile away a third bomb fell, but did not explode.The area was roped off and the people from neighbouring houses evacuated until the bomb was dealt with.

Three days after his house had been wrecked by bombs at Abersychan, Mr Evan Tom Davies was searching the wreckage when he found, in a battered cage his two budgerigars, apparently none the worse for the experience.

Members of the signalling section of the Home Guard at Blaenavon advertised for a gramaphone to assist them to obtain proficiency in Morse. They possessed a series of recorded Morse lessons but had no instrument on which to reproduce them.

Among the airmen who qualified for membership of the RAF 'Caterpillar Club' for those who had saved their lives by making a parachute jump, was Sgt.-Pilot S.J. Hitchings of Cwmbran Road, Pontypool. He and all four members of his crew made their jump in September 1941 over Germany and spent the next four years as prisoners of war.

In March 1941, a stick of ten high explosive bombs which were dropped in the vicinity of the Pontypool golf course broke some windows in a farmhouse; embedded a large stone in the middle of No 17 green; frightened several courting couples; threw an air raid warden from his bicycle; interrupted a game of table tennis in the clubhouse; tilted a service bus which was in the neighbourhood and so upset some dairy cows that their output of milk next morning was two gallons less than usual.

A contribution of sixteen dollars (£3 12s 6d) to the *Free Press* Fund was sent from a tiny village named Pontypool in Ontario, Canada. It arrived just before the fund was closed in April, with a grand total of £3,508 5s 2d. The fund had been started during the Battle of Britain and an historic donation was that of Mrs Fred Taylor, who gave £9/5/- one shilling for each of the 185 German planes brought down by the RAF on Sunday 15 September.

Pontypool MP, Alderman Arthur Jenkins accompanied Clement Attlee, Lord Privy Seal, as his Personal Parliamentary Secretary on a three week visit to the United States. On his return, Alderman Jenkins said that the tour had been a great success. The vast majority of Americans felt that what was happening in Europe was of vital concern to them. Most of the American people were friends of Great Britain and anxious to do the right thing.

People of the Eastern Valley continued to do their utmost to raise money to help the war effort. A 'Warship Week' held in Blaenavon from 7th - 14th February, 1941, set a target of raising £35,000 to cover the cost of the hull of a motor torpedo boat. The total figure raised in fact reached £62,816. Likewise, 'Cwmbran and District Warship Week' which was held during the previous month had also raised £60,000 and *HMS Turquoise* , a trawler minesweeper was adopted.

Scrap metal was collected throughout the Valley, but a criticism at one point arose in Blaenavon over the ripping out of so many iron railings to feed the war factories. The point was made that it was all very well giving up the railings but at the same time there was enough scrap metal lying around the vicinity of Blaenavon, to build a battleship. One local man was heard to comment, ' We would give our pen knives let alone our railings if there were no scrap metal about.'

A magnificent air-raid shelter was constructed by the people of Victoria Row, Blaenavon. It was situated under a tip of waste material from the ironworks and the inside was boarded, lit with acetylene lamps, heated by an iron stove and well ventilated. The interior, resembling a long compartment in a railway carriage was fitted on both sides with plush tip-up seats, bought second-hand from the local cinema. Not only was the shelter a place of refuge, but it also served as a meeting place for the women of Victoria Row (which consisted of twenty houses), where they held tea parties and even concerts.

One day a banana, which was a rare commodity in those times, was raffled at the Blaenavon Works by Mrs A. Pritchard for the local War Comforts Fund and the bidding reached 35 shillings. Further money was raised by a 'Wings for Victory' week with the aim being to cover the cost of six Mosquito two-engined bombers. The target was £120,000, but the total raised reached £186,320.

A Canadian soldier, who fought in the First World War and later in Mexico, Nicuaragua and with the Republican army in the Spanish Civil War, lectured the Home Guard at Pontypool in August 1941 on guerilla and irregular warfare. He declared that the existence of the Home Guard 'would spike Hitler's designs on Britain after the evacuation from Dunkirk.'

Geoffrey Bailey of Pontnewynydd was decorated by the King with the Distinguished Service Medal he had won at the Battle of Norvik. His hand was shot off in the action aboard *HMS Hardy* , which was hit and ran ashore. He dived into the icy water, swam 200 yards to the snow-covered shore and then walked 15 miles to hospital.

The Forge Hammer Assembly Rooms in Blaenavon, hosted an RAF exhibition and Flight Lieut. Landon Sorral, the man in charge of it, also put on a demonstration in an RAF rubber dinghy, which was watched by a large crowd at the local swimming baths. It was soon after this display that an RAF pilot in difficulties, successfully manouvered his Halifax bomber to avoid crashing into the inhabited part of Blaenavon. The plane came down near Milfraen Colliery, Garn-yr-erw, and all the crew escaped uninjured. They were part of 51 squadron, based at Snaith in Yorkshire and had been on a routine training flight over Wales, when the plane developed a problem. The crew of seven all baled out safely - two landed in Blaina, 3 at Nantyglo and 1 on the Blaenavon road.

Leading Wireless Telegraphist Robert Howell Powell of Griffithstown arrived home in May 1942 from Columbo after escaping with 250 others from Singapore, two days after it fell to the Japanese.

In November 1942 Pilot Officer Arnold Stanley Meara, Royal Air Force Volunteer Reserve, of Abersychan, with the rest of the crew of his bomber, was reported missing after his 27th operational flight over enemy territory. He was awarded the DFC for his services as a navigator of the highest skill on all of the heavy raids on the Ruhr. A week after the award had been announced, his mother and wife were overjoyed to receive a letter in his own handwriting from a German prison camp.

In July 1944 over 200 schoolchildren, teachers and escorts, evacuated from the South of England, arrived in Blaenavon. They were accorded a reception by Mr A.J. Bevan, the Chairman of Blaenavon Council. Evacuees who came to Pontypool numbered over 2,500 and in the Blaenavon area there were at one time over 700 evacuated children and parents.

Private Horace Prosser (23) of Cwmavon arrived home after escaping from an Italian Prisoner of War Camp. His mother was the widow of a soldier who had served in the Zulu and Boer wars. Another Blaenavon lady, Mrs Edmunds of Queen Street, had six sons who were all serving in HM Forces and they had previously all been playing members of Blaenavon RFC.

An unfortunate Blaenavon soldier was Private Evans, who must have been feeling pretty sick in 1944. He had joined the Army in preference to working underground in a local colliery. But by an irony of fate, on being taken prisoner he was put to work underground digging coal in Germany.

In September 1944, Corporal Lee Davies of Talywain was honoured by local people when he returned home after escaping from a German prison camp at the fourth attempt. He worked at Blaenserchan Colliery before joining the Army 12 years previously. He fought in the North West frontier of India, Iraq and the Middle East, was captured at Tobruk, and became an Italian prisoner of war. When the Italians capitulated he made a get-away, was re-captured and made three more attempts before regaining his freedom.

Towards the end of 1944, the end of the war appeared to be not too far away and compulsory drills and training of the Home Guards were ended. The black-out was replaced by half-lighting and the obligation to carry out fire-watching drills was also suspended. The 9th and 12th Battalion Mon. Home Guard paraded in Pontypool Park for the last time, 'unless an emergency arises which necessitates their standing to again.'

On May 7th, 1945, the Germans announced their surrender and the British Government declared that the following day (Tuesday) would be celebrated as 'VE Day' to mark the unconditional surrender of Germany to the three Allied Nations of Great Britain, Russia and the USA. For the British people, the war had lasted 2,094 days, (just over five years and eight months). This was 526 days more than the war of 1914 - 18.

Throughout the Eastern Valley VE Day was celebrated with great rejoicing. Flags and bunting appeared in profusion in every street and there was much dancing and music. However, the merrymaking was tempered by the thought that victory over Japan still had to be achieved before the war was really over.

Talywain Cross was turned into an open-air dance floor and bonfires were lit on the Monday evening at various points on the hillsides. Councillors of the North Ward at Garndiffaith organised a victory parade. It started from the Workmen's Hall and was marshalled by Major F.H. Bees. Headed by Varteg Band and including several excellent tableau the procession proceeded via Varteg to Cwmafon, Victoria Village and back.

Blaenavon had been well prepared for VE Day. A programme for Thanksgiving Service had been arranged and printed beforehand and festivities in the town commenced soon after the Prime Minister's historic announcement. The Tuesday evening service held at the Workmen's Hall was probably unprecedented in the town. Such a spacious hall was not large enough to accommodate all those seeking admission, but the Council were well prepared, for they had installed loud speakers outside the hall which were connected to a public address system. By this means, the hundreds of people gathered outside, were able to participate in the service.

Before this united service, short services had also been held in practically every church and chapel in the town, with crowded congregations everywhere. Children in all corners of Blaenavon were frantically gathering all kinds of fuel for bonfires, which were to light up the sky for the greater part of the night.

As the evening shadows lengthened, flood-lighting added to the general festivities. The tree foliage at St Peter's Church became fairy like, while the clock cenotaph and Park House were also among the places lit by floodlights.

There were few streets in the town which did not organise parties, chiefly for the benefit of the children, who would always remember the great occasion. In Elgam Avenue, for example, tables were set up in the roadway between the avenues. Flags fluttered from windows and houses were gaily decorated with flowers.

Miss May Lewis, Chairman of Blaenavon Council, walked around visiting many of the street parties, expressing her appreciation of everything that was being done for the children and her hopes that the same friendly and generous spirit in the town would continue.

The five hundred inhabitants of Cwmavon held a Thanksgiving Service at the local church on the evening of VE Day and this was followed by the lighting of bonfires on the hillside, which continued to burn until the early hours of the next morning.

Pontnewynydd people enjoyed an atmosphere of competitive spirit in the decoration of streets and organisation of parties. Commercial Street and Chapel Street in particular presented a colourful scene of flags of the Allies and bunting stretched from window to window. These continued to the boundary of the village where the Forge Hammer was a blaze of colour. Between 600 - 700 children were entertained to an excellent tea at the Pontnewynydd Works canteen, by the generosity of the Management. This was followed by sports and games in the Works Welfare Grounds. Street parties were held everywhere and at a merry pace. In the evening, Chapel Street was floodlit, with dancing and community singing continuing until a late hour.

Celebrations were opened in Blaendare Road, Pontypool, by Councillors C. Jones and C. Grey. About 100 children and the adults were provided with tea. A wireless set was playing in the background and in the afternoon sports were held. These were followed in the evening with community singing around a bonfire and the proceedings drew to a close with Councillor Grey thanking the organisers and everyone who had attended.

A victory thanksgiving concert was held at Pontypool's Market Hall and it was the greatest musical occasion that the town had seen since the Welsh National Eisteddfod in 1924. The concert was attended by nearly 3,000 people. There were two ladies' choirs, three male voice choirs and a choir of 300 voices was formed by two mixed choral societies.

In Cwmbran numerous street parties were organised for the children and these were followed by games and races. Later in the evening the adults participated in community singing and dancing in the streets. Victoria Street and Ventnor Road amalgamated their resources to provide a very special party for the children. Someone loaned a piano and the children were well provided with food and pop. The money contributed was well beyond that required and it was decided to retain the surplus for even greater 'Victory' celebrations at the conclusion of the Japanese war.

In June a special train pulled into Crane Street Station to take a large group of evacuees and mothers back to their homes in London. Waving handkerchiefs and shedding tears they departed, leaving the officials and foster-parents with their families on the platform. Local people had indeed opened their homes and hearts to provide shelter and care for the children and mothers who came to the Eastern Valley to escape the murderous V-bomb attacks. They had been billeted in houses from Blaenavon to Sebastapol.

The Eastern Valley celebrated the end of the Japanese war on 15th and 16th of August with street dancing, bonfires, fireworks and singing. Council preparations for the celebrations had to be made hurriedly, for until a fortnight previously few people had expected the capitulation of the Japanese to be so near.

Pontypool Park was floodlit on both nights and numerous bonfires were to be seen along the ridges on both sides of the valley. Dancing in the streets was going on throughout the locality and Clarence Street for example was supplied with music by Cliff King who had run lines to loudspeakers opposite his shop and at Clarence Corner. Massed choirs, ladies, mixed and male sang the 'Hallelujah Chorus' and other pieces in Pontypool Park and at Talywain Rugby Ground.

Floodlighting was also a special feature at Blaenavon with the Workmen's Hall, War Memorial and St Peter's Church receiving special treatment as did the home of Mr C.F. Sullivan in the Park. The Council arranged for the attendance of Blaenavon Colliery Silver Band at the Keeper's Road, where hundreds of people assembled around a huge bonfire and danced and sang to the music provided.

A large crowd gathered at Pontnewydd and danced to music provided by Bert Poulton, butcher, who also arranged special lighting effects. A fireworks display added to the general merriment, which continued until about 3 o' clock in the morning.

The children of Stanley Road, Garndiffaith, were provided with tea and when dusk fell a bonfire was lit by the oldest inhabitant of the district, Mr Tucker. Dancing then continued until the early hours in the arena which was floodlit. At Penygarn the children of James Street had a carnival and bonfire and the next day a Victory tea, which was also attended by about twenty old age pensioners.

Blaenavon's thanksgiving service was held at the Recreation Ground and the parade comprised members of Blaenavon Council and officials, Army Cadets (with their new Bugle Band), Air Training Corps, St John's Ambulance, Red Cross Services, representatives of Civil Defence and other organisations. The parade headed by Blaenavon Colliery Band, marched through the main streets of the town to the Recreation Ground, where the service was conducted by Canon D. Ivor Jones MA (Vicar), Rev G.L. Jones (King Street Baptists), and Rev Harry Thomas (Broad Street Baptists). Miss May Lewis JP (Chairman of Blaenavon Council) addressed a fairly large gathering, and the Band accompanied the singing of hymns.

Station Street, Abersychan, was alive with people participating in VJ celebrations which continued nightly throughout the week. Saturday was a great climax, when between 1,000 and 1,500 packed the street where Messrs Rickett's Band (later joined by a Jazz Band from Pontnewynydd) provided music for dancing. There were fairy lights, exploding fireworks, solo artists and community singing that could be heard for miles.

Pontnewydd streets were alive with people who made the most of the great occasion. At Freeholdland a jazz band was playing and there were many bonfires and fireworks.

Many streets in Griffithstown and Abersychan arranged celebrations, but generally speaking people seemed slightly more restrained than on VE-Day. Bonfires and squibs added to the general excitement and fun. In the evening dancing and singing took place around a very large bonfire in a field.

In September, the Pontypool War Comforts Fund was wound up and the £7,000 plus that still remained was equally divided among the eligible men and women serving in HM Forces on VJ-Day or who had served before that date.

The first local man to be re-patriated after being a prisoner of war in Japanese hands was Stoker Charles Jenkins of Charles Street, Blaenavon. He had been serving in *HMS Mata Hari* , a coaster taking women and children to Australia, when she was captured by the Japanese. Throughout his captivity he had hidden the ship's ensign which he brought home with him in October 1945.

Gordon Davies, returned to his Griffithstown home in Commercial Street in November 1945 after being a prisoner of war in Japanese hands for 3.5 years. At one period during his captivity he lost 2.5 stones in a fortnight but regained some weight later. His worst experiences were while employed night and day making the Thailand-Burma railway, on which every POW had to work, irrespective of rank. There was little food, and those who were ill were given even less and still forced to work.

The first Pontnewydd POW to return was Gnr. Bernard William John Fisher RA who came home in November after spending four years in a Japanese camp. Also on the same day, Craftsman Douglas Llewellyn Witchell REME, aged 26, a prisoner in Japanese hands for over 3 years arrived at his Blaenavon home and was given a tremendous welcome in Phillip Street. Before the war he had been a blacksmith's striker at Blaenavon Company's works and was 6ft in height and well built. But at one period of his captivity his weight dropped from 12st 10 lbs to 6st 8lb. He had been called up shortly after the outbreak of war, and was captured at Singapore. He was a prisoner in Thailand and worked at the quarries there and on the railroad. Hundreds of his mates had died during captivity.

**The Gulf War**

During the Gulf War in February 1991, a Torfaen Support Group was set up to sendparcels of home comforts to the 28 local people who were stationed in the Gulf. The packages included a letter from the Mayor of Torfaen, Mrs Sarah Richards, in which she sent the servicemen and women the good wishes of all the council members and officers and prayers for their safe return. The parcels also contained small luxuries like sweets, packet soups, a local newspaper and necessities such as toothpaste and toilet paper.

In February 1991 Corporal David Denbury (26) a Royal Engineer from Ponthir was killed while with the SAS regiment behind enemy lines in Iraq. His parents ran the Star Inn at Ponthir. He had served for 12 years in the army, joining the 22nd regiment of the SAS in 1989 and received the Queen's Gallantry Medal (QGM) for special duties in Northern Ireland.

David's funeral took place at All Saints' Church, Llanfrechfa, a few weeks after his death and he was buried with full military honours. The coffin draped in a Union Jack was carried by six soldiers from the 9th Parachute Squadron of the Royal Engineers to the graveside. Three rifle volleys were then fired above the grave, followed by the sounding of the Last Post, played on the bugle by 28 year old Royal Engineer, Chris Ellis. Corporal Denbury has since been commemorated in a stained glass window at the church.

A cenotaph bearing the names of about 150 local soldiers was unveiled at Panteg Cemetery in 1921.

## ---13---

# Here and there in Torfaen

*'Henllys is neglected by visitors to this part of the country, unless they are directed there by kind friends, or become entangled in the lanes by misdirection or accident; yet there are those who know Henllys and become so attached to it that their walks are taken in no other direction.'*

Olive Phillips 1951

### Abersychan

At the start of the nineteenth century this place, a few miles north of Pontypool, where the Sychan joins the Afon Lwyd, was just an area of woods and meadows. The Sychnant (dry brook) occasionally dries up in summer time and over the years the name Aber-sych-nant has been corrupted into Abersychan. A farm bearing this name used to be situated on the western side of the road near the bridge over the Afon Lwyd.

Financed by the British Iron Company, work commenced on the construction of Abersychan parish church in April 1831 and the contractor was John Lane of Pontypool. Dedicated to St Thomas, the church was built with fourteen windows made out of heavy cast iron. (These were replaced in 1958 by leaded lights in cathedral glass).

The first service was held on 10th September 1832, with the church filled to its utmost capacity of 500. Weekly services were conducted in English and Welsh alternately. From 1832 to 1844 the church was in the charge of the Vicar of Trevethin, the Rev Dr Casbard, the Rev D. Jones, curate, the Rev T. Davies and other assistant priests.

In 1844 Abersychan was formed into an ecclesiastical parish and the Rev F.R.P.C. Bluett BA., was appointed the first vicar. He resided in the parish at a farm called 'Bailey Glas' until a vicarage was built for him. He died on 10th October 1871 and a tablet in the church was erected by the parishioners in his memory.

Abersychan was later constituted a civil parish under the provisions of the 'Local Government Act 1894.' It contains Garndiffaith, Pontnewynydd, Talywain and the hamlets of Cefn-y-crib, Cwmavon, Cwmffrwdoer, Cwmnantddu, Freeholdland, Golynos, Pentrepiod, Snatchwood, Tranch and Varteg.

'Lock-up Lane' recalls a lock-up that was built in 1837 by the Trevethin Parish Police to house their local constable and it was replaced in 1885 by a police station built by the Monmouthshire Constabulary.

On the east bank of the Afon Lwyd, immediately north of Rising Sun Bridge, is an interesting estate lodge built in about 1835 by Capel Hanbury Leigh in the Tudor Gothic style as a home for the estate forester for Lasgarn Wood.

Abersychan was once a thriving mining town with its own swimming pool, thriving shopping centre and railway station, but during the last two decades, largely due to the death of the local coal industry it has become a depressed area that is much in need of regeneration. Fortunately, funds are now available to the tune of £1.6m through the Industrial Village Scheme to finance the regeneration of this one-time thriving mining village.

**Croesyceiliog**

One would assume that this village takes its name from a cross erected by St Ceiliog some time in the Dark Ages. Well, if such a cross ever existed, it has long since vanished. Also no longer to be seen is the large sculptured figure of a cock that is reputed to have once stood on a hillock in a field near the Upper Cock inn. The cock was depicted in the act of crowing and was no doubt a medieval momento of St Peter's denial. This strange monument is said to have been destroyed in 1646 by a band of Roundheads, who ransacked the neighbourhood on their way to the siege of Raglan Castle.

'With its pretty symmetry, its decorated barge boards, its hood mouldings and mock Tudor windows, and its general air of a cottage out of Never-never Land, designed by Lewis Caroll, Jim Crow's Cottages miles serenely on our matter-of-fact world,ready at any moment to be swept up on th e wings of a cloud and transported to Fairy land.'

Fred Hando 1964

An interesting old building in Croesyceiliog is **Jim Crow's Cottage** which has a particularly fine front fascade. It takes its name from an old seafaring man who was a friend of Benjamin Evans the village postmaster, shopkeeper and schoolmaster who resided in this cottage. When Jim Crow the ancient mariner passed away, Ben Evans and his wife decided to commemorate him by naming their cottage and nearby fields after him. Today, Croesyceiliog Comprehensive School stands on 'Jim Crow's Fields'. This early 19th century building was fortunately in recent years saved from proposed demolition, renovated and fitted into a small new housing development.

Pontrhydyrhn Baptist Chapel was built in 1836 and extended in 1889 and 1905. Members ofhe Conway family who financed its construction are buried in the graveyard.

Standing at the top of Chapel lane in Croesyceiliog is the **Pontrhydyrhn Baptist Church** which in its present form dates to 1836, when it replaced a smaller chapel built in 1815. Until that time a small room in the tinplate works had been utilised. There were additions to the building in 1889 and 1905 to provide a Baptistry and Sunday School accommodation. The building is a fine example of Greek influence, as demonstrated by its Ionic portico and pediment. Finance for building this Chapel came from the tinplate proprietors - the Conway family, whose tombs lie in the adjacent graveyard.

At the entrance gates of the church stand a giant cedar tree with its huge branches spreading far and wide. It is the only remaining tree of many brought back from Lebanon, in the Holy Land, by members of the Conway family who once went there on holiday.

**Garw Row** is a small cul-de-sac off The Garw, an old lane passing through the village, just to the west of the Upper Cock Inn. The Row contains fifteen old cottages which were built in the mid nineteenth century to house workers in nearby colliery and tinplate works. They were considered of interest as typical workers' housing of their time and careful conservation of these dwellings was undertaken in fairly recent years by Cwmbran Development Corporation. The aim was to bring the houses as close as possible to present day standards whilst at the same time preserving their character.

## Cwmavon

Situated midway between Pontypool and Blaenavon is the hamlet of Cwmavon(Cwmafon), which was once the site of a forge, thought to be operated by the first ironmasters of Blaenavon Ironworks. It was erected on a small area of flat land beside the Afon Lwyd and its history is somewhat obscure.

On the 1792 map of the Pontnewynydd to Blaenavon tramroad it is not even shown, yet it is clearly marked as 'Farteg Works' on the preliminary survey made in 1813 for the one inch O.S. map. The only relic of significance visible on the site is a large arch keystone, set into a wall (G.R. 26970657) and dated 1804. Some workmen excavating a trench for a subsidiary sewer in July 1951 unearthed some brick and ironwork relics of the forge, but these are no longer in evidence. The Forge Manager, Mr Partridge, resided in Cwmavon House which was built in about 1825.

Forge Row, Cwmavon, consisting of 12 cottages was the first workers' housing in South Wales to have back doors. The cottages date back to 1804 and are relatively unaltered in appearance.

Of particular interest is the terrace of twelve houses known as **Forge Row** perched on the hillside above the site of the forge. They were constructed in 1802-3 and apart from Stack Square, Blaenavon (built in 1792), this is the only surviving example of housing from the first phase of the Industrial Revolution in old Monmouthshire.

Each of the twelve dwellings originally had four rooms on two storeys, the front door opening directly into what was a kitchen /dining room, from which a passage / larder led to the rear door and a small back bedroom. The rear door was an unusual feature for this time and Forge Row was perhaps the only row in the 1820s to have a back door. A small winding staircase adjacent to the fireplace in the living room /kitchen gave access to the first floor. The stairs led into a front bedroom, through which there was access to a small rear bedroom. Roofed with random slates, the underside was plastered to act as insulation and help retain heat in the building.

When the Varteg Forge closed in 1840, many of the workers moved away from the locality and as a result most of the cottages in Forge Row became vacant. According to the 1852 census only six of the dwellings were occupied at an average of 4.3 persons per house. In later years the Row came into the ownership of the proprietors of the Varteg Hill Collieries, located on the west side of the valley. Forge Row was then fully occupied by employees of that company. People continued to live in the Row until 1975, when the last resident was re-housed by the local authority.

In 1980 Forge Row was in serious danger of demolition by the National Coal Board who were then the owners. Fortunately, Torfaen Museum Trust had the foresight to purchase the buildings and thus ensure their survival. This row of cottages is certainly of historic importance for they are relatively unchanged from their original design and appearance. The high standard of construction and (for its time) relatively generous floor areas makes Forge Row a prototype of industrial housing design and it has been listed as a Grade II Ancient Monument.

In 1989 the British Historic Buildings Trust and the National Trust undertook restoration of the cottages in a unique £200,000 scheme which was supported by Cadw and the Prince of Wales Committee. A great deal of care and attention was applied in order to preserve the original charm and character of the buildings, while at the same time providing modern facilities.

The original cottages 1 & 2 were combined to form one large end-of-terrace cottage with extra accommodation on the ground floor. The original cottages 3 & 4, 5 & 6, 7 & 8 and 9 & 10, were combined to form large middle-of-terrace cottages while the original No. 11 was retained to form a single bedroom, middle-of-terrace cottage and the original No. 12, a large end-of-terrace, single bedroom cottage.

Fireplaces and original stairways were retained in all the cottages, while a second stairway was installed in the halls of the five larger cottages. These were also provided with ground floor cloakrooms to compliment the first floor bathrooms.

The total cost of the scheme was £200,000 and this was covered by the subsequent sale of the restored cottages. It was necessary for the new owners to sign a strict covenant which prevented the cottages from being altered or spoiled in any way.

Westlake's Brewery at Cwmavon.

The Manager's House

Situated on the east bank of the Afon Lwyd, just below the main road at Cwmavon, is a five storey building constructed in local stone with red brick dressings and a slate roof. It was built in 1900 by Charles Westlake for the purpose of brewing beer. The designer was George Adlam and Sons of Bristol, leading brewery architects of that time. It succeeded a previous brewery in Blaenavon that had been opened in the 1880s by Charles Francis Westlake. Difficulties in obtaining a reliable water supply in Blaenavon had resulted in the Cwmavon site being chosen for the site of the new brewery.

By 1907 Westlakes Brewery Ltd (founded in 1889) had a chain of pubs and its beer was regarded very highly. In 1911 the Company took over the Castle Brewery in Pontypool but by 1920 the business was in decline and brewing ceased eight years later.

During the depression of the 1930s an independent experiment in self-help known as the 'Order of Friends' took over the building as its headquarters. The scheme was designed to assist the unemployed in maintaining their moral. Here bakers, cobblers, carpenters and other skilled tradesmen exercised their crafts on behalf of their fellow unfortunates and in return received the produce of various small-holdings that were cultivated by the less skilled. Every day the place was a scene of intense activity. The farm adjoining the brewery was acquired by the Order as part of the scheme and the ground was subjected to intense cultivation, to cater for the needs of those who had come to rely upon its productivity for their livelihood.

In later years part of the building was taken over by Dunlop of Brynmawr who used it for the manufacture of a range of technical products and employed 50 - 100 people. These products included specialised components for leading manufacturers of accumulators, dividing strips for terrazzo flooring and sheets, rods and circles of ebonite, often for export. They also set up a Latex Department there. Rubber gloves, bowls, mats and an assortment of rubber goods were produced. Childrens' clothes were made by another firm on the two top floors where large numbers of women were employed as machinists. Railway uniforms were also produced.

The building is now used as a plastics factory and it has been listed as a Grade II Ancient Monument, being a fine survival of an impressive Victorian brewery which was built by well known architects who specialised in the design of such buildings.

### Garndiffaith

The ecclesiastical parish of **Garndiffaith** was formed in 1937 when St John's Church was built and the village also has several Non-conformist churches including Calvinistic, Methodists, Congregational, Primitive Methodist, Wesleyan and United Methodist.

In 1905 a Workingmens' Institute was built with a wide range of facilities including baths, reading room, recreation and billiard rooms.

This impressive viaduct which spans Cwm Ffrwd and connects Garndiffaith with Talywain. It was built in 1876 by the engineer John Gardner and the line opened on 18th September 1879. Although the railway has long since closed this stone viaduct remains as a fine example of Victorian engineering.

### Griffithstown

**This village** one mile south of Pontypool, is named after Henry Griffiths who was the founder of the settlement in the mid-nineteenth century. He was born in Chepstow in 1824 and at the age of twenty, was working for the Great Western Railway Company at Swindon. Some years later he was promoted to the position of Station Master at the newly opened station in Pontypool Road in his home county of Monmouthshire. His responsibilities extended as far north as Pandy and as far west as Crumlin and he was able to boast that he had crossed the great viaduct in the first loaded train in 1857.

Now feeling well established in the Pontypool area, Henry Griffiths looked around for a suitable site on which to build himself a house. He chose a plot of ground on the hillside above the canal and overlooking the woodlands of Panteg. Jointly, with two other railway officials, ten acres of ground were purchased from the Hanbury estate. They divided the land into plots and formed a 'Building Committee', with the aim of building houses to accommodate railway employees. At one of their early meetings it was decided to name the new settlement after the chairman of the committee.

Henry Griffiths, himself, had bought four of the plots and on one of them in 1860, he built himself a fine dwelling which was named **St Dunston's House**, after his second wife. He in fact married three times. First in May 1851, he married Elled Ogdon Parke, eldest daughter of Mr Fenning Parke, schoolmaster of Minchinhampton, Gloucestershire. In 1859, having been widowed, he married Ann Dunston, daughter of Samuel Dunston of the parish of St Clement in Cornwall. His third marriage in 1867, following the death of his second wife, was to her sister Margaretta Dunston and it took place at St Mary's Church, Chepstow. In total he had six children.

Up until 1864 Griffithstown formed part of the parish of Llanfrechfa. It was a large parish, with the mother church of All Saints situated in the part of the parish known as Llanfrechfa Lower. It extended from the boundaries of Pontymoel to those of Llangattock juxta Caerleon. In about 1884, about 270 acres were taken from the north western corner of the parish of Llanfrechfa to form the village of Griffithstown.

On the deeds of the land purchased by Henry Griffiths and his committee it is stipulated that no licensed house should be built on it and this explains the absence of any public house in Griffithstown. Henry Griffiths died at the age of 90 on 19th February 1915 and a memorial plaque to him can be seen inside St Hilda's Church.

*St Hilda's Church, Griffithstown, from Greenhill Road.*

Constructed in 1887 in the Early English style, **St Hilda's Church** consists of chancel, nave, aisles and a south porch. On Whit Sunday, 1905, a fine carved screen was dedicated as a memorial to the Rev James Edwin Dunn (vicar from 1898 - 1904) and his wife.

The west window was erected in 1962 by Mr and Mrs I. Butler in commemoration of their golden wedding anniversary. Another memorial window is dedicated to the Rev E. J. Dunn, first vicar of the parish. Mr J. E. Dunn and Dr O' Keefe are commemorated by a window erected in 1920 and the stained glass window near the font was presented by Mrs Butler.

A memorial plaque commemorates Henry Griffiths, the founder of Griffithstown:-

'In memory of Henry Griffiths,
Died 19th February 1915, aged 90.
Whose pioneer work as a founder of this Town
is recognised in its name Griffithstown.'

Nearby is **Panteg House** which was originally built in the 1830's as the residence of the Managing Director of Panteg Works and was then known as "Belvedere". During the First World War it became a hospital for wounded soldiers and it later became the Social Club of the Panteg Works with reading rooms, games rooms, a lounge with bar and a large room for concerts, dinners and social meetings of all kinds. For a time during World War Two it housed the office staff of the firm's London headquarters during the blitz on London.

In 1956 the Panteg House Committee removed the ban on the admittance of women and this alteration in the club's constitution was reported to have been welcomed by the male employees of Panteg works, who hitherto had exclusive use of the club.

The old Goods Shed on Station Road, Griffithstown celebrated its 120th anniversary in 1999. It is situated near the Avesta Sheffield main entrance and has been derelict since the closure of the passenger line in 1962. A preservation society has been formed by local people who are working to turn the building into a railway museum. Funding has been provided by Pontypool Community Council while Avesta Sheffield have donated building materials.

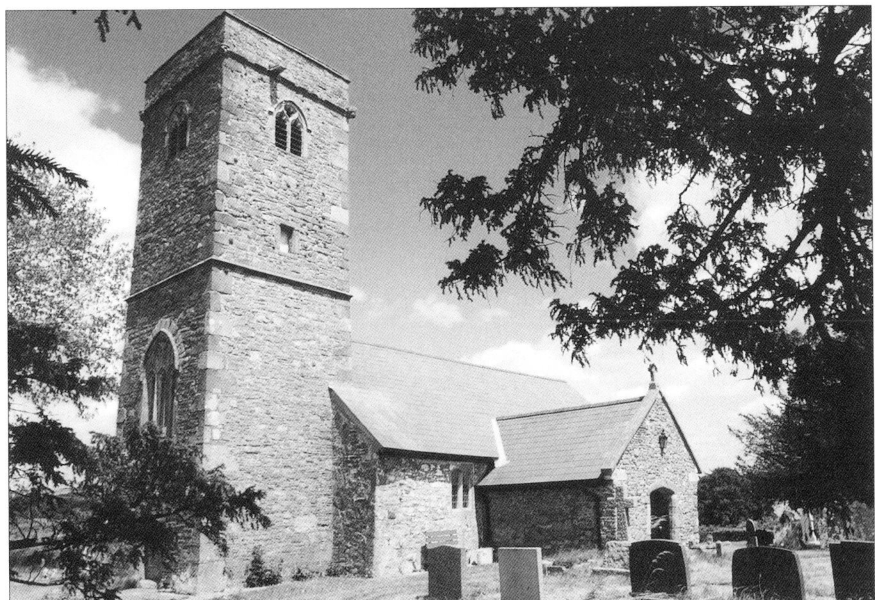

**Henllys Church**

Dedicated to St Peter, this is an ancient building comprising chancel (with an embossed roof), nave, south porch and a western tower in two stages. A projecting embattled stair turrett can be seen in the north corner of the tower and above the 14th century windows runs a course decorated at each corner by stone faces and one strange animal. Within the the tower are two bells, one of them being dated 1350.

Under the floorboards of the pews are many ancient tombstones, while a memorial stone on the north wall tells us:-

> 'Consider then and be not
> proud,
> Thy time will come to wear a
> shroud
> With me and them that's gone
> before
> To lie with worms which Craves
> for more.'

The churchyard cross has four steps leading to the base and stump of the column and nearby is an immense yew with a stone seat squared around its trunk.

**Henllys** signifies 'Old Court,' a name which suggests that some important chieftain of ancient times had his court here. It may well have stood on the site of a farmhouse on the southern slope of Twmbarlwm, a mile beyond the church at an altitude of 600 feet above sea level. It bears the confusing name of 'Cwrt Henllys' which translates 'Court Old Court.'

**Llanderfel**

The ruined church of Llanderfel stands at an altitude of about 1,000 feet above sea level on the slopes of Mynydd Maen and probably dates from about 550AD, which makes it the oldest known building in Torfaen. It is reputed to have been established by St Derfel who died about the end of the sixth century and was said to have been a contemporary of King Arthur. As a young man he was a noted warrior who became known as Derfel Gadarn (Derfel the Valiant) and is said to have distinguished himself at the Battle of Camlan in 542. His might and prowess in war are constantly alluded to in the writings of the medieval Welsh bards. In the latter part of his life he is reputed to have become a member of the Llanilltyd Fawr (Llantwit Major) community where his father Hywel Farchog was buried. Derfel himself is said to be buried on Bardsey Island off the Lleyn Peninsula in North Wales.

St Derfel is commemorated on April 5th and his festival is marked in more than twenty Welsh 'Kalendars' of the 15th and 16th centuries. This church on the hillside above Cwmbran is one of only two foundations dedicated to St Derfel in Wales and it was once a place of some importance. When it was acquired by the monks of Llantarnam it was treated with the greatest veneration and became a place of pilgrimage.

St Michael's Church Fred Hando

The Horse and Jockey Inn Fred Hando

**Llanfihangel Pontymoile**

Situated one mile to the east of Pontypool, this church is one of the very few Llanfihangels (Church of St Michael) situated on low ground, for churches dedicated to the Archangel Michael are generally to be found on hill tops. Church and inn are often to be found rubbing shoulders and adjoining the church is an attractive thatched hostelry which stands beside the old coach road to Abergavenny. Fred Hando, a local author, in 1949, summed up the one-time tranquillity of this spot when he wrote:-

> 'Pleasant it is to pull in here (as our forebears did in their coaches) to recapture some of the atmosphere of old Gwent and to be calmed by the serene beauty of the hamlet, where the cream walls and brown roof of the church and the cream walls and brown thatch of the inn are set against the dark green of the yews and the pale green of the larch plantations on the hillside.'

The church was first mentioned in documents dating from the thirteenth century, when the Bishop of Norwich in 1254 produced a valuation of the churches in England and Wales for the Pope. By 1536 it was referred to in documents as 'Kylegoyane' and recorded as being annexed to the Parish of Panteg.

It may be assumed that the church was rebuilt in 1736, for this date is engraved above the south porch with the initials I.H.C.W., which no doubt refer to a local man who was the church warden at that time.

The western belfry contains two bells, one of which is dated 1598, but the most interesting feature inside the church is the 'waggon' style roof which can be seen in both the chancel and the nave. Such a name is taken from the shape of the canvas shelter that was often attached to old carts.

A single central corbel above the chancel arch is probably the only relic of the roof loft which would have been reached by a flight of stone steps. Two other items of interest include an oak chest and a circular font with a flower-patterned bowl.

On the east wall is a tablet commemorating the Rev Christopher Cook who was incumbent of this church for 75 years. He in fact held the longest tenure of any parish in Wales. Born in Clydach, he was the son of a naval surgeon (who served in the Battle of Trafalgar and died a nonagenarian). Christopher Cook was ordained in 1850 and the following year he became Minister of Llanfihangel Pontymoile and Mamhilad. At first he conducted services at his two churches in Welsh, then in both English and Welsh and later in English entirely. He was affectionately known as 'Parson Cook' and during his long tenure he conducted 910 weddings which was indeed a very large number for such a small parish church.

Living in retirement for seventeen years, he still kept up his interest in the church by regularly reading the lessons, while his curate conducted the services. During his 100th year, the Rev Cook must have had quite a shock when the roof of St Michael's Church, suddenly decided to fall bodily into the churchyard below. The ancient nails had rusted and strong winds proved the final straw. However, workmen from the Pontypool Park Estate soon arrived on the scene to repair the damage.

In 1927 'Parson Cook', suffered a fall at his home which resulted in a fractured thigh and the shock of his injury led to his deat at the age of 102. He was buried in the grave of his wife at St Illtyd's Church, Mamhilad.

Dedicated to All Saints, Llanfrechfa Church, with the exception of the south porch and the impressive tower was rebuilt in 1873.

**Llanfrechfa**

The name of this village translates as 'the hill top church of the speckled land,' which stems from the fact no doubt that it was built on a lightly wooded ridge. All Saints Church was rebuilt in the fifteenth century and the existing tower added. We may deduce from the remains of a former roof line on the inside of the east wall that the reconstructed church was the same width as the tower and lower than the present nave.

In 1872 the main body of the fifteenth century church was demolished and rebuilt, with the outer walls extended into the churchyard. Also, at this time, the belfry's original three bells were increased to six, all being inscribed with verses from a fourteenth century Latin hymn called 'Salutatio Jesui.' (Two more bells were added in 1936).

The embattled tower is constructed of rectangular stone blocks in a plain Perpendicular style, with battlements and a small staircase leading to the turret. On the south side of the tower is a sundial, and the western side bears a stone carved with part of a Maltese cross.

Inside the church, the nave is separated from the chancel by two steps and a carved wooden screen which is surmounted by three carved wooden figures representing the Holy Family.

The Altar is made of a thick slab of white marble set onto a table of carved oak. Four small crosses on each corner of the Altar and a larger one in the middle have no doubt been carved to represent the five wounds of Christ. Above the Altar is a reredos constructed of Caen stone which was brought here from Normandy. It depicts in fine detail, Jesus celebrating the Holy Eucharist and blessing the chalice. Built into the wall on the right of the Altar is a small stone piscina. This was used for ceremonial washing after the celebration of the Eucharist.

At the end of the north aisle is the baptistry where if desired the ordnance of baptism by immersion may be performed. Shields on the front of the baptistry are decorated with the ark, the fish and the Chi-Ro monogram. The baptistry is covered with a large wooden lid.

Several wall tablets are to be seen inside the church and it is of interest that many of them must have been taken from the earlier building. The oldest tablet, dated 1696, is dedicated to Charles Griffiths of Llanyrafon Farm.

A plaque on the inside of the tower wall commemorates Frank Johnstone Mitchel and his wife Elizabeth Harcourt Rolls of Llanfrechfa Grange. She was the aunt of Charles Stewart Rolls, the famous pioneer aviator and co-founder of Rolls Royce.

**Llanfrechfa Grange**, a short distance away, was built in about the middle of the 19th century in the grounds of an old manor house in the style of the Elizabethan period. The Grange was built by Charles Prothero, clerk of the peace for the county, 3rd son of Thomas Prothero of Malpas. He created 140 acres of parkland out of the existing fields. In about 1865 the property was sold to Francis Johnstone Mitchell, who added to it and much improved it. It was later purchased by Sir John Cecil Davies.

During the Second World War Llanfrechfa Grange was used as a maternity home for women from heavily-bombed areas. It subsequently became a psychiatric hospital.

Llantarnam Abbey was rebuilt in 1834-6 by Reginald James Blewitt, an important Monmouthshire industrialist and politician.

The building is now owned and occupied by the Sisters of St Joseph.

### Llantarnam

Llanfihangel Llantarnam is the more accurate name of this village and while the first part translates as the Church of St Michael, the origin of the name Llantarnam has been given at least two different explanations. Some historians have claimed that it is a corruption of Llantorfaen after the ancient name of the river Torfaen, now known as the Afon Lwyd. But writers of the past have also claimed that the name is derived from Nant Teyrnon (Teyrnon's Brook). As a mythical Lord of Gwent Iscoed, Teyrnon is described in one of the ancient tales of the *Mabinogion* as 'the best man in the world.'

It was a 12th century Lord of Caerleon, Howel ap Iorwerth, who founded a Cistercian abbey, dedicated to St Mary, at Llantarnam in 1175, the year of his death. At that time Llantarnam was considered to be part of Caerleon for it was in the Lordship of that locality.

Llantarnam Abbey endowed with lands at Abercarn, Panteg and Trevethin, within a short time became one of the richest religious houses in this part of Wales, with sixty monks in residence. These monks of the Cistercian order were known as the White Monks, according to the colour of the habits that they wore. The rules of their Order were obeyed in the strictest way and they never partook of wine nor meat and fasted frequently.

In 1272 the Lordship of Caerleon was taken over by the De Clare family, who typically in the Norman fashion had seized a great deal of monastic property. By 1317 the number of monks at Llantarnam had dwindled to twenty. A disastrous fire, in 1398, razed the Abbey to the ground, but through the prodigious efforts of the Abbot, John ap Gruffydd, it was restored with the work being completed within two years.

In 1405 the abbot, John ap Howell, was apparently a militant churchman and appears to have been active on the Welsh side when forces of Owain Glyndwr, attacking Usk Castle, were defeated by the king's troops. The abbot personally heard confessions and gave absolution before the battle , but was himself killed in the engagement.

By Act of Parliament, dated 4th February 1536, the Abbey with all its valuable possessions was surrendered to the king. Three years later the monastic site, together with the neighbouring church was granted to a certain John Parker. He died without issue in 1552 and his possessions at Llantarnam reverted to the Crown. Leland described the abbey as 'standing in a wood' and at the Dissolution of the Monasteries it was worth £71 3s 2d per annum and six monks were in residence.

Queen Elizabeth on 26 May 1554, granted the site and its lands to William Carpenter and William Savage. Within a very short time they conveyed Llantarnam to William Morgan ( of Pentre-bach), the eldest son of John Morgan of Caerleon, a son of Sir Thomas Morgan of Pencoed Castle in south Gwent. William Morgan claimed descent from the princes of Gwent and he had previously resided at Pentre Bach to the north of Llantarnam.

From 1555 to 1571, William Morgan was an MP and undoubtedly a man of some wealth and importance, being connected through both his father and his mother with the chief families of Gwent and Glamorgan. His wife was Elizabeth, a daughter of Sir Rice Mansell and when William died on 29th March 1582, it is most likely that he was buried in the Morgan Chapel of Llantarnam Church, where the framework of an alabaster monument can be seen. His only son and heir was Edward Morgan who is believed to have built a portion of the Tudor house which now stands on the site of Llantarnam Abbey.

Edward Morgan suffered considerable financial impositions, by his unwavering loyalty to Roman Catholicism, for these were times when such faith involved great risk to life and property. By refusing to attend divine service at the (Anglican) parish church, he made himself liable to a fine of £20 per month under Elizabeth's 1581 Recusancy Act. He paid the fine consistently from 1606 up to his death in 1633, a total of £7,900. This sum included £1,000 which Edward paid in July 1612 in order to be excused taking the 'Oath of allegiance.'

The Morgans of Llantarnam were devout Catholics and their loyalty to the old faith persisted through the years of persecution. In defiance of the law the family secretly maintained a resident priest and as a result the Calvinist Member of Parliament, John Arnold of Llanfihangel Crucorney, denounced Llantarnam as an illegal rendezvous for Roman Catholics. It was here that the Jesuit priest, Father David Lewis, was arrested in November 1678. He was taken prisoner, 'a little before day by six armed men,' in a little hut at Llantarnam 'under a clay floor cunningly contrived.' This hut is said to have stood opposite the church and next to a blacksmith's forge. David Lewis was subsequently hanged, drawn and quartered at Usk on 27th August 1679. His last words were:-

> 'I was condemned for reading Mass, hearing Confessions, anointing sick, christening and preaching. As for reading the Mass, it was the old, and still is, the accustomed and laudable liturgy of the Holy Church, and all the other acts are acts of religion and worship of God. And for religion I die.'

He was buried near the porch of St Mary's Priory Church in Usk and in 1970 was canonised with about forty other English and Welsh Roman Catholic martyrs at a ceremony conducted in Rome by Pope Paul.

Edward Morgan's eldest son, also named Edward, inherited the property but died at the age of 25 in 1682. He left no son to inherit his estates. His two daughters, Anne the elder and Frances, in 1707 agreed on a partition of their inheritance, by which Anne received the manors of Edlogan and Pulpen, the two together representing the greater part of the parish of Panteg, Llandewi Fach, Llanfrechfa Upper and Lower, Llanhennock, Llandegfedd, Caerleon and Llantrissent, totalling about 3,702 acres. To Frances was allocated the manor of Wentsland and Bryngwyn, including part of Llanhilleth, that part of the parish of Trevethin which lies to the west of the Afon Lwyd, Llanfihangel Pontymoel and part of Llantarnam, totalling 4,483 acres.

Anne died a spinster in 1712 and she willed her property to her step-father, John Grubham Howe of the county of Gloucester, who had by then married her mother Mary after the death of her first husband, the third baronet. As a result of marrying a Morgan of Llantarnam, the name of John Grubham Howe turns up frequently in documents relating to Monmouthshire and it is relevant that it was he, who in 1689 applied to King William for permission to set up a market in Pontypool. Following a public enquiry held at 'The Golden Lion,' Abergavenny, a Royal Charter was granted on 25th January 1690 for three fairs a year to be held in the town and a market on each Saturday 'for the buying and selling of livestock and merchandise'. Anne's younger sister, Frances, married Edmund Bray, of Barrington Co., of Gloucester and it is her name which appears on the plaque that can be seen on the front of the old Corn Market in Pontypool. Frances Bray nee Morgan had two daughters, Mary, who married John Blewitt and Frances, wife of John Fettipace.

The manor of Edlogan eventually passed from John Grubham Howe to his grandson, John Thynne Howe, 2nd Lord Chedworth, and thence to John Hanbury and today is in the ownership of the Lord Lieutenant, Sir Richard Hanbury Tenison.

In 1832 the property was inherited by Reginald James Blewitt, the great great grandson of Mary Blewitt. He was born in 1790 and was to become an important figure in the commercial, industrial and political life of Monmouthshire. He was Mayor of Newport in 1837- 38 and 1841 - 42, and a Member of Parliament from 1837 - 1851. Also he is noted for having founded, and for a short time edited, the county's first newspaper, *The Monmouthshire Merlin.* For thirty years this was the only newspaper covering the whole of the county and it is now of great interest to historians. The issue of the paper for 15th December 1832 announced that, 'Mr R. J. Blewitt had come to occupy the noble mansion (at Llantarnam) of his ancestors.'

On taking up residence in the noble mansion of his ancestors at Llantarnam, Blewitt announced that he was going to have repairs carried out to the roof at an estimated cost of £50. However, the condition of the mansion was much worse than at first realised and a vast rebuilding of the entire structure had to be undertaken. It was also decided in 1836, to re-route the road from 'The Three Blackbirds' to 'The Greenhouse' and to also construct a long wall as a boundary to the park. The total cost of all this work amounted to nearly £60,000. Above the main entrance in the wall (the new Magna Porta) can be seen a stone bearing the date 1836 and the name Magna Porta, together with a shield bearing the arms of the Morgan family.

'Magna Porta'- the main entrance to Llantarnam Abbey, constructed by R.J. Blewitt in 1836.

Following the retirement from Parliament of Benjamin Hall as Member for the Monmouth Boroughs in 1837, Blewitt stood as Liberal candidate against the Tory ironmaster, Joseph Bailey, and won the seat by polling 440 votes against Bailey's 386.

Blewitt was responsible, with Philip Jones of Llanarth, for founding the Monmouth and Glamorgan Bank in 1837. It paid good dividends for a number of years, but collapsed suddenly in 1851. As a result, Blewitt withdrew from public life in the county, resigned his seat in Parliament and went to live in France, Following the death of his elder brother, Edward Francis Blewitt, he returned to England in 1868 to dispute the title of his widowed sister to the family estates. After a long legal battle which Blewitt lost, he ended his connection with Monmouthshire. He died on 11 September 1878 and the *Monmouthshire Merlin* of 20th September carried the following obituary notice:-

> 'We have this week to record the death of a gentleman who, in years long past, occupied a prominent position in this county... Mr. Blewitt, having withdrawn from this neighbourhood more than 20 years ago, his name is familiar only to a small proportion of those residing in the county; many who were his contemporaries and supporters during an active political career have long since passed away. For years Mr. Blewitt took a conspicuous part in local affairs and, as a genial friend, a man of culture and extraordinary energy, was much esteemed and respected...A cloud having fallen upon his fortunes, he withdrew from the county and his connection with it was never afterwards resumed. He had, we believe, reached his eightieth year and retained his characteristic energy of mind almost to the close of his life.'

In 1895 Llantarnam Abbey was purchased by Sir Clifford Cory who resided there until his death in 1941. A description of the grand house during this period is provided by Winifred Graham in a book entitled, *Observations - casual and intimate*, which was published in 1946:-

> '...the huge fireplaces blazing on all sides camouflaged the lack of central heating and were even sufficient to warm the entrance hall with its Minstrel Gallery and long church-like stained-glass windows. We were given comfortable adjoining bedrooms where fires also blazed. Then, in this home of luxury, came a surprise. My astonishment was great to see an old-fashioned round bath placed on the hearth rug with large steaming cans of water for my ablutions. The Abbey, with its numerous apartments for visitors, boasted no bathrooms. The large staff seemed to think nothing of carrying cans down the endless corridors and stoking fires from morning till night.
> Only a few years before he died at the age of eighty he decided suddenly to inaugurate bathrooms and central heating. He never did things by halves. Stately marble bathrooms were installed and owing to the great thickness of the walls these alterations cost over £3,000. The floor of the gunroom, when taken up for central heating pipes, revealed buried human skeletons, hundreds of years old, probably monks.'

The sisters of St Joseph bought the Abbey in 1946 and turned it into a centre from which to provide facilities for others in their Order and carry out the works of the congregation. Part of that work was ensuring the necessary peace and quiet for the convalescence and rehabilitation of sisters working in towns and cities. As well as having elderly, retired and invalid sisters residing there, the Abbey serves as a religious retreat, a novitiate and a house of study for younger sisters.

Rear courtyard of Llantarnam Abbey.

Llanfihangel Church stands beside the Greenhouse Inn at Llantarnam.

**Llanfihangel church**

Dedicated to St Michael, Llanfihangel Church, stands next to the Green House Inn and alongside the old main road from Newport to Pontypool. The building is mostly 15th century, but between the north chapel and the chancel are two curious arches which probably date back another five hundred years.

Restoration of the church was carried out in 1869, in the Gothic style and it now consists of a battlemented tower, nave, chancel and a chapel, generally known as the Morgan or Blewitt Chapel. This was probably built by William Morgan who purchased Llantarnam Abbey in 1554. It is also likely that the two depressed arches through which it is entered were brought here from the old abbey.

There are several stone memorials in the Morgan Chapel, including some to the Blewitt and Dowling families, but the most prominent monument is the massive tomb of the 16th century Morgan family on the north side. It has been converted into a back-ground for a communion table.

A seemingly out of place monument commemorates a certain 'Martin Kuych Van Mierop Esq., of London, Merchant. He died by a fall at the Mynydd Mane. Aug 1775.'

On the north wall a tablet commemorates Martha Absalam who died in 1770 aged 82:-

'Death in a very good old age
Did end my wery Pilgrimage
A sweet deliverance from my
Pain
That I may Enter life Again
An happy Change and ever blest
When grife and Pain
Is turn'd to Rest.'

Beneath, on another stone, between an hour-glass and a skull, is the inscription to Ann Dentt of Llanfrechfa who died in 1686, aged 18.

In a vault underneath the chapel are deposited the remains of Edmund Blewitt, son of Edward Blewitt of Llantarnam Abbey. He died at Gloucester on 3 July, 1831 in the 31st year of his age. The vault was erected by his widow Mary Blewitt in 1831.

The memorial to Edward Blewitt reads:-

'Sacred to the memory of Edward Francis Blewitt Esq., of Llantarnam Abbey, who died on the 20th February 1808 in the 71st year of his age.'

The ancient looking font may be pre-Norman and its fish decorations may be associated with the early Christian symbol based on the Greek word for fish. This is ichthus and is composed of the intitial letters of words which anglicised would be Iesous Christos Theo Uios Soteer (Jesus Christ, Son of God, Saviour).

A window in the east wall depicts Christ, St George and St Peter and it was erected as a war memorial.

In 1919 some beautiful mural paintings were discovered on a wall in the nave, one of them depicting St Christopher. They were described at the time as being painted in 'gorgeous blue, gold and red.' Sadly they were later destroyed.

Outside in the churchyard can be seen the base and shaft of an ancient cross. It is surmounted by a comparatively modern cross. Of more recent interest at the Greenhouse end of the churchyard is the grave of Private John Williams of the South Wales Borderers, a local hero who won the Victoria Cross at the famous battle of Rorke's Drift, during the Zulu War of 1879 (see chapter twelve).

The 18th century Green House Inn

Carved sign above the door

**The Green House Inn**

Standing next to the church is an attractive inn which is noted for the quaint sign that can be seen above the entrance. It depicts on a wooden tablet, two jolly old men sitting at a table, one smoking, with a large tankard before him; the other holding a smaller mug or glass and a candlestick between them. Their coat tails drop over the chairs as they sit there. Below are the words:-

Y Ty Gwyrdd
1719
Cwrw da
A Seidr i chwi
Dewch y mewn
Chwi gewch y brefi

(Translation)
The Green House
1719
Good Beer
And Cider for you
Come in
You shall taste it.

Llanyrafon Farm is one of Torfaen's former manor houses. Dating back to the 16th century it was altered and extended in the 17th and 19th centuries. It is now being developed by the Torfaen Museum Trust as a museum of the agricultural history of the valley.

**Llanyrafon Farm**

For centuries this large grey house has stood near the Afon Lwyd and its original name was probably 'Glanyrafon' - implying 'on the bank of the river'. Today, it is known as Llanyrafon Farm and the historian Bradney tells us that this was the most important mansion in the parish of Llanfrechfa and the seat of a family named Griffiths. Charles Griffiths, the last of the name, was steward of the manor of Edlogan. The present house may have its origins in the Middle Ages but it is from the end of the 16th century to the middle of the 19th century that the surviving buildings relate. It would seem that the oldest part of the house is the eastern wing which dates back to the last quarter of the 16th century and includes a parlour and hall separated by an oak post and panel partition, which bears the initials 'CG' of one of the Charles Griffiths who lived at the farm between 1630 and 1836. The central section of the house was constructed by 1616 and it very much reflects the growth in prosperity of the Griffiths family.

In about 1800 William Griffiths moved from Llanyrafon to Gloucester, where he was a successful solicitor, but he made regular visits to Llanyrafon to manage his estate. The property was sold to Richard Laybourne in the 1890s, and then the Pillinger family who continued to farm there. But in the 1900's they moved to a new red brick villa built a short distance away by Alfred Massey Pillinger. This was known as Llanyrafon House and is now part of the Commodore Hotel.

In the 1950's the Llanyrafon estate comprising 1,000 acres was sold to the Cwmbran Development Corporation and a wide range of possible uses for the house were considered, including the drastic suggestion of demolition. Fortunately at the end of the 1970's it was decided to retain the building and the Torfaen Museum Trust took it over in 1987 and work was started on restoring the building with Messrs Capps & Capps of Hay-on-Wye undertaking the specialised work. The building is now open to the public on weekends from April to September.

Front entrance to Llanyrafon Farm.

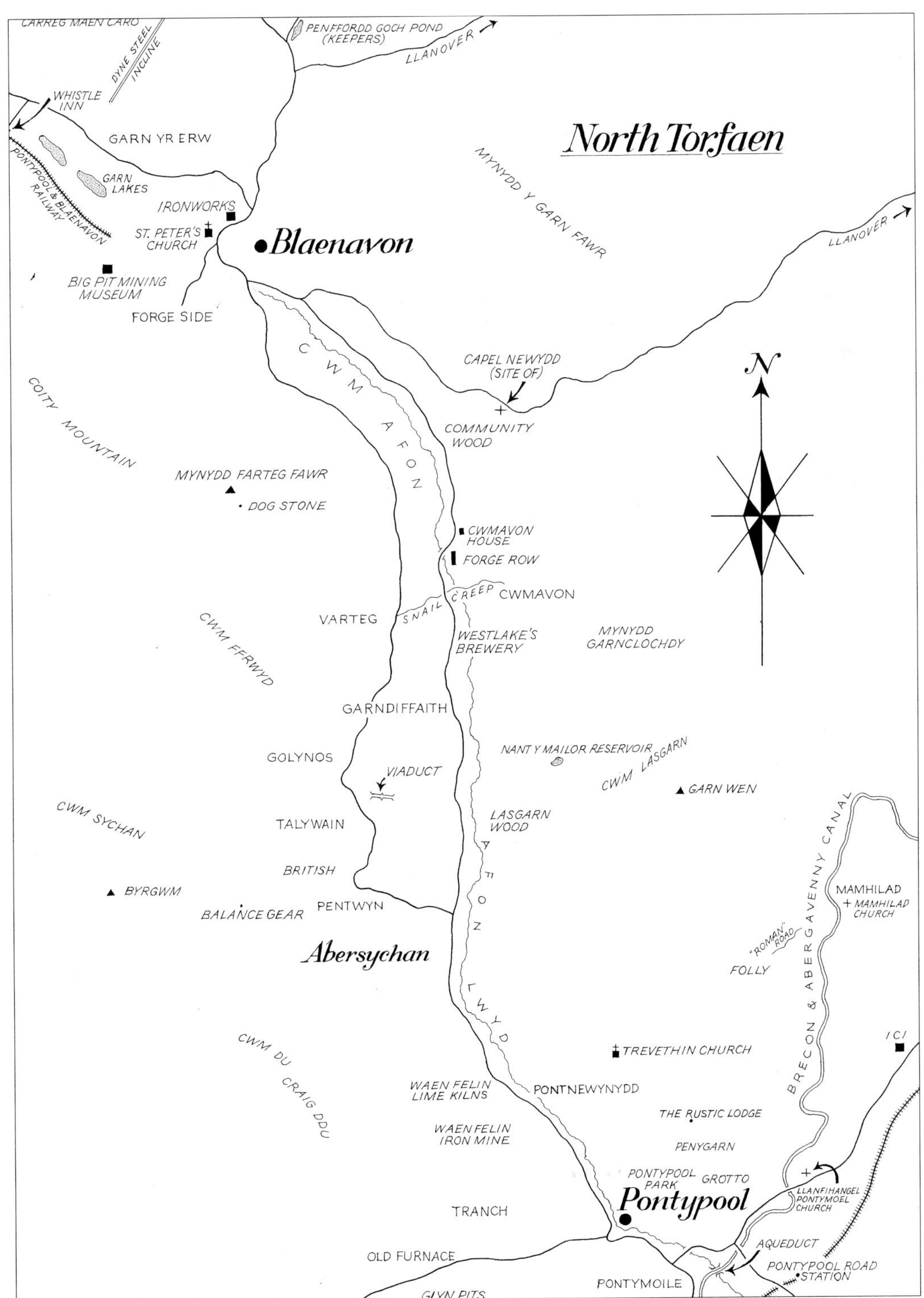
CARREG MAEN CARO
DYNE STEEL INCLINE
PENFFORDD GOCH POND (KEEPERS)
LLANOVER
WHISTLE INN
GARN YR ERW
North Torfaen
PONTYPOOL & BLAENAVON RAILWAY
GARN LAKES
IRONWORKS
MYNYDD Y GARN FAWR
LLANOVER
ST. PETER'S CHURCH
Blaenavon
BIG PIT MINING MUSEUM
FORGE SIDE
CWM AFON
CAPEL NEWYDD (SITE OF)
N
COITY MOUNTAIN
COMMUNITY WOOD
MYNYDD FARTEG FAWR
DOG STONE
CWMAVON HOUSE
FORGE ROW
SNAIL CREEP
CWMAVON
VARTEG
WESTLAKE'S BREWERY
MYNYDD GARNCLOCHDY
CWM FFRWYD
GARNDIFFAITH
NANT Y MAILOR RESERVOIR
GOLYNOS
VIADUCT
CWM LASGARN
GARN WEN
CWM SYCHAN
TALYWAIN
LASGARN WOOD
BRECON & ABERGAVENNY CANAL
BRITISH
MAMHILAD
MAMHILAD CHURCH
BYRGWM
BALANCE GEAR
PENTWYN
AFON LWYD
"ROMAN" ROAD
Abersychan
FOLLY
CWM DU
CRAIG DDU
TREVETHIN CHURCH
ICI
WAEN FELIN LIME KILNS
PONTNEWYNYDD
THE RUSTIC LODGE
WAEN FELIN IRON MINE
PENYGARN
PONTYPOOL PARK
GROTTO
Pontypool
LLANFIHANGEL PONTYMOEL CHURCH
TRANCH
AQUEDUCT
OLD FURNACE
PONTYPOOL ROAD STATION
PONTYMOILE
GLYN PITS

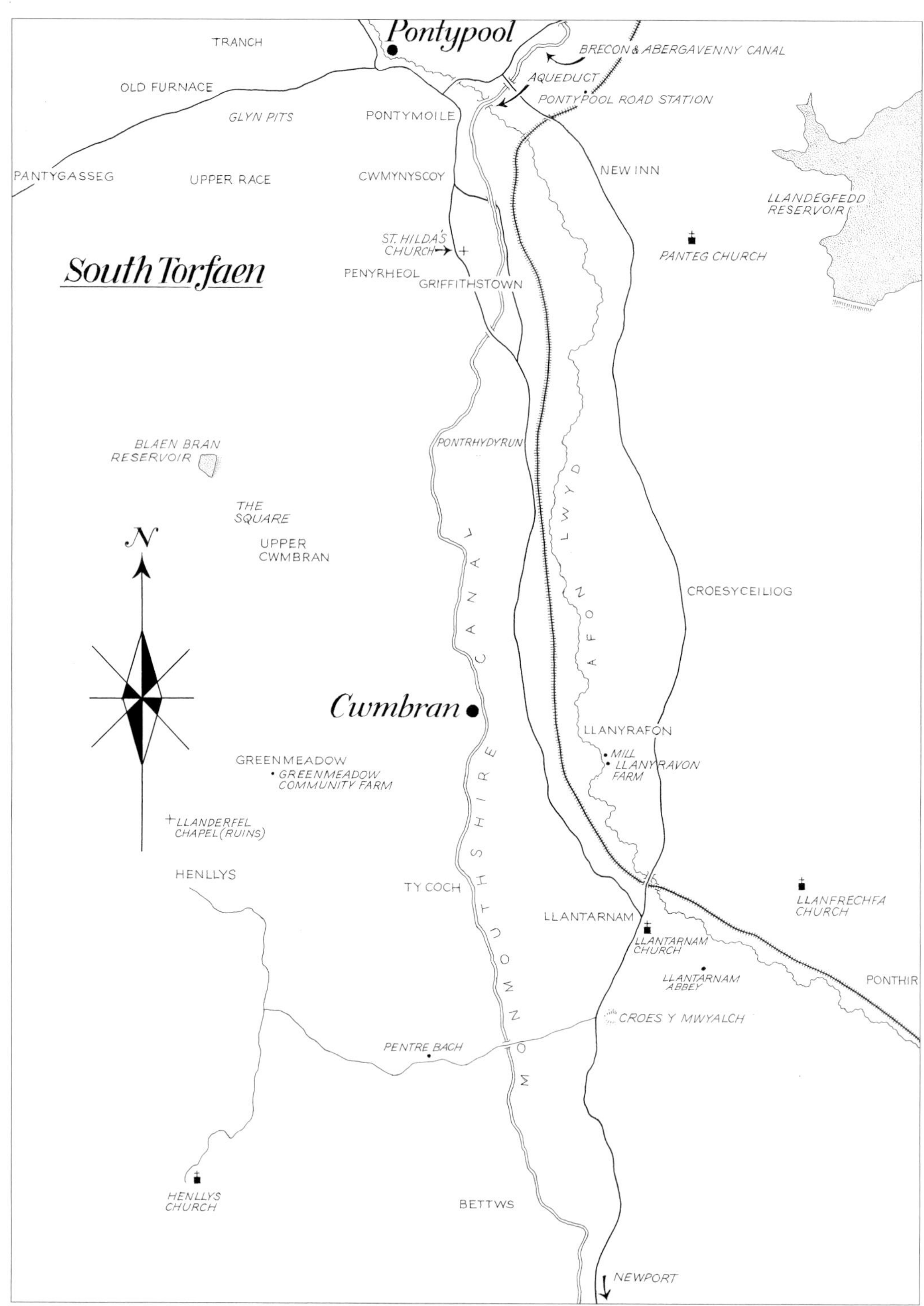
South Torfaen
Pontypool
TRANCH
OLD FURNACE
GLYN PITS
PONTYMOILE
BRECON & ABERGAVENNY CANAL
AQUEDUCT
PONTYPOOL ROAD STATION
PANTYGASSEG
UPPER RACE
CWMYNYSCOY
NEW INN
LLANDEGFEDD RESERVOIR
ST. HILDA'S CHURCH
PANTEG CHURCH
PENYRHEOL
GRIFFITHSTOWN
BLAEN BRAN RESERVOIR
PONTRHYDYRUN
THE SQUARE
UPPER CWMBRAN
N
AFON LWYD
CROESYCEILIOG
MONMOUTHSHIRE CANAL
Cwmbran
LLANYRAFON
MILL
LLANYRAVON FARM
GREENMEADOW
GREENMEADOW COMMUNITY FARM
LLANDERFEL CHAPEL (RUINS)
HENLLYS
TY COCH
LLANTARNAM
LLANFRECHFA CHURCH
LLANTARNAM CHURCH
LLANTARNAM ABBEY
PONTHIR
CROES Y MWYALCH
PENTRE BACH
HENLLYS CHURCH
BETTWS
NEWPORT

The 16th century Llanyrafon Mill is one of the few remaining examples of a triple stone water mill. It is open to the public on weekends during the summer.

**Llanyrafon Mill**

This mill was part of the Manor of Edlogan and was owned by the Griffiths family from the 1600's until 1880. After that date it changed hands several times and finally ceased production in 1951.

Water to drive the mill wheel was taken from the Afon Lwyd about half a mile to the north and it flowed down a mill race to turn an overshot wheel which still survives. The route of the old mill race can be traced along Miller's Ride on the Llanyrafon Estate.

The mill is unusual in that it had three sets of grinding stones which were made of hard wearing French burr and it served many of the important farms in the area including Tredegar House, the home of the Morgan family just outside Newport.

A voluntary organisation known as 'The Friends of Llanyrafon Mill' was formed in December 1995 and their aim is to restore the mill to a working facility.

The church of St Mary the Virgin at Panteg is one of the earliest in the area. Although largely rebuilt in 1849 it retains its medieval tower.

**Panteg**

Pleasantly situated 2 miles south-east of Pontypool the original foundation of St Mary's Church is said to have been given to St Cybi (a cousin of St David) by King Etelic of Edlogan in about 560 AD. The old register dates from 1598 and records the names of various parishioners connected with the Race Ironworks. A blank occurs in them from 1640 to 1646 when Presbyterianism predominated in England.

During this period the Civil War occurred and a body of Roundheads marched through the lower part of the parish and came to the church. They smashed the windows, pews and doors, pulled up the flooring, broke the churchyard cross, mutilated the gravestones and then departed.

The slender embattled western tower with a projecting stair turret contains three bells and is the oldest part of the building, dating from the mid 15th century.

The Hanbury family became responsible for the church from 1769 and in 1836 the living was accepted by the Rev Dr David James who was responsible for building the National Schools at Pontymoel and Sebastapol.

The oldest part of the County Hospital building at Panteg stands beside the Monmouthshire Canal and was originally constructed as a workhouse.

**Panteg Workhouse**

Panteg Workhouse (County Hospital building) was founded following the 1834 Poor Law Act. Before this Act, poor relief had been the responsibility of individual parishes. Rigid standards were set down by the Act and England and Wales was divided into 365 unions.

The site for Panteg Workhouse was favourable in that it was accessible by road and canal (which brought the stone for its construction) and, later in 1852, by railway. The Workhouse even had its own sidings to bring coal to the boilerhouse, and the abutments of the bridge which carried it over the canal can still be seen.

The Pontypool Board of Guardians, who were responsible for the Workhouse, decided on stone for its construction on the advice of the quarryman employed by Capel Hanbury Leigh. It was he who had donated the site, and plans were drawn up for a building to house 100 people, but if necessary capable of housing 150.

By April 1838, the Workhouse had is first inmates, and gradually other staff, such as chaplain, porter, teacher and a nurse, were appointed as numbers grew. The occupants from that time were classified into two groups - casuals (who called in for a night's lodging) and the permanent residents, made up of only the most destitute and infirm of the area, since conditions in the workhouse were such as to discourage all but the most destitute from admission.

From the beginning, the Workhouse was intended to be a last resort for the destitute and homeless, with the hardest taskmaster and worst paymaster imaginable. Paupers were vetted before being admitted, and discouraged from staying by the harsh conditions which included restrictions on movement and visitors, a ban on alcohol and tobacco and having to wear a uniform, They slept in dormitories on rough mattresses with the sexes separated, although later, couples over 65 lived together if space permitted. All new arrivals at the Workhouse were first scrubbed clean, and their clothes fumigated and hair cut.

Inmates were later given a distinctive uniform, and a warrant was issued for their arrest if they dared to abscond with it. Cleanliness and discipline were very important and strict regulations governed every aspect of life. There was a special record book for punishment, detailing the use of birch, cane and rod, floggings, deprivation of food and privileges and confinement, presumably solitary.

The inmates also had to work very hard for their keep - the men maintained the grounds and paths, chopped sticks and carried coal. The women helped with cooking, cleaning, scrubbing and mending. They survived on three meals a day. It was an unexciting diet of bread, cheese, gruel, suet pudding, rice, and a little meat and potatoes. Only special events, such as Christmas and Queen Victoria's Coronation warranted special meals. Children were housed in two separate buildings, and educated in a school-room under the same harsh discipline as the adults.

After the opening of the main Infirmary buildings in 1914, the Workhouse moved closer to becoming a hospital, and the children were by then being educated in ordinary schools. In January of that year the master of the Workhouse reported to the Guardians that the number of inmates was 152, vagrants numbered 55, the majority being professional tramps and the rest Army, Reserve and Militia men. After 1914, it was classed as a Poor Law Institution and in the First World War admitted wounded soldiers. Diet and treatment improved between the wars and in 1930 the County Council took over from the Guardians, who had run it for nearly 100 years. But it was the Second World War which was finally responsible for the change into a hospital.

In 1939 the women and children were transferred to Ty-Bryn, Tredegar, and the men to Regent House, Chepstow. Plans were drawn up to protect the buildings from air raids, and more medical staff and equipment were introduced. It thus became an Emergency Hospital for the wounded soldiers of the Second World War. After the war, it was decided to open a Maternity Unit in Panteg as Llanfrechfa Grange House could not cope with the spiralling birthrate. Several long low buildings were erected well away from the road, and the Unit opened in 1950. Although intended to be temporary structures, these buildings were still in use until the hospital closed.

The National Health Service was formed in 1948 and took over the running of the hospital. After that time it had various additions built in a variety of styles, but the original Workhouse buildings still remained in use. In its final days it was a General Hospital with Maternity, Geriatric, Gynaecological, Acute Medical and Orthopaedic Departments and was administered by the Gwent Health Authority.

In 1989 a two-year fight to save the maternity unit at the County Hospital, Griffithstown, by councils and people of the Eastern Valley came to an end when the unit officially closed on September 4th. From that time onwards, the mothers-to-be have had to have their children born outside the Valley, either at Newport's Royal Gwent Hospital or at Nevill Hall, Abergavenny.

The manor of Pentre Bach dates back to the 16th century but there was probably a building on the site even before that time.

**Pentre Bach**

Situated about a mile along the road leading to Henllys Vale from the cross roads near the Three Blackbirds Inn at Llantarnam, and dating from the thirteenth century, is a former grange of Llantarnam Abbey. In early documents it was referred to as 'Mynydd-tir-Waun' (i.e. 'The Monks' Meadowland') and Cefn Vynach (the Monks' Ridge) but, even before the closing of the Abbey by King Henry VIII in 1536, the building was leased as a private residence by a minor branch of the Morgans of Tredegar.

Thomas Morgan, a Roman Catholic and an arch-conspirator was born here in 1543. He was a devoted follower of Mary Queen of Scots and was able to deliver her letters while she was imprisoned at Tewkesbury, for he was secretary to Lord Shrewsbury until he was caught out. He was imprisoned in the Tower of London for ten months and afterwards compelled to find refuge in Paris. On more than one occasion he plotted for the assasination of Queen Elizabeth and is credited with a scheme for blowing up Parliament long before Guy Fawkes attempted it!

During Edward VI's reign the building was granted to John Russell, the Earl of Bedford, having previously been held by Lewis Blethyn. Not long afterwards it became the possession of William Morgan

William Morgan enlarged the building in 1554 and developed the estate so that by the time of King Charles II (1660-1685) it had acquired the name by which it is still known, Pentre Bach (the little village). It subsequently became a farmhouse and by the 19th century it had passed into the hands of the Blewitts, who had inherited much of the Abbey lands.

Penygarn Baptist Chapel was built in 1727 on the hillside to the east of Pontypool.

**Penygarn**

Situated on the hillside overlooking Pontypool is the community of Penygarn which has become virtually a part of Trevethin. On the north side of the parish road leading to Trevethin stands Penygarn Baptist Chapel which from the valley below looks just like a whitewashed cottage. Before it was built in 1727 services were held in Penygarn farmhouse which became known as Sheperdson's Farm.

The Rev Miles Harris, better known as Miles Harry of Blaenau Gwent, took charge of its congregation of fifty and the power of his preaching drew worshippers from far and wide, some travelling to the chapel on horseback.

Penygarn had only been intended to serve as a mission centre and school, but by 1729 it had become a proper church. It was designed as a house - a house of God - and it was intended that it would contain none of the trappings of religion; the words of God formed its rules and instead of being in front of an altar, the people held their communion services around a table.

The influence of Penygarn became substantial. In 1736 only nine years after the chapel was built, the first academy in Wales was set up at Trosnant for training young men for the Baptist ministry, and Miles Harry was one of the tutors. This was the progenitor of the academy at Abergavenny and the Baptist College at Pontypool.

In front of Penygarn chapel can be seen the grave of Thomas Allgood (the third) who died in 1779. He was involved in the manufacture of Pontypool Japan ware.

The Rustic Lodge is situated in the depths of the American Gardens and it was constructed in the 19th century as a woodman's cottage. It is now a grade III listed building.

Another interesting building near Penygarn is the **Rustic Lodge** which is built of 'pudding stone' or conglomerate and stands on the private road through the American Gardens. Large cubes and prisms of this stone intermix with smaller lumps in the walls and porch. Larger, clean cut stones lie above the supporting wall-plates and roof-timbers while the pediment of the porch and the hip-roof are decorated with graceful oaken designs. Lead-lights add daintiness to the heavy stonework.

Capel Zion, Ponthir was built in 1834. It was refubished and decorated in 1981 and designated as a listed building.

**Ponthir**

The name of this village relates to a bridge spanning the Afon Lwyd and it means 'Long Bridge,' as currently spelt. In 1605 it was Pontheere and at a later period Pontheer. Sometime later it was changed to Ponthier and when the railway station was built in 1878 it was given its present spelling of Ponthir. It is of interest that this bridge was once the longest one-arch span to be found at any point along the course of the Afon Lwyd.

No doubt the first bridge would have been a wooden structure which would have been frequently damaged during periods of floods. In 1800 a stone bridge was built by Rowlin Paul and the one-arched structure was of a hump backed nature.

A railway station was opened in Ponthir in 1878 and the coming of the railway put an end to the old tramroad which connected the Monmouthshire & Brecon Canal with the wharf on the side of the River Usk at Caerleon. Strong horses, some of which were kept at the local tin-plate works were employed in hauling the trams carrying metal and coal along this route for over a century.

The first church in Ponthir was converted from a house and called 'Capel Sion' and it was opened in 1903. It was a mixed church and its total membership at that time consisted of nine Baptists and three Independents.

In 1834 the original building was demolished and another one erected in its place with the cost borne by the members of the congregation. According to one writer the dimensions of it were '42 feet long and 28 feet wide, and it has a roomy gallery at one end.' A clock was placed on the front of the gallery which had previously been on one of the walls of the old building.

On the inside walls of the church, about six feet from the floor, were wooden racks on which hats could be placed. About a century ago it was customary for the male members to wear top-hats, and undoubtedly the racks were used for this aristocratic type of headgear. The racks unfortunately have since been removed.

Services in English as well as Welsh were given in Zion during the early years of the 19th century. In about 1837 it appears that sermons were given in the two languages - probably a Welsh sermon was given in the mornings and an English version in the evenings.

The total membership of the church in 1864 was 140 and in 1870 it consisted of 148 Baptists and 2 Independents. The highest membership in the history of this church was 233 in the Revival of 1872. During that year the Rev J. Williams baptised 104 people.

In 1870 a spacious vestry was added to the church and a room above it became known as 'The Lecture Room'. The foundation stone of the new vestry was laid by Mr David Jenkins of Brodawel, Caerleon, with a silver trowel.

At one time there was a stable next to the church which was used to shelter the horses of worshippers who used to travel to services from some way off on horseback or in carriages drawn by horses.

A library containing 200 volumes was opened at the church in November 1887. Books were borrowed weekly and fines of 1d were imposed when they were kept longer than a week.

In 1898 funds were raised for the renovation of the church which was carried out in 1901. New seats and a pulpit were installed and eleven years later a new pipe organ was purchased at a cost of £250. Electric light was installed in 1921.

### Pontnewynydd

In 1911 Pontnewynydd was described as a 'thickly populated and very prosperous ironworks and colliery district with plans underway for a further 300 houses to ease chronic overcrowding.' There were also plans for a Tinplate works to be built nearby.

Ebenezer Chapel opened in 1742 and Edmund Jones, its famous founder preached there for more than fifty years.

On the hillside above Pontnewynydd can be found the **Ebenezer Chapel** which was founded in 1741 by Edmund Jones who was known as the 'Old Prophet' due to the fact that he had an uncanny habit of foretelling the future. He was born in 1702 at Penllwyn in the parish of Aberystruth (now part of Nantyglo) and was the son of John and Catherine Lewis who were farmers. Following the ancient Welsh custom, Edmund adopted his father's Christian name as his surname and became known as Edmund Jones.

He was a studious and intelligent child, who could read the Bible in Welsh even before he was nine years of age. His parents were advised to send him to a good school so that he might become a preacher. But his only education seems to have been a few years at a school kept by Mr Howell Prosser, curate of his native parish, who, judging by his pupil's literary efforts in later years, must have given him very good tuition.

In 1721, at the age of nineteen, Edmund began preaching at Penmaen in Mynyddislwyn, where a chapel had been founded. Bradney records that Jones was present at a meeting at Abergavenny which was addressed by Miles Parry, the Welsh revivalist, and that he soon afterwards moved to Pontypool. It has been suggested that he moved to that place because he was disappointed at not being made pastor of the Penmaen chapel on the death of the then minister and Mr Philip Davies was appointed instead. The appointment was made in 1739 and Jones departed soon afterwards.

By 1740 Edmund was residing in Pontnewynydd where he proceeded to raise funds for a new chapel. Out of his life's savings of £40 he presented £30 and to augment that he sold some of his prized books for £15. In the same year he went to live in a cottage at Lower Tranch where he became known as Edmund Jones, 'Prophet of the Tranch'.

He then set about building a place of worship for his newly formed church and congregation and by 1742 his chapel had opened. For over fifty years he preached there and also held services occasionally in various remote farmhouses. Being a very generous man, his charitable deeds became part of the local folklore. On one occasion he is said to have even taken the shirt off his back to give to a poor, starving vagrant he met on the nearby hills. When reprimanded by his wife for his foolishness, his only reply was, 'The Lord will provide! ' The following day a lady in Mynyddislwyn sent him a roll of flannel to make new shirts.

Omens played a very important part in his life and an often quoted story is that of the mysterious rainbow shaped cloud which bridged two mountains near his home in 1739, and was regarded by the local inhabitants with superstitious awe. Edmund assured them that it was a sign that God would soon visit the valley. In the same week scores of converts resulted from a mighty religious revival, of whom at least five became ordained ministers of much renown. This was considered by Edmund as his most successful year as a minister in his home district.

In later years Edmund Jones was ridiculed for his belief in fairies, but it should be remembered that such a belief was quite common amongst the country people of his day. In his book entitled *On Apparitions, Fairies and other Spirits of Hell* described them as children dancing to music, and seriously exhorted his readers not to view them in the light they had generally been considered, but as happy spirits, .

> 'If any think I am too credulous in these relations and speak of things of which I myself have no experience, I must let them know they are mistaken. I also reasonably apprehend that a well attested relation of apparitions and agencies of spirits in the world is a great means of preventing the capital infidelities of Atheism and Sadduceeism, which get such ground in some countries, for in Wales, where such things have often happened, and sometime still do in some places, though but seldom now, we scarce meet with any who question the being and apparition of spirits.'

He had a particular fear of witches and on one occasion refused to enter a house in Crumlin to pray for a dying woman. 'Pray with that old creature? No, not I. That old creature is a witch,' he said, but his ministerial companion had no such fears and entered the house and prayed for the dying woman. Just as the last spark of life left her, a large hound approached the house and put its paws on the window-sill. Edmund was then convinced that she was a witch and that the devil, in the form of a dog, had come to collect her soul. In his books he confesses that he was afraid to travel in the dark along certain roads and paths for fear of meeting evil spirits.

The most famous of his books *A relation of Apparations of Spirits in the County of Monmouth and the Principality of Wales*, was first published in 1767. A second edition appeared in 1780, and the third edition was published in 1813, twenty years after his death.

Edmund had married whilst quite young, but had no children. His wife was noted for her piety, good temper and intellectual and conversational powers. She died twenty-three years before her husband in July, 1768.

Although Edmund Jones lived in the Eastern Valley for more than fifty years, he was also a great traveller and, at the age of eighty, he travelled on foot through North Wales, preaching as often as twice a day if called upon. His diaries for nine years record that he preached 104 times in 1731; 76 in 1732; 240 in 1739; 300 in 1768; 337 in 1770; 511 in 1773; 260 in 1778; 340 in 1780; and even in 1789, in the 88th year of his age, he preached no less than 405 times.

He also carried on an extensive correspondence with the great men of his age, such as Howell Harries, George Whitefield and John Wesley.

For nearly a year before his death he was confined to his house, spending most of the time in bed. He died on 26th November 1783, at the age of 92 and in the 69th year of his ministry.

He was buried in the graveyard of Ebenezer Chapel, Pontnewynydd, a mile north-west of Pontypool, which he had founded over fifty years earlier. Mr John Griffiths of Abergavenny preached his funeral sermon to a large and tearful congregation, from 2 Timothy iv. 7-8, a text he had chosen himself, and a most appropriate one for such an old warrior - 'I have fought the good fight, I have finished my course, I have kept the faith.'

Lower Tranch, home of Edmund Jones   Fred Hando

Grave of Edmund Jones

Edmund left a good library, part of which he bequeathed to his successor in the ministry at Ebenezer Chapel. The remainder, together with all his manuscripts, including the history of the first fifty years of his life, were bequeathed to his sister's son. Unfortunately, this nephew did not appreciate their value, and sold two cartloads to a Pontypool grocer as waste paper. Fortunately, some of his diaries are held by the National Museum at Aberystwyth. The diaries date from 1731 but are incomplete. They give accounts of his many preaching tours and the number of sermons preached.

Ebenezer Chapel was so called because Edmund Jones prophesied that his successor would bear that name, and so it turned out to be, for the next minister proved to be the Rev Ebenezer Jones. Inside the chapel on the south wall is a memorial stone of 1793 commemorating Edmund Jones. It reads:

> 'In this Yard are deposited the Remains of the
> Rev Edmund Jones late Minister of this Church who
> was faithful in Christ's Vineyard for 70 years,
> he died Nov 26th 1793 Aged 91 years and 7 months.
> Who also erected this house and Settled it for the
> use of ye Independent Religious Society here
> Assembled till time shall be no more.'

Outside in the graveyard a simple stone was erected over his grave and alongside it is a portion of a very large stone which once bore nine stanzas of the panegyric which he composed on the death of his wife, but just five stanzas survive. It is said that Edmund chose to be buried in a separate grave from his wife as he didn't want there to be any difficulty on the day of resurrection. In February 1907 a red granite memorial to the memory of Edmund Jones, founder of Ebenezer Chapel was unveiled here.

The name of Ebenezer Chapel is linked with Ebensberg, a steel town in Pennsylvania in the USA. This is due to Edmund's assistant pastor, Rees Lloyd, who was ordained in 1795 at the Ebenezer Chapel in Pontnewynydd, where he preached many times.

Soon after the death of the 'Old Prophet', Rees Lloyd and his family emigrated to America, taking with them a number of Welsh families from this district. While the Napoleonic wars were raging in Europe, this small band of people landed in Cambria Co. Rees Lloyd bought some land for a Dr Benjamin Rush for 57,873 dollars and built a small cabin where he and his family first lived. In 1797 he established the first Congregational Church of Ebenezer (Ebensberg), where he was pastor for twenty-two years, before leaving to become pastor of the Congregational Church at Paddy's Run, where he stayed until his death at the age of 79 in 1838.

The Rev Ebenezer Jones proved a worthy successor of Edmund Jones and he was much respected in the county. He was appointed interpreter at the Monmouthshire Assizes, and fulfilled the duties of that difficult position for twenty years with considerable tact and ability, which gained him the admiration of all concerned with criminal matters. He was medical and legal adviser to his own people and was held in the highest esteem by the gentry of the neighbourhood, as well as other parts of the country. It is said of him that on one very critical occasion, when two lives were in the balance, he addressed the Court in such a manner that even the Judge on his seat wept, and who was afterwards heard to exclaim, 'Pity this man was not a bishop.'

Capel Hanbury Leigh, of Pontypool Park, held him up as a model agriculturalist, and whenever he had any new project in view, he would seek advice from Ebenezer Jones. On one occasion, after inviting Ebenezer to examine some new project he was to undertake, the Squire's agent happened to be present and because the Squire paid such deference to Ebenezer's opinion, the agent took offence. On the following Saturday he came in contact with him in the town, and did not forget to refer to the matter in rather contemptuous terms, remarking that 'You know no more about farming than his old hat,' to which Ebenezer replied, 'I am not aware what may be the farming capabilities of your old hat, but this I will say, that I know a great deal more about farming than the head that is under that hat.'

Ebenezer Jones died in his 60th year on the 31st January, 1829.

### St Catwg's Church, Trevethin

The ancient parish church of Trevethin occupies a commanding position and its prominent tower is a local landmark. Dedicated to St Catwg (Cadoc), it is a 12th century foundation and the mother church of Pontypool.

A local legend recalls that when the first church here was being built in the sixth century, St Catwg became much bothered by the fact that the work carried out during the day was torn down at night and the materials carried away. He decided that the culprit had to be the devil and had a large bell made which would make a loud noise when Satan was making off with his spoil. In due course the noise startled the devil so much that he dropped the stones that he was carrying and quickly sped away. In memory of this event the spot on the hillside where the pile of stones can be found has been named Garn Clochdy (stones of the belfry).

Early records show that this parish was originally in the Deanery of Bergavenny. In the Norwich Taxation of 1254 it is referred to as *Ecclesia de Throvethin* and in the taxation of Pope Nicholas in 1291 it is called *Ecclesia de Trevelion*, and also in the Deanery of Bergavenny. Mention of Trevethyn is made in the *Valor Ecclesiasticus* of 1535 in the Deanery of Abergavenny and it was still in the same Deanery in 1835.

Until the year 1843 Trevethin was a Chapelry attached to Llanover and it was then made a separate parish. The gift of the living was assigned to the Dean and Chapter of Llandaff Cathedral, who made the appointment up to the year 1916.

Many new parishes were formed as a result of population increase during the Industrial Revolution and a new Deanery was formed which was known as Blaenau Gwent. Trevethin formed part of that Deanery until 1922 when it became one of the parishes of the new Deanery of Pontypool formed from the parishes in the Deaneries of Blaenau Gwent, Usk, Newport, and the old Deanery of Caerleon.

St Catwg's Church, Trevethin.

The old building, of which only the tower remains, was described by William Coxe who came here during his tour of Monmouthshire in 1800:-

> 'The Parish Church of Ponty-pool, called Trevethin, is situated on an eminence at the distance of a mile from the town. The Church consists of a square tower of stone, with white-washed battlements, a nave, a north aisle, and a chancel; it appears to be an ancient structure, the nave being separated from the aisle by four low arches reposing on massive columns scarcely five feet in height. The chancel is divided from the Church by a Gothic arch, over which is inscribed 'John Hanbury, Charles Rogers, mercer, Church wardens, 1730.' On the pulpit I saw an inscription in large old characters "1637, God save the King, C.R. 13, J.H. A.H. R.H. A.H.," which were the initials of John and Richard Hanbury and their respective wives, with the arms of the family rudely carved.'

In 1843 the Rev Thomas Davies became the first incumbent of the new parish of Trevethin and movd into a house donated for the purpose by Capel Hanbury Leigh. Three years later he decided that it was time to rebuild and enlarge the church, with the main purpose of doubling the seating to accommodate a much increased congregation, which had resulted from the rapid rise in population of that area. During the next year the church, with the exception of its Early English tower, was completely rebuilt. The work was started by a Mr Carter, but he died within a few months and the job was then completed by his brother-in-law, Mr J.F. Williams.

The tower was raised by about 8 feet and a large window inserted. Four pinnacles were also erected on top of the tower, but these can no longer be seen for three of them were blown off during a fierce gale in November 1928 and the remaining one was so badly damaged that it had to be removed.

On July 8th,1847, the re-constructed church was consecrated by Bishop Copleston of Llandaff.

Inside the tower is a belfry and a bell chamber containing eight bells, which were originally hung in part of the famous London Exhibition of 1887 as part of a display described as the 'Village of Old London'. They were afterwards purchased by Mr. Pegler of Pontypool and erected in this tower by public subscription.

Of particular interest inside the church are the monuments of the Hanbury family, and the family pew in which they worshipped. In the north transept a portrait bust of John Hanbury in Carrara marble is accompanied by a memorial which reads:-

'Here lies the body of JOHN HANBURY Esqr
of PONT-POOLE in the County of MONMOUTH,
Who by his great Understanding and Humanity
Made the people of this Place and Neighbourhood Rich and Happy.
And they will tell their children to latest Posterity
That he was a wise and Honest Man.
He was chosen in eight Parliaments,
And was Knight of the Shire for the County of MONMOUTH
at his Decease.
He was appointed by the Great Duke of MARLBOROUGH
One of his Executors to his last Will
He married BRIDGET daughter of Sr EDWARD AYSCOUGHE
of Kelfey in the County of LINCOL
By whom he left fve sons, JOHN, CAPEL, CHARLES, GEORGE
and THOMAS.
He died the 14th day of June 1734 in the 70th Year of his Age.'

A second bust is of Capel Hanbury Leigh with a memorial reading:-

'Sacred to the Memory of
Capel Hanbury Leigh Esqr of Pontypool Park,
Lord Lieutenant of the County of Monmouth.
Born October 6th 1776, died Sept. 28th 1861
Deeply lamented by all who knew him.'

On the west wall beneath the north gallery, is the tablet of Molly Ann Hanbury Leigh, wife of Capel Hanbury Leigh, Esq., of Pontypool Park. This tablet was formerly near the Hanbury Pew, but was moved when the new Choir Vestry was erected. There is a family vault underneath the pew, in which some members of the family are buried.

Three other memorials are also of special interest: The first to Sergeant Rosser Francis, of the 3rd Volunteer Battalion, South Wales Borderers, bears the inspiring motto of the battalion - 'Gwell Angau na Gwarth' - 'better death than dishonour' (1901). The second makes John Dunlaplate, colour sergeant, exclaim (1842):

'Billeted by death
I quartered here remain;
When the last Trump sounds
I'll rise and march again.'

The third is to John Summerfield, landlord of the Yew Tree Inn across the road, who died in 1855, aged 38 years. He was 5ft 10in high, he weighed 476 lbs (324 stone), his waist measured 67 inches, and his calf 25 inches. Sometimes he travelled for exhibition in shows and when at home, crowds of people used to come to his Inn to see him. He was a descendant of James Somerfield a London barber. When he died it was necessary to remove his bedroom window to permit the removal of the coffin. His grave is on the north west side of the churchyard.

A window in the east wall portrays Christ receiving the sick and was erected to commemorate the 1811 colliers who lost their lives in the Llanerch Colliery disaster of 1890. On Sunday 23rd February 1890, a Memorial Service was held here for those bereaved by the Llanerch Colliery Explosion. The Rev. J.C. Llewellin conducted the service, and the preacher was the Rev. W.R. Thomas, M.A., Vicar of Abersychan.

The formal unveiling of the window by Mrs. J.C. Hanbury took place on 3rd November 1890, and the inscription reads:

> 'To the glory of God and in affectionate Memory of 181 Colliers of whom 5 lost their lives in the Glyn Pit on 23rd January 1890, and 176 perished in the disaster at the Llanerch Pit on 6th February 1890. Erected by the Pontypool Fire Brigade. Gus Bevan, Capt. Nov. 3rd 1890.'

The graves of some of these men and also those killed in an accident at Glyn Pits can be seen in the churchyard.

The War Memorial Chapel in the south transept was erected in 1923, in what was formerly the organ chamber and was dedicated on 15th September 1923, when the screens and chapel were unveiled by John Paton. On entering the chapel one is immediately struck by its beauty and dignity and it has been described as one of the most beautiful War Memorials in the county. The chapel vestry, organ chamber, altar, reredos, and a window with pictures of Christ, St David and St Cadoc commemorates 160 men of this parish and over 500 men of the Second Battalion of the Monmouthshire Regiment (later named the Royal Regiment of Wales) who laid down their lives in the First World War. The names of all those who died in battle are inscribed in beautiful gold leaf on a remembrance plaque. In 1984 the chapel was restored to its former splendour at a cost of £15,000.

The 'Dog Stone' on the slopes of Mynydd Farteg Fawr marks the grave of H. M. Kennard's dog 'Carlo' who was accidently shot on the 'Glorious 12th' in 1864.
H. M. Kennard was one of the chief share-holders of the Blaenavon Co.Ltd..

**Varteg**

High on the south eastern slopes of Coity Mountain, just below the trig'point on Mynydd Farteg Fawr is a large iron monument which was erected in memory of Carlo, a dog once owned by H.M. Kennard. The simple inscription on the iron tombstone tells the story of a tragedy which was occurred on that spot on August 12th, 1864. Mr H.M. Kennard, of Crumlin Hall, general manager of Blaenavon Works, was shooting with a party of sportsmen on that side of the valley. Carlo, Mr Kennard's famous setter, was one of the dogs used, and the story goes that after raising a covey of grouse, Carlo was accidently shot. His death cast a gloom over the party and Mr Kennard ordered that he be buried where he fell. The iron gravestone was cast at the Blaenavon Works and transported by horse and cart up the ancient bridle track past High Meadows and the old Shepherd's House to the side of Coity Mountain. It marks the spot where the dog met his untimely death and is still an item of interest to people who wander across the Varteg Mountain and it is known locally as the 'Dog Stone'.

Two other gun dogs owned by the Kennards were 'Billy' and 'Bones' and inscribed stones marking their graves can be seen in the grounds of Ty Mawr at Blaenavon.

# CHRONOLOGY OF SIGNIFICANT EVENTS

1179 Howell ap Iorwerth, Lord of Caerleon founded the Abbey of Llantarnam.

1407 John ap Howell, the Abbot of Llantarnam was killed in an attack on Usk Castle during the Owain Glyndwr rebellion.

1425 The Grant brothers set up an ironworks at Pont-y-moel.

1535 Llantarnam Abbey was dissolved.

1544 Henry VIII granted the Manor and Lordship of Edlogan and Mynydd Maen with all its courts and waste grounds as part of his dower to his sixth wife Lady Katherine Parr.

1558 The Manor of Edlogan passed to William Morgan.

1577 Services were being held in Capel Newydd near Blaenavon.
The first ironworks was established near Pontypool by Edmund Brode, whose partner was Richard Hanbury.

1600 First iron furnace established at Blaenavon - site unknown.

1626 James Leonard of Pontypool arrived in America to survey the hills for iron on behalf of the Massachusets Bay Company. In 1642, with his brother Henry he established the first successful ironworks at Lynn, Massachusets. In due course Pontypool people emigrated to America in search of employment in the iron industry.

1645 Old Trosnant Furnace was partially demolished by some of Cromwell's troops.

1657 George Fox, the famous Quaker visited Richard Hanbury at Pontymoel.

1660 Thomas Algood, a native of Northamptonshire, introduced the process of lacquering iron plates. This invention was afterwards brought to perfection by his son, and distinguished by the name of 'Pontypool Ware.'

1667 The Quaker, George Fox visited Richard Hanbury again and persuaded him to join the Society of Friends.

1680 The Hanbury family purchased land beside the Afon Lwyd.

1695 Death of Richard Hanbury, who was buried in the Quakers' burial ground at Pontymoel.

1697 Invention of the rolling mill by Thomas Cooke, manager of the Hanbury Works.

1703 The first successful commercial production of tinplate in Britain began at Pontypool.

1707 Francis Bray inherited the manor of Wentsland and Llantarnam. Her sister Anne received Edlogan (including Panteg).

1709 Charles, the third son of Major Hanbury was born at Pontypool. He was to assume the name of Hanbury Williams in consequence of the will of his godfather, Charles Williams Esq. of Caerleon, and thus obtained the estate at Coldbrook, near Abergavenny.

1716 Death of Thomas Allgood and his son Edward succeeded him as manager at Pontypool.

1717 The technique of 'Japanning' tinplate was successfully developed at Pontypool.

1720 Pontypool Ironworks were commissioned to make iron gates for the Governor's Palace at Williamsburg.

1729 Penygarn Baptist Chapel was erected.

1730 Mrs Frances Bray, Lady of the Manor of Llantarnam financed the building of the Corn Market in Pontypool. This building is now occupied by shops but still has the family arms on the facade.

1732 A Baptist academy was founded at Trosnant, near Pontypool.

1739 Howell Harris visited Pontypool and as a result of serious disturbances in the town, Capel Hanbury, as magistrate had to read the Riot Act. Harris was arrested but released on bail.

1740 One of the earliest printing presses in Wales was set up at Pontypool by Miles Harry, the Baptist Minister of Penygarn. Three books in the Welsh language were published in the town during that year.

1742 Ebenezer Independent Chapel at Pontnewynydd was opened by Edmund Jones.
1759 Death of Charles Hanbury Williams.
1760 Benjamin Franklin visited the Pontypool Ironworks.
1782 Thomas Hill and Thomas Hopkins opened Bridge Level at Blaenavon.
1788 Three blast furnaces built at Blaenavon at cost of £40,000.
1789 Blaenavon Ironworks commenced operating.
1792 The first Monmouthshire Canal Act was obtained.
1793 Death of Edmund Jones ('The Prophet of the Tranch') aged 91 years. He was succeded in
his ministry by the Rev Ebenezer Jones.
1795 Completion of the tramroad from Blaenavon to the canal basin at Pontnewynydd.
Death of Benjamin Pratt, one of the first three Blaenavon Ironmasters on 24th May. 1796
Completion of the Monmouthshire Canal to Pontymoel.
1797 Second Monmouthshire canal Act was obtained.
Capel Hanbury assumed the name of Leigh.
1798 Archdeacon William Coxe visited Blaenavon, during his tour of Monmouthshire.
The earliest known use of the term 'tramroad' was written into the minutes of the Brecknock and Abergavenny Canal Company.
1799 David Tanner erected furnaces at Blaendare.
1801 Death of 'Billy' Allgood.
1802 The third Monmouthshire Canal Act was obtained.
Monmouthshire Canal extended to Pontnewynydd.
1803 Varteg Ironworks began production.
1804 Construction of Forge Row, Cwmavon to house workers at nearby Varteg Forge.
1805 St Peter's Church, Blaenavon was opened.
An Act of Parliament was passed to create a new parish of Blaenavon.
1812 The Monmouthshire Canal was joined with the Brecon & Abergavenny Canal.
14,579 tons of iron were sent by canal to Newport during this year.
1814 The Fossett family founded their circus in Blaenavon.
1815 Battle of Waterloo, which was followed by an industrial slump in Britain.
The longest tramroad tunnel in Britain was built near Blaenavon.
Death of Samuel Hopkins.
1816 St Peter's School, Blaenavon, opened with 120 pupils. It was built and endowed by Sarah Hopkins in memory of her brother Samuel and was the first school to be established in Wales by an industrial concern for the benefit of their workers' children.
1817 Garnddyrys Forge was completed and production began.
1818 Flat races were held at Pontypool on a course at Cilgoigan Mill Farm. The land later became the Polo Ground.
1819 264 acres of land were leased by the Hanburys to the Varteg Iron Company.
1823 Pontypool Gas Works was established.
A school was opened at Varteg by the Varteg Iron Company.
1824 Death of Thomas Hill.
1825 Pentwyn Ironworks were erected by the Hunt brothers.
1826 Abersychan Ironworks were erected.
1827 A new Market House was built at Pontypool.
Death of Thomas Hill the second.
1829 The British Iron Company was formed to take over the Abersychan Ironworks.
1830 A Welsh Wesleyan chapel was built at Varteg.
Capel Hanbury Leigh swore in 2,060 special constables among the employees of the various ironworks in and to the north of Pontypool.
The Varteg Ironworks, with five furnaces were started by G. Kendricks & Co.
1831 Anti-Truck Act introduced.
1832 Independent chapel erected at Cefn-y-crib.
Anti Truck Act passed by Parliament.
1835 Pontypool Charity School was established by the Rev Thomas Davies.

1835 Capel Hanbury Leigh was appointed Lord Lieutenant of Monmouthshire.
1836 Blaenavon Iron & Coal Company was formed by R.W. Kennard.
The Old Town Forge was demolished.
1837 The Peoples' Charter was drawn up by the Chartists' movement.
The West of England and South Wales Bank was opened in Pontypool.
A Baptist College was erected at Penygarn near Pontypool.
Glyn Pit was sunk in the Glyn Valley.
Golynos Ironworks began production.
1838 Pontypool Town School was built by the Rev Thomas Davies as a church school, to accommodate 300 pupils.
1839 The Eastern Valley contingent of the ill-fated Chartists' march on Newport was led by William Jones, 'the Watchmaker.'
Water balance tower built at Blaenavon Ironworks by James Ashwell.
1840 A school was built at the bottom of Twmpath Hill, Pontypool, by Capel Hanbury for his employees' children.
1842 Mines Act passed by Parliament.
Capel Hanbury Leigh built a school at Twmpath for the children of his employees at Lower Race and in the Glyn Valley.
1843 Milfraen Pit was sunk. (It was first known as Jayne's Pit).
1844 Hill Pit, Blaenavon was sunk by the Blaenavon Iron & Coal Company Ltd.
1847 Forgeside, Blaenavon, was established.
The Turnpike road was built from Pontypool through Abersychan and Varteg to Blaenavon.
George Street School opened in Pontypool.
1850 The Blaenavon - Pwlldu incline was re-constructed by Thomas Dyne Steel for use by standard gauge wagons.
1851 The British Iron Company went bankrupt after spending £400,000 on their works.
1852 The GWR line from Newport to Pontypool was opened.
Abraham Darby took over Cwmbran Town Forge, eventually selling to Messrs Weston and Grice five years later.
1853 A decision was made to move the forge at Garnddyrys to Forgeside, Blaenavon.
1854 The foundation stone of Pontypool Town Hall was laid by Mrs Hanbury Leigh.
Pontypool to Blaenavon railway opened on route of old tramroad.
1855 Work at Kay's Slope, Blaenavon, started.
1856 Pontypool Town Hall was officially opened.
1857 J.C. Hill established the Oakfield Wireworks. It had 25 puddling furnaces and produced an average 300 tons a week.
The British Ironworks were taken over by Messrs Darby & Co., for £8,000.
Crumlin Viaduct, built with Blaenavon iron, was completed.
1858 Cwmnantddu Colliery (later named Llanerch Colliery) was sunk by the Ebbw Vale Company.
1859 *The Pontypool Free Press & the Herald of the Hills* was established by David Walkinshaw. .
1860 A new blast engine was started at Blaenavon Ironworks.
Kear's Pit was sunk at Blaenavon (later re-named Big Pit).
Varteg Pit was sunk.
Blaenavon adopted the Local Government Act of 1858 and the Urban District of Blaenavon came into being.
Pontymoel School was opened by the National Society for the Education of the Poor and financed by the Ebbw Vale Company.
R. W. Kennard was elcted Chairman of the Blaenavon Company Ltd.
1861 A new mill for the manufacture of railway tyres opened at Blaenavon.
Services were held at Capel Newydd for the last time.
Mrs Hanbury Leigh laid the foundation stone of the Wern National School.
British Top Pits was sunk.

1861 Death of Capel Hanbury Leigh, aged 85. His funeral at Trevethin Church was attended by 15000 people.
Lord Llanover was appointed Her Majesty's Lieutenant in Monmouthshire.
1862 Blaenavon Town Hall opened in Lion Street.
Races were held in Pontypool for the first time since 1850.
At the Great Exhibition in London, the Blaenavon Iron Company were awarded prizes for pig and manufactured iron of excellent quality, especially for solid rolled wheel tyres.
1862 News of the vast fortunes to be made in the newly discovered gold fields of Vancouver Island reached Pontypool. Dozens of families sold their belongings and set off to stake their claims.
1863 Varteg Furnace was blown in by Messrs Partridge & Jones.
1864 Blaenavon Company Ltd., formed with nominal capital of £400,000 in £50 shares.
Capel Newydd near Blaenavon ceased to be used for services.
1865 New tyre mill and steel works opened at Blaenavon.
Blaendare Pit was sunk.
1868 LNWR opened the Blaenavon - Brynmawr line.
First furnace at Forgeside came into blast.
Death of Thomas Hill the third.
1869 A new furnace was blown in at Blaenavon (No.9), the last of three that had recently been built on the Coity side of the valley.
1870 LNWR station opened to the public at Blaenavon.
Telegraph wires were extended to the Post Office, Pontypool, the entire telegraph system being placed in the hands of the Post Office authorities.
Death of R. W. Kennard.
1871 Pontymoel Tin Works began production. Tinplate Co.'
The printing and publishing office of *The Pontypool Free Press* was removed from the Corn Market to the old Assembly Room over the Butter Market.
1873 Panteg Steel Works was established by Sampson Copestake.
1874 Official opening of Tynewydd Iron and Tin-plate Works at Pontnewydd.
1875 Zion Baptist Church was built serve the growing population of Forgeside, Blaenavon.
General miners' strike and lockout which lasted 5 months.
1876 Closure of the British Ironworks.
1877 Thomas and Gilchrist began their experiments at Blaenavon.
Fire broke out in the old Japan House in Crane Street, Pontypool.
1878 Blaenavon-Talywain Railway was completed.
Tirpentwys Pit was sunk.
The open-hearth method of steel-making using phosphoric ores, which revolutionised steel production was developed at Blaenavon by Gilchrist and Thomas.
1879 Blaenavon Ironworks Company was reformed and the name shortened to Blaenavon Company Ltd., with a new board of directors.
1880 Big Pit was created by deepening a shaft sunk 20 years earlier, known as Kearsley's Pit.
1883 Tynewydd Tinplate Works stopped trading.
1885 Henllys Firebrick Works was re-opened following a change of ownership.
1887 A serious epidemic of measles at Sebastapol affected more than fifty houses. There were more than 130 cases of which 14 proved fatal.
1889 Pontypool Cattle Market was erected at a cost of £2,000. It accommodated 250 cattle, 3,500 sheep and 2,000 pigs.
H. J. Kennard was appointed Chairman of the Blaenavon Company Ltd.
1890 Llanerch Colliery disaster at Cwmnantddu, claimed the lives of 176 miners.
1891 It was decided by the Haberdashers' Company and the Charity Commissioners that Pontypool would be the site of the new west Monmouthshire school to be erected in accordance with the will of the late William Jones of Monmouth..
A complaint was made that bicycles were making the streets of Pontypool unsafe for children and old people. It was suggested that a byelaw should be made making it an offence to ride a bicycle or tricycle in any street.

1892 A banquet was held at the Crown Hotel, Pontypool to celebrate the selection of the town as the site for the proposed West Monmouthshire School.

1894 Pontypool Council was established by an Act of Parliament.
Pontypool Market was officially opened on 1st December by Mr J.C. Hanbury.
Blaenavon Workmen's Hall, built at a cost of £10,000 was officially opened.

1896 The foundation stone of West Mon School was laid by Mr J.C. Hanbury.
Tirpentwys Colliery claimed a record one day's output of 814 tons.
Death of H. J. Kennard.

1897 Pontypool was one of the first places in Wales to establish an electric light and power company. The Pontypool Electric light Company advertised that they would install wiring free of charge in order to induce more people to have electric light installed.

1897 Official opening of the Girls Grammar School at Penygarn by Mrs J.C. Hanbury.
Trosnant Cycle Stores, Pontypool advertised their latest machines and offered purchasers a free course of six lessons at the South Wales Riding School in Cardiff.

1898 Official opening of West Mon School, built at a cost of £30,000.

1900 Furnaces at the old Blaenavon Ironworks shut down.
Gwenallt (Cwmffrwdoer) Pit was sunk.

1901 Pontypool RFC was formed.

1902 Foundation stone of Pontypool Hospital laid by Mrs J.C. Hanbury.

1903 Closure of Garn Pits, marking the end of ironstone mining at Blaenavon.
R. W. Kennard was elected Chairman of the Blaenavon Company Ltd.
The Hanbury Assembly Rooms in Pontypool, which had been in existence for over twelve years were converted into a theatre and music hall, known as the 'Theatre Royal.'
The first Convent School was set up by the sisters of the Order of the Holy Ghost in Osborne Road. It was later moved to a house in Albion Road.

1904 Andrew Carnegie gave £2,000 for the purpose of erecting a free public library in Pontypool.
*The Free Press of Monmouthshire* turned to electricity for its motive power.
Redbrook Tinplating Co. Ltd., erected a Tin box factory adjacent to the Tynewydd works and registered it as 'Pontnewydd Tinplating Co. Ltd.'

1905 Mount Pleasant Congregational Church was built in Hanbury Road, Pontypool.
Abersychan Working Mens' Institute built at a cost of £1,050 was opened.
A fire at West Mon School gutted the gymnasium. The swimming bath was saved but the roof and contents of the gymnasium were destroyed.

1907 Panteg Steel Works was transferred to Messrs Alfred Baldwin & Co., Ltd.
The Theatre Royal in Pontypool was acquired by George Henry Pitt who turned it into a musical hall and playhouse, seating 800 people.

1908 Pontypool Library in Hanbury Road was officially opened by Mr J.C. Hanbury.

1909 General Booth, veteran head of the Salvation Army paid a visit to Pontypool in the course of a scheduled tour of 1,400 miles during which he delivered 82 addresses, received 43 receptions and spoke to the prisoners in four gaols.
The Free Library was built on Hanbury Road, Pontypool at a cost of £1,889 with assistance from the Carnegie Trust. It included both Reference and Lending Libraries, Reading and Committee Rooms and a small Lecture Hall.

1910 The Empire, Abersychan was opened after reconstruction at a cost of £3,000.
Tom Griffiths, Pontypool's MP for 17 years retired.

1911 Pontypool contributed 101 and Abersychan 30 singers to the mammoth Welsh choir of 5,000 voices which sang before 12,000 people at the Crystal Palace, London, in the Welsh Musical Festival.

1912 It was announced that Mr J. C. Hanbury was to give up his residence at Pontypool Park.

1913 A new Cinema built in Crane Street was opened. It was announced that the pictures would be shown by two of Tyler's Indomitable Bioscopes.

1914 St Alban's Convent School was established in Pontypool Park House.
Britain's first flag-day took place at Griffithstown in aid of the National Relief Fund.
A new Palace Electric Theatre was opened in Commercial Street, Griffithstown.

1915 The Nurses Home at Pontypool Hospital was opened.
1917 Pontypool Gas and Water Company opened a new reservoir at Penyrheol 770 feet above sea level with a storage capacity of 23,000,000 gallons.
1918 Outbreak of the First World War.
1920 Pontypool Park was formally opened as a public park on Easter Monday. The event was attended by 15,000 people despite wet and windy weather .
An Electricity Power House was built in red brick at Forgeside, Blaenavon.
1921 Commencement of the first Eastern Valley passenger motor service by Mr W. Barratt and his brother, with just one bus, a 32 seat Commer, supplying a service every two hours.
Pontypool's new picture-house, The Park Cinema, with a seating capacity of 1,250, opened on Boxing Day. Charlie Chaplin appeared in 'The Idle Class.'
John Capel Hanbury JP DL, died at his home at Sevenoaks, Kent at the age of 68 and was cremated at Golder's Green Crematorium.
Kay's Slope and Milfraen Collieries closed down.
Pontypool Park House was purchased for £6,000 by the Sisters of the Holy Ghost thus ensuring the future of St Alban's School.
1923 Woolworths opened in George Street, Pontypool.
Pontypool's Crane Street Cinema closed and the building later became the 'Palais de Danse.' It boasted one of the best sprung dance floors in South Wales.
1924 The old Town Bridge in Pontypool was demolished and replaced by one costing £7,250.
The Royal National Eisteddfod of Wales held in Pontypool Park.
The first radio broadcast made from a national eisteddfod was at Pontypool.
Opposing a proposal for a new road through Pontypool Park, Mr G.H. Pitt at a meeting of Pontypool Council, said it seemed that the new road would be built and George Street never widened unless the Council took a firm stand. He prophesied that if the new road was made Pontypool would be shifted up to Penygarn and grass would be growing in the streets of the town.
1925 The new Town Bridge in Pontypool was officially opened by Major General Lord Treowen.
The Empire, Abersychan was re-opened under new proprietorship as the Capital Cinema.
1926 A Chamber of Trade was formed in Pontypool by local businessmen.
1927 Twmpath Central School, Pontypool was opened by Alderman W. C. Watkins JP.
Pontypool Educational Settlement was officially opened by Lord Macmillan. It was the first building in Wales to be specifically designed for adult education.
1928 A scheme for widening George Street in Pontypool was turned down by the rate-payers.
1929 Garn-yr-erw Welfare Hall, built at a cost of £1,600, was opened by the Right Hon Thomas Richards, Secretary of the South Wales Miners' Federation.
Llantarnam Council decided to embark upon an electric lighting scheme for the district, following a report submitted by the electrical engineers Messrs Arthur Ellis & Partners.
1930 Garn Drift opened at Blaenavon.
New Council offices were built at Blaenavon.
1932 Official opening of Penygarn Junior School at a cost of £8,000.
1934 Extra classrooms and a science block at West Mon School were erected at a cost of £20,000.
Greyhound racing was held for the first time at Blaenavon.
A new automatic telephone exchange opened at Talywain.
The Blaenavon Works were bought by Daniel Doncaster & Co., Ltd., of Sheffield.
1935 Fifty two nominations were received for the 24 seats on the new amalgamated Pontypool Council.
Alderman Arthur Jenkins was adopted as the Labour Party parliamentary candidate for Pontypool in succession to Tom Griffiths.
Between 2,000 and 3,000 able bodied unemployed men, with hundreds of women, some carrying children, marched to Pontypool from all parts of the Eastern Valley to protest against cuts in unemployment pay.
1936 Royal visit of Edward VIII to the Eastern Valley.
Park Terrace School, Pontypool was officially opened By Alderman Michael Murphy.

1936 Demolition started on the old GKN blast furnaces at Forge Hammer, Cwmbran.
Obediah Evans the Eastern Valley miners'agent, alarmed at the shrinking population of the valley, prophesied that in the next decade the Eastern Valley would be finished industrially unless something was done to attract new industries.

1937 The new post office in Blaenavon was opened by Major J.H. Lones.
Glynsychan House and grounds in Abersychan were acquired by Pontypool Council as a park and recreation ground.
It was announced that a biscuit factory would be built at Llantarnam at a cost of £100,000.
Work began on the Eastern Valley trunk sewer scheme, estimated to cost £254,000.
The Educational Settlement at Rockhill Road, Pontypool was opened by Lord MacMillan.

1938 Pontypool Town School celebrated its centenary.
Blaenavon's last furnaces closed down.
Pilkington's Glass factory at Pontypool Road began production.

1939 The new £100,000 engineering works of the Saunders Valve Co. Ltd., at Cwmbran was opened by Alderman Arthur Jenkins MP in the presence of over 300 guests.
New pithead baths opened at Big Pit Colliery.
Steel was produced at Blaenavon for the first time in twenty years. The new steel works had been built as the result of assistance by the Nuffield Trust and was only a few hundred yards from the place where the cousins Gilchrist and Thomas carried out their famous experiments.

1940 Abersychan Brick and Slag Works closed down owing to a shortage of labour.

1941 Pontypool Hospital was the first institution of its kind to put into operation the new increased scale of salaries for its nursing staff. The increase meant an additional expenditure of £527 per annum of which the Government paid half.

1942 Open cast mining started at Blaenavon.

1943 Mrs Eleanor Edmunds JP of London, formerly of Abersychan made a gift to the public of 22 acres of Lasgarn Wood, Abersychan.

1944 Talywain's Bob-a-day Road was mentioned in the House of Commons by Alderman Arthur Jenkins MP during a debate on employment policy. He asked for definite action to ensure hat there would be no large scale unemployment after the war.

1945 Alderman Arthur Jenkins, MP for Pontypool was appointed Parliamentary Secretary to the Ministry of Education. He resigned later that year due to ill health.
Hugh Dalton, President of the Board of Trade announced that a large new factory for the spinning and processing of nylon yarn was to be erected at Mamhilad between Pontypool and Usk. It was expected to employ about 1,700 people.
The first four completed pre-fabricated houses in Wales were ercted in Golf Road, New Inn and formally handed over to Pontypool Council. The houses had an estimated life of ten years and were valued at approximately £1,085 each.

1946 Alderman Arthur Jenkins M P (62) died at St Thomas's Hospital, London.
Abersychan Brick and Slag Works was restarted under a new company, employing 20 men.

1947 The first oil-fired tinplate mill in the Eastern Valley went into operation at Tynewydd Works, Pontnewydd.
The Abersychan Roman Catholic Church of St Francis of Assisi was destroyed by fire.

1948 The Blaenavon Medical Society which had served the town since 1891, ceased to exist when the new National Health Service started.
Work began on a new maternity unit at Panteg County Hospital.
Pontypool Council voted against steps to rebuild the Folly Tower.
Roy Jenkins (27), son of the late Alderman Arthur Jenkins was elected MP for Central Southwark.
Field Marshal Montgomery was greeted by a crowd of several hundred at the Pontypool Drill Hall. He arrived in his famous open car which carried him from Normandy to Berlin.

1949 Designation of Cwmbran New Town, the first new town to be built in Wales.
Pontypool Chamber of Trade voted in favour of supporting the Eastern Valley Licensed Victuallers Association in their attempt to restore Sunday opening in the valley.

1949 Anthony Hopkins (destined to be a famous actor) became a boarder at West Mon School.
Blaendare Colliery was closed down by the NCB.
A giant new £600,000 gas producing station was formally opened at New Inn by Alfred Robens, Parliamentary Secretary to the Ministry of Fuel and Power. The works was able to produce over 4,000,000 cubic feet of gas daily for the Pontypool area.

1951 Cwmbran Development Corporation moved into their new headquarters in Old Cwmbran.
The old Bath Beerhouse on the corner of The Cross, Pontypool was demolished by the council as the first step in the widening of George Street.
A collection of Pontypool Japanware was presented to the town by Mrs Kay Booker, in memory of her husband, Gordon Booker, late of the Clarence Hotel.
Pontypool Gas and Water Company drew up a scheme to flood a valley to the north of the village of Llandegfedd to provide a new reservoir.

1952 The first two houses built by Cwmbran Development Corporation were occupied at provisional rents of 36/6 a week.
Pontypool's 'Palais de Danse' became the 'Queen's Ballroom' and was often used for staging wrestling and boxing bouts.
Mr James Kegie, the county planning officer told the Rural Community Council at Usk that Monmouthshire must find more water, otherwise by 1970 there would be a deficiency of seven to eight million gallons a day. Alternative proposals were for reservoirs in the Honddu Valley, and the Pontypool Company's Llandegfedd scheme. He hoped the latter would be the one adopted.
A memorial clock to Alderman Arthur Jenkins MP for Pontypool (1935-46) was unveiled in Pontypool Park by James Griffiths MP for Llanelly.

1953 Pontypool Urban District Council purchased Glantorfaen House.
Coronation celebrations at Pontypool Town Forge coincided with the 250th anniversary of the beginnings of tinplate making in the town. Sheets were being tinned on the site of the works as far back as 1703, when Queen Anne was on the throne.
Pontypool RFC converted Elm House into a new social and administrative HQ.

1954 Pontypool's new fire station, built at a cost of £33,000 was opened at New Inn by Mr H.M. Smith, Chief Inspector of fire services.
West Mon School, Pontypool became a County Grammar School.
Field Marshall, The Viscount Montgomery of Alamein opened the new foundry extension of Messrs Guest, Keen & Nettlefolds Ltd., at Cwmbran, which was to provide work for at least 500 people. He threw a golden sovereign into a mould of molten metal and then poured the first mould.
A new £50,000 building erected to adjoin Pontypool park House as an extension to St Alban's School was officially opened by Archbishop McGrah of Cardiff.

1955 A fully retained fire station costing £9076 was opened at Abersychan in Limekiln Road.
Death of Tom Griffiths, MP for Pontypool from 1918 until his retirement in 1935.

1956 Plans for a Civic Centre at the rear of Pontypool Town Hall were approved in principle by Pontypool Council.
Thirty-three vehicles, nose to tail, from the Cross to the Town Hall was the largest traffic jam yet seen in Pontypool. The problem was discussed by the Pontypool Chamber of Trade, and one member was in favour of a scheme to make George Street one way, while another argued that the only answer was a Pontypool by-pass to meet the needs of the future.
Lord Raglan opened Panteg's new Public Hall and commented that Panteg had grown into a sizeable town of about 4,000 people and should no longer be considered a village.
The controversial film 'Rock around the Clock' was booked for the Pontypool cinemas. It had been banned in some places because it was alleged that it was likely to lead to public disorder.

1957 During its first seven years of existence, Cwmbran Development Corporation had built 2,417 houses, 18 miles of road and 54 miles of sewer.

1957 In November, the last of the Blaenavon Company's employees received their final pay packets from the old company. Messrs Doncaster & Son were to take over the building and plant during the following month.
Avondale Tinplate Works, Pontnewydd closed down following a shortage of orders. The works had been in existence for over sixty years and employed about 250 people.
Pontypool voted to allow Sunday cinemas by 4,981 votes to 1,976 in a poll in which only 24% of the electorate participated.

1958 Publication of *Rape of the Fair Country* by Alexander Cordell..
Pontypool's Town School closed and was demolished as part of the Council's plan for the re-development of High Street.
Leo Abse was elected as MP for Pontypool became the first Welsh peer.
Granville West, former Labour MP for Pontypool.
Sir Ben Bowen Thomas, Permanent Secretary to the Welsh Department officially opened Pontypool's College of Further Education, built at a cost of £140,000.
The Royal Cinema in Pontypool closed and was later demolished. Constructed at the end of the nineteenth century it used to be known as the Hanbury Assembly Rooms.
Town School was closed and demolished as part of Pontypool Council's plan for the re-development of High Street.
Official opening of Pontypool's College of Further Education, built at a cost of £140,000.

1959 Work started on the new Police HQ and courtroom at Pontypool, estimated to cost £86,000.
*The Free Press* celebrated its centenary.

1960 A memorial obelisk to Sidney Gilchrist Thomas and Percy Carlyle Gilchrist was unveiled at Forgeside in front of Coity House.
Mr Ernest Marples, Minister of Transport, made a grant of £75,225 towards the estimated £100,300 cost of widening George Street, Pontypool.
The Cwmbran factory of GKN Ltd., where railway fastenings were made, was converted into a malleable iron foundry to produce parts for the car industry.

1961 Pontypool's first Community College was opened at the new Trevethin School.
Ernest Marples, Minister of Transp[ort, made a grant of £75,225 towards the estimated £100,300 cost of widening George Street in Pontypool.
The £3.5m Llandegfedd Reservoir was inaugurated by Alderman Charles Horwood, Chairman of Cardiff Waterworks Committee. Using a stainless steel spade, he cut the first sod of the project to build an £84,000 dam 120ft high and 1,100 ft long, holding back 5,000 million gallons of water. The reservoir affected twenty farms in the valley of the Sor Brook.

1962 Work started on the £20,000 sports stadium at Cwmbran.
Cwmbran Railway Station was closed for passenger service.
The Shell Grotto at Pontypool Park, St Alban's Convent, Crane Street Baptist Chapel and the Horse and Jockey Inn, were among local buildings listed by the Ministry of Housing and Local Government as being of special architectural interest. Also listed were the three oldest churches in the Pontypool urban area, St Cadoc's Trevethin, St Mary's Panteg and St Michael's Llanfihangel. The minister also named the former stables to Pontypool Park House and the house known as 'Ty Gwyn' in Hospital Road, Pontnewynydd.

1963 Work started on the long-awaited demolition of Pontypool's George Street to remove a bottleneck by widening the road. The plan was first devised in 1910.
Closure of Deakin's Slope which had opened in 1899.
Monmouthshire County Council opened a £60,000 infants school at Pontnewydd. This was the sixteenth primary school to be built in the new town.

1964 The Queen's Ballrom was purchased by Pontypool Council for £16,000.
St Alban's Roman Catholic Secondary School was opened by the Archbishop of Cardiff.
Pontypool Council bought for £17,500 all the buildings in Pontypool owned by Partridge Jones and John Paton Ltd., and the buildings on the site of the Pontnewynydd works, the Central, Osborne and Pontypool forges and Bristol House for a further £2,500.
Pontypool's first ever Christmas lights were switched on by the Chairman of the Council.

1965 The first carriageway of the 1.75 miles long Croesyceiliog by-pass was opened for traffic.
A new infants school at Penygarn to accommodate 480 pupils was officially opened by Alderman T. Wellington.
Fifty-five years of worship at St James' Church, Blaenavon ended with the closure of the church because of declining congregations and rising costs.

1966 It was announced that Crane Street Station, Pontypool was to close with the result that the town lost its direct goods and parcel service and 20 staff lost their jobs.
Pontypool Council agreed to the establishment of a permanent gipsy encampment at Lower Race which had been occupied by gipsy families for over 60 years.
Leo Abse MP opened Llantarnam Grange, which had been renovated to provide a social meeting place and arts centre for Cwmbran.
The Oak Brick Company at Pontnewynydd ceased production.
Monmouthshire's new County Hall committee recommended the council to approve plans for a six-storey building at Croesyceiliog costing between £1.5m and £2m.
The first sheltered workshop for disabled people in Wales was opened by Monmouthshire County Council at Pontnewydd. It was named the Monwel Works and provided useful occupation for handicapped people in the area.

1967 B.I.G. Batteries Ltd., went into production at Lower Pontnewynydd, producing car and commercial batteries.
A new production record was set up at Pilkington's Pontypool factory of 1,853,443 square feet of standard glass per week. This is equivalent to a fifty mile length of glass, seven feet in width. It broke the old record for the factory of 1,833,563 square feet a week.

1968 It was announced that one of the world's largest pharmaceutical firms, Parke Davis & Co., was to build premises at a cost of £2m on a 35 acre site adjacent to the ICI Fibres factory.
A rare Pontypool japanned knife-box decorated with gold chinoiserie figures, made in 1760 and containing contemporary silver knives, forks and spoons was sold by auction at Christie's sale-rooms, London for 800 guineas.
Daniel Doncaster & Sons Ltd., opened a new 125 ton rolling mill at Blaenavon.

1969 Pipes for North Sea Gas were laid through the streets of Blaenavon.
A revolutionary town centre re-development plan for Pontypool prepared by the County Planning Officer, Mr James Kegie, was adopted by the Council. It provided for a town centre square in George Street, completely free of traffic, a new bus station on the site of the market and a new market in Crane Street. Housing estates were to border the town centre with a new bypass along the old railway line.
Tirpentwys Colliery closed down.

1970 Pontypool's only cinema (The Park) was destroyed by fire. It was built in the 1920s at around the time of the 1924 Pontypool Royal National Eisteddfod.
Tabernacle Baptist Chapel at the top of Crane Street, Pontypool was demolished.
Large scale demolition at the top of Crane Street, Pontypool, resulted in the disappearance of several shops and public houses, including The Swan, The Three Cranes, The Tabernacle Baptist Chapel School Room and the town's first cinema which later became the Queen's Ballroom.
Blaenavon's old peoples' home was opened and named the Arthur Jenkins Home in memory of the father of Roy Jenkins, now Chancellor of the Exchequer, who was asked to perform the opening ceremony.

1971 The Gilchrist Thomas Industrial Estate was commenced by Blaenavon Urban District Council as a means of bringing desperately needed jobs into the area.
Revised plans for the development of High Street, Pontypool were accepted by the Council's design and development committee.
James Kegie, County Planning Officer recommended that the 18th century stable block of Pontypool Park House would be the most suitable site for the proposed town museum.
An African born barrister, Mr M.B. Mehta was appointed Clerk to Pontypool Council.
Radio and TV star Bob Monkhouse opened the new Tesco Store in George Street,

Pontypool. It was said that the store would be a prototype of the one-stop shopping centre of the future.

1972 Cwmbran Library opened in the town centre block known as Gwent House.
The Tirpentwys Valley, high above Pontnewynydd was chosen as the location for a refuse tip for Pontypool.
ICI Fibres confirmed their intention to transfer their research and development department from Pontypool to Harrogate. This resulted in the loss of 629 white collar jobs.
GNKN Works at Cwmbran closed on 31 December and intensive efforts were made to find jobs for more than 500 steelmakers.

1973 Plans to use 100,000 sq ft of vacant office space at the ICI Fibres plant at Pontypool, for housing a Government department were put forward by Mr Leo Abse MP.
Torfaen, the name chosen by local councillors to cover Blaenavon, Pontypool, Cwmbran, Llanyrafon, Croesyceiliog, Ponthir and Henllys, came into effect.
George Spencer was appointed as the last Chairman of the Blaenavon Council which was to become part of the new Torfaen Council.
Paul Murphy (24), a Labour member for Fairwater became one of two youngest members of Torfaen Council. The youngest was John Vaughan Jones (23), a Labour member for Cwmbran Central and Llantarnam.
The first meeting of the new Torfaen District Council took place on Friday 18th May in the council chamber of the Town Hall. George Day was elected as the first chairman.
For the second time in its 114 years existence, ownership of the *Free Press* changed hands. The new owners were F. Bailey & Son Ltd., of Dursley, Glos., a family firm established 100 years previously, who owned a series of weekly news papers.
Plans were unveiled for a man-made lake of 150 acres at Garn-yr-erw.

1974 Pontypool Leisure Centre opened a a cost of £600,000. This was the last major project completed by the old Pontypool Urban District Council.
Pontypool's new luxury cinema with 210 seats opened on Osborne Road. The first film to be shown there was 'The Three Musketeers.'
Each member of Cwmbran Council was presented with a scarf or tie displaying the 'Valley of the Crow' to mark their final meeting before phasing out to the new Torfaen authority.
The coat-of-arms for Torfaen Council prepared by staff of the East Mon College of Further Education at Pontypool was approved. Each of the four quarters represents a part of the Torfaen District. Black diamonds and the keys of the Kennard family of Blaenavon, a Japanware vase for Pontypool; three wheatsheafs for the Pontypool rural area; and a crow in flight representing Cwmbran. The upper and lower quarters of the coat-of-arms are separated by horizontal blue and white stripes depicting the Afon Lwyd which flows through the length of Torfaen.
Mr George Day, leader of the Labour majority on Torfaen Borough Council was sworn in as the first Mayor of the Borough of Torfaen before the start of the Council's first meeting.
Development of the Gilchrist Thomas Industrial Estate in Blaenavon was well advanced with a total of ten factories either completed or in the course of construction.
It was announced that Siebe Gorman Ltd., manufactures of diving, underwater and industrial safety equipment would be moving to Cwmbran and would employ between 450 and 500 people at their new works.
Re-chem International Ltd's new industrial waste treatment plant at New Inn came into operation. The cost of building the plant was £242,000.

1975 Official opening of Pontypool's ski-slope, built at a cost of £65,000. At 200 metres it was the longest in Europe and it was expected that Pontypool would become the skiing centre for Wales.
Alfa Laval's new £1. 2 million factory at Cwmbran was opened by Lord Raglan, Chairman of the Cwmbran Development Corporation.
Pilkington's glassworks at Pontypool ceased production.

1976 Blaenavon's new Leisure Centre opened at a cost of £188,000.
It was announced that a Leisure Centre would be incorporated into the new Abersychan

comprehensive school, at a cost of £240,000, which would be shared by Gwent County Council and Torfaen Borough Council.
Saunders Valves, the Cwmbran based company won its third Queen's Award in ten years.
Blaenavon Ironworks were taken into the care of the Scretary of State for Wales.
The £20 million fibreglass factory at Pontyfelin, owned by Pilkingtons, started production.

1977 Daniel Doncaster, Blaenavon, were given a £400,000 investment by their parent company Inco, to develop a new process at the plant for producing gas turbine parts for the aero industry.
A new town bridge was constructed to carry the Pontypool centre inner-relief road over the Afon Lwyd. Fourteen prestressed concrete beams, 55 feet long and weighing up to 15 tons each were used in the construction.
Hundreds of residents from New Inn marched on Pontypool's Town Hall in protest against the controversial Re-Chem waste disposal plant.
The first UK athletics championships were held at Cwmbran.

1978 Torfaen Museum Trust began operations with the aim of preserving and interpreting the heritage of the Eastern Valley for the benefit of the community, both local and world-wide.
The final plans for the £1,362, 500 conversion of West Mon Grammar School into a seven form entry mixed 11-16 comprehensive school were given the go-ahead.

1979 Ferranti announced plans to build a £15m factory on the former brickworks site at Ty Coch Industrial Estate. It was expected to employ 1,000 people by 1984.
Work started on a £3.5 million expansion at the Daniel Doncaster works at Forgeside, which would create 1,000 new jobs. The expansion was expected to double the capacity of the company which produces specialised components for aircraft.
ICI Fibres announced a £50m investment at their Pontypool works. But five months later they announced plans to slash their workforce by 450.

1980 Big Pit, Blaenavon closed on January 31st, due to geological problems.
The Welsh Development Agency granted £200,000 towards the Big Pit Museum project.
Torfaen Council announced a proposal to establish a cycleway along the towpath of the former Monmouthshire & Brecon Canal.
The Welsh Water Authority announced plans to construct a reservoir capable of holding 60 million gallons of water at Court Farm, Ponthir at a cost of £1.5m.
It was announced that Snatchwood Hospital, Pontnewynydd would be closed and the patients transferred to nearby Pontypool & District Hospital.
Cwmbran New Town was twinned with the West German town of Bruchsal.

1981 A few weeks before his wedding, Prince Charles visited the Eastern Valley on part of a two-day tour of South Wales during which he visited projects carried out by voluntary groups and assisted by the prince of Wales Committee. His stop in Blaenavon included a visit to Big Pit, Wales' first coal mining museum and then Blaenavon Ironworks. He also visited the Valley Inheritance Museum at Pontypool.
The Valley Inheritance Museum at Pontypool was opened to the public on International Museums Day, concluding three years of hard work by the Trust.

1982 Twmpath Central School was merged with West Mon Grammar School to form a large comprehensive school.
West Mon and County Girls Grammar Schools became comprehensive and admitted pupils of the opposite sex for the first time.
Wern Secondary Modern School was badly damaged by fire and later demolished.
The Welsh Development Agency awarded a £160,000 contract to start development of a high technology industrial park at Mamhilad near the ICI and Parke-Davis factories.
Blaenavon Workmen's Hall Committee opened a new 'mini-cinema.'
Griffin Press (Hughes & Sons Ltd.), one of the oldest commercial printers in the Eastern Valley was put up for sale.

1984 Blaenavon Town Council in May, abolished the office of Mayor and appointed Mrs Bernice Price as chairman instead. But in three years time when a new council was elected the office was to be be re-instated.

1984 Fears were mounting in Blaenavon that a fault in a wall at the Workmen's Hall could signal the end of the historic building.
Another building within an uncertain future was the Clarence Hotel in Pontypool which was now closed and boarded up by the owners Ansells, because no one was interested in buying it. The asking price was £120,000.
Demands were made by Torfaen MP Leo Abse for the closure of Re-chem until a public inquiry had established the safety of the plant.

1985 The *Free Press* entered its 126th year of publication and entered the new technological age. Linotype machines now became redundant with the introduction of the computer.
An environmental improvement grant of £115,000 for landscaping and tree planting in Blaenavon was announced by the Welsh Office.
Publication of *Cordell Country* by Chris Barber thus identifying the area around Blaenavon with the well known novelist Alexander Cordell and attracting visitors to the area.

1986 New offices of the Pontypool *Free Press* at Pontymoile Corner were officially opened by the actor Anthony Hopkins.
The old Pontymoel National School, a fine example of Gothic /Revival architecture was demolished.
Torfaen Council revealed plans for a massive re-shaping of Pontypool. They all depended on the construction of a new relief road along the line of the disused mineral line.
Cadw began a £300,000 ten year restoration programme at Blaenavon Ironworks.
A new railway station was opened near Edlogan Way in Cwmbran.

1987 Torfaen Councillors agreed to a massive £3m extension of Pontypool Town Hall to provide 55,000 square feet of office space. Gwent House in Cwmbran would become redundant.
In October work began on the £500,000 link road from Clarence Corner to the Western relief road which would in due course bypass Pontypool town centre.

1988 Cwmbran Development Corporation was wound up and its various responsibilities transferred to Torfaen Borough Council.
The £2.5m link road between Lower Race, Pontypool and Hafodyrynys was opened.

1989 George Street School, Pontypool was demolished and a new school erected on the same site.
The bi-centenary of Blaenavon Ironworks was celebrated.
The people of the Eastern Valley demonstrated their opposition to the Re-chem plant at New Inn and demanded a public inquiry into the toxic waste firm, Re-chem International.
The Maternity Hospital at Panteg was under threat of closure. Torfaen Council said that they would fight the plans 'tooth and nail.'

1990 Torfaen MP Paul Murphy tabled a motion in the House of Commons to commemorate the centenary of the Llanerch Colliery disaster in which 175 men and boys lost their lives on February 6th 1890. Mr Murphy's grandfather Jeremiah Murphy worked at the colliery when the disaster occurred but was fortunately ill at the time of the explosion and not involved as a result.
Varteg Memorial Hall was destroyed in a fire. It was built in 1923 as a war memorial and paid for directly by the people of Varteg, many of them miners who paid 1d a week from their wages. The Hall was a focal point for the village and had been due to be sold by British Coal to the community association for use as a social centre.
Paul Murphy, Torfaen MP officially opened the Council's new 282 berth multi-storey car park behind the Town Hall by breaking a ribbon with the first car.

1991 Greenmeadow Community Farm opened on the hillside above Cwmbran.
Trico, the windscreen wiper manufacturer moved from Brentford to a £15m purpose-built factory at Skewfields, near Pontypool. The firm is a subsidiary of American based Trico-Products Corporation and its founder JR. Oshei invented the windscreen wiper in 1916 after colliding with a cyclist, while driving his car in heavy rain.
Gwent Health Authority announced that it would be closing Pontypool Hospital and transferring its geriatric patients to the County Hospital Griffithstown.

1991 County Planning chiefs unveiled detailed plans of a multi-million pound scheme to relieve traffic congestion at Pontymoile.

Cwmbran-based Radio Gwent was closed down by the BBC as part of a £2.8m cost-cutting package. Radio Gwent was one of only two community radio stations in Wales and its closure was a major blow to the county.

The new six-storey Pontypool Civic Centre opened and for the first time since Torfaen's formation in 1974 all the headquarter's staff of nine departments was united on one site. Paul Murphy MP for Torfaen declared the building officially open and immediately afterwards the first council meeting was held in the new 70 seat chamber built on the upper floor of the town hall.

Torfaen MP, Paul Murphy opened the new Springvale Wildlife Valley at Greenmeadow Community Farm. The project included six ponds with the top three forming the basis of a Wildfowl Sanctuary.

1992 Panteg Steelworks were taken over by Avesta Sheffield, carrying on the 125 year tradition of making high quality steel.

Snatchwood Hospital, Abersychan was demolished. It was originally the private residence of a mine owner and later became an orthopaedic recovery unit attached to St Lawrence Hospital, Chepstow, dealing with war injuries.

Blaenavon's Community Woodland site with picnic site and adventure playground area was officially opened.

1993 North American firm Du Pont took over the former ICI plant at Mamhilad in a multi-million pond trans-atlantic factory swap. Later in the year Du Pont announced the loss of 400 jobs.

Torfaen MP, Paul Murphy officially opened Pontypool's £5 million Western Relief Road.

Restoration work began on the Shell Grotto in Pontypool Park.

1994 The re-built Folly Tower was officially opened by Prince Charles.

Blaenavon Workmen's Hall celebrated its centenary.

Pontypool & District Hospital was officially closed on 27th January.

Pontypool Road Railway Station was re-opened after a long-awaited £150,000 facelift.

St Alban's Roman Catholic Comprehensive School opted out of Local Education Authority control.

Proposed opencast mining at the British, Talywain was strongly opposed by the local community.

1994 Local Government re-organisation resulting in the creation of Torfaen County Borough Council.

1995 Brecon Beacons National Park gave a conservation award for the rebuilding of the Folly Tower. The CROFT team received a Prince of Wales Award.

Pontypool Settlement (founded in 1937) re-opened in a new building on Trosnant Street and was re-named Pontypool Community Education Centre.

1996 Pontypool's open air market returned, bringing people back into the heart of the town.

Courtyard Arts, a unique outdoor performance venue, opened in the cobbled courtyard of the Valley Inheritance Museum.

Greenmeadow Community Farm was one of 27 sites in Britain to receive an award under the Local Agenda 21 scheme which was set up following the 1992 Earth Summit in Rio de Janiero to encourage greater co-operation between the public sector and local people.

1997 Restoration work was completed on the Shell Grotto in Pontypool Park. The project was jointly funded by the old Borough Council in conjunction with the European Regional Development Fund and Cadw.

The new canal basin at Five Locks, Cwmbran was officially opened.

Torfaen & Blaenau Gwent County Borough Councils published a leaflet describing a 'Cordell Heritage Trail.' This 25 mile route takes the visitor through the former industrial heartlands of Pontypool, Blaenavon, Nantyglo and Blaina, taking in twelve locations on the way, that relate to some of the novels of Alexander Cordell.

1997 Death of Alexander Cordell, author of world-wide best selling novel *Rape of the Fair Country*, at the age of 83.

The Bailey Newspaper group which published *The Press Series* was taken over after 125 years in the Bailey family, by Southampton based Southern newspapers.

The Congress theatre in Cwmbran celebrated its 25th birthday with a week of Gala Entertainment and a special commemorative plaque was unveiled by Sir Richard Hanbury-Tenison KCVO, HM Lord Lieutenant of the County of Gwent.

Paul Murphy, MP for Torfaen was appointed Minister of State for Northern Ireland.

1998 Completion of the Pontymoile road improvement scheme at a cost of £20m.

Torfaen's Development Committee agreed to the expansion of the Valley Inheritance Museum into three neighbouring cottages, originally built to provide homes for servants of the Hanbury family. The extra space will be used to house exhibitions, archives, and part of the local history reference library.

West Mon School celebrated its centenary.

The first seven cameras monitoring Pontypool town centre were unveiled by Cllr Bob Wellington at a ceremony at the civic centre. Monitored by a surveillance team round the clock it was expected that they would help to improve safety and reduce crime in the town.

Culture Secretary Chris Smith announced Blaenavon as one of 32 recommended UK sites for World Heritage status. It was one of only two sites in Wales to be nominated.

1999 Pontypool was twinned with the Portuguese town of Coneixa (population 15,000). The town was already linked with Bretten in Germany and the French town of Lonjumeau.

The 'Drill Hall' TA centre in Osborne Road, Pontnewynydd shut its doors for the last time as a result of the Pontypool Territorials, part of the Royal Regiment of Wales, being amalgamated with the Royal Welch Fusiliers.

Paul Murphy, Torfaen MP, officially opened a new science, library and resource facility costing £225,000 at the Welsh Comprehensive School, Ysgol Gyfun Gwynlliw.

Garndiffaith Methodist Church celebrated its 150th anniversary.

Pontypool Market was given a £250,000 facelift.

Big Pit Mining Museum's future was secured when it officially became part of the National Museums & Galleries of Wales.

Neil and Glenys Kinnock officially opened the Pontymoile road improvement scheme (£20 million). Neil Kinnock, the acting European Transport Commissioner praised Torfaen's policy of expanding the local web of cycle paths.

Torfaen's Development Committee approved plans for a multi-screen cinema and leisure complex on the site of the multi-storey car park in Glyndwr Road, Cwmbran.

Torfaen Council proposed to change Blaenavon's former council offices, a Grade II Listed Building into a public library with a coffee shop, retail and exhibition facilities.

A Tourist Information Centre was opened at Blaenavon Ironworks, as part of the Blaenavon Heritage Regeneration Study.

Torfaen Museum Trust celebrated the 21st birthday of the Valley Inheritance Museum with a party during which the guests sang Happy Birthday to the Museum.

Paul Murphy, Torfaen MP was appointed the 13th Secretary of State for Wales.

He commented, 'My job as a Member of Parliament is to reflect the opinions of the people I represent. Now I can do that at the very highest level - in the Cabinet.'

## RECOMMENDED READING

### Non-Fiction


Atkinson, M., *Blaenafon Ironworks: A Guide to its History and Technology* (1983)
Barber, C., & Blackmore, M., *Portraits of the Past*, (1997)
Barber, C., *Cordell Country* ,(1985)
Bowen, R., *Blaenavon in Old Picture Postcards*, (1982)
Bradney, J. A.., *History of Monmouthshire*, : the Hundred of Abergavenny (part 2), (1906), (1992)
Browning, L., *A Brief History of Blaenavon, Monmouthshire*, (1906)
Byles, A., *The History of the Monmouthshire Railway and Canal Company* ,(1982)
Caldwell, M., *Upper Cwmbran - A Search into the Past* , (1979)
Coxe, W., *An Historical Tour in Monmouthshire*, (1801)
Clarke, A.., *The Story of Monmouthshire* Vol I (1961), Vol II (1979)
Clarke, A., *The Story of Pontypool*, (1958)
Crane, A., Derrick, B., & Donovan, E., *Pontypool's Heritage*, 2 Vols (1991/93)
Crane, A., Donovan, E., Smith, Al., & Harris, J., *Pontypool's Pride* , (1988)
Davies, E. J., *The Blaenavon Story*, (1975)
Evans, C. J. O., *Monmouthshire, its History and Topography*, (1953)
Foster, B., *The Llanerch Colliery Explosion* (1998)
Foster, B., *A Tribute to the Eastern Valley Colliers and Miners* , (1999)
Grey Davies, T., *Blaenavon and Sydney Gilchrist Thomas*, (1978)
Hanbury Tenison, R., *The Hanburys* , (1995)
Hadfield, C., *Canals of South Wales and the Border*, (1960)
John, W.D., *Pontypool and Usk Japanned Wares*, (1933)
Knight, J. K., *Blaenavon Ironworks - A Bicentennial Guide* , (1989)
Lloyd, J., *Early History of the Old South Wales Ironworks*, (1905)
Lloyd, W. G. *Roll of Honour*, (1995)
Lewis, J., & Thomas, M., *Blaenavon through the years in Photographs*, Vols I, II & III. (1987, 1998, 1993)
Morgan, H., *South Wales Branch Lines*, (1984)
Nichols, R., *Pontypool and Usk Japan Ware*, (1981)
North, F. J., *Coal and the Coalfields in Wales* , (1931)
Preece, J., *Blaenavon Remembered*, (1985)
Riden, P., *Rebuilding a Valley: A History of Cwmbran Development Corporation* , (1988)
Roden, B.,*Pictorial Memories of Old Pontypool* , (1998)
Sambrook, W., *Pontypool and its Environments*, (1973)
Scrivenor, H. A., *Comprehensive History of the Iron Trade*, (1841)
Shaw, M. A., *Scrappbook of Abersychan, Talywaun, Garndiffaith ,Varteg & Cwmavon* in 3 vols (1983, - 86)
Stevens, R. A., *The Brecknock & Abergavenny and Monmouthshire Canals*, (1975)
Wilkins C., *The History of the Iron, Steel, Tinplate and other Trades of Wales*, (1903)


### Newspapers and Journals


Monmouthshire Merlin
Pontypool Free Press
Pontypool Local Register
Presenting Monmouthshire
South Wales Argus

**Fiction**

Cordell, A., *Rape of the Fair Country* , ( 1959) (1998)
Cordell, A., *This Proud and Savage Land* ,(1987)
Shaw, M., *We Shall Sing Again*, (1990)
Shaw, M., *Shall We Meet Again*, (1991)
Shaw, M, .*Love Will Come Again*, (1996)

## OTHER TITLES BY CHRIS BARBER

*Walks in the Brecon Beacons* , Pridgeon (1976)
*Exploring the Waterfall Country* , Pridgeon (1976)
*Ghosts of Wales , John Jones*, Cardiff (1979)
*Exploring the Brecon Beacons National Park* , Regional Publications (1980/85)
*Exploring Gwent* , Regional Publications (1984)
*Mysterious Wales* , David and Charles (Hardback) (1982), Granada (Paladin Paperback) (1983)
*Cordell Country* , Blorenge Books (1985)
*More Mysterious Wales* , David and Charles (Hardback) (1986), Grafton (Paperback) (1986)
*The Romance of the Welsh Mountains* , Blorenge Books (1986)
*Hando's Gwent* (Volume I), Blorenge Books (1987)
*Hando's Gwent* (Volume II), Blorenge Books (1989)
*The Ancient Stones of Wales* (Jointly with John G. Williams), Blorenge Books (1989)
*The Seven Hills of Abergavenny* , Blorenge Books (1992)
*Journey to Avalon* (Jointly with David Pykitt), Blorenge Books (1993), Samuel Weiser (1997)
*Abergavenny in Old Picture Postcards* , European Library (1995)
*Walks in Cordell Country*, Blorenge Books (1996)
*Portraits of the Past*, (Jointly with Michael Blackmore) Blorenge Books (1996)
*Classic Walks in the Brecon Beacons National Park* Blorenge Books (1997)
*In Search of Owain Glyndwr* Blorenge Books (1998)

## ACKNOWLEDGEMENTS

During my wanderings around Torfaen, researching and photographing locations for this book I was given assistance by many people. In particular I express my gratitude to the following:-

Dr Clive Grace, Chief Executive Office of Torfaen County Borough Council, for asking me to undertake this project.

Considerable research was undertaken with kind assistance from the staff of the Pontypool Free Press, Newport Reference Library, County Record Office, Cwmbran Library, Pontypool Library and the Valley Inheritance Museum. Individuals who gave assistance included Bill Gascoine, John van Laun, Alison Turner and Peter Walker.

Comments on my manuscript and suggestions for its improvement were made by Dick Cole, David Ludlow, Sir Richard Hanbury-Tenison, John Rodger, Jim Russell and Ann Waller.

Assistance with the provision of illustrations was kindly given by Chris Howes, David Boddington, John Lewis, Francis Keen, Pat Clarke, Sir Richard Hanbury-Tenison, Brian Jones, Margaret Pead and Arthur Crane.

I am most grateful to Michael Blackmore for providing artwork and to Mid Wales Litho for their high quality printing.